The Original Australians

The Original Australians

STORY OF THE ABORIGINAL PEOPLE

Josephine Flood

ALLEN&UNWIN

First published in 2006

Allen & Unwin
83 Alexander Street
Crows Nest NSW 2065
Australia
Phone: (61 2) 8425 0100
Fax: (61 2) 9906 2218
Email: info@allenandunwin.com
Web: www.allenandunwin.com

National Library of Australia
Cataloguing-in-Publication entry:

Flood, Josephine.
    The original Australians : story of the Aboriginal people.

    Bibliography.
    Includes index.
    ISBN 978-1-74114-872-5.

    1. Aboriginal Australians – History. 2. Aboriginal
    Australians – Historiography. 3. Australia – History. I.
    Title.

994.0049915

Maps by Map Graphics, Brisbane
Typeset in Dante 11/15 pt by Midland Typesetters, Australia
Printed in China by Everbest Printing Co Ltd.
10 9 8 7

Photos
Inside cover: This panel was painted in the Anbangbang gallery at Nourlangie Rock in Kakadu National Park (open to the public) in 1964 by Najombolmi, the last great rock painter of Arnhem Land, who camped there and decided to 'put the people back into the rockshelter'. He painted two family groups, some of the women with drops of milk in their breasts, ready to people the land again. Then he built a platform and painted mythic beings high on the wall. **Inside back cover:** The largest figure is the dangerous spirit of Namandjolk. At top right is Namarrkon, the lightning man. Lines of lightning join his hands and feet. The stone axes attached to his head, elbows and knees produce thunder and lightning when struck against clouds or the ground. Underneath him are some saratoga fish, 'to feed the people'. **Inside front cover:** Namarrkon's wife Barrkinj is painted above one of the groups of women.
p. vii: A Wandjina at the Kalingi Odin site, west Kimberley, Western Australia.

This book is dedicated to the Aboriginal people of the Northern Territory, who for the last two decades have been generously and patiently teaching me about their traditional life and culture.

CONTENTS

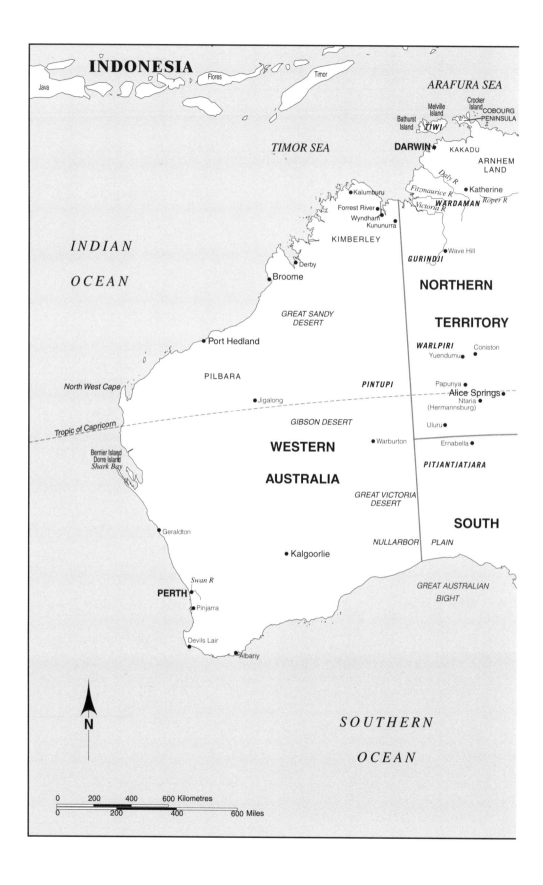

PREFACE

The Original Australians tells the story of Australian Aboriginal history and culture from their distant beginnings to the present day. As an archaeologist, my aim is to try to explain what happened in the past and place traditional Australian indigenous societies into their global context. My mission is to present an accurate, objective, informative account of this continent's first inhabitants. Australia is a country where, for archaeologists, the ancient past and the present converge, for it is here that people survived through major climatic changes, suffered huge loss and pain as a result of European colonisation, and, almost against the odds, managed to maintain their cultural identity, now recognised and respected throughout the world. The resilience of Aboriginal people is one of the great human stories of all time.

During a long career as an archaeologist, I have excavated ice age caves, searched the landscape for ancient campsites and recorded rock paintings and their associated myths. In that time, I have worked with many Aboriginal people and admire and respect them. They have suffered much, yet have survived, bridging the gap between their culture and history and the contemporary world.

Of course, the Aboriginal story has not finished, and I bring it up to the present, covering current issues and hopes for the future. The most difficult section of this book to write has been the story of the last two centuries, for recent history has become extremely polarised. In the 1980s, a critical view of Australian history arose among a younger band of historians in reaction to an earlier self-congratulatory approach. Henry Reynolds' book *The Other Side of the Frontier* pioneered this new direction of 'committed history'. Reynolds' strong sympathy for Aboriginal victims led to him and his followers being dubbed 'black armband' historians by Geoffrey Blainey, a distinguished historian of the older school. Blainey's book *Triumph of the Nomads* is an extremely positive portrayal of traditional Aboriginal society, but by 1993 he considered historical writing in Australia had 'swung from a position that had been too favourable, too self-congratulatory, to an opposite extreme that [was] even more unreal and decidedly jaundiced'. Blainey agreed that 'the treatment of Aborigines was often lamentable' but was disturbed by 'mischievous statements that the Aborigines' numbers were drastically reduced primarily by slaughter. In fact, diseases were the great killer by a very large margin.'[1] (One reason I wrote this book was to evaluate this claim.) In 2002, Sydney historian Keith Windschuttle published *The Fabrication of Aboriginal History, Vol. 1, Van Diemen's Land 1803–1847* and sparked off what are known as the 'History Wars' between left and right leaning historians. Much heat and personal invective surround questions such as exact casualty figures, which both sides concede

can never be accurately known. One positive result of all this verbal violence has been that it has made some historians re-evaluate earlier work. However, many of the general public now have no idea what to believe, which is why in this book I concentrate on generally agreed facts and how we know what we know.

This book, like my previous ones, has been written in response to a specific request, this time from overseas friends planning their first visit and wanting an introduction to indigenous Australia. I searched the bookshops but found nothing suitable that dealt with both the past and the present. My goal in writing, therefore, is to provide an up-to-date account that answers the most commonly asked questions about the First Australians.

My target audience is the general public, especially those who would like to try to understand Australian Aboriginal society from a wide perspective, whether their interest lies in origins, traditional life and art or more recent history. I have also written for those readers who, like me, grew up elsewhere and didn't study Australian history at school. Some may say that only Aborigines should write about Aboriginal Australia, but the reality is that the interests of the few indigenous historians or archaeologists usually lie in other areas, such as oral history and autobiography. Inevitably, my viewpoint is different and I tell the story from an outsider's perspective, based on research and knowledge gained in Aboriginal studies since I arrived in Australia in 1963.

My first step was to ask family and friends in Australia, Britain and the United States for lists of questions. Replies were equally divided between past and present, leading me on a fascinating seven-year-long detective hunt. After several false starts I almost gave up the concept, until I recalled the words of Goobalathaldin (Dick Roughsey) round a campfire in Cape York: 'I want to hear the whole story.' 'Where shall I begin?' I asked. 'Begin at the beginning,' he replied. In previous books on Australian archaeology and rock art I had taken the 'beginning' as the moment, perhaps 60 000 years ago, when the first human footprint appeared on an Australian beach. This time Aboriginal society is revealed to the reader as it was gradually discovered by the outside world. My tale therefore begins with first contact between foreigners and Aborigines.

My interests lie in the 'why' rather than the 'what' of history. As polar explorer Apsley Cherry-Garrard said, 'The best stories are not what people do, but why they do it.' I therefore seek to understand both white and black motives for past actions, such as why Aboriginal responses to outsiders were so varied or why a treaty was made with the indigenous people of New Zealand but not Australia. Of course, causes of past events must be seen in the context of their time, not through the lens of the twenty-first century. We must constantly remind ourselves of the first explorers' and colonists' total ignorance about Aboriginal society. Only very slowly did understanding improve. In Australia the discipline of anthropology is barely a century old and archaeology is even younger. While this book summarises modern understanding about traditional Aboriginal Australia, it seeks to explain past events in their own context rather than with the benefit of hindsight.

Amalgamation of my questioners' interests produced a list of key topics:

- Where did the First Australians come from?
- What are their genetic origins?
- Did they all speak the same language and is it related to any other language?
- What impact have Aborigines had on the Australian environment?
- Did Aboriginal hunting cause the extinction of Australia's megafauna?
- Was traditional Aboriginal life idyllic?
- Did the First Australians have a religion or shamans?
- How much violence was there in traditional society?
- Why did Australian Aborigines not become gardeners or farmers?
- Are there any 'nomads' left?
- Why did Captain Cook believe Australia to be *terra nullius*—ownerless?
- Why were treaties not made with Australian Aborigines?
- Who introduced smallpox into Australia?
- Was conflict or imported new disease the main factor in Aboriginal depopulation?
- Did the colonists attempt genocide?
- How have government policies of protection, integration and self-determination worked?
- Were Aboriginal children 'stolen'? If so, why and with what result?
- What are land rights?
- What are the problems in modern Aboriginal communities?
- What do Aboriginal people want?
- How can these aspirations be achieved?

This is an extremely challenging list. My attempted 'answers' are based on evidence ranging from rock paintings to DNA, First Fleet diaries to Aboriginal web sites. Sources include indigenous communities, archaeologists, anthropologists, linguists, ethnographers, historians, journalists and government officials, and I am most grateful for the overwhelmingly positive responses I have received to my many requests for information and comment. Inevitably, such a book has to be selective but I have tried to give a representative account. In the story of the colonial period, most attention is given to the best-documented accounts of the first three decades of interaction in the Sydney region and Tasmania.

As an archaeologist, my approach is an evidence-based examination of culture and history in search of the 'truth'. My interpretations are assessed in terms of how well they account for *all* the evidence, not whether they can be proved to be true in any absolute sense. Scientific methods are used but it is seldom possible to confirm or refute hypotheses with the same certainty as in the hard sciences. Discovering what happened in the past is like doing a jigsaw puzzle with most of the pieces missing and no picture on the box as a guide. The archaeologist is both a detective and a scavenger, hunting among historical documents and field evidence. Archaeologists are today's explorers, whether excavating ice age caves or investigating a nineteenth-century massacre site. As historian Sir Keith Hancock said, 'There is only one way to do history, with boots on your feet and a pack on your back.' The geography behind history is essential to our understanding of events and place, whether ancient or modern.

References to primary sources and further evidence are provided in the notes. Consultation on the book has been carried out with various colleagues and with the friends and family members who originally asked the questions.

Particular thanks are due to Nigel Peacock, Ursula Fraser and Barbara Roscoe, who gave me invaluable comments on my first draft. I much appreciate the useful feedback I received at the next stage of preparing the manuscript from Val Attenbrow, Richard Broome, Frank Fenner, Alan Frost, Campbell Macknight, Betty Meehan, Rod Moran, Denise Robin, Lyndall Ryan, Peter Sutton and Mike Westaway. In addition, the final draft of the whole text was checked by historian Campbell Macknight and anthropologist Peter Sutton.

Finally, I would like to thank Elizabeth Weiss and Angela Handley of Allen & Unwin in Sydney for their encouragement, wise advice and meticulous editing.

It is hoped that this book is both factually accurate and observant of Aboriginal sensitivities, but I apologise in advance for any errors or problems. Feedback on the book would be most welcome to my email address < josephineflood@compuserve.com>.

PLEASE NOTE
In traditional Aboriginal communities it is customary not to
mention the name of, or reproduce images of, the recently deceased.
Care and discretion should therefore be exercised in using this book
within Arnhem Land, Central Australia and the Kimberley.

NOTES ON TERMINOLOGY

Over the last four decades, terminology in Australian Aboriginal studies has been constantly changing. Today two distinct groups of indigenous Australians are officially recognised—the people of the Torres Strait Islands and the Aboriginal people of mainland Australia and Tasmania. Each has their own flag, which is flown at official functions across the nation. The term 'indigenous' is used to describe people who originally, before intermarriage with newcomers from overseas, had no other race history except from the country in which they live. Nowadays the term 'indigenous Australians' is used to embrace both Aboriginal Australians and Torres Strait Islanders.

'Aboriginal people' or 'Aborigines' (always capitalised) are used in Australia to distinguish mainlanders from the people of Torres Strait. I follow correct grammatical forms in using Aborigine/s as a noun and Aboriginal as an adjective. ('Aboriginals' is considered more politically correct, but some Aboriginal people have told me they don't like being just an adjective!) Regional names such as Murris or Kooris applied by contemporary Aboriginal groups to themselves are inappropriate to describe the whole of Australia or the deep past. The term 'Aborigines' includes people of variously mixed ancestry; when it is necessary to distinguish between people of mixed and of non-mixed descent, the latter are called people of full Aboriginal descent. Terms such as 'half-caste' are only included if they are part of a quotation from a historical source.

For the sake of clarity, the term 'prehistory' is retained for the period before records were written down; in Australia this is 'pre-contact', usually taken as pre-1770, the date of Captain Cook's first visit to Australia. History relies on documentary and recorded oral evidence, whereas prehistory is reconstruction based primarily on archaeological evidence. This does not in any way imply that societies without writing were inferior or that history is more important than prehistory. In 1988 the Australian Institute of Aboriginal Studies resolved to use 'history' to refer to the Aboriginal past before written records as well as post-contact, but this has proved confusing and has not been widely adopted; for example, the respected journal *Aboriginal History* deals only with post-contact history.

I have had some difficulty in finding a term for the modern 'non-indigenous' people of Australia. It is unsatisfactory to define people by what they are not, but Australia has become such a multiracial society that no racial description is appropriate. I therefore use the terms mainstream or dominant society, as well as non-indigenous people. Anglo-Australians is also used in a broad sense to denote non-indigenous people, where their racial origins are not important to the story.

EXPLORATION
European discovery of Australia

Few things are as intriguing as a question mark on a map. For more than a thousand years, mystery surrounded the possible existence of a great, unknown continent in the southern hemisphere. Greek and Roman philosophers argued for it and first-century geographer Ptolemy sketched a huge landmass in the southern ocean. Ptolemy saw an unknown southern land—*Terra Australis Incognita*—as necessary to balance the lands of the northern hemisphere, and later cartographers agreed.

It wasn't until the sixteenth century that European merchant adventurers reached the remote island continent.[1] The Renaissance was a time of discovery, of charting unknown lands in search of riches and, ultimately, empire. European ocean travel became possible through advances in shipbuilding and navigation.[2] Superpowers Spain and Portugal struggled for global control and in the 1494 Treaty of Tordesillas the Pope divided the non-Christian world between them. In the Pacific the line of demarcation followed line of longitude 129 degrees East of Greenwich, bisecting Australia and now forming the Western Australian border. Portugal thus 'acquired' what is now Western Australia, and Spain the rest of the continent. The Portuguese were the first Europeans to reach the Australian region and by 1516 had built a fortified trading post in Timor, only 460 km (285 miles) north of the Kimberley coast.[3]

›› Dutch encounters and the first kidnappings

The first recorded encounters between outsiders and Australian Aborigines involved the Dutch, whose merchant fleet reached the East Indies, as the Malay Archipelago was called, in 1596. The Dutch East India Company (Verenigde Oostindische Compagnie or VOC) established its headquarters in Batavia (Jakarta) on Java in 1619. Trade with the Spice Islands, where nutmeg and cloves were available, helped turn Holland into the wealthiest country of its time, and the Dutch replaced the Portuguese as masters of the eastern seas. Exploration of New Holland, as the Dutch named northern and western Australia, was motivated by the search for trade goods, especially gold, silver, sandalwood and above all nutmeg, a small sack of

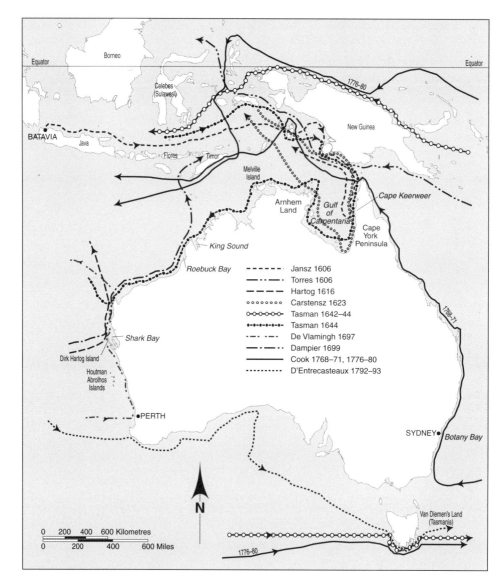

» *European voyages of discovery.*

which had a 60 000 per cent mark-up in Europe and could set a merchant adventurer up for life.[4]

Indigenous Australians gave their first Dutch visitors a hostile reception in 1606, when Willem Jansz sailed his ship *Duyfken* down the western edge of Cape York Peninsula, reaching a place he called Cape Keerweer ('Turn-Again'). His journal is lost, but fragmentary reports tell us his brief landfall (near modern Weipa) was marred by violence from naked 'savage, cruel, black barbarians'.

Later that year, Spaniard Luis Vaes de Torres sailed through the narrow strait between New Guinea and Australia now called Torres Strait. He spent weeks negotiating innumerable reefs and islands, where he kidnapped 'twenty persons'. The hostages reached the Philippines but nothing is known of what happened to them there. This kidnapping was the first of several aimed at training interpreters for use as intermediaries.

The VOC's instructions to Jan Carstensz, the captain of the *Pera*, before his 1623 voyage were to kidnap 'some full-grown persons but especially young boys and girls, to the end that the latter may be brought up here [Batavia] and turned to useful purpose in . . . their own country'.[5]

Carstensz and other voyagers were still searching for the fabled islands of gold, which, according to Marco Polo's fantasies, lay south of Java. They were doomed to disappointment. After sailing down Cape York, Carstensz reported:

> This is the most arid and barren region that could be found anywhere on the earth. The inhabitants, too, are the most wretched and poorest creatures that I have ever seen . . . as there are no large trees anywhere on this coast, they have no boats or canoes . . . These men are . . . of tall stature and very lean to look at . . . they are quite black and stark naked, some of them having their faces painted red and others white, with feathers stuck through the lower part of the nose . . . with twisted nets round their heads.[6]

Carstensz's first encounter with Aborigines, on 18 April 1623 near the Edward River, began well when they were met by many inquisitive people, some armed and some unarmed, who 'showed no fear and were so bold as to touch the muskets of our men . . . while they wanted to have whatever they could make use of'. Sadly, peace was shattered when the Dutch kidnapped a man, the sailors were attacked, and one Aborigine was shot. Two weeks later, a second man was seized and another was shot. Two hundred men brandishing spears opposed the next landing. When one was wounded, he was seized as a captive, but died soon afterwards.

Until the English invention in the mid-eighteenth century of an accurate chronometer, mariners had no means of establishing their longitude. Errors in navigation, and the prevailing westerly winds, blew some Dutch ships onto the dangerous shoals of Western Australia. In 1629, a large Dutch ship, the *Batavia*, was shipwrecked in the Houtman Abrolhos islands off the western coast. Fellow Dutchmen murdered 125 of the survivors. The Dutch rescue party from Java responded by executing eight of the perpetrators and exiling two of them on the adjacent coast. These two murderers were Europe's first living 'gift' to Australia.

In 1642, Dutchman Abel Tasman headed further south in search of the elusive southern continent and became the first European to set foot on the island of Tasmania, which he named Van Diemen's Land. Dense clouds of smoke told him the island was inhabited. The men who went ashore found a tall tree with notches freshly cut up its trunk. 'They measured the shape of the steps and found each were

» *Aboriginal men of the Kolaia tribe, Cambridge Gulf, Western Australia, in the 1920s. They have cicatrices (scars) on their bodies and wear their hair bound around a pad of emu feathers, enabling small sacred objects to be carried hidden from view.*

fully five feet [150 cm] from one another so that they presumed here were very tall people or these people by some means must know how to climb up trees.'[7] In fact, the Tasmanians proved to be small people with good tree-climbing skills.

›› Dampier

In January 1688, Englishman William Dampier, a literate buccaneer, spent two months in King Sound near Derby in the Kimberley (northwestern Australia) with his shipmates, repairing their beached trading ship, the *Cygnet*. Dampier, an acute observer, kept detailed notes preserved in waterproof bamboo cylinders sealed with wax. His vivid account was both successful and influential. In 1699, Dampier commanded an English naval expedition to explore the region further in the *Roebuck*. He voyaged along the western coast from Shark Bay to Roebuck Bay just south of Broome and produced another book.

Dampier paints a grim picture of the arid northwest and its naked people:

The inhabitants of this country are the miserablest people in the world. The Hodmadods [Hottentots of Africa] . . . for wealth are gentlemen to these. They have no houses, or skin garments, sheep, poultry, fruits of the earth . . . They are tall, straight-bodied and thin, with small, long limbs. They have great heads, round foreheads and great brows. Their eyelids are always half closed, to keep the flies out of their eyes . . . They have great bottle noses, pretty full lips and wide mouths. The two fore-teeth of their upper-jaw are wanting in all of them, men and women, old and young . . . Nor have they any beards . . . Their hair is black, short and curled like that of the Negroes, and not long and lank like the common Indians. The colour of their skins . . . is coal-black like that of the Negroes of Guinea. They have no sort of clothes but a piece of the rind of a tree, tied like a girdle about their waists, and a handful of long grass, or three or four small green boughs full of leaves thrust under their girdle, to cover their nakedness . . . They had such bad eyes, that they could not see us till we came close to them.[8]

This is important evidence that pre-contact Australia was no paradise. Eye ailments were especially prevalent among desert Aborigines, and trachoma, a contagious inflammation of the eyelids, is still a chronic disease, often leading to blindness. Indeed, in the Western Desert language, the words for 'old' and 'blind' are interchangeable. This is also the first mention of Australian bush flies. Dampier complained that 'no fanning will keep them from coming to one's face; and without the assistance of both hands to keep them off, they will creep into one's nostrils and mouth too'.

Lack of the two front teeth indicates tooth avulsion, a widespread initiation ritual in Australia. More puzzling is the mention of men's lack of beards, for in the Kimberley and elsewhere older men usually sported beards, although sometimes they shaved them with a sharp shell or stone 'knife'. The people's main food was fish, caught in stone fish traps. Similar traps are still used by Bardi people as the most efficient way of harvesting fish. Dampier also remarked on other key aspects of Aboriginal life—small-scale societies, close communal living and the habit of sharing all procured food:

They have no houses but lie in the open air without any covering . . . they live in companies of twenty or thirty men, women and children together. Their only food is a small sort of fish, which they get by making wares [weirs or traps] of stone across little coves . . . Every tide brings in the small fish . . . at low-water they seek cockles, mussels and periwinkles. There are very few of these shellfish . . . At their places of abode . . . the old people . . . and tender infants await their return; and what providence has bestowed on them they presently broil on the coals and eat it in common . . . Whether they get little or much, every one has his part . . . When they have eaten, they lie down till the next low-water, and then all who are able march out, be it night or day, rain or shine . . . They must attend the wares or else they must fast.[9]

When Dampier first anchored, 'seeing men walking on the shore, we presently sent a canoe to get some acquaintance with them, for we were in hopes to get some provision among them. But the inhabitants, seeing our boat coming, ran away and hid themselves. We searched three days in hopes to find their houses, but found none. Yet we saw many places where they had made fires.' Later they went over to an island, where they found 40 men, women and children. At first, they were threatened with spears, but no violence ensued. Surprisingly, on this coast Aborigines had no visible watercraft. Dampier's crew saw 'a drove of these men swimming from one island to another'. They picked up four and gave them boiled rice, turtle and fish. 'They greedily devoured what we gave them, but took no notice of the ship or anything in it, and when they were set on land again, they ran away as fast as they could . . . Nor did they seem to admire anything we had.' Fear, shyness, lack of curiosity and indifference to foreign goods—except food and weapons—characterised most first encounters between Aborigines and outsiders.

Another incident involved the first European attempt to persuade Aborigines to work for them. The task was to carry small barrels of freshwater from earthern wells down to the boats. Dampier gave the men some old clothes, filled the casks and put a barrel on each man's shoulders, but nothing happened: 'all the signs we could make were to no purpose, for they stood like statues without motion, and grinned like so many monkeys, staring one upon another. For these poor creatures do not seem accustomed to carrying burdens . . . So we were forced to carry our water ourselves. They very fairly put the clothes off again, and laid them down as if clothes were only for working in.'[10]

A chasm of misunderstandings yawns here—Aborigines saw trade as exchange of artefacts not of labour, they laid down the clothes because they did not want them, and they had no concept or words for 'work'. Aboriginal men did not carry burdens, except their weapons, so that their hands were free for hunting—the women carried household items and small children when moving camp.

Dampier's account is especially valuable in showing us the rigours of traditional life in a harsh, arid environment. Although he could not understand their language, the scarcity of food and lack of watercraft was clear enough. By the time of colonisation, however, the Bardi were using mangrove rafts to hunt turtle and dugong with long fishing spears.

›› Further Dutch voyages

Dampier's books rekindled Dutch suspicions of English intentions in New Holland, so in 1705 three ships commanded by Maarten van Delft set out for northern Australia. They visited Arnhem Land and Bathurst and Melville Islands, home of the Tiwi people. There was prolonged contact with Aborigines and they reported that the people:

possess nothing which is of value . . . and have . . . only a stone which is ground and made to serve as a hatchet. They have no habitations, either houses or huts; and feed on fish which they catch with harpoons of wood, and also by means of nets, putting out to sea in small canoes, made of the bark of trees . . . Some of them had marks on their body, apparently cut or carved . . . Their diet seems to consist of fish, and a few roots and vegetables . . . No one was able to understand their language.[11]

The crew of Jean Etienne Gonzal's ship *Rijder* in 1756 have the dubious distinction of being the first Europeans to introduce alcohol into Australia. The liquor was arrack, a strong spirit made from fermented palm juices, which Cape York Aborigines reportedly enjoyed and made 'merry and even struck up a kind of a chant'.[12] Despite their genuine interest in the region, the Dutch neither claimed nor settled it.

›› The Macassans

Dugout sailing canoes were first introduced to tropical Australia by Macassans—Indonesian fishermen, who made lengthy annual visits but never settled on Australian soil. From around 1720, trade through the Dutch port of Makassar in Sulawesi included increasing quantities of trepang (*bêche-de-mer* or sea cucumber), which was sold to China.[13] In Australia's shallow tropical waters these worm-like, cucumber-sized animals were abundant, a food that neither Europeans nor Aborigines ate but one which was prized by the Chinese as a delicacy and aphrodisiac. Indonesian beds had been exhausted by 1720, and so the exploitation of Australian trepang began. The trepang were caught by Macassan fishermen along 1100 km (700 miles) of Australian coast from the Kimberley to the eastern Gulf of Carpentaria. The trepang-bearing western coast they called *Kayu Jawa* and that to the east *Marege'* (pronounced Ma-rey-geh). The Macassans called themselves, and were known to Aborigines as, *Mangkasara'—Makasar* people from the southwest corner of Sulawesi. They had a long and proud history and had been officially Muslim since the early seventeenth century. Their voyages to Australia were carefully regulated with formal contracts and sailing passes.[14] The Macassans used praus—wooden sailing ships that had rectangular sails raised on a demountable tripod-mast and were guided with two rudders hanging from a beam across the stern. Similar praus carried goods and people throughout the Malay Archipelago.

Tropical Australia's climate is monsoonal, with a wet season from December to February and a dry season from June to September. When the monsoon winds began to blow from the northwest in November or December, praus sailed the 2000 km (1250 miles) from Makassar to Australia. The ships left carrying weapons but no cargoes and, after five months of fishing, headed north again, laden with dried trepang, beeswax and tortoiseshell, when the winds blew from the southeast in late April to May.

Macassan camps are identifiable from shards of red pottery, green glass from square-necked gin bottles, bronze coins and tall, feathery, imported tamarind trees. Camps were located on easily defended islands or promontories and were furnished with stone fireplaces, huge boiling-down cauldrons, smoke-houses and wells for drinking-water. Some of these items appear in Aboriginal rock paintings.

In February 1803, while circumnavigating Australia, Matthew Flinders came across eleven Macassan praus off Arnhem Land. With his Malay cook translating, Flinders talked with Pobasso, the commander, who told him there were 60 praus in their fleet, crewed by over a thousand men.[15] He described how 'they get the trepang in from 3 to 8 fathoms water [5–14 m, 18–48 ft]; and where it is abundant, a man will bring up eight or ten at a time'. They were also caught by net or spear. Trepang were first cured by boiling. They were then gutted, cooked again (with mangrove-bark to give flavour and colour), dried in the sun, and smoked. After this, they would keep almost indefinitely. The end-product, according to naturalist Alfred Wallace, resembled 'sausages which have been rolled in mud and then thrown up the chimney'.[16]

Relations between Macassans and local Aborigines varied; Dutch records testify to hostility and some Macassan deaths at Aboriginal hands and Pobasso himself had been speared in the knee and issued strong warnings 'to beware of the natives'. Yet at times relations were friendly and there was cohabitation (one prau captain fathered nine children by three Aboriginal women). Some Aboriginal men even travelled overseas by prau and by 1876 seventeen were living in Makassar.

Arnhem Landers adopted hundreds of Makasar words, including their name for white people—'balanda', derived from 'Hollander', as the Dutch were known in the East Indies. They acquired new songs, ceremonies and art forms, including wooden sculpture, 'Van Dyke'-style goatee beards, long pipes for smoking imported tobacco and small dugout sailing canoes, which the Macassans kept on deck and used for trawling for trepang. Macassans called these 'lepa-lepa', which became 'lippa-lippa' in Arnhem Land. Aborigines obtained them through exchange or by salvage from the many praus wrecked on the coast, but eventually made their own, using metal tools acquired from Macassans and later from the British. They also incorporated Macassan items into ritual life and some ceremonies apparently referred to new, introduced diseases, such as smallpox (see chapter 4) and syphilis.[17]

Arnhem Land stands out as the major exception to the general rule that Aboriginal culture was one of the most conservative on earth. Had there been cultural dynamism we would have seen variations in economic mode such as occurred in the Americas, major revisions of art styles, the production of textiles and pottery, and much more extensive trading with the outside world. The Yolngu of Arnhem Land, unlike any other Aboriginal Australians, had made adjustments so that new things were adopted and new people were given a place in their cosmology. In contrast with this hot-bed of innovation, indigenous artefacts reported by the earliest visitors to

Cape York and the Kimberley are closely matched by those of three centuries later, suggesting greater cultural conservatism and far less contact with the outside world.

›› Captain Cook

The primary aim of Lieutenant (later Captain) James Cook's 1768–71 voyage in the *Endeavour* was scientific—he was to sail to the Society Islands (Tahiti) to observe the transit of Venus on 3 June 1769. His task completed, Cook opened his secret, sealed orders. They confirmed that he should try to find the supposed great southern continent thought to lie far south between New Holland and Cape Horn. Besieged by young Tahitians wanting to accompany him, Cook took a priest called Tupaia as an interpreter. He searched the South Pacific and circumnavigated New Zealand, proving conclusively that the 'land of the long white cloud' was *not* the northern tip of an undiscovered southern continent. Tupaia's presence was invaluable in establishing good relations with Maori warriors, with whom he conversed with ease. (Close similarities between Tahitian and Maori are demonstrated in comparative word lists compiled by Joseph Banks—later Sir Joseph—the expedition's chief naturalist.)[18]

From New Zealand, Cook wanted to return by way of Cape Horn because:

> by this route we should have been able to prove the existence or non-existence of a Southern Continent which yet remains doubtful; but . . . the condition of the ship . . . was not thought sufficient for such an undertaking . . . It was therefore resolved . . . to steer to the westward until we fall in with the East coast of New Holland and then to follow . . . the direction it may take until we arrive at its northern extremity.[19]

Believing himself a failure for having missed the southern continent, Cook set sail for the unexplored eastern coast of the island of New Holland (Australia). Ironically, New Holland proved to be the only inhabitable continent-sized island in the southern hemisphere, but it was not until Cook's second voyage in 1772 that, by a thorough criss-cross search of the 15 000-km-wide (10 000-mile-wide) South Pacific, he finally disposed of the myth of the southern isles of gold.

On 19 April 1770, *Endeavour's* crew sighted the 'gentle sloping hills . . . clothed with trees of no mean size' of the southeastern corner of Australia. Sailing northwards up the coast, they saw a number of 'natives of a very dark or black colour' and several 'smokes'—fires lit either by lightning or Aboriginal hunters.[20] The fires were too large and sporadic to have been smoke signals lit to alert neighbours. Traditional enmity between neighbouring tribes makes it unlikely that they warned of a ship's arrival by prearranged signals and on landing Cook met no organised resistance. Aborigines lived in small groups that seldom combined against mutual enemies.

On 29 April, in search of freshwater, the *Endeavour* entered the large bay of Gamay, which Cook later named Botany Bay because of the innumerable plants collected there by botanists Banks and Daniel Solander. The tall ship with its great sails passed within 400 m (¼ mile) of fishermen in four canoes and provoked a most unexpected reaction—apparent indifference. The fishermen did not even look up. Then, when the ship anchored close inshore, a naked woman carrying wood appeared with three children. 'She often looked at the ship,' Banks recounts, 'but expressed neither surprise nor concern. Soon after this she lighted a fire and the four canoes came in from the fishing; the people landed, hauled up their boats and began to dress their dinner, to all appearance totally unmoved by us.' So huge and alien was the *Endeavour* that it probably seemed a mirage or monster, and by ignoring it they conceivably hoped it might disappear. The Englishmen thought them so peaceful that they expected their landing to be unopposed, but when two boats carrying 30 men approached the shore the Aborigines clearly recognised them as humans rather than spirits, and all 'made off except two men who seemed resolved to oppose our landing'. Cook spoke to them but 'neither us nor Tupaia could understand one word they said'.

> We then threw them some nails, beads, etc ashore which they took up and seemed not ill pleased in so much that I thought that they beckoned to us to come ashore; but in this we were mistaken, for as soon as we put the boat in they again came to oppose us, upon which I fired a musket between the two, which had no other effect but to make them retire back where the bundles of their darts [spears] lay, and one of them took up a stone and threw at us which caused my firing a second musket load with small shot, and although some of the shot struck the man, yet it had no other effect than to make him lay hold of a shield . . . to defend himself.
>
> Immediately after this we landed, which we had no sooner done than they throwed two darts at us, this obliged me to fire a third shot, soon after which they both made off . . . Mr. Banks being of the opinion that the darts were poisoned, made me cautious how I advanced into the woods. We found there a few small huts made of the bark of trees in one of which were four or five small children with whom we left some strings of beads etc . . . Three canoes lay upon the beach the worst I think I ever saw, they were about 12 or 14 feet [3.6 or 4.2 m] long made of one piece of the bark of a tree drawn or tied up at each end and the middle kept open by means of pieces of sticks by way of thwarts.[21]

Cook felt that firing overhead or at the legs from 40 yards (36 m) could do little harm, and Banks justified it because 'we suspected their lances [spears] to be poisoned from the quantity of gum which was about their points'. (Aborigines did sometimes put poison on spear-tips to cause infection in a wound; spearheads were dipped in a putrid corpse before use in fighting or smeared with grass-tree gum or milky mangrove juice. Even when no poison was used, victims often died of tetanus.)[22] In southeastern Australia, Aborigines had lived so long in isolation that intruders from an outside world were probably inconceivable. They mounted a courageous opposition against the strange white beings and the thunderous noise of their magical sticks, but the English were very surprised that they fled leaving their children behind. During their eight days at Botany Bay, Cook and Tupaia kept trying to communicate and 'form some connections with the natives', but 'we could neither by words nor actions prevail upon them to come near us', 'they all fled at my approach' and 'all they seemed to want was for us to be gone'. Others found that, 'they had not so much as touched the things we had left in their huts'. Banks reported that, 'Upon every other occasion both there and everywhere else they behaved alike, shunning us and giving up any part of the country which we landed upon at once.' Cook judged Aborigines to be a 'timorous and inoffensive race' compared with Maori and their great war canoes carrying a hundred men, fortified hilltop settlements, war dances, tattooing and elaborate dress. Relations had varied, but often Maori warriors had paddled canoes out to the *Endeavour* and traded fish for cloth and beads. In Cook's view:

> The natives [of Australia] do not appear to be numerous, neither do they seem to live in large bodies but dispersed in small parties along by the waterside; those I saw were about as tall as Europeans, of a very dark brown colour but not black, nor had they woolly frizzled hair, but black and lank much like ours. No sort of clothing or ornaments were ever seen by any of us . . . Some we saw that had their faces and bodies painted with a sort of white paint or pigment.[23]

Sailing northwards, Cook later wrote 'this eastern side is not that barren and miserable country that Dampier and others have described the western side to be'. He observed smoke all the way up the coast, and then became acquainted with Aborigines at Endeavour River (near modern Cooktown, Queensland), where *Endeavour* was beached for seven weeks after being holed and almost lost on the Great Barrier Reef. It took three weeks for Aboriginal men to approach the beached ship. Friendly contact was finally established and over twelve consecutive days eight meetings occurred. The first involved giving presents such as cloth, nails, beads and a small fish. The fish was greeted 'with the greatest joy imaginable', and the next day the gift was reciprocated. The only presents that were valued were food items, and trouble arose only when eight Aborigines who had ventured on board the *Endeavour* asked for two of several large turtles lying on deck. Their request was refused and attempts to remove turtles were thwarted, whereupon they leapt into their canoe, went ashore and set fire to the grass upwind of the tents and fishing-nets. Warning shots were fired but no one was hurt, the fire was put out, peace overtures were made and they were invited onto the ship again, but 'could not be prevailed upon to come on board'. The moral Banks drew from this incident was not that food should be shared out generously, but that firebreaks should be burnt before pitching camp, observing, 'I had little idea of the fury with which the grass burnt in this hot climate, nor of the difficulty of extinguishing it when once lighted.'[24]

Artist Sydney Parkinson was struck by the 'diminutive' size of north coast Aborigines. Banks measured some men and found them 'in general about 5 feet 6 inches [168 cm] in height and very slender; one we measured 5 feet 2 [157 cm] and another 5 feet 9 [175 cm], but he was far taller than any of his fellows'. Their skin colour was described as 'chocolate', and hair as 'straight in some and curled in others; they always wore it cropped close round their heads; it was of the same consistence with our hair, by no means woolly or curled like that of Negroes. [Cropping of the hair and beard was done by singeing.] Their eyes were in many lively and their teeth even and good; of them they had complete sets, by no means wanting two of their foreteeth as Dampier's New Hollanders did.'[25]

Men had raised cicatrices on arms and thighs and bodies painted in red and white lines with white circles around the eyes. Some wore shell necklaces, string armlets, waist-belts made of human hair or kangaroo-skin and impressive nose ornaments of long bird bones 'as thick as a man's finger' worn through the pierced septum. They carried spears tipped with sharpened wooden points or stingray barbs. They had spear-throwers but no bows and arrows, which were used in New Guinea and the Torres Strait Islands but nowhere on the mainland. 'One man who had a bow and a bundle of arrows' was observed by Cook on Possession Island 11 km (7 miles) off the tip of Cape York, but they were the first Cook had seen.

Physical similarities between all east coast Aborigines led Cook and Banks to assume (wrongly) that they all spoke the same 'New-Holland language'. The language, of which they recorded brief word lists at Endeavour River, was Guugu Yimithirr. Here the word 'kangaroo' first entered the English language. Cook and Banks thought it a generic name for any macropod (long-footed marsupial), whereas it applies only to large black kangaroos, for each species has a different name in Guugu Yimithirr, as in all other Aboriginal languages. (The story that the true meaning of kangaroo is 'I don't know' is apocryphal.) Cook observed that New Hollanders 'are a different people and speak a different language' from New Guineans, since there seemed to be no contact or 'commerce' between the two.[26] The only clear cultural difference noticed between northern and southern Australians was in watercraft, for southerners fished from small, fragile bark vessels, whereas north of the Whitsunday Islands outrigger canoes able to carry four people were used—narrow, roughly hollowed-out tree trunks about 3 m (10 ft) long with a single or double outrigger to prevent them overturning.

Describing Australian Aborigines presented a challenge. The primitivist school of thought had taught observers to assess indigenous people against their own background; there were no longer inbred assumptions of European superiority. In the mid-eighteenth century, the notion of 'the noble savage'—naturally virtuous and innocent native people—had been advanced by French philosopher Jean-Jacques

« SPEARS, SPEAR-THROWERS AND SHIELDS »

The main Aboriginal weapon was the spear. Spear length varied from 1.5 to 5 m (5–18 ft) and the weight from 50 grams to 1.8 kilograms (2 oz–4 lb). Longer spears were used for fighting, shorter ones to hunt game such as kangaroos and emus (one of the large flightless birds of Australia). Spears could kill at 27 m (90 ft). Plain wooden javelins with sharp, fire-hardened tips served for hunting and fighting. Tasmanians used nothing else, but mainlanders developed many elaborate types. Some spears had barbs cut in the shaft while others had detachable heads. The notorious 'death' or 'war' spears of southeastern Australia had rows of a dozen or more sharp pieces of stone set in resin on the shaft to cause maximum tissue damage and make dislodgement difficult. Shafts were made of wood, reed, bamboo or grass-tree (*Xanthorrhoea*) stalks and detachable heads were fixed with sinews or resin.

Some spears were used with a spear-thrower or 'woomera' (the name comes from the Sydney language). This resembles the atlatl of North America, and both probably originated in Asia. Woomeras have shaped wooden shafts 45–150 cm (18–60 inches) long, with a short peg or hook at the butt end. This fits into a hole in the end of the spear. Woomeras add extra force to the thrower's arm by keeping it in touch with the spear for longer and increasing

» *Pitjantjatjara men (pronounced pigeon-jar-jarrah) demonstrate the art of spear-throwing at Uluru (Ayers Rock) at the handing back of native title on 26 October 1985.*

leverage. When the spear shaft is given a flick with the forefinger as it is thrown with a woomera, it rotates in flight, giving greater accuracy. The projectile force of a spear propelled in this way far exceeds that of the bow and arrow, but is less accurate. In Central Australia, woomeras are multipurpose implements used for hurling spears, kindling fire or disembowelling game with the sharp stone chisel set in resin on one end. The maximum distance travelled by hand-thrown javelins is 60 m (200 ft) but ultra-light spears thrown by a woomera have covered 180 m (600 ft).

Spear shields were designed to deflect barbed spears thrown in battle, whereas narrow parrying shields with handles cut in the dense hardwood were for defence against clubs in individual combat. Outer surfaces were incised with stone or tooth implements or painted with ochre, charcoal, pipe-clay, blood or fats. Geometric and figurative motifs were combined in designs identifying the shield's owner. Southeastern Australian shields boasted the most intricate carving and greatest motif range. Styles varied, the most spectacular being the huge, painted shields of northern Queensland (see the Queensland, South Australian or Australian Museums). Shields were used over most of Australia, except Tasmania, and toy shields were made for young boys to practise with.

In August 1770 at Botany Bay, Joseph Banks noted in his journal that the bark of many trees had been cut into shield shapes and prised up with stone wedges but not removed, 'which shews that these people certainly know how much thicker and stronger bark becomes by being suffered to remain upon the tree some time after it is cut round'.

» *Aborigines of Hastings River, northern New South Wales, remove bark from a grey mangrove tree to make a shield, c. 1910. A 'blank' for the shield was removed, a handle made from pliable vine or wood was added, and the shield was decorated with painted designs. One man carries two boomerangs in his string belt, the other a fighting club.*

» «

Rousseau. His concept of Arcadia, an earthly paradise inhabited by happy, healthy, beautiful people whose every want was supplied by bountiful nature, was just a theory until the first French and British ships visited Tahiti and discovered its apparent reality.

The Tahitians' 'soft primitivism', which was much admired by Banks, was later found to encompass licentiousness, infanticide and human sacrifice. Cook was more impressed by the 'hard primitivism' of Maori warriors, with their elaborately tattooed faces, even if they did feast on their slain enemies, and of 'New Hollanders', such as the two who so courageously opposed his landing, although vastly outnumbered. Both Banks and Cook appreciated the contentment, self-sufficiency and Spartan simplicity of Aboriginal life; as Cook expressed it in apparent deliberate contradiction of Dampier:

> the natives of New-Holland . . . may appear to some to be the most wretched people upon Earth, but in reality they are far more happier than we Europeans . . . They live in a tranquillity which is not disturbed by the inequality of condition: The earth and sea . . . furnishes them with all things necessary for life . . . they live in a warm and fine climate, . . . so that they have very little need of clothing . . . they seemed to set no value upon any thing we gave them, nor would they ever part with any thing of their own . . . this in my opinion argues that they think themselves provided with all the necessarys of life and that they have no superfluities.[27]

Sir Joseph Banks, a wealthy Londoner whose opinion was to be far more influential, concluded that New Hollanders were 'the most uncivilised savages perhaps in the world'. A major factor in this judgement was the nudity of Aboriginal women as well as men, for even the women of Tierra del Fuego wore a 'flap of seal skin' over their 'privities'. Cook judged Fuegians rather than Australian Aborigines as 'perhaps as miserable a set of people as are this day upon earth'. He described them as 'a little ugly half starved beardless race, . . . almost naked', and found it 'distressing to see them stand trembling and naked on the deck'. Cook was struck by Fuegian suffering from cold even in the middle of summer, something he did not witness in Australia. Similarly Charles Darwin, who met both Aborigines and Fuegians in the 1830s, classed the 'shivering tribes' of Fuegians as 'the most abject and miserable creatures I anywhere beheld . . . The Australian, in the simplicity of the arts of life, comes nearest the Fuegian'. From these views came the concept that these societies in 'the uttermost parts of the earth' were living representatives of the oldest phase of human development.[28]

» The question of consent

On 22 August 1770, Cook landed on Possession Island off Cape York.

> we saw a number of people . . . we expected that they would have opposed our landing but as we approached the shore they all made off . . . the Eastern coast from the latitude

The Original Australians

of 38° South . . . to this place I am confident was never seen or visited by any European before us, and . . . I now once more hoisted English Colours and in the name of His Majesty King George the Third took possession of the whole Eastern Coast . . . by the name of New South Wales.[29]

Cook claimed 3.8 million km² (1.5 million sq. miles) from latitude 20°37' to 43°39' south and inland as far as longitude 135°. This claim only gave the English preliminary title, and settlement in 1788 gave actual possession of just the region occupied by the colonists—the Sydney Basin. The name New South Wales came from the resemblance of eastern Australia's wooded hills, headlands and beaches to the south coast of Wales.

The Admiralty's instructions to Cook were:

You are also with the consent of the natives to take possession of convenient situations in the country in the name of the King of Great Britain or, if you find the country uninhabited, take possession for his Majesty by setting up proper marks and inscriptions, as first discoverers and possessors.[30]

The problem was that these instructions referred to mythical isles of gold inhabited by civilised people able to negotiate treaties. The 'natives' Cook met were not. He could not seek their consent in the absence of any common language and his interpreter, Tupaia, could not understand the Australians, which was not surprising as about 250 separate languages were spoken in Aboriginal Australia, all unrelated to any in the outside world.[31]

No signs of houses, villages, fields, domesticated animals, cultivation nor any system of land ownership or government were apparent, in contrast with the complex agricultural societies and large populations of Tahiti and New Zealand. Banks described Aborigines as 'wandering like the Arabs from place to place' and their huts as 'framed with less art or rather less industry than any habitations of human beings probably that the world can show'.[32]

Cook was also frustrated in following the Admiralty's instructions by the Aboriginal tendency to 'make off' when strangers appeared and the lack of leaders with whom to negotiate, unlike New Zealand where chiefs were identifiable by their special garb. The new land seemed to be sparsely populated by small nomadic groups; Banks said they never saw more than 'thirty or forty [persons] together'.[33] He decided the land was 'thinly inhabited' and that the unseen interior was probably 'totally uninhabited', in view of a lack of smoke far inland and the apparent scarcity of animal life or 'wild produce' away from the sea coast. Banks therefore argued that because there was no cultivation on the coast, there was none inland, and that people could not exist inland without cultivation.[34]

Cultural anthropologists have identified a broad pattern of development in human societies from bands to tribes to chiefdoms to states, while acknowledging some exceptions, variations and overlap between categories.[35] Australian societies were all of the band variety, characterised by small group size and nomadism—regular mobility and the lack of any permanent single base of residence. Aboriginal nomadism, however, was highly restricted geographically, except in the most arid regions. This is in stark contrast with nomads such as the Kurds, who moved between Turkey and China over time.

A band is a residential group of people that live and forage together. The 'Pygmies' and the San People of Africa, the Inuit and Fuegians have comparable band-type societies. Australian bands comprised one or more extended families but composition was fluid. Core members were close relatives by birth or marriage but individuals were extremely mobile and the band's size and membership varied with food resources and personal circumstances. Band numbers ranged from 8 to 70 persons but were usually between 14 and 33, with an average of 25.[36] Each band had its own 'range' (the area from which it won its living) but with permission could forage more widely in a neighbouring band's territory. Bands were land-using 'residence groups', whereas 'clans' were 'country groups' with a common identity, often based on claimed descent from a single Ancestral Being. Each clan held a defined 'estate', generally identified by a focal point such as a waterhole.[37]

The next major stage of social organisation is the tribe or regional linguistic grouping, usually distinguished by numbers in the hundreds. A 'tribe' is what anthropologists call a set of people sharing a common linguistic identification and hence a common identification with the area with which that language is traditionally identified. There are direct links between particular tracts of country and particular languages that were planted in the landscape by Ancestral Beings. For example, the Wardaman people of the Northern Territory are not Wardaman because of the language they speak, but because they are linked through their parents to places in which their language was installed in the era of creation. The 600 or so Australian tribes were primarily loose linguistic groupings that bore little relation to classic tribes with their fixed settlements, such as villages in New Guinea. Aboriginal Australia had neither fixed settlements nor political units in the form of villages, nor did tribal members act collectively as a social, economic or military unit. There was no racial solidarity and tribesmen did not regularly fight together against invaders. Australian societies are therefore classed as primarily of band rather than tribal type.

Some anthropologists now argue that the term 'tribe' is inadequate to express the complexity and diversity of Aboriginal social organisation. Many indigenous Australians disagree. Belonging to a particular 'tribe' or 'nation' (strictly a group of tribes) has become central to the identity of Aboriginal people, who use the terms proudly to indicate their origins and ancestral territory or 'country'. I therefore continue to use the traditional 'tribe' here rather than suggested replacements such as 'linguistic grouping' or 'regional identity'. Traditional Australian tribes numbered from 25 to several thousand persons with a mean size of 450.[38]

» Were treaties possible?

Australia is the only continent where no treaties were made between colonists and prior occupants, because the unique characteristics of its indigenous society made negotiated agreements impossible. Even had the communication problem been overcome, a separate treaty would have been required with each tribe. Cook's critics forget that traditional Aboriginal Australia was never united. Elsewhere the British did make treaties, for example the Treaty of Waitangi in New Zealand in 1840. Like the Aborigines, in Cook's time the Maori did not read or write. The major differences were that all Maori spoke the same language and their society was of the chiefdom type, with a developed tribal organisation governing thousands of subsistence gardeners living in villages and fortified hill-forts. Maori warrior bands fought organised battles against newcomers, but were also prepared to sell land to foreigners.[39]

Similarly, treaties were successfully made with tribal chiefs in North America, where the culture and structures of intertribal councils were not unlike European ones. One striking difference between early American and Australian history is that stories of the American frontier abound with names of tribes and great tribal federations, whereas early Australian history lacks named groups.

» *Terra nullius*

In the eighteenth century, the three recognised ways of acquiring legal sovereignty were by conquest, cession or occupation of land that was ownerless. The American colonies were mainly acquired by conquest or cession, but in 1770 Australia was regarded as 'common land' occupied only by 'wandering tribes'.

Politicians at the time were strongly influenced by the 1690 doctrine of John Locke that: 'As much land as a man tills, plants, improves, cultivates, and can use the product of, so much is his property. He by his labour does, as it were, inclose it from the Common.'[40] If a man improves common land 'for the benefit of life', it becomes his inalienable property. The much-quoted 1760 opinion of Swiss international law writer, Emerich de Vattel, was that:

> Nations, incapable by the smallness of their numbers to people the whole, cannot exclusively appropriate to themselves more land than they have occasion for, and which they are unable to settle and cultivate. Their removing their habitations through these immense regions, cannot be taken for a true and legal possession; and the people of Europe, too closely pent up, finding land of which these nations are in no particular want, and of which they make no actual and constant use, may lawfully possess it, and establish colonies there.[41]

De Vattel did not sanction total dispossession of indigenous people but argued that colonists had a limited right to land: they could take possession of 'a part' of the country but should confine themselves 'within just bounds'.

Since there was no sign of any chiefs or private land ownership, the claim that Australia was common land was not as unreasonable then as it may seem to us now. Elsewhere British colonies were planted in places where indigenous people understood, and defended, the concept of property. In America, Africa, India, the East Indies and New Zealand colonists encountered societies of gardeners and farmers who had houses, villages, fences and cultivated plots of land. Such evidence of prior ownership was clear and could not be ignored. Newcomers adjusted their views according to the level of development they observed.

The British followed the conventions adopted by European nations over the previous two centuries for legally acquiring unowned land, or *terra nullius*. This Latin phrase translates as 'nobody's land', and was actually not used with regard to the colonisation of Australia until the later twentieth century.[42] In legal terms, *terra nullius* means 'land over which no previous sovereignty has been exercised' or more simply 'land of no sovereign power'.

The clearest statement of the three possibilities for treating newly discovered lands is in Schouten's codicil to Abel Tasman's Instructions of 1641:

1. With a friendly sovereign power, make a treaty (as Tasman did in Japan and tried to do in Tonga).
2. With an unfriendly sovereign power, declare them an enemy (as Tasman did in New Zealand when the Maori attacked him).
3. In lands manifesting no sovereign power or visible government, whether uninhabited or *not* uninhabited, claim the land for the Dutch State (e.g. Tasman claimed Van Diemen's Land for the Dutch State as a sovereign power, not for the VOC, which was not a sovereign power).[43]

Cook's decision not to negotiate a treaty but to claim the land for the British Crown under the right of *terra nullius* was therefore not illegal by the terms of the day, or 'Captain Cook's mistake', as one school textbook labels it. As leading historian Alan Frost says, 'had the British not seen New South Wales to be *terra nullius*, then I believe they *would* have negotiated for the right to settle the Botany Bay area'.[44]

Later, in 1889, the Privy Council confirmed that 'from the outset' the law of England was New South Wales law, because the colony 'consisted of a tract of territory practically unoccupied, without settled inhabitants or settled law, at the time when it was peacefully annexed to the British dominions'.[45]

The urge to explore is a basic human instinct. Only Australia's remoteness and adverse reports from all its early visitors preserved it long after Europeans had colonised all other inhabitable continents. In the age of maritime expansion, Australian hunter-gatherers had no hope of permanent reprieve from intrusion by more developed nations. Throughout much of human history invasion, warfare and violence have been the norm. Thomas Hobbes in 1651 defined 'a state of nature' as 'a state of war', in which existence must be one of 'continual fear, and danger of violent death; And the life of Man solitary, poor, nasty, brutish and short'. European countries suffered endless invasions, and even sea-girt Britain endured innumerable incursions over 7000 years from Neolithic hunters, megalith builders, Celts, Romans, Angles, Saxons, Jutes, Vikings and Normans. Almost none of this immigration was peaceful.

Fortunately, by 1788 the rule of law was firmly established in Europe. As Frost points out:

> Cook and Banks were percipient, tolerant of racial and cultural difference, and empathetic to a remarkable degree . . . If any group of Europeans of this time might have adjusted their perceptions and modes of procedure to accommodate the fact of the Aborigines, it was this one; the Aborigines were simply too un-European for them to comprehend truly.[46]

» The question of cultivation

'We see this country in the pure state of nature, the industry of man has had nothing to do with any part of it,' Cook exclaimed.[47] Some now describe Aborigines as 'cultivators' because of their regular burning of the landscape for hunting, to keep paths open and to provide new, sweeter grass to attract game (see chapter 6). Burning had a huge impact on Australian vegetation but was not cultivation in the usual sense of the word. In Aboriginal Australia there was no sign of horticulture, agriculture or animal or plant domestication.

Australia is drier and flatter, with generally shallower soil and less biomass than any other inhabited continent, with the world's most unpredictable climate. Lack of food production in arid regions did not surprise early voyagers, but the absence of gardens, crops or domesticated animals on the fertile east coast was a puzzle. Why weren't pigs, chickens or gardening imported from Australia's near neighbours in the Torres Strait or New Guinea? Arnhem Landers adopted many other elements from outsiders—shell fishhooks, painted skulls and various art designs, cults and rituals, so why not animal husbandry and cultivation? Some Aborigines while trading with Torres Strait Islanders encountered vegetable plots, banana and coconut trees, and pigs but didn't import any species or adopt their neighbours' gardening techniques. Aboriginal men of the tropics were selective in what they adopted from their northern neighbours. Useful items, such as harpoons and fishhooks, were acquired and later copied, together with exotic ceremonial drums and masks. One reason why horticulture was not imported may simply be that digging was considered women's work but it was men rather than women who saw taro, yams and coconuts being cultivated on Torres Strait islands.

Australian soils and climate permit modern agriculture and were amenable to Stone Age horticulture. At least ten plants domesticated in Southeast Asia are also endemic in northern and central Australia, where they are used but not cultivated. These include taro, arrowroot, yams, wild rice, native millet, two fruit and three nut trees, including the macadamia, with its large nuts.[48]

Some animals and birds could also have been domesticated. Candidates were koalas, wombats, kangaroos, wallabies, pelicans, brush turkeys, cassowaries, emus, ducks and geese, but none are herd animals, none furnish milk or, while alive, any other useful product like wool, hair or horns, and none could be used for riding, pulling or carrying loads. The nearest the Aborigines came to animal domestication was when rainforest people tethered cassowary chicks for a few days until tamed. The young birds then roamed the camp until large and fat enough to provide a feast. But they were not kept for breeding, presumably because adult birds are large and very aggressive, with lethal talons.[49]

Were Aborigines too well furnished with food to bother about producing more? No, for anthropologist Jon Altman's research has shown that the influential concept that hunter-gatherers were 'the original affluent society' with abundant food and leisure time is a myth, even in the richest environments. The mistaken idea that Australian hunter-gatherers needed only about four hours per day to feed themselves came from a brief, flawed 1948 study in Arnhem Land: the all-adult group was unrepresentative, and the study didn't cover the seasonal cycle, with its lean as well as good times. Even in the relatively rich environment of coastal Arnhem Land, archaeologists Rhys Jones and Betty Meehan found during a year living with Gidjingali people that Aborigines needed far more than five hours each per day to produce the minimum food to survive (estimated at 2000 calories per day per capita) for a group that included young children and old people as well as active food collectors. Nor was the food supply reliable; in the year of the study a single freshwater flood almost wiped out the shellfish along 12 km (7 miles) of coast, a resource that the previous year had been a major food. The uncertainty of survival, the unremitting labour of the food quest and frequent hunger cast serious doubts on nostalgic concepts of a lost utopia.[50]

There was a strict division of labour in food-collecting. In Arnhem Land, men hunted animals, large fish and birds, and women gathered plant foods and shellfish. Over the seasonal cycle, men and women contributed roughly equal amounts of calories to the diet, but the women's provision of carbohydrates—from the collection of vegetables, fruits, seeds and nuts—involved far longer hours of work than the men's hunting, which provided protein. The calorific return per woman-hour collecting bush food over four months in different seasons ranged from 115 to 276 calories,

» *A Wardaman traditional owner, Julai Blutja, with a goanna in the Katherine region, Northern Territory, in 1992.*

averaging only 181. Food was shared according to a strict formula, but during the wet season, the lean period for vegetable foods, or when hunters came home empty-handed, there was hunger in the camp.

In spite of occasional food shortages, tribal Aborigines saw nature as their garden, a resource that didn't need cultivation or improvement. An Arnhem Lander once said, as she watched a Fijian missionary digging his vegetable plot, 'You people go to all that trouble, working and planting seeds, but we don't have to do that. All these things are there for us, the Ancestral Beings left them for us . . . we just have to go and collect the food when it is ripe.'[51]

Why did food production not develop in the more fertile, well-watered southeast, now a breadbasket for the world? Australia was an 'unlucky country' in its prehistoric flora, fauna and thin soils, but there are species that could have been domesticated. Only two of the world's 56 large-seeded grass species—native millet (*Panicum decompositum*) and pigweed or purslane (*Portulaca oleracea*)—are native to Australia and their grain size is only 13 mg, against 40 mg for the heaviest grains elsewhere. Yet Australian millet belongs to the same genus as broomcorn millet, a staple of early Chinese farming.

In semiarid and arid Australia, seeds were widely harvested but never cultivated. Millet was reaped with kidney-shaped stone knives and gathered when the seed was full but the grass still green. The grass was then stacked in small heaps and the seeds left to dry and ripen. When the seeds were ripe, the grass was threshed so that the seeds all fell in one place. This system cleverly overcame the problem of wild cereal seeds ripening at different times. When explorer Sir Thomas Mitchell travelled down the Darling River in July 1835, he observed that, 'the grass has been pulled . . . and piled in hayricks, so that the aspect of the desert was softened into the agreeable semblance of a hayfield . . . we found the ricks, or hay-cocks, extending for miles.'[52]

The grass was later threshed by hand to separate seed from stalks. Then, if not eaten immediately, seeds were stored in pits, kangaroo-skin bags or large wooden dishes. In Central Australia, in the 1870s, 1000 kg (1 ton) of seed was stored in 17 wooden dishes each about 150 cm long by 30 cm (5 ft long x 1 ft) deep, probably to feed participants at an initiation ceremony.[53] Women ground seeds into flour on millstones and baked loaves of unleavened 'bread' in the campfire. Processing was extremely time-consuming. Each kilogram (2 pounds) of native flour cost 5–8 hours of a woman's labour (3 hours harvesting time and 2–5 hours for processing, depending on the species). Seed-processing was women's work, but men did some reaping. It is no wonder that English bread and flour proved such powerful magnets, drawing Aboriginal people into towns and away from traditional life. Another problem with a diet based on stone-ground flour was that grit from the millstones caused severe wear on teeth, leading to chronic periodontal disease. All the adult skeletons found at the prehistoric burial site of Kow Swamp, Victoria, had first molars so worn that the roots were exposed and worn halfway down.[54]

Some other foods were managed, for example, permanent traps were built to catch eels and other fish and the tops of yam tubers were sometimes left in the ground 'so that the yam would grow again', as tropical Aborigines explained.[55] Some fruits such as *Solanum centrale* (desert raisins) and wild figs were stored for later use, particularly to feed ceremonial gatherings, but the heat and predation by dingoes (the wild dog of Australia), termites and locusts made most food storage impractical. Instead, desert Aborigines developed 'living larders' or 'game reserves' as last resorts in times of drought. They drove kangaroos into 'oases' with permanent water and broke their legs to keep them there. In the colonial period the same method was used: sheep were stolen, driven into the bush and their legs broken to keep the meat fresh until needed.

All such measures involved management, not production, of food resources. Worldwide, agriculture developed roughly simultaneously around 10 000 years ago, a time of major post-glacial climatic change.[56] Temperatures rose everywhere, and food supplies improved. Greater availability of plants and animals led to higher human population numbers, while rising seas displaced people into already inhabited areas. These changes increased population densities so that in some regions they eventually exceeded levels that could be sustained by hunting and gathering alone. Significantly, the change from collection to production of food occurred only in particularly fertile parts of the world, as they were the first to become overpopulated. As the saying goes, 'necessity is the mother of invention'. Domestication of plants and animals increased food supplies by ten- to a hundredfold.

Some have argued that agriculture is the natural end point to which all societies evolve, and Australia's slowness in this respect was due to the lack of animals and plants suitable for domestication. Others maintain that food production is by no means inevitable. In Australia, pressures for domestication were outweighed by those against, especially extreme religious conservatism, which was diametrically opposed to change. Ceremonies were performed for the maintenance of food plants and animals but Aboriginal beliefs strictly opposed the concept of actual food production. Taboos and totemism (spiritual linkages between people and the natural universe) forbid modification of the environment, for there is a strong belief in the interrelatedness of all living things. Likewise, storage of food for future private consumption is incompatible with the ubiquitous practice of sharing, and the use of food surpluses to support large ceremonial gatherings.

» Conservatism

Conservatism, or at least a very slow rate of change, is normal in human societies but seems exceptional to us because we live in a period of constant, rapid development. Aboriginal society is renowned for its cultural conservatism—the long-term continuity of specific traditions. There was great pressure against innovation. Central Australian artists consistently stated that artistic motifs did not change and were reproduced exactly as they always had been since the Dreaming or Dreamtime, the era when Ancestral Beings created the landscape and all living things. The Law established in the Dreaming must continue for ever unchanged. The Creative Ancestors told of in myths instituted a way of life that they introduced to humans, and because they themselves are believed to be eternal, so are the patterns of life they brought into being. The traditional Central Australian artistic repertoire is unchanged from the ice age.

Throughout Australian prehistory, basic forms of technology, religion and economy remained the same. For instance, the rite of cremation has endured for over

« A LACK OF COCONUT TREES »

The absence of coconut trees in Australia puzzled Cook. Neither he nor Flinders saw a single one. Why, they wondered, were coconut trees absent from Australia but flourishing on the coasts of the Torres Strait islands and Pacific Islands? Coconuts were extremely scarce but not entirely absent at the time of European settlement. Close examination of the Queensland coast in the mid-nineteenth century did reveal some tall, old coconut trees on remote Russell Island, southeast of Cairns, which probably germinated from buoyant, drifting nuts. 'It is obvious to anyone who walks the beaches, particularly of the east coast,' says Australian coconut expert, Mike Foale, 'that coconut seeds arrive fairly frequently, and that some of the seeds are capable of establishing palms.'[a]

Aboriginal languages of northeast Queensland had names for the coconut, and coconut fruits were traded between Torres Strait Islanders and Cape York Aborigines, yet no coconut palms grew in inhabited pre-colonial Australia. Why not? Hungry foragers consumed nuts washed up on beaches, thankful for the ease of collecting this nutritious, tasty food. Others competing for the prized meal were white-tailed rats (*Uromys caudimaculatus*) that could gnaw through the husk. A seedling also yields a quick meal for human or rodent from its residual kernel and spongy 'apple' but is destroyed in the process. Young trees were eaten by termites. Even mature coconut trees died after Aborigines harvested the succulent growing bud or 'heart of palm'. The same thing happened to several native species, such as 'cabbage palms' (*Livistonia* sp.).

Fruits are still washed up on the beach and eaten, but not planted, by Arnhem Landers. The direction of prevailing currents means that relatively few coconuts wash up on Australia's northern shores but they are plentiful in northeastern Queensland where, in the mid-twentieth century, anthropologists reported that Aborigines had learnt to plant them. Foale suggests that 'but for the presence of Aboriginal food-gatherers and the foraging white-tailed rat, the coconut would have been well established on at least the most favourable tropical shores of the Australian northeast before European settlement'.

Now coconut palms have become widespread and successful in Australia and on the northeast coast many coconut groves thrive without any management.

« »

40 000 years. The pattern of life set by the first Australians 50 millennia ago proved exceptionally successful and long-lasting. In Tasmania, isolated from the rest of the world for the last 14 000 years, change was minimal. Mainland Australia saw more innovations but no major ones, such as the development of pottery or the use of

metals. Some developments were indigenous while others, such as fishhooks, diffused from Asia. Non-indigenous commentators emphasise change in Aboriginal society, as change is equated with dynamism and progress in Western eyes. Aboriginal people disagree—they are proud of their conservatism and justifiably boast of having the world's longest continuing art tradition, oldest enduring religion and most ancient living culture. Traditional indigenous belief maintains that Aboriginal society has remained essentially unchanged since its beginning in the Dreaming.

» Nomadism

Native Australians have long been regarded as classic nomads—'peoples who live in no fixed place but wander periodically according to the seasonal availability of food . . . [and] usually live in small bands that spend anything from a few days to a few weeks in a vicinity, moving within a loosely defined territory'.[57]

In deserts, where food and water were scarce, people were constantly on the move, seldom camping for more than a few nights at each waterhole. In contrast, the inland fishermen of western Victoria spent around two months each autumn tending traps to exploit the annual downriver migration of eels to their marine breeding grounds. Such seasonally resident people have been termed 'semi-sedentary' but were still nomads, in that they had no home base and moved perhaps six times a year in the course of a regular seasonal round. Other semi-sedentary Aborigines lived along the banks of Australia's largest river, the Murray, where the arid hinterland limited most excursions to a 20-km-wide (12-mile-wide) corridor, the maximum distance hunter-gatherers could walk carrying a skin waterbag. It is no coincidence that these people developed the continent's most structured and hierarchical societies and the closest approach to tribal councils for conflict resolution.

» A sparse population

Aboriginal population density was greatest in environments that were rich in food, such as coasts, estuaries, large rivers and lakes. It is important, therefore, that, even after spending several weeks on the east coast, Cook and Banks considered Australia 'thinly inhabited'.

Much subsequent research has shown their judgement to be correct, although the size of the pre-contact Aboriginal population is inevitably uncertain. For the first 50 years, European settlement was confined to the coastal fringe. Often the only sign of Aboriginal presence was smoke from distant fires, and estimating numbers inland was impossible. In the 1920s, anthropologist Alfred Radcliffe-Brown was asked to assess the Aboriginal population in 1788. Using figures collected in the early 1800s, he concluded in the 1930 *Australian Yearbook* that 'the available evidence points to the original population of Australia having been certainly over 250 000, and quite possibly, or even probably, over 300 000.'

This figure of 300 000 doubled earlier estimates. It also fitted well with anthropologist Norman Tindale's identification of 600 tribes in Australia, with a mean of 450 members each. If Radcliffe-Brown's estimate is roughly right, it means that numbers declined from around 300 000 in 1788 to roughly 60 000 in 1921, a drop of 80 per cent. The major cause was the deadly impact of new diseases on people with no prior immunity. Epidemics of smallpox, influenza and tuberculosis killed most sufferers, and venereal diseases virtually sterilised a generation. Another factor was the devastating effect of alcohol. Modern historians emphasise violence on the frontier as responsible for Aboriginal depopulation, while barely mentioning disease. However, historian Henry Reynolds' estimate of 20 000 Aboriginal deaths in a century of frontier conflict accounts for only 8 per cent of the indigenous population decline. The vast majority of the 20 000 were men, whereas what matters most for population maintenance is female fertility.[58]

Some have put the Aboriginal population in 1788 much higher. Economic historian Noel Butlin estimated it as over a million, but archaeologist Keryn Kefous showed that his calculations involved incorrect assumptions concerning different environments' carrying capacity (the number of people an area of land can support). Butlin used maximum figures but actual hunter-gatherer population density is much lower because of droughts and uneven, unreliable resources. Most researchers now consider Radcliffe-Brown's figure too low but Butlin's far too high. A realistic estimate for Aboriginal population size in 1788 is half or, at most, three-quarters of a million.[59]

Europeans found traces of Aboriginal presence wherever they went in the 7.4 million km² (3 million sq. miles) of a country almost the same size as the continental United States. A prehistoric population of half a million would have averaged one person to fifteen km² (6 sq. miles) across the continent, although density varied widely according to local resources, climate and topography. Australian environments range from tropical rainforests to alpine peaks and from rich coastal and riverine shores to waterless deserts. Only one in ten Aborigines lived in the arid zone in the central third of the continent, which receives only 120–250 mm (5–10 inches) of rain a year. Western Desert people averaged one person to 150–200 km² (58–77 sq. miles).

Population was highest in the Murray and Darling River valleys and on the tropical coast of Arnhem Land, where it reached two people per km² (per ½ sq. mile). This density approaches that of coastal New Guineans who live by hunting, gathering and low intensity slash-and-burn agriculture, but their horticulturalists, who practise intensive shifting cultivation of sweet potato and taro in the central highlands, live at much higher densities (4–10 people per km²). New Guinea has only a tenth of Australia's land area but agriculture raised its pre-colonial indigenous population to about one million.[60]

» «

In short, European explorers found on Australia's shores a naked, 'wandering' people fishing, hunting and gathering with stone-age implements. Nakedness was equated with primitiveness, as was the lack of houses, villages, cultivation or any apparent system of chiefs, government or land tenure. In Europe, uncultivated land was regarded as ownerless, common land that could be legally colonised and settled without a treaty with the nomadic inhabitants. Australia's apparent lack of tradeable commodities and its vast distance from the European superpowers meant that it was the last inhabited continent to be colonised, but colonisation became inevitable once its splendid harbours and seemingly infinite supply of usable land were discovered.

COLONISATION
Early Sydney

Colonisation of such a remote land as Australia after only one visit was a remarkably bold venture that almost ended in disaster for the British. The primary motivation was the sudden need to find an alternative place to house convicts. British society was based on the sanctity of private property but theft was rife and the prisons were consequently overflowing. Until 1776, convicts were transported to colonies in North America, where they were indentured to plantation owners as labourers. The successful revolt of these colonies and their subsequent independence as the United States of America largely ended this practice, and New Zealand was never considered as an alternative because of the Maoris' extreme hostility. Pending another solution, convicted felons were kept in floating prison-hulks on the River Thames. Banks suggested Botany Bay as an alternative and, after much debate, in 1786 Lord Sydney (after whom Sydney would be named) announced the King's decision to send a fleet the following year. Eleven ships were to transport 717 convicts, mainly Londoners convicted of minor theft, and 290 seamen, soldiers and officers.

A cheaper solution than sending ships 19 000 km (12 000 miles) across the world was to build new gaols in Britain, but Australia had other attractions. Britain needed a port of call between the Indian and Pacific Oceans, and Norfolk Island was a promising source of timber for masts and flax for sailcloth. Ports and tradeable items were the focus of early colonisation; it was not until the nineteenth century that unexplored country was valued for its own sake.

Captain Arthur Phillip, a naval officer, was appointed the first governor. His instructions were:

> To endeavour by every possible means to open an intercourse with the natives, and to conciliate their affections, enjoining all our subjects to live in amity and kindness with them. And if any of our subjects shall wantonly destroy them . . . it is our will and pleasure that you do cause such offenders to be brought to punishment according to the degree of the offence.[1]

Phillip was equally keen to have no 'dispute with the natives, a few of which I shall endeavour to persuade to settle near us, and who I mean to furnish with everything that can tend to civilise them, and to give them a high opinion of their new guests'. Importantly, the British perceived themselves not as invaders but as guests, albeit uninvited ones, and their mission not as dispossession but as peaceful establishment of a small colony among the natives.

» New arrivals

After a gruelling eight-month voyage from Portsmouth, the First Fleet reached Australia and sailed into Botany Bay on 18 January 1788. Around 40 armed Eora people on the southern shore rattled their spears and shouted 'warra, warra', meaning 'go away'—the first Eora words ever spoken to the colonists.[2] Phillip avoided an encounter by instead landing, unarmed, on the northern side where there were only six men. According to eyewitness Watkin Tench, a captain of the marines,

> An officer in the boat made signs of a want of water . . . The natives directly comprehended what he wanted, and pointed to a spot where water could be procured. The Indians [Aborigines], though timorous, showed no signs of resentment at the Governor's going on shore. An interview commenced, in which the conduct of both parties pleased each other . . . the natives . . . seemed highly entertained with their new acquaintance, from whom they condescended to accept of a looking glass, some beads, and other toys.[3]

While at Botany Bay, David Collins, the colony's judge-advocate, commented: 'the natives had hitherto conducted themselves sociably and peaceably toward all the parties of our officers and people . . . and by no means seemed to regard them as enemies or invaders of their country and tranquillity'.[4]

Early meetings were marked by nervousness on both sides. When surgeon-general John White came upon an armed group, he decided to demonstrate the power of his gun. Borrowing a wooden shield, he fired his pistol at it. Panic ensued at the loud bang and the hole the invisible missile left. Fortunately, White calmed things down by turning to that universal language—music. Rapidly he whistled the catchy tune we know as 'We won't get home till morning'. Aborigines are great mimics and soon fear turned to laughter and singing.[5]

Watkin Tench was perhaps the most sensitive newcomer. On his first walk on the beach he took along a little English boy. Holding the lad's hand, Tench strolled along until they met a dozen naked Aboriginal men. Both parties were armed, but Tench, seeing the interest aroused by the boy, opened his shirt to display his dazzling white skin. An elder came close and 'with great gentleness laid his hand on the child's hat and afterwards felt his clothes, muttering to himself all the while'.[6]

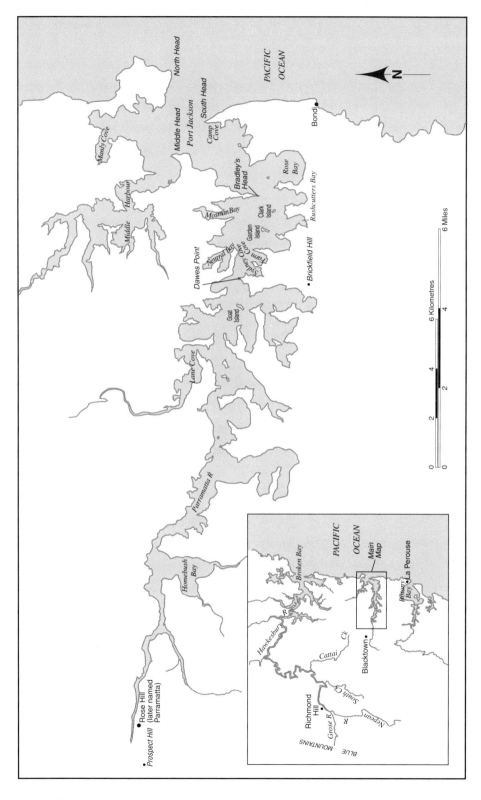

» *The Sydney region.*

Aborigines were puzzled about the newcomers' gender and took them for women, as they lacked beards. They poked at marines' trousers until Lieutenant Philip King ordered one to undo his fly, whereupon 'they made a great shout of admiration'. King was a young officer with a laddish interest in the opposite sex:

> We saw a great number of women and girls, with infant children on their shoulders . . . all *in puris naturalibus*, not so much as a fig-leaf. Those natives who were around the boats . . . made us understand their persons were at our service. However, I declined this mark of their hospitality but showed a handkerchief, which I offered to one of the women . . . she suffered me to apply the handkerchief where Eve did the fig leaf; the natives then set up another very great shout.[7]

King's rejection of the Aboriginal men's offer led to the first of innumerable misunderstandings. The widespread Aboriginal custom of offering wives to visitors was a sign of friendship. Acceptance imposed obligations for reciprocal services or future gifts; rejection may have signalled the mission was an unfriendly one.

Botany Bay proved an unsatisfactory site for the colony. There was no trace of the fast-flowing stream or 'vast quantities of grass' reported by Cook and Banks, who had visited during a wet autumn, which they mistook for a dry season under the false impression that the whole east coast had the same climate. So much was strange about Australia: seasons reversed, four-legged animals that hopped, trees that shed bark rather than leaves and no familiar animals apart from a dog—the dingo—that howled like a wolf. Deciding to look for a better place, on 21 January Phillip set out to explore Port Jackson (Sydney Harbour) about 20 km (12 miles) to the north, which Cook had passed but not investigated.

As they sailed up the coast, Aborigines again shouted, 'warra, warra'. Then on entering Sydney Harbour, they passed a small bay where twenty men 'waded into the water unarmed, received what was offered them, and examined the boats . . . their confidence and manly behaviour made me give the name Manly Cove to this place'.[8]

They found to their delight 'the finest harbour in the world', with deep water right up to the rocky shore, so that the ships could be moored to large trees. A site was chosen for the settlement at the head of Sydney Cove, the small bay called 'Warran' by the Aborigines (now known as Circular Quay) immediately west of where the Opera House now stands. It was 'near the run of freshwater, which stole silently along through a very thick wood', and 'every man stepped from the boat literally into a wood', according to Collins. Much tree-felling was necessary before camp could be established. Contemporary accounts and pictures show thick forest around the harbour except in a very few places, which occasioned special comment. Captain John Hunter, Phillip's second-in-command, wrote that in one place 'the trees stand very wide of one another, and have no underwood; in short, the woods . . . resemble a deer park'—the result of Aboriginal burning. Such 'parklands' were rare, open areas in a wilderness of 'immensely large trees', 'sour grass' and a 'jumble of rocks and thick woods'.[9]

On 26 January 1788 (now Australia's national day), the British flag was raised at Sydney Cove, and the land became a 'settled colony' and a dominion of the Crown. Under common law, all those born in dominions were British subjects. Aborigines therefore became British subjects but lost any proprietary rights in the land they inhabited. Upon annexation of the colony, ultimate title to all land was vested in the Crown.

What did Aborigines think of the new arrivals—huge floating objects and white-skinned people with strange things on their heads, bodies and feet? Eora people called the ships 'buruwang', meaning island, because they thought they were floating islands, and that sailors climbing up the rigging were devils or possums.[10] On closer view, white people were seen as ancestral spirits returning from the dead, for white was the colour of death. Eora believed the spirits of the dead travelled out to sea. White people coming from the ocean were therefore returning spirits. (Eora had no ocean-going craft nor any idea that other inhabited countries existed.) They believed that on death the spirit left the body. Unless correct rituals were performed, spirits might linger in their tribal territory, but normally they returned to the land of the dead, variously located in the sky, beyond the horizon or on a distant but visible island. This was a logical belief for a society with a small, geographically isolated population, as Professor Eliade, expert on comparative religions, explains:[11]

> Owing to the Australian kinship system everybody is—or can be—related to everybody else. If a friendly stranger approaches a camp, he is always finally recognised as being related to someone of the group. Consequently, for the Australians, only one 'world' and only one 'human society' exist. The unknown regions outside familiar lands do not belong to the 'world'—just as unfriendly or mysterious foreigners do not belong to the community of men, for they may be ghosts, demonic beings, or monsters.

Fortunately for the British, they were regarded as ghosts rather than monsters, and by a lucky chance Phillip had one of his front teeth missing. Lack of a right front tooth distinguished initiated Eora men; when Phillip showed them he, too, lacked that tooth, 'it occasioned a general clamour and I thought gave me some little merit in their opinion'.[12] This belief sheltered the new arrivals from the normal hostility towards strangers.

» Lapérouse

On 26 January, as the last British ships were leaving Botany Bay for Sydney Cove, two French ships unexpectedly arrived. The French commander, Jean-François de Lapérouse, had instructions to treat Aborigines well during his voyage of discovery, but was understandably nervous after Samoans had massacred twelve of his crew. The French built a stockade around their camp and in early February were 'obliged to fire on the natives . . . to keep them quiet'.[13] Later French officers informed Phillip: 'the natives are exceedingly troublesome . . . whenever they meet an unarmed man they attack him'. Frenchmen who had been attacked told a British sailor:

> The natives before had been very friendly to them and at this time one of the boats was aground and when they came down to murder them the French supposed their intent was to assist them with launching the boat . . . upwards of 500 stones was thrown in the first shower. The French immediately discharged a volley of small arms at them and it is supposed above 20 of the natives must have been killed—several of the French were also wounded . . . afterwards some hints dropped that it was one of their sailors had behaved very ill to some of the natives.[14]

The nature of the French ill-behaviour is unknown, for after their ships left early in March 1788, they vanished. The wreckage of their ships was found on Vanikoro in the Santa Cruz Islands in 1826. The French legacy was that Botany Bay Aborigines became extremely aggressive towards the colonists.[15]

» The first year

There are over 24 eyewitness accounts of race relations during the settlement's first five years, although they are all from the colonists', rather than an indigenous, perspective. Especially valuable sources are Governor Phillip, David Collins, John Hunter, Watkin Tench, lieutenants William Bradley and Philip King, surgeon George Worgan and midshipman Newton Fowell. Detailed observations from the first fifteen months are particularly important as they are a record of Aboriginal life *before* Aborigines suffered the ravages of smallpox and other new diseases. It was also a period when Aborigines were regarded and treated as individuals. All primary sources agree that fairly good relations existed between black and white.

Only three days after the British landed at Sydney Cove, local Aborigines were dancing with the newcomers. When surveying the harbour, Bradley's party was welcomed ashore by unarmed men who showed them a good landing place and greeted their arrival with excited shouting and capering. Bradley continues—'these people mixed with ours and all hands danced together'.[16] The dancers were all men, for women were kept at a distance and guarded by an armed man—clearly these women were *not* being offered to the young sailors. Bradley, an accomplished artist, later painted the scene. One threesome shows an Aborigine in classic dancing position with knees wide, holding hands with a sailor in blue and a red-coated soldier. The next day, there was more dancing with another group, followed by hair-combing 'with which they were much pleased'. Later, haircuts were requested and given with scissors, and, as confidence grew, men allowed their beards to be shaved with 'cut-throat' razors.

Most early interaction occurred while sailors were fishing and officers were out surveying the harbour. Some of the fishermen shared their netted catch, and found Aborigines 'very thankful'. Sometimes Aboriginal men helped haul in the seine— huge vertical fishing nets—and received a fair share of the catch, but there were some violent incidents and two boats were pelted with stones. On 21 February, the first Aborigines approached the settlement by canoe and were given some fish. Next day 20 to 30 men came back and landed on nearby Garden Island, where they made off with two shovels, 'but not without their skin being well peppered with small shot'. Midshipman Hill had ordered marines to load bird-shot rather than ball ammunition and to fire only at their legs.[17]

After this, Aborigines kept away for more than a year. They particularly feared marines with their long-barrelled muskets that they termed 'gerubber'—the name for a firestick.[18] At Botany Bay one man 'was bold enough to go up to a soldier and feel his gun, and felt the point of the bayonet, looked very serious and gave a significant Hum'.[19] Marines' bright red jackets with white cross-straps were probably interpreted as fighting men's garb, for many Botany Bay warriors were painted with similar diagonal white stripes.[20] Although Aborigines avoided the soldiers and settlement, in July 1788 one group took up residence in a nearby cove. These people were 'visited by large parties of the convicts of both sexes . . . where they danced and sang with apparent good humour . . . but none of them would venture back with their visitors'.[21] In the early years there were few sexual contacts, because both societies found the other ugly and alien. Aborigines apparently disliked whites' 'weak blue eyes and thin noses'; one description characterises Europeans as 'those whose noses walk first'.[22] They also prevented an escaped Madagascan convict, 'Black Caesar', from joining them. For their part, the newcomers were repelled by the foul-smelling fish oil that Aborigines smeared on their bodies to ward off mosquitoes.

In mid-1788, Phillip reported:

> The natives have ever been treated with the greatest humility and attention . . . every means shall be used to reconcile them to live amongst us and to teach them the advantages they will reap from cultivating the land, which will enable them to support themselves at this season of the year, when fish are so scarce that many of them perish from hunger . . . every possible means shall be used to . . . render their situation more comfortable. At present I think it is inferior to that of the beasts of the field.[23]

The British were anxious for peace and friendship. As Collins expressed it: 'It was much to be regretted, that none of them would place a confidence to reside among us; as in such case, by an exchange of languages, they would have found that we had the most friendly intention toward them, and that we would ourselves punish any injury they might sustain from our people'.

Aborigines were 'far more numerous' than Phillip expected, and in 1788 he estimated the coastal population between Botany and Broken bays as 1500 people, spread over 2000 km² (770 sq. miles). This gives a population density of about one person to 1.3 km² (½ sq. mile) of coast or 2 km² (¾ sq. mile) of the wooded hinterland with its scarcer food resources.[24] Nine named bands lived around Sydney Harbour, which the British called 'tribes'. Each band had between 6 and 10 small canoes, and 67 canoes were observed on the harbour on one day in 1788. In the same year, 49 beached canoes and 212 armed men were encountered at Botany Bay, but no violence ensued.

» Winter food shortages

Almost every confrontation in the early years was about food. Aborigines seemed perpetually hungry and understandably sought a share of whatever fish were caught. Fish were their summer staple, yet even in summer were not particularly plentiful. Tench commented: 'the universal voice of all professed fishermen is that they never fished in a country where success was so precarious and uncertain'. Winter was worse; as Worgan said: 'since the approach of winter, the fish have become scarce'. This scarcity has often been blamed on British overfishing, but fish supplies in the harbour always decline in winter, because shallow-water fish move into deeper water in the colder months.[25] In June 1788, Collins noted, 'The cold weather which we had at this time of year was observed to affect our fishing, and the natives themselves appeared to be in great want. An old man belonging to them was found on the beach of one of the coves, almost starved to death.' In winter (from June to September), 10 of 35 edible plants became unavailable. The main winter food was 'fern root', the thin starchy rhizomes, eaten raw or roasted, of ferns or native bracken, although the latter were woody and unpalatable.[26]

Scarcity of kangaroos and other game was widely remarked in early accounts and in the 1840s by Mahroot, then the last surviving Aborigine of unmixed race in Botany Bay. Mahroot reported that a shortage of animals meant local Aborigines had no skin cloaks, so blankets and jackets were stolen 'to keep them warm in winter'.[27]

Winter was a time of relative hardship for most hunter-gatherers in temperate Australia. All early observers described Aborigines as 'spare', 'thin' or 'emaciated', especially at the end of winter. Tench measured many Eora men and found them 'more diminutive and slighter made, especially about the thighs and legs, than the Europeans . . . Baneelon [Bennelong], who towered above the majority of his countrymen, stood barely 5 feet 8 inches [172 cm] high.'[28]

For its part, the infant colony was anything but self-sufficient. Gardens were planted around each cottage and there were vegetables by spring 1788 and fruits by

1790, but there were over a thousand mouths to feed. When the first crops failed, the settlement was threatened with starvation. Phillip therefore ordered more fertile land to be cleared on the upper Parramatta River and the resulting small harvest just kept the colonists alive until the first supply ship, the *Justinian*, arrived in June 1790.

» Conflict

In 1788, three Aborigines were killed by convicts, while one soldier and seven convicts received fatal spear wounds. Some Eora attacks were revenge for theft, as when two convict rush-cutters stole a canoe. Another murder of two convicts was probably provoked by a different convict's earlier knifing of an Aborigine who had stolen some of his possessions. In a 1791 letter a convict commented: 'The natives are pretty peaceable here—but if they catch any of our people in the woods, they will kill them.'[29]

On 4 October 1788, a convict strayed from a herb-gathering party and was murdered and 'mutilated in a shocking manner' in a seemingly unprovoked attack. Then, on 24 October, several Aborigines threw spears at another convict building a fence. The governor immediately went there with an armed party, 'where some of them being heard among the bushes, they were fired at; it having now become absolutely necessary to compel them to keep at a greater distance from the settlement'.[30] No one was killed but it is unclear whether anyone was injured. This change in racial relations clearly troubled Phillip's conscience and he admitted: 'it is not possible to punish them without punishing the innocent with the guilty'. Yet, his first duties were to protect his own people and to maintain authority. The settlers were ever fearful of being attacked, although most fears proved groundless. For instance, on 18 December, terrified messengers reported 'two thousand' warriors at the brick kilns, but those sent to repulse the attack found only 50, who fled into the woods after convicts pointed their spades at them like guns.

Phillip hoped to 'persuade a family to live with us', but by October 1788 wrote: 'the natives still refuse to come amongst us . . . I now doubt whether it will be possible to get any of these people to remain with us, in order to get their language.' In December, Phillip's determination to establish communication led to the drastic action of kidnapping. The first to be kidnapped was Arabanoo, who quickly picked up English and became a great favourite, deciding to stay at Government House and frequently dining at the governor's table.

» Disaster

In April 1789, a smallpox epidemic struck:

> Early in the month . . . the people whose business called them down to the harbour daily
> reported that they found, either in excavations of the rock, or lying upon the beaches
> and points of the different coves . . . the bodies of many of the wretched natives of this

country. The cause of this mortality remained unknown until a family was brought up [to the settlement], and the disorder pronounced [by doctors] to have been the small-pox . . . That it was the smallpox there was scarcely a doubt; for the person seized with it was affected exactly as Europeans are who have that disorder; and on many that had recovered from it we saw traces, in some the ravages of it on the face.[31]

An empty house was prepared for the rescued family where they were given nursing care. Arabanoo nursed two victims, only to die of smallpox himself on 18 May. He was buried in the governor's garden, 'much regretted by everyone', according to sailor Newton Fowell, 'as it was supposed he would have been of infinite service in reconciling the natives to us'. It seems the need for reconciliation goes back to the very beginning of race relations in Australia.

Only two out of six sufferers brought back into Sydney Town survived—an 8-year-old boy, Nanbaree, and a girl of about fourteen, Abaroo (later corrected to Boorong). Both children were adopted, rapidly learnt English and became useful go-betweens, but later Boorong went back to the bush when she wanted a husband.

The epidemic was certainly smallpox and killed over half the Eora. Mortality was up to 95 per cent in some bands; only three survived out of the 50-strong Cadigal. The disease was so disastrous that the dead went unburied. As Hunter reported:

> It was truly shocking to go around the coves of this harbour, which were formerly so much frequented by the natives, where in the caves of the rocks, which used to shelter whole families in bad weather, were now to be seen men, women and children lying dead. As we had never seen any of these people who had been in the slightest degree marked with the smallpox, we had reason to suppose that they had never before now been affected by it.[32]

The only colonist affected was an indigenous North American sailor, who succumbed after visiting Aboriginal child sufferers.[33] Most of the British were immune, either through prior infection or variolation, the pre-cursor of vaccination. Variolation involved inoculation by incision or injection of pus or scabs from smallpox patients.[34]

Aborigines were demoralised by the mysterious disease that killed blacks but spared whites, as if whites had such strong magic they were invincible. Aboriginal numbers declined drastically, especially the number of women, for smallpox killed 10 per cent more women than men. It caused almost certain death to pregnant women, a fatality rate of at least two thirds among the under-fives and up to a third among the rest. This led to fewer children and a significant drop in the ratio of women to men. The first official counts of the mainland Aboriginal population in the 1840s revealed very low numbers of children and a general preponderance of men, and all the pockmarked survivors observed were male.

By late 1789, Phillip's need for interpreters 'to reconcile [the Aborigines] to live amongst us' was becoming urgent. The colonists' chronic food shortage was another factor, according to Tench: 'Intercourse with the natives, for the purpose of knowing whether or not the country possessed any resources, by which life might be prolonged, as well as on other accounts, becoming every day more desirable, the governor resolved to make prisoners of two more of them.' On 23 November, Bennelong and Colbee were seized as they came to take fish offered at Manly Cove. Bennelong, aged about 30, was from the Wangal band whose territory was Darling Harbour westwards to Parramatta, and the rather older Colbee was from Cadigal, whose land stretched from the southern harbour entrance to Sydney Cove.

Phillip gave instructions 'to treat them indulgently and guard them strictly'. Bennelong and Colbee had both survived smallpox and bore its scars; Tench commented, 'Colbee's face was very thickly imprinted with the marks of it'. Both had huge appetites: 'Twelve pounds [5.4 kg] of fish does but little towards satisfying them for one meal'. This was when the colony was threatened with starvation because the only supply ship had been wrecked at Norfolk Island, the Second Fleet had not yet arrived, and colonists' weekly food rations were reduced to 2 lb (900 g) dried pork and rice and 2.5 lb (1.1 kg) flour, a diet supplemented by rats, crows and fish. Colbee escaped in December but Bennelong remained for another five months. Tench recounts:

» *An engraving of Bennelong by James Neagle, produced in
1798 after Bennelong's return from England.*

Our friend Bennelong, during this season of scarcity, was as well taken care of as our desperate circumstances would allow . . . Had he penetrated our state, perhaps he might have given his countrymen such a description of our diminished numbers and diminished strength as would have emboldened them to become troublesome. Every expedient was used to keep him in ignorance . . . but the ration of a week was insufficient to have kept him for a day. The deficiency was supplied by fish, whenever it could be procured, and a little Indian corn [maize].[35]

These measures to hide the colony's weakness from Bennelong remind us of the newcomers' almost total ignorance about the Aborigines. They feared an army of warriors might attack the tiny, unfortified settlement, for they did not know that the Aboriginal population was low, dispersed and fragmented into small bands. Colonists therefore tended to overreact to any imagined threat.

» The governor is speared

Bennelong escaped on 3 May 1790 and was not seen again until 7 September, when a party went ashore at Manly Cove and found many Eora on the beach feasting on a dead whale 'in the most disgusting state of putrefaction'. The feasters rushed to pick up their spears but Nanbaree explained the visitors were friendly. Then Bennelong came to the water's edge. He was barely recognisable, being 'so greatly emaciated', with a long beard. He had also acquired a large scar over one eye and a spear wound through his upper arm.[36] Colbee joined them and Bennelong inquired after the governor. He asked for metal hatchets but there were none so he was given other small gifts, including hair clippers that he immediately began to use. This was reciprocated with some chunks of whale blubber, the largest for the governor. Bennelong sent word that he would return to the settlement if the governor would come to meet him at Manly. As it happened, Philip was in another boat not far away and eagerly accepted Bennelong's invitation.

The story of Phillip's spearing has often been told but new information was discovered in 1998, when Sydney's Mitchell Library purchased previously unknown letters from Lieutenant Henry Waterhouse to his father. Waterhouse was one of only four eyewitnesses, the others being Collins, a sailor and Phillip himself. It now seems clear that Bennelong masterminded a payback spearing, presumably as revenge for his kidnapping. Bennelong chose the time and place by inviting Phillip to Manly Cove. Phillip landed and walked up the beach to greet Bennelong, unarmed except for his pistol. Bennelong and Colbee were also unarmed but directed nineteen other warriors into a semicircle round the governor. Bennelong handled an unusually long barbed spear, then put it down on the ground, from where the assailant, Willemering, picked it up with his toes, fixed it to a spear-thrower and threw it with great force at Phillip. The spear hit near his collarbone and came out behind the shoulderblade. As

Bennelong, Colbee and Willemering ran off, Phillip staggered back towards the boat dragging the 3-m long (12-foot-long) spear. Waterhouse tried to break off the shaft and eventually succeeded but not before he was slightly wounded by a flight of spears thrown at the fleeing men. Only one sailor's musket would fire but miraculously they escaped. Phillip was bleeding heavily but gave explicit orders 'to prevent any of the natives being fired on'. In two hours they rowed back to Sydney Cove, a surgeon extracted the wooden point, and in six weeks Phillip had fully recovered.

Was the aim to kill? Almost certainly not. Willemering had an uninterrupted view and was only 20 yards away from Phillip, who was approaching him with hands outstretched in a gesture of friendship. The spearing did *not* result from Willemering's fear or misunderstanding, for we now know that he was a 'koradgee' or 'clever man' from the Carigal band to the north. Bringing a 'clever man' to do the spearing with a special wooden spear has all the hallmarks of ritual punishment, whereby victims are wounded in a formal peace-making ceremony. Moreover, Bennelong was remarkably confident of Phillip's recovery.[37]

» 'Coming in'

To his credit, Phillip ordered no reprisals, and a week later Bennelong returned to the settlement and a peace conference was held. Two days later Phillip was rowed across the harbour to pay a friendly return visit to Bennelong's camp, and on 8 October Bennelong returned to Government House. King reported that Bennelong 'sits at table with the governor, whom he calls "beanga", or father, and the governor calls him "doorow", or son'. A brick house, 3.6 m² (12 sq. ft), with a tiled roof was built for him on his chosen spot—now Bennelong Point, site of the Opera House. Although superior to most Sydney dwellings and one of the first brick buildings in Australia, the house did not appeal to Bennelong, but was much used as a meeting place. 'Neither he nor his family will live in it,' a contemporary observed. 'They will sometimes stay in the place for a day, then make a fire on the outside of it . . . they prefer living in the woods.'

When Bennelong returned, other Aborigines began to come into the settlement, probably driven by hunger at winter's end. As Hunter recounted, 'Whenever they were pressed for hunger, they had immediate recourse to our quarters, where they generally got their bellies filled.' A year later, Sydney resident George Thompson commented 'the people can scarcely keep them out of their houses in daytime'. European food, especially bread, must have seemed like a gift from the gods—good, tasty, filling fare obtainable without any effort. Begging became rife; 'hungry' and 'bread' were the first English words Aboriginal children learnt. The settlement provided both food and relative safety. As Collins remarked in 1793: 'their attachment to us must be considered as an indication of their not receiving any ill treatment from us'. The following year 'two female natives, wishing to withdraw from the cruelty which they, with others of their sex, experienced from their countrymen, were allowed to embark [for Norfolk Island] . . . and were consigned to the care of the lieutenant-governor'.

Inevitably, at Government House Bennelong was also introduced to alcohol. Wine was scarce and imported rum was the main alcoholic drink available—beer was too expensive to transport and was not produced in Australia until 1795. Aboriginal introduction to alcohol was therefore anything but gentle. Arabanoo had treated liquor 'with disgust and abhorrence', but Bennelong acquired a taste for it, although it did not become a problem till the end of his life. He also became reasonably proficient in English. Only one man, Lieutenant William Dawes, learnt much of the Eora language and compiled a vocabulary, aided by an Aboriginal girl, Patyegarang. (His researches may have gone a trifle further, for some language of love appears in his phrasebook.)

Gradually it became clear that Aboriginal languages were very different from Indo-European ones and even from each other. When Phillip, Tench, Dawes and Eora guides Colbee and Boladeree went inland on a five-day exploration expedition in 1791, they were surprised to discover that Aborigines who lived in such close proximity were unfamiliar with each other's country and spoke different dialects. Collins was amazed that 'People living at the distance of only 50 or 60 miles [80–95 km] should call the sun and moon by different names'. Similarly, Elizabeth Macarthur, wife of John Macarthur, the founder of Australia's merino wool industry, wrote from Parramatta in 1791 that 'the natives visit us every day, more or less. We can learn nothing from them respecting the interior part of the country. It seems they are as much unacquainted with it as ourselves. All their knowledge and pursuits are confined to that of procuring for themselves a bare subsistence.'[38]

When Phillip returned to England in 1792, Bennelong and his young kinsman Yemmerrawanyea accompanied him, and were presented to King George III. Bennelong stayed in England until 1795 but Yemmerrawanyea died there in 1794. Bennelong's health also suffered from the British climate and on 2 January 1813, only eight years after his return, he died an alcoholic who no longer fitted well into either Aboriginal or white society.

Like Bennelong, the Eora came to rely on the settlement for their survival. By winter 1791 they had become fringe-dwelling beggars, enjoying settlers' bread, tobacco and rum, which they called 'tumble-down'. Brawling, drunken Aborigines provided a regular, pitiful spectacle, as contemporary art attests. Both in town and on board visiting ships, prostitution of Aboriginal women became a standard means of obtaining food, alcohol, tobacco, blankets and clothes. At this stage there was no money in the colony, so payment in rum was normal currency, leading to inevitable alcoholism and degradation. Interaction soon led to the birth of mixed-race babies and the spread of venereal disease (see Chapter 4).

» *A lithograph by Augustus Earle (1793–1838) showing a group of Aborigines affected by drink in Sydney Town.*

» Violence

If a convict stole a chicken he was flogged, and if he stole a sheep he was hanged, but Aborigines were not. Indigenous people were free British subjects with (in theory) the full protection of British law. Aborigines speared any convicts caught straggling in the bush, but for three years Phillip strictly forbade any retaliatory expeditions. Indeed, when sixteen convict brick-makers set out in March 1789 armed with stakes to avenge the death of a comrade killed by Aborigines, not only was one killed and seven wounded, but they were each sentenced to 150 lashes. The governor had them severely flogged in front of Arabanoo, who was meant to be impressed by British justice but instead expressed terror and disgust.[39] Many convicts hated Aborigines as a result, a hatred that bore bitter fruit when they gained their freedom. The other component in this explosive mixture was the Marine Corps, as the marines hated convicts and Aborigines alike.

Phillip tried to keep relations amicable, but on 9 December 1790 his convict huntsman, McEntire, was mortally wounded. McEntire was one of only three convicts allowed to keep a musket to shoot wild game for the officers' tables. Bennelong and other Aborigines regarded McEntire 'with dread and hatred', probably because of his sour disposition, misdeeds in the bush and killing of kangaroos and a dingo.

McEntire had gone with three others to hunt at Botany Bay; they were resting in a hide, waiting for game to emerge for a twilight drink, when they heard rustling. Five Aborigines, armed with spears, were creeping up. When McEntire saw one was clean-shaven and with short hair, a sure sign of a visit to the Sydney Cove barber, he said, 'Don't be afraid, I know them', laid down his gun, stepped forward and spoke to them in Eora. He accompanied them a hundred yards, 'talking familiarly all the while', but then the beardless man jumped up on a fallen tree and used his spear-thrower to launch a 'death spear' at McEntire, lodging it in his side. Death spears were meant to kill. Jagged pieces of stone were fastened in two long rows of barbs on the spear-head. When surgeons extracted it, most of the barbs were torn off and stayed inside his body, and he died six weeks later.

The culprit was a young man with a cast in his left eye, identified by Colbee and others as Pemulwuy of the Bidjigal band from Botany Bay. (Pemulwuy is one of the few names of which the meaning is known—'man of the earth'.)[40]

When McEntire was speared in this seemingly unprovoked attack, Phillip ordered an avenging party to:

> make a severe example of that tribe. At the same time the governor strictly forbids (under pain of the severest punishments), any soldier or other person not expressly ordered out for that purpose ever to fire on any native, except in his own defence, or to molest him in any shape, or to take away any spears or other articles . . . The natives will be made severe examples of whenever any man is wounded by them, but that will be done in a manner which may satisfy them that it is a punishment inflicted on them for their own bad behaviour.[41]

Some Aborigines agreed with this policy. Phillip recounts that 'Bennelong, Colbee and two or three others now lived at Sydney three or four days in the week, and they all repeatedly desired those natives might be killed who threw spears'. They also agreed with reprisal on a group, because this was also the Aboriginal way. Phillip decided on a punitive expedition to bring in ten Bidjigal adult men or their heads.

Phillip's justification for punitive action was that by this time 'no less than seventeen of our people had either been killed or wounded by the natives' and it was time to teach them a lesson. The problem with such reprisals is that the innocent rather than the guilty suffer, and in disproportionate numbers, and the vast gulf between the two societies meant that the 'lessons' Europeans tried to teach were simply not understood. Others strongly disapproved of Phillip's plan. Dawes initially refused to go, and Tench successfully negotiated for the proposed number of captives to be reduced to six. The party of 50 red-coated soldiers assembled on the barracks square to beating drums, but the reprisal expedition was predictably unsuccessful. Phillip could scarcely have expected any other outcome, for he had led enough expeditions to know the difficulty of finding any Aborigines with their superb bush skills. As his secretary, Collins, later explained:

> There was little probability that such a party would be able so unexpectedly to fall in with the people they were sent to punish . . . The very circumstance, however, of a party being armed and detached purposely to punish the man and his companions who wounded McEntire, was likely to have a good effect, as it was well known to several natives, who were at this time in the town of Sydney, that this was the intention.[42]

It seems the colourful parade and body bags were just a show of force, equivalent to Aboriginal rattling of spears to frighten enemies. It is not clear whether Phillip realised that his own life had been spared by the use of a relatively benign wooden-barbed spear, whereas McEntire was deliberately murdered with a stone-armed one.

Bennelong often sought British assistance to attack his enemies: 'Indeed from the first day he was able to make himself understood, he was desirous to have all the tribe of Camaraigal killed.' To combat ever-present dangers of attack, Aborigines rapidly sought terrier or spaniel puppies, and soon 'not a family was without one or more of these little watch-dogs, which they considered as invaluable guardians during the night'.[43] English dogs were used as watchdogs and for hunting whereas dingoes, which occasionally were seen accompanying an Aboriginal group in the bush, were never truly domesticated. Dingoes were acquired as puppies but usually returned to the wild to mate.

Collins' verdict was that Aboriginal men were 'revengeful, jealous, courageous and cunning . . . the management of the spear and the shield, dexterity in throwing . . . clubs, agility in either attacking or defending, and a display of the constancy with which they endure pain, appearing to rank first among their concerns in life.' He deplored their constant violence and 'savage mode of living, where the supply of food was often precarious, their comforts not to be called such, and their lives perpetually in danger.'

The only Aboriginal death caused by soldiers during the first three years of settlement occurred on 28 December 1790. According to Collins, Bigon—a constant companion of Bennelong—and two other Aborigines wounded a convict-gardener, who had caught them stealing potatoes, a serious offence in a hungry colony. Seven marines were sent after the three potato thieves with orders to shoot only if attacked, but when they found the group encamped there was a fight. One of the Aborigines, Bangai, threw his club and the soldiers opened fire. The men ran off but Bangai was badly wounded and later bled to death.[44]

During the first 35 months, fewer than a dozen Aborigines had died from conflict with the newcomers, and these, except Bangai, were all killed by convicts. There are several reasons for such a low death rate on both sides. Initially Aboriginal attacks were confined to payback killings and British violence was held in check by official policy and the severe punishment of anyone who harmed a native. However, the settlers had not yet intruded far onto Aboriginal lands.

By late 1790, many Eora lived in town and a few dined regularly with the governor. Theft was the main problem—Aborigines took metal axes, clothes and food, and convicts stole artefacts to sell to visiting ships as souvenirs. Floggings of convicts for such thefts were viewed on at least two occasions by Aboriginal people. Their reaction to British justice was horror, for floggings were much bloodier than the traditional Aboriginal punishment of ritual spearing in the thigh. On the first occasion, Arabanoo was reduced to tears. On the second, 'there was not one of them that did not testify strong abhorrence of the punishment and equal sympathy with the sufferer'. The victim of the theft of her fishing lines, Colbee's wife Daringa cried and Bennelong's wife Barangaroo, 'kindling into anger, snatched a stick and menaced the executioner'.

» Aboriginal treatment of women

While inhuman treatment of convicts upset Aborigines, the brutal violence with which the women were treated by local Aboriginal men horrified the British officers. Tench observed:

> The women are in all respects treated with savage barbarity . . . When an Indian [Aborigine] is provoked by a woman, he either spears her or knocks her down on the spot. On this occasion he always strikes on the head, using indiscriminately a hatchet, a club or any other weapon . . . Colbee, who was certainly in other respects a good tempered merry fellow, made no scruples of treating Daringa, who was a gentle creature, thus. Baneelon [Bennelong] did the same to Barangaroo.[45]

Some violence was witnessed firsthand. Love and war seemed to be Bennelong's 'favourite pursuits'. When asked about a wound on his hand, Bennelong 'laughed and owned that it was received in carrying off a lady of another tribe by force. "I was dragging her away: she cried aloud and stuck her teeth in me." "And what did you do then?" "I knocked her down, and beat her till she was insensible, and covered with blood."' Early chroniclers record dozens of similar examples of Aboriginal men's violence towards women, whether from their own or other tribes. Elizabeth Macarthur described Aboriginal women as 'slaves to their husbands'.[46]

Some children were also neglected or victimised. 'We often heard of children being injured by fire', Collins said; 'never were women so inattentive to their young as these'. (At night children slept between two small fires and often rolled into them.) Young children were sometimes victims of payback killings, since vengeance was exacted on any relatives of supposed wrongdoers. For instance, a young girl, Gonanggoolie, was

deliberately killed in a reprisal raid. Then in 1796 'a little native girl, between six and
seven years of age, who for some time had lived at the governor's house, [was] most
inhumanly murdered by two of her savage countrymen'. She was an orphan and had
'become a great favourite with her protectors. This, and her being a native of the
country near Broken Bay, excited the jealousy of some of the natives who lived at or
about Sydney, which manifested itself in their putting her to death in the most cruel
manner'. Her mutilated body was found 'speared in several places and with both the
arms cut off'.[47]

Australian Aboriginal society must be one of the few societies to have virtually
no rituals of courtship or marriage, although customs varied regionally. Marriage was
usually outside one's own group but was not necessarily marriage by capture (see
chapter 5). A more formal wedding ceremony was observed near Sydney in 1819,
when the bridegroom first daubed the young woman with spit and ochre and the couple withdrew from the crowd. He then stood her against a tree and knocked out her
two front teeth by setting a small hardwood stick against them and hitting the stick
hard with a stone axe. The bride bore this without a single cry and it seems the pro-
cedure was normal practice.[48] Collins observed that, 'We have known several
instances of very young girls having been much and shamefully abused by the males.'
Even in the case of 'marriage', 'the prelude to love in this country . . . is violence, of
the most brutal nature'. The women are:

> unfortunate victims of lust and cruelty. The poor wretch is stolen . . . being first stupefied
> with blows inflicted with clubs and wooden swords, on the head, back and shoulders,
> every one of which is followed by a stream of blood, she is dragged through the woods by
> one arm . . . The ravisher . . . conveys his prize to his own party, where a scene ensues too
> shocking to relate. This outrage is so constantly the practice among them, that even the
> children make it a game.

Collins, Dawes and others were horrified. They found even unmarried girls 'bore on
their heads the traces of the superiority of the males . . . We have seen some of these
unfortunate beings with more scars upon their shorn heads, cut in every direction,
than could be well distinguished or counted.' While some of these may have come
from funerals, where it was customary for women to beat their heads until blood ran,
it is clear from many eyewitness accounts that violence was endemic in Aboriginal
society, as in many other hunter-gatherer groups.[49]

Monogamy prevailed among younger men but older, more powerful men usually
had two or more wives. Polygyny led to raids to acquire women, who were then
sometimes abused by husbands and older wives. Britons made their disapproval clear,
but violence continued and in 1797 Collins wrote: 'every endeavour to civilise these
people proved fruitless . . . A young woman, the wife of a man named Ye-ra-ni-be,

both of whom had been brought up in the settlement from their childhood, was cruelly murdered at the brick-fields by her husband.'[50]

Increasing knowledge rapidly destroyed illusions of a pre-colonial Utopia. Gradually, in the face of reality, Rousseau's romantic concept of the 'noble savage' was abandoned; changing attitudes are revealed both in written accounts and in pictures, which began with idealised, classical figures and ended in caricature.[51]

» Spiritual life

Race relations improved during 1791. Perhaps as a gesture of reconciliation, some Britons were invited to Bennelong Point in late February to witness a 'corroboree'— a word from the Sydney language that means a performance of music and dance. It began soon after dark by the light of several small campfires. The singer was accompanied by clap sticks and the dancing was 'truly wild and savage, yet in many parts

» Sydney rock engraving of Daramulan, supernatural Great Spirit Father, who shaped the world. Eora believed their medicine men's magical powers came from Daramulan, who once lived on earth, where he taught men, gave them their initiation ceremonies and told them what foods to eat. When a young man was initiated he was told Daramulan's name and heard his terrifying voice in distant thunder and the weird, high-pitched humming produced by sacred bullroarers, oval pieces of wood swung on strings. Eora believed in a fertile land beyond the sky with trees, rivers and plentiful game, where the spirits of the dead were cared for by Daramulan. Belief in an 'All-Father', a supreme creative being, was widespread in southeastern Australia, but not elsewhere; other names for this omnipotent creative being were Baiami and Bunjil.

there appeared order and regularity'. Men performed distinctive dance movements in formation: 'One of the most striking was that of placing their feet very wide apart and by an extraordinary exertion of the muscles of the thighs and legs, moving the knees in a trembling and very surprising manner, such as none of us could imitate.'

Earlier an initiation ceremony was held at nearby Farm Cove. Collins witnessed this and another in 1795 and published detailed descriptions of rituals culminating in tooth avulsion.[52] Otherwise, colonists learnt little of spiritual life and thought Aborigines had no religion, although placement of artefacts in graves implied a belief in an afterlife. At Port Jackson, young people who died were interred but elders were cremated.

December 1791 saw Australia's first cross-cultural funeral—that of a fine young man, Ballooderry, who succumbed to a fever despite desperate attempts to save him by white and black healers alike. He was buried in the governor's garden near the shore. His body was wrapped in an English jacket and blanket instead of traditional paper-bark and then laid in his canoe together with spears, a spear-thrower and his waistband of woven hair. As the canoe was carried to the grave, Ballooderry's father threw two spears towards a watching group of Aboriginal women and children, a sign that the death would be avenged. (Sorcery was believed to cause all natural deaths except in the very young or old.) Red-coated marines beat a drum tattoo as the canoe was interred. The body was placed on its right side with the head towards the northwest, and shrubs were cut down so that 'the sun might look at it as he passed'.[53] Spectators were enjoined not to speak the name of the deceased but refer to him as the 'nameless one', a universal taboo in Aboriginal Australia.

» British expansion

The need to make the infant colony self-sufficient led in mid-1791 to the grant of arable land beyond Parramatta to 37 convicts who had served their time. This took settlement into the land of the Darug or 'woods tribe', who occupied the undulating Cumberland Plain between Parramatta and the Blue Mountains. The Darug reacted violently to the newcomers and soon set fire to a settler's hut. Soldiers were then dispatched to guard each settlement until all lands were cleared of timber. Yet the death toll remained low—by December 1792, when Phillip departed for England, only one more European and one more Aborigine had been killed.

Governor Phillip's first task had been to establish a viable settlement, and after five years the new colony was thriving. In a letter in October 1792 convict James Lacey wrote: 'The convicts . . . are much better off than the labouring people in England, few of them being without a garden, pigs, poultry etc etc'. Phillip also kept interracial conflict low, but failed to persuade Aborigines to take up any form of labour. Some barter did develop, Aborigines trading fish and artefacts for food.

« CORROBOREE »

Dancing is important in Aboriginal life and 'play-about' corroborees of song and dance were held by the campfire most nights. Traditional dance was segregated by gender and generation. Men danced directly in front of the singers, women in a line or group behind the men or in the shadows. In traditional communities, women still dance with young children on their shoulders. Babies soon learn to cling to their mothers' hair as they sit, asleep or awake, astride her neck.

Women's dance is noted for its graceful hand and leg movements. Women seldom lift their feet fully from the ground, but move up and down on heel and toe, gliding one toe in front of the other foot or sliding or shuffling in jerks forwards and sideways, keeping the feet together.

Men's dance is often much more vigorous and dramatic, with continuous running, hopping, leaping and turning in time with the beat of clap sticks or 'drumming' on skins folded across the knees. There is much rhythmic knee, foot, arm and body movement and stamping. Children learn to dance by copying adults, and when boys are becoming proficient, elders have commented that their 'knees are talking' as Aboriginal male dancing emphasises stamping, trembling and outward movement of the knees. Often dancers act out the story of a contemporary or mythological event or imitate a successful hunt with wonderfully realistic miming of animals and birds.

A public non-segregated corroboree by firelight was often the prelude to a sacred ritual the following day. Men's sacred corroborees are particularly elaborate and usually involve lengthy body painting, making of large, decorated headdresses and sometimes preparation of a painting or sand-sculpture on the dancing ground. Before ceremonies, hours are spent on body decoration, applying special designs with paint made from pigment mixed with water. White comes from pipe-clay, lime or crushed gypsum rock, black from charcoal, and red, yellow and brown from ochre. Designs denote the relationship of individuals to their kin group. Body decoration ranges from simple daubing to complex, finely drawn geometric designs. When the ceremony is completed, all such ground paintings, sculptures and body decorations are obliterated.

The great initiation, increase and fertility ceremonies were usually held in early spring or at the end of the wet season in the tropical north. Sacred corroborees were held in daylight in a restricted area, from which women were strictly excluded. Women had their own secret corroborees, involving body decoration, dance and singing, in a secluded place away from the camp. Spectators were only allowed at public rituals.

» *Dancers in this depiction of a corroboree from 1854 hold boomerangs and shields. Their knees are wide apart and their arms raised in the distinctive Aboriginal men's dancing style.*

» «

Phillip's successor, John Hunter (1795–1800), was also a naval officer, as the British Government still regarded its Australian penal colonies, Sydney Cove and Norfolk Island, as maritime settlements. Sydney's potential as a trading port was beginning to be realised, and an ocean-fishing industry developed. Some Aborigines, such as Mahroot, obtained work in the whaling industry. Whales and seals abound on Australia's eastern coast and the first whale was caught in November 1791. A master whaler 'declared that he saw more sperm whales in one day off the Pigeon House [south of Sydney] than he had seen in six years' fishing on the coast of Brazil'.[54]

» Frontier conflict

Until Hunter became governor in 1795, the colony was run by its principal army officer, Major Francis Grose, who was succeeded by Captain William Paterson. Their focus was on land rather than sea, and they encouraged major expansion inland. By

1794, a 53-km (32-mile) track joined Sydney to the Hawkesbury River ('Derrubbin'). By mid-1795, there were 546 farms, growing maize and wheat, spread over 50 km (30 miles) on both banks.

When Hunter first saw these fertile river flats, he exclaimed 'these low banks appear to have been ploughed up, as if a vast herd of swine had been living on them . . . we put ashore . . . and found the wild yam in considerable quantities, but in general very small, not larger than a walnut'. Evidently Aboriginal women had been digging for tubers of daisy 'yams', for, although small, these were an Aboriginal staple—as important a food as potatoes were for colonists.[55] The daisy yam grounds belonged to the Darug. Their diet consisted of eels, fish, crayfish, mussels, ducks, emus, kangaroos, possums, honey, bracken roots and, above all, tubers.

When the yam grounds were cleared and ploughed by settlers, 'open war . . . commenced between the natives and the settlers'. It was Australia's first conflict over land. In Sydney, blacks and whites had shared the sea's resources but the rich alluvial river flats could not be shared so easily and conflict became inevitable.[56]

Settlers were vulnerable because their farms were backed by thickly wooded country, which provided perfect cover for raiders. Aborigines plundered huts and stripped fields, carrying corn cobs away in blankets and fishing nets. In response, armed watchmen fired on them, with reprisals on both sides following each incident. It was a fairly even contest, for Aborigines could kill with death spears at 27 m (90 ft) and throw three or four spears in the time it took to reload a musket. Most Hawkesbury settlers were unarmed former convicts but from 1795 soldiers were stationed there to protect them, and were effective but ruthless. It was a lawless frontier of which the Parramatta magistrate wrote, 'It would be impossible to describe the scenes of villainy and infamy that pass at the Hawkesbury.'[57] The death toll between 1794 and 1800 was 26 whites and up to 200 Aborigines.[58]

Pemulwuy, murderer of McEntire, became notorious for raids, violence and arson. He headed every party that robbed maize grounds or burnt wheatfields. Arson was another Aboriginal weapon, which drove farmers out by torching their thatched wattle-and-daub huts and destroying their crops. By the time Governor King (1800–06) succeeded Hunter, a price had been put on Pemulwuy's head. In 1802 King wrote: 'The natives about Sydney and Hawkesbury continued as domesticated as ever, and reprobated [deplored] the conduct of the natives in the neighbourhood of Parramatta and Toongabbie, who were irritated [stirred up] by an active, daring leader named Pemulwuy.'[59]

Loss of life among Pemulwuy's band was high, but violence continued until late 1802 when he was shot by soldiers. Some fellow-tribesmen, who had been expelled from Parramatta because of Pemulwuy's misdeeds, asked that his head be carried to the governor and they be allowed to return to the town. This was done, and Pemulwuy's head was forwarded in a barrel to London for research. King ordered that no other Aborigines should be harmed. Today Pemulwuy is acclaimed as the first hero of the resistance but he was also regarded by parties on both sides as an impediment to peace and friendship. Relative quiet followed Pemulwuy's death, although his son, Tedbury, carried on hostilities for some time. By no means all Eora had fought; some worked for the governor, or farmers or as guides for the soldiers.[60] Some Aborigines were given land, some became fully integrated into white society, some married settlers and several groups had land allocated to them. King also agreed to Aboriginal requests that no more settlements should be made on the lower Hawkesbury River.[61]

In 1802 King issued a proclamation reminding colonists that any 'instance of injustice or wanton cruelty towards the natives will be punished with the utmost severity of the law' but that 'the settler is not to suffer his property to be invaded, or his existence endangered by them'.[62] His predecessor, Hunter, had taken the unprecedented step in 1799 of having five Hawkesbury farmers arrested and charged with murder for the barbarous slaughter of two Aboriginal youths as revenge for killing a settler. The men were found guilty but the court could not agree a sentence and wrote to England for advice; a change of governor intervened and eventually the men were pardoned.

Although Aborigines were classed as British subjects, their legal position differed from that of the convicts. The problem was that the concepts behind British law and the trial system were completely alien to their way of thinking, and they could not swear upon the Bible before giving evidence. Legal opinion held: 'The natives of this country (generally speaking) are at present incapable of being brought before a Criminal Court, either as criminals or as evidence . . . the only mode at present, when they deserve it, is to pursue and inflict such punishment as they may merit.'[63]

» Bungaree's circumnavigation of Australia

Bungaree, an elder from Broken Bay who was skilled at hunting, fishing and boating, became the first Aborigine to circumnavigate Australia when he accompanied Matthew Flinders on his 1801–03 voyage of exploration. Nanbaree also came on the first half of this voyage. Their demanding role was to strip off and approach armed warriors to negotiate for the visitors to get freshwater. This was not easy, as the other groups did not understand the Eora language. Fortunately, Flinders found the Aborigines he met timid and usually friendly. Indeed, when two of the ship's company became disorientated Aborigines took them to their camp, fed them on roast duck, and conducted them back to the ship in safety. There was only one indigenous fatality on the voyage. When an officer was speared after a misunderstanding, the captain responded with a reprisal attack in which one Aborigine was shot.[64] Torres Strait Islanders in sailing canoes gave the strangers a different reception—they were keen to trade their bows and arrows, coconuts, plantains and water in bamboo containers for metal axes.[65]

« BOOMERANGS »

A boomerang is a bent or curved thin hardwood missile. Returning boomerangs sweep in a near-circular arc of up to 50 m (160 ft) radius and were used to kill birds or drive them into nets set across flightways. Straight-flight, non-returning boomerangs were used for hunting and fighting. Hunting boomerangs have a range of up to 200 m (650 ft) and were thrown at possums, gliders, flying-foxes (fruit bats), goannas, bandicoots, flocks of pigeons, ducks or cockatoos, and even soaring wedge-tailed eagles, whose feathers were prized for ceremonial decoration. Fighting boomerangs were heavier and longer with a shallower curve and sharper edges. They were thrown through the air, ricocheted from the ground or used as clubs or 'swords'. Boomerangs were also used for digging, fire-making, cutting and as clap sticks. Boomerangs can be C-, V- or occasionally X-shaped. Some were painted or finely carved.

A boomerang actually flies, its sophisticated aerodynamics exploiting an ingenious combination of lift and spin. Its design employs the same principle as an aeroplane wing, with a curved upper and flat lower surface. A straight-flight boomerang is launched in a horizontal position, but the returning variety is near-vertical when thrown with a wrist-flick, so that most of the lift directs it sideways to the thrower. This allows it to spin and cut through the air at an oblique angle, generating lift. Because of its spin, the upper part of the wing cuts through the air more quickly than the lower part, generating more lift. This creates a turning force on the boomerang, which starts to follow a circular path, rather like a spinning gyroscope. Its flight path continues to curve until it returns to the point from which it was thrown.

The word 'boomerang' comes from the language of the Tharawal people south of Botany Bay. Returning boomerangs were first seen in action in a formal Aboriginal fight beside Sydney Harbour in 1804, where Britons were 'justly astonished at the dexterity and incredible force with which a bent, edged waddy [club] resembling slightly a Turkish scimitar was thrown by Bungary [Bungaree]'.[a]

Boomerangs probably developed as a modification of throwing-sticks, use of straight-flyers leading to the discovery of returning types. The oldest Australian boomerangs were excavated from a 10 000-year-old layer in Wyrie Swamp peat-bog, South Australia, and are now displayed in the South Australian Museum in Adelaide and the National Museum of Australia, Canberra. The nine boomerangs are thin and light with wing spans of only 29–50 cm (11–19 inches), the arms joining in a sharp elbow with one end twisted up slightly and the other down. Their curvature, lateral twist, small-ness and lightness are classic properties of returners.

Returning boomerangs have turned up at archaeological sites as far apart as India and Arizona and were evidently independently invented. The oldest known boomerang—about 23 000 years old and carved from mammoth tusk—comes from a cave in Oblazowa Rock in southern Poland. Wildfowling with returning boomerangs is pictured in Egyptian tombs and wall-paintings. Others were used until quite recently in India to hunt partridge and small deer and by Hopi Indians to hunt hares.[b]

» Boy with a toy boomerang and shield in Central Australia in the early 20th century.

» «

» Culture clash

Lachlan Macquarie, who was governor from 1810 to 1821, instituted an annual charitable feast and gift day to benefit Aborigines and in 1815 founded a school for Aboriginal children, the Native Institution at Parramatta. Pupils aged 3–15 were taught Christianity, reading, writing, arithmetic, agriculture, craft and domestic skills. Some children had difficulty with arithmetic, for most Aboriginal languages have no numbers beyond three or four. However, this schooling demonstrated Aboriginal intelligence, for the daughter of Yarramundi, Maria Lock, came first among 100 white and 20 Aboriginal children in an 1819 public examination.[66] She later married a white man and acquired her own land grant. The Native Institution was transferred from Parramatta to more remote Blacktown in 1822, but closed for want of pupils in 1829.

Macquarie tried hard to convert Aboriginal men into farmers. In 1815 he settled sixteen Aboriginal families, including Bungaree and his family, on land on Sydney Harbour, providing them with a boat, huts, gardens, pigs, rations, clothes and a convict. This proved largely abortive—the families stripped the huts of saleable items, and ate, sold or lost the pigs, but used the boat to sell fish in Sydney Town.

Compliant Aboriginal leaders were given brass 'king plates' to hang round their necks, such as the breastplate given to Bungaree, which read 'Boongaree—Chief of the Broken Bay tribe—1815'. Later, Macquarie gave Bungaree a general's uniform, complete with plumed cocked hat, and he acquired another brass plate proclaiming him 'King of Sydney Cove'. He became well-known, as he was rowed out to visiting ships to exact his 'king's tax', but after all the display he and his followers would go fishing, exchange their catch for rum and tobacco and then row back across the harbour to their camp on the northern shore. In this way Bungaree kept his people together and free from white supervision. Alcohol took its toll and he was seen in the Government Domain 'in a state of perfect nudity, with the exception of his old cocked hat, graced with a red feather'.[67] He fell ill in 1830, was cared for in Sydney Hospital, and then by a Catholic priest, and died among his own people on Garden Island.

In 1816 Macquarie granted Colbee and another man, Narragingy, 12 ha (30 acres) of land on Richmond Road in recognition of their 'recent good conduct'. Others joined them and the area became known as 'Black Town', now a Sydney suburb. This was the first formal land grant made to indigenous Australians.[68]

However, a spate of murders and robberies in the same year forced Macquarie to make the following proclamation:

- Armed Aborigines are forbidden from coming 'within one mile of any town, village or farm'.
- Aboriginal punishment duels and fights are banned as 'a barbarous custom repugnant to British laws'.
- Peaceful, unarmed Aborigines wishing to place themselves under the protection of the British Government are issued with certificates that protect them from injury.[69]

From 1817 to 1825 the *Sydney Gazette* reported only nine cases of interracial violence in NSW, none of which occurred in the Sydney region. Indeed, visitors commented on Sydney's relaxed race relations in contrast with the armed Aborigines encountered outside the towns.

Whites were perplexed by what they saw as the paradoxes of Aboriginal character. As Reverend Samuel Leigh exclaimed:

> What an anomalous race of beings! Shrewd and intelligent, yet not possessing even the first rudiments of civilisation; utterly ignorant of all the principles of art or science, yet able to obtain a ready livelihood where a civilised man would perish; knowing nothing of any metal, possessed of no mechanical tool and yet able to formulate weapons of a most formidable description . . . looked down upon as the lowest in the scale of humanity, yet proudly bearing themselves, and condemning the drudgery of the men who despise them.[70]

Popular opinion agreed with the colony's judge during Macquarie's time, Barron Field, who wrote that in contrast with Maori and South Sea islanders, Aborigines had 'no aptitude for civilisation'. Nevertheless, the British found them good-natured, friendly, cheerful, healthy people with a great sense of humour. They were also brave and stoical, apparently inured to discomfort and pain.[71]

« »

Two societies could hardly have differed more than Georgian England and Aboriginal Australia. English society was based on the Christian work ethic and the sanctity of private property, whereas Aborigines saw no value in work except the food quest and believed in the sanctity of communal property. Each society tried to make the other change. Aborigines expected Europeans to share their food and other goods; Europeans tried to instil principles of private ownership and regular work into Aborigines. Instead of mingling, they lived uneasily side by side, and, as the pastoral frontier spread, there was accommodation and cooperation but inevitably conflict.

CONFRONTATION

Early Tasmania and Victoria

In 1772, over a hundred years after Abel Tasman's visit, Frenchman Marion Dufresne also visited Van Diemen's Land, or Tasmania as it was later called. Dufresne espoused Rousseau's belief in the 'noble savage . . . in an intermediate state between the primitive and the civilised'.[1] Dufresne believed all people shared a common humanity and 'would send naked Frenchmen on shore whenever naked inhabitants were encountered . . . and then present gifts to show that the inhabitants of "civilised" France were greeting the noble savages of the South Seas in peace and friendship'.[2]

Alas, these good intentions ended in tragedy. When Dufresne's ships reached Tasmania, two cutters were rowed towards Aborigines on the beach. The women and children immediately 'took refuge in the woods', but a man made welcoming signs, whereupon two sailor volunteers stripped and swam ashore. There they were presented with a firebrand, a customary way of receiving strangers. Duclesmeur, who was second-in-command, wrote:

> Our men accepted it and gave a mirror to the old man. His astonishment and that of the other savages showed incomprehension as one after another saw themselves in it. The colour of the two sailors did not surprise them less and after they had examined them closely they put down their spears and danced before them. This reception was such as to give confidence and M. Marion determined on landing . . . they appeared greatly alarmed at the arrival of a third boat and made all sorts of menacing demonstrations to prevent a landing . . . The savages rained on us a shower of spears and stones, one of which wounded M. Marion . . . We discharged several shots at them and at once they took to flight uttering frightened cries.[3]

Crozet, Dufresne's lieutenant, later reported that several Aboriginal men were wounded and one killed. Dufresne survived this encounter but met his end in New Zealand where, with 25 of his crew, he was killed and eaten by Maori warriors. When

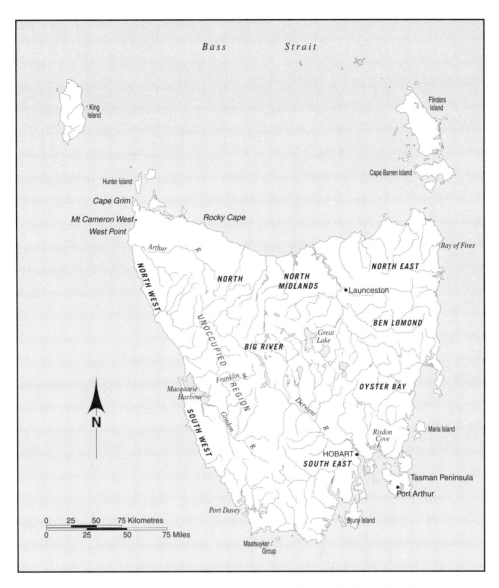

> Tasmania has a temperate marine climate and is ecologically varied, with a cool, windy, oceanic western
> coast, a sub-alpine mountain core, temperate rainforest in the southwest and a dry temperate eastern half.
> Its area is 67 800 km² (26 172 sq. miles)—about the size of Ireland. Tasmania lies between latitudes 40 and
> 44 degrees south, in the teeth of southern gales circling the globe known as the 'Roaring Forties'. It
> has thousands of lakes and its mountains rise to 1617 m (5307 ft) and are snow-covered in winter. Yearly
> rainfall in the west averages 3.75 m (150 inches).

Crozet recounted their experiences, Rousseau was horrified, exclaiming: 'Is it that the
good Children of Nature can really be so wicked?'[4]

Two more French exploratory expeditions followed—Bruny d'Entrecasteaux
(and naturalist Jacques de Labillardière) in 1792–93 and Nicolas Baudin in 1802, who
was accompanied by zoologist François Péron, the first man to call himself an anthropologist. There were no further hostilities and these explorers described Tasmanians

as shy, cheerful people living in family groups and subsisting largely on shellfish. The d'Entrecasteaux expedition had the most prolonged, friendly contact, and a black member of the crew quickly became a favourite. Aborigines were puzzled that all their visitors were men—Europeans were as strange to them as Martians would be to us. The first sight of a sailing ship occasioned much amazement, and we know that mainlanders later speculated whether they were huge birds, trees growing in the sea, or drifting islands.[5] The Frenchmen took a goat and a monkey ashore 'to see what effect the sight of them would have upon the natives'. The Aboriginal reaction was to treat them like the other strange humans and 'they solemnly invited them to sit down beside them'. On Baudin's expedition, a Tasmanian was presented with his first bottle of 'grog' (alcohol, actually arrack); startled by the brightness of the glass, he threw it into the sea. Later, glass became prized for cutting.[6]

» Tasmanian society

Tasmanians seemed generally healthy, although explorers commented on the protruding bellies of both adults and children, probably caused by malnutrition. They were covered with vermin but seemed free of disease apart from some skin complaints. One blind woman was encountered, and two people with congenital defects— a dislocated hip and a hunchback: 'the most curious, inquisitive and busy man amongst them was a little deformed hump-backed fellow, he expressed great joy by laughing, shouting and jumping'.[7]

When Labillardière met a group of 42 people, he found a healthy ratio of children to adults—7 men, 8 women, and 27 children. Elsewhere he encountered a group of 48, comprising 14 women, 10 men and 24 children, eating a meal of shellfish around seven fires.[8] Both sexes wore shell and fibre necklaces and were decorated with raised cicatrices in patterns of lines and circles on their shoulders, chests, arms, backs, stomachs and buttocks. Circles represented the sun and moon, for 'The cicatrice of the sun and moon is intended to remove inflammation . . . Some of those cicatrices are 3 and 4 inches [7–10 cm] in diameter.'[9]

In spite of the cold, wet climate, most went naked except for the mixture of animal fat, charcoal and ochre covering their heads, faces and bodies. No cloaks were worn, although one woman 'wore a kangaroo skin . . . for the convenience of carrying [a] child'. Cremation of the dead was usual but some of the deceased were interred or placed erect in hollow trees. Péron recorded a recent Aboriginal cremation site. Burnt human bones of several individuals were wrapped in bark, weighed down with stones and placed in a 'wigwam' of bark sheets decorated with linear designs similar to body markings.[10]

Similarities with mainland Aborigines were nudity, skin colour and the custom of wearing the bones of deceased kin around the neck as tokens of affection. They also shared the mainland habit of standing with one leg braced on the other. One difference was the Tasmanians' generally peaceful nature—when Labillardière

» FIRE-MAKING «

Tasmanians carried firebrands, but could they kindle fire? The necessary materials for fire-making—flint and iron pyrite—were available in Tasmania and several explorers found baskets containing 'a stone they strike fire with and tinder made of bark'. These materials require the percussion method (see below), which was also used on the mainland.[a]

The evidence of George Augustus Robinson, who led the 1829–34 Friendly Mission to Tasmanian Aborigines, suggests that the knowledge of how to make fire may have been lost. By then no one still kindled fire, but in 1830 Robinson 'obtained a stone from one of the Brune [Bruny] natives with which they . . . strike fire. It has the resemblance of a flint; . . . they call it "my.rer"'. Words for firestone differ from those for ordinary stone.[b] On the west coast, Robinson recounted that 'as the chief always carried a lighted torch I asked them what they did when their fire went out. They said if their fire went out . . . they were compelled to eat the kangaroo raw and to walk about and look for another mob and get fire of them. They must give fire and sometimes they would fight afterwards.' Fire was the most valued Aboriginal possession, and had to be given whenever requested, even if the request came from traditional enemies.[c]

Elsewhere in Australia, fire was produced by the drilling method or the percussion method. In the Cooktown region, Banks described the drilling method as follows:

> They get fire very expeditiously with two pieces of stick . . . the one must be round and 8 or 9 inches [20 or 23 cm] long and both it and the other should be dry and soft; the round one they sharpen a little at one end and pressing it upon the other turn it round with the palms of their hands . . . often shifting their hands up and running them down quick to make the pressure as hard as possible; . . . they will get fire in less than two minutes and when once possessed of the smallest spark, increase [it] in a manner truly wonderful.[d]

The drilling method of twirling a round-ended stick in a depression in a wooden base was used in northern Australia, but elsewhere rubbing hardwood against softwood in a sawing motion was more common. Some desert Aborigines still demonstrate this method. They find a piece of dry softwood, split it lengthways, place the split facing upwards and put some kindling such as dry kangaroo dung into it. Then one man holds the branch down by putting a foot firmly on each end and another rubs crossways on the split wood, usually with the sharp edge of a hardwood spear-thrower. Rapid sawing soon heats the wood and the kindling begins to smoulder in about half a minute. Once the kindling is aglow, dried grasses are added and a few puffs of breath produce a flame. Sometimes a piece of hardwood is used on a grooved softwood shield. Grass-tree stems provide ideal softwood in southeastern Australia.

In the percussion method, a piece of flint is embedded in dried grass, furry bark or emu feathers, and struck with iron pyrite until a spark ignites the tinder. It is then gently blown, placed in more kindling and held in the wind until it is all alight. Percussion is the world's earliest method of kindling a flame, and was used in Tasmania, southern Australia, Tierra del Fuego, the Solomon Islands, British Columbia and the Arctic.[e]

» *A man makes fire by the drilling method.*

《   》

discovered someone had reconnoitred their campsite overnight but left them unharmed, he wrote: 'Where else in this part of the world [the Pacific] could we have escaped attack and possible massacre under similar conditions?'

Tasmanians were small in stature, men averaging 160 cm (5 ft 3 inches) and women 152 cm (5 ft). The French described their hair as 'woolly' or 'frizzy' as it was tightly curled and springy, resembling that of New Guineans rather than mainland Aborigines. Uniquely in Australia, distinctive hairstyles distinguished different tribes. West-coast people shaved their heads into monk-like tonsures, northern men wore ringlets and northern women cropped their hair very short, leaving only a narrow ring round the skull.[11]

Although curly hair, small stature and dark skin characterised Tasmanians, analysis of DNA and physical form shows they are related to mainlanders. The differences that emerged after 14 millennia of isolation are due to genetic drift (accidental loss of lineages).[12]

The most striking thing about Aboriginal Tasmania was what was missing. They had no dogs because dingoes only reached the mainland long after the formation of Bass Strait at the end of the ice age, which totally isolated Tasmania from the outside world.[13] The Tasmanians' only weapons were spears, clubs and stones, which could be thrown 100 m (330 ft). They had hand-held stone tools for chopping, cutting and scraping, but did not develop hafted axes or grinding technology. Their equipment amounted to roughly fifteen items, a clear contrast to the adjacent mainland, which had four times as many, or the tropical north, which had eight times the number. Tasmanian equipment is the basic Australian tool kit, the irreducible minimum for nomads' long-term survival. Except when there was a glut of seals or muttonbirds, they 'rarely remain two days in the same place'.

Women used digging sticks and collecting bags and sometimes wore skin capes. Men had spears, clubs, stone chopping tools for heavy-duty cutting and scrapers for butchering carcasses. Other artefacts were canoe-rafts, necklaces, waterbags and possum-skin pouches for carrying firestones and ochre. Unmodified items used opportunistically included shells as drinking cups, wooden wedges for prising shellfish off rocks, rolled bark as firesticks, and rocks for pounding vegetables or smashing bones to extract marrow.

Tasmanians used seaweed for water containers, made baskets from grass and rolled grass ropes for climbing trees to obtain possums and honey. Both sexes climbed trees, sometimes with a stone chopper for cutting toeholds balanced on the head. Tasmanians in the west and south developed watercraft to cross rivers and estuaries and reach nearer islands. Canoe-rafts were about 4.5 m (15 ft) long by 1 m (3 ft) wide, made of three sausage-shaped rolls of rushes, paperbark or stringy-bark bound with a network of bark fibre and grass string. Fire was carried on a bed of clay. These frail craft carried 2–6 men, who stood and propelled them with long poles. When too deep for punting, people swam alongside, pushing the raft forward. Craft were quickly made and performed well in rough water. They resemble Maori 'mokihi'—small canoes made from reeds and flax stalks. Independently, similar problems of crossing icy, fast-flowing rivers gave rise to similar solutions.

Buoyancy was a problem: 'When saturated, the bark had a density similar to water, so that buoyancy depended on air cavities trapped within the bark itself. The rate of saturation meant that after a few hours, a craft tended to lose its rigidity and thus to wallow like a bundle of kelp in the sea.'[14] Nevertheless, prehistoric camps on Maatsuyker Island reveal that over the last 500 years Aborigines journeyed 10 km (6 miles) offshore to hunt seals and nesting muttonbirds. Similarly, archaeologist

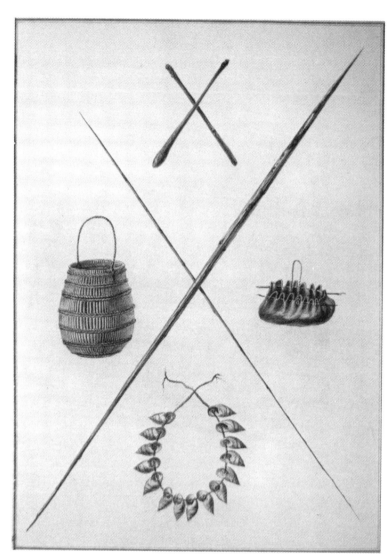

» *An illustration from 1807, showing the Tasmanians' main artefacts: men's wooden spears with fire-hardened tips used for hunting and fighting, of which there were two types—thrusting lances about 1 m (3 ft) long and throwing javelins up to 4 m (13 ft) long; a woman's multi-purpose digging stick, which was also used as a club or chisel, and a man's throwing-stick around 60 cm (2 ft) long, used for hunting birds, knocking possums out of trees and dispatching injured or cornered game (top); a water carrier made of seaweed (bull kelp) (right); a woman's large basket made of grass or rushes tightly woven in two-ply to carry shellfish—slung behind the back by a cord of rolled grass or bark looped round the forehead (left); a shell necklace, the only non-utilitarian Tasmanian artefact (bottom).*

Sandra Bowdler has shown that Hunter Island, 6 km (4 miles) off northwestern Tasmania, has been visited for 2500 years. Large islands (greater than 90 km²/35 sq. miles) less than 4 km (2½ miles) away were permanently inhabited. Smaller ones up to 8 km (5 miles) offshore were visited seasonally. Islands involving single water crossings of 13–15 km (8–9 miles) were *never* visited. Long voyages across open sea were extremely dangerous. Daring Aboriginal men voyaged to offshore islands to spear seal, but 'many hundred natives have been lost on those occasions', Robinson was told.[15]

» Social organisation

In spite of rapid depopulation, Tasmania's social structure was still in place during Robinson's expeditions in 1829–34. He became fairly fluent in the two main languages (western and eastern) and his two teenage sons often accompanied him and developed useful language skills. (Unfortunately from what Robinson recorded of the languages, modern linguists have been unable to reconstruct them.)[16]

Tasmanian society exemplifies basic Aboriginal social organisation. The smallest social unit was a 'hearth group', a family who cooked and camped round a fire and shared a hut. Each hut accommodated an extended family. Hearth groups averaged seven people, and groups of seven or eight huts housed a whole band in wintertime.

The band was the land-using unit. Leaders were mature men who were distinguished as hunters and warriors. Rhys Jones estimated Tasmanian bands on average originally included 40–50 individuals belonging to about 10 families. Each band had hunting rights to their own 'country', often centred on an important food-collecting zone such as an estuary and bounded by mountains or other landmarks. It also foraged widely, with permission, on the territory of other bands.

» *A hut decked with porcupine grass in the Arltunga district of Central Australia, 1920s. On the stormy west coast of Tasmania, substantial domed huts were built of branches thatched with grass or bark and lined with muttonbird feathers, but elsewhere shelters were simple windbreaks or half-domes made of bark sheets and pliable branches.*

Bands occasionally met to share seasonally abundant foods, hold ceremonies and arrange marriages. Women married men from outside their own band but usually within the same tribe. Wars were fought between tribes over such issues as broken trade agreements regarding the supply of ochre. People were highly mobile and the seasonal round involved travelling 160–500 km (100–300 miles). Band territories combined coastal and inland areas and each occupied 500–800 km² (200–300 sq. miles). One third of Tasmania (the western mountains and temperate rainforests) was unoccupied at British settlement. Jones estimated average population density in inhabited regions to be one person per 10–12 km² (4–5 sq. miles); for inland tribes it was one person per 20 km² (8 sq. miles) and for richer coastal areas one person per 6 km² (2⅓ sq. miles). There were markedly fewer people in Tasmania than in similar temperate coastal environments on the mainland. Archaeologist Harry Lourandos compared Aboriginal population density on the Tasmanian coast with that on the western Victorian coast and found the Victorian density significantly higher: one person per 2 km² (⅘ sq. mile). Likewise, inland densities in Victoria's Western District were twice those of inland Tasmania.[17]

» Population size and disease

The only detailed analyses of pre-contact indigenous population numbers in Tasmania are by Plomley and Jones, who each calculated the pre-colonisation number of bands and multiplied it by average band size. Plomley arrived at 3990 (57 bands averaging 70 people each) and Jones' figures were 2800–4250 (70–85 bands with 40–50 people each).[18] Historian Keith Windschuttle has suggested that Jones overestimated the number of bands (Jones allowed for an extra 30 unnamed bands in the Midlands region) and that Plomley set the average size of a band too high, since those observed by French explorers were smaller. (Duclesmeur noted in 1772 that the inhabitants seemed to 'live in troupes of 50 to 60 men and women altogether'.) Windschuttle, using Jones' lower figures and disregarding Duclesmeur's higher estimates, concluded: 'Fifty bands at an average of forty members per band equals 2000 people. Given the generosity of the assumptions involved in this estimate, we should thus regard the total pre-colonial Aboriginal population of Tasmania as less than 2000.'[19] Jones' most recent estimate was 3000–5000. This figure resulted from two different calculations— one from the number and size of bands and the other by multiplying the number of tribes (nine) by their average size on the mainland (350–500 people).[20]

A strong oral tradition indicates that a catastrophic epidemic occurred even *before* British settlement. Robert Clark, a teacher at Wybalenna Aboriginal Establishment, reported that Aborigines told him they were originally 'more numerous than the white people were aware of' but 'their numbers were very much thinned by a sudden attack of disease which was general among the entire population previous to the arrival of the English, entire tribes of natives having been swept off'.[21] Before 1803,

» *1. Aboriginal boys standing on an engraved rock at Spear Hill, Western Australia, in the heart of arid Australia. Early explorers had no concept of the size of Australia or its vast interior.*

» *2. Broad, thin, spear-deflecting shields from Victoria with zigzag designs and finely incised cross-hatching.*

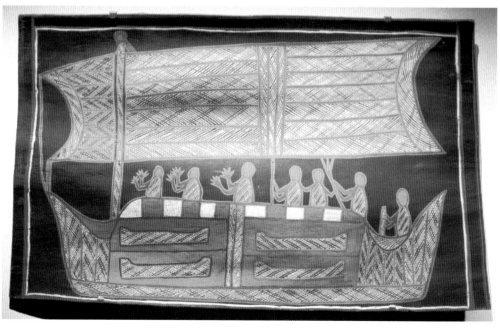

» *3. A Macassan prau with crew and four dugout canoes painted on bark by the artist Nakinyappa on Groote Eylandt and collected in the 1960s. A replica of a prau can be seen in the Northern Territory Museum in Darwin.*

» **4.** *Aboriginal women collecting water lilies, Cape York Peninsula, Queensland. Small, sweet tubers of water lilies (Nymphaea sp.) are eaten after they are lightly roasted in hot ashes. The ripe seeds are also eaten raw or stored and later ground into flour to make damper—unleavened bread baked in wood ashes.*

» **5.** *Aboriginal woman from Central Australia decorated for a corroboree—a combination of dance, song and dramatic performance.*

›› *6. Painting by F. Péron of canoe-rafts and Schouten Island, Tasmania.*

›› *7. Robinson on his Friendly Mission, in* The Conciliation, 1836, *by B. Dutterau.*

» **8.** View in Broken Bay, New South Wales, March 1788, *showing Aboriginal canoes, British boats and the newcomers and Aboriginal men dancing together, by William Bradley.*

» **9.** *Nipper Kapirigi fashions a stone tool in Kunawengayu rock-shelter, Arnhem Land, Northern Territory.*

›› **10.** *The Devil's Marbles, south of Tennant Creek, Northern Territory. The Aboriginal name for these huge granite boulders is Karlwe Karlwe, meaning 'sacred meeting place'. The area is rich in creation stories and was the site of major ceremonies.*

›› **11.** *Namarakain spirit figure painted at Mt Borradaile, northwest Arnhem Land, Northern Territory.*

›› **12.** *Anthwerrke, an Arrernte caterpillar dreaming site in a small gorge in Emily-Jesse Gap Nature Park east of Alice Springs, Northern Territory.*

» **13.** *Dreaming landscape at Watarrka (Kings Canyon) National Park, Northern Territory, 300 km (200 miles) west of Alice Springs.*

disease may have come from sailors or early sealers. If so, it was probably influenza, which had a disastrous effect on people with no prior immunity, as smallpox never reached Tasmania.

Corroboration of depopulation through disease in the northeast comes from Robinson: 'from observations made during this [1831] journey combined with the testimony of the natives themselves, I ascertained beyond a doubt, that many of those districts which had been formerly peopled by the Aborigines are now unoccupied; the once resident tribes being utterly extinct, a fact which was evinced by the dense overgrown [unburnt] underwood'.[22] The northeast was far from settled districts and the sealers' depredations affected the numbers of women but not of men, so new diseases would seem to be the primary cause of depopulation.

Jones' higher estimate of 5000 may therefore be most realistic for pre-colonisation Tasmanian numbers. A population of 5000 fits well with ethnographic evidence, is plausible compared with mainland densities in similar environments and readily explains the Tasmanians' rapid near-extinction under the dual impact of incomers' germs and guns. [23]

» Marriage

Tasmanian men were monogamous. Only two exceptions are known, both special cases. One man had two wives because when his first wife became dangerously ill she was left behind to die. Her husband married again but she recovered, so 'he continued them both'. The second was a 'chieftain, too old to fight', who needed the care of two women. The two wives 'agreed together admirably well' and both outlived their husband. One later became lame, so she lived by a river and 'subsisted on kelp and herbs'.[24]

In Tasmania, both sexes married in their late teens. A woman was regarded as her husband's property and was taken to his territory. On the death of a spouse, women remarried quickly and the new partner took over responsibility for children from the earlier union. There was no marriage ceremony and 'courtship' often involved violence. The French explorers lamented that Aboriginal women were 'often the victims of the brutality of their tyrants'. Robinson personally witnessed men forcing women to their beds by stabbing them with sharp sticks or stone knives. For instance, in 1830 he wrote: 'Mannerlelargenner had cut Tencotemainner with a knife because she would not stop with him . . . Tonight was another scene of confusion, the men running after the women with knives in their hands and the women running away.'[25] Murder of women was frequent. A jealous man named Nappelarleyer killed 'quite a young girl'; the murderer was then himself killed.[26] In another incident, a man named Montpeliatter murdered a 'tall, fine young woman' because she rejected his advances.[27] At seventeen, Truganini was married against her will to Woorrady, twenty years her senior, when his first wife died. Robinson commented that 'though highly

» *Woorrady, Robinson's main informant and Truganini's husband, in 1834.*

averse to her suitor . . . she is fearful to betray her feelings by a word or a look . . . This arises out of the fear of offending and a dread apprehension for its consequences.[28] Truganini's fears were well grounded, as Woorrady told Robinson:

> plenty of mothers and fathers kill their daughters on account of their attachment to men whom they dislike and to prevent their marriage. He knew a mother kill her daughter whilst sitting at the fire by jabbing a spear through her body, in at her back and out at her belly . . . The lover hearing of it watched an opportunity when the men were away hunting, and went and killed the mother. The natives form very strong attachments and they bear implacable enmity to their foes.[29]

» Rock art

Aboriginal Tasmania had both the world's smallest toolkit and its simplest, scarcest rock art. Only 28 linear motifs, mainly circles, occur in its eight engraving sites and the only paintings that have been discovered are a few red ochre patches and hand stencils in three ice age caves. Unlike the mainland, no figurative, representational motifs exist. Only three bird 'tracks' (footprints) have been found among 1000 engravings and one site has only circles. The closest mainland parallels are ice age engravings. By the 1700s, Tasmanians no longer made engravings and were unaware of their meaning or even existence, but they drew circles and lines inside their bark huts and by the 1830s were adding figurative Western motifs such as dogs, bullock-teams and boats.[30]

» Beliefs

Like mainlanders, Tasmanians believed in supernatural beings. Woorrady told how Lal.ler put his hand on the ground and created kangaroos that came out and ran away. Drome.mer.deen.ne arose from the sea and made kangaroo-rats and now is the bright southern star Canopus. According to Woorrady, 'Moi.nee and Drome.mer.deen.ne fight in the heavens and that Moi.nee tumbled down at Louisa Bay and dwelt on the land, that his wife came after him and dwelt in the sea, and . . . the Moi.nee children came down in the rain and went into the wife's womb and that afterwards they had plenty of children'. Moi.nee 'cut the ground and made the rivers, cut the land and made the islands'. When he died he turned into a large rock and still stands at Coxes Bight in Louisa Bay. Other Ancestral Beings came with the west wind or took animal form, like Tarner, the boomer kangaroo, who sat down and made all the lagoons.[31]

One creation story was current throughout Tasmania. It told how Moi.nee made the first man, Parlevar, who had a tail but no joints in his legs, so could not sit down. Another spirit saw his plight and cut off his tail, cured the wound with grease and made joints to his knees. He told Parlevar to sit down, which he did, declaring it 'very good'. By 1831 when Woorady and others told these stories much had been lost, but enough survives to show that Tasmanians' mythical beings resembled those of the mainlanders. They created humans, fire, the landscape and all living creatures and then were transformed into huge rocks or stars. Tasmanians' fire myth refers to two men in the sky—the stars known as Castor and Pollux—who made fire by rubbing their hands together and threw it down to men who were initially fearful but later returned and made a fire with wood. This resembles a fire story from Victoria.[32]

Some indisputable ceremonial sites exist. In the Bay of Fires, two lines of flat stones resembling a paved path lie above charcoal that has been radiocarbon-dated to 750 years ago. Such stone arrangements are common in mainland Australia and were used during initiation ceremonies.[33] Other links with mainland culture are art, dance and song. There were prolonged mourning songs but also light, secular airs. The women sang very sweetly and Labillardière compared their songs to those of 'the Arabs of Asia Minor. Two of them frequently sang the same air together; but the one constantly a third above the other, forming this harmony with the greatest exactness.'

» *Rock engravings at Mt Cameron West, northwest Tasmania. Circles typify Australia's earliest rock art. Motifs were pecked out of the rock with stone hammers. These engravings are unusually deep, giving them a sculptural quality. They are at least 2000 years old and may be much older.*

For their part, Aborigines loved Robinson's flute music, but when a Frenchman played his violin they put their fingers in their ears.

The basic belief system of Aboriginal Australia known as the Dreaming clearly existed long before Tasmania was isolated. This shows that the Dreaming is of ice age antiquity, not a mere 1500 years as has recently been claimed.[34]

» Artefacts

European explorers regarded Aborigines as 'children of nature'. Tasmanians even lived in the base of hollow trees: 'Many of their largest trees were converted into more comfortable habitations [than windbreaks]. These had their trunks hollowed out by fire, to the height of six or seven feet [1.8–2.1 m]; and the hearths, made of clay, to contain the fire in the middle, leaving room for four or five persons to sit round it.'[35]

Tasmania is the coldest, windiest part of Australia, yet, unlike mainlanders in their voluminous skin cloaks, its inhabitants almost never wore protective clothing. Early visitors concluded that Tasmanians were on the lowest rung of the 'chain of being', a now-discredited view that later formed the basis of Social Darwinist belief that Tasmanians were the missing link between apes and humans.[36]

People entered Tasmania across the land bridge exposed by the low sea level between 43 000 and 14 000 years ago.[37] The oldest occupied site to be excavated is 40 000 years old, in Warreen Cave in the southwest. Ice age Tasmanians lived within sight of glaciers in limestone caves, where they left hand stencils on the walls. They developed trading networks and used specialised tools, such as bone-tipped spears, to hunt wallabies; use of such sophisticated weapons so early was a surprise to archaeologists but the evidence is clear. Use-polish on spear-tips also indicated skin-working. It seems Tasmanians 'sewed' skins together and used bone-tipped spears in the ice age just as early as contemporary reindeer hunters in the northern hemisphere. (Bone points were eyeless awls rather than needles, so there was no true 'sewing' in Aboriginal Australia.)[38] Ice age hunters tightly targeted slow-moving wallabies on alpine grasslands until impenetrable temperate rainforest invaded the region and drove their prey and them out.[39]

» Why didn't the Tasmanians eat fish?

Total isolation of a few thousand people for fourteen millennia explains the ensuing simplification of culture and the loss of some useful arts. Archaeological evidence shows that about 3500 years ago Tasmanians stopped eating fish and making bone tools. The key site is Rocky Cape Cave, where the lower layers contain the bones of 31 different fish species—rocky-reef fish caught in baited box traps and estuarine fish from tidal-traps—but which are then absent from more recent occupied layers.[40] Bone tools vanished at the same time as scaled fish, probably because they were used to spear or gut them.

Whenever offered fish, whether raw or cooked, Tasmanians rejected it with cries of horror. Why they stopped eating fish is an unsolved mystery. Did they deliberately switch from fish to seals, a fattier, higher-energy food? As archaeologist Harry Allen said, 'Had the Tasmanians the service of a consultant nutritionist, they would probably have been advised to give up fishing and concentrate their energies on more profitable foods. There is evidence . . . that this is just what they did.' A climate shift about 3500 years ago to cooler, drier conditions led to increased Aboriginal burning of rainforest margins and expansion into uninhabited areas such as the west coast, with greater access to sealing grounds.[41] Yet why not eat both fish and seals? Especially when seals were hunted-out on sites, such as West Point, that were then abandoned.

Clearly there was a strong taboo against eating scaled fish, which Tasmanians regarded as non-food. Hostile tribesmen taunted Aborigines accompanying Robinson that he would 'feed them on fish, and mimicked the pulling up of the fish with a line'. (When an Arnhem Land fisherman was told about coastal people who did not eat fish, he exclaimed 'Silly bugger, eh?')[42]

Food taboos were observed at certain times, such as initiation or pregnancy, but the Tasmanian taboo on fish was unique and lasted for 3500 years. No previously advanced explanation is convincing, but I believe that the total ban on fish followed a major poisoning event remembered ever since. Fish are prone to natural toxins. Ciguatera, a poison that occurs naturally in algae and plankton, enters the food chain and may build up to lethal doses in larger fish.[43]

Ciguatera poisoning causes more human illness than any other toxicity from seafood. On tropical and subtropical islands, 10 000 to 50 000 individuals are affected annually, with 10–12 per cent mortality. Captain Cook suffered mild poisoning twice in 1774 in Vanuatu, probably from red bass. On the 1748 British naval expedition to Mauritius, 1500 men died from ciguatera poisoning. It is not possible to detect the poison before eating the fish, which appear healthy, and cooking does not remove the toxin. No immunity develops after an attack and the second time much less toxin is required to produce symptoms. There is no vaccine or antidote.

High-risk fish species live in tropical waters, but were they also around temperate Tasmania? One of the species most often identified as carrying the greatest risk of ciguatera poisoning was also identified in the early layers of Rocky Cape Cave—the wrasse. A rocky-reef species, wrasses were caught in baited box traps and are still common in Tasmanian waters today. Wrasse was the most abundant species in Tasmanian prehistoric deposits until 3500 years ago, when fishing abruptly ceased. Toxic fish are often confined to a small area and toxicity varies seasonally, but it seems that 3500 years ago Tasmanian fishermen suffered such severe poisoning that no Aboriginal Tasmanian ever risked eating fish again. The Aboriginal custom of sharing all food means that a single meal could wipe out a whole band. News of such a calamity would have spread quickly, leading to the universal taboo.

Significantly, the only other widespread, long-term Aboriginal food taboo concerns toxin-prone shellfish. The coastal Nyungar people of southwest Australia never consumed shellfish although they ate scaled fish.[44] Like Tasmanians, Nyungar were extremely isolated, the southwest being a remote 'oasis' in the corner of a vast arid expanse. Although furnished with a long, rich coastline, Nyungar obtained most food from the land. They lacked watercraft, nets and fishhooks and abhorred all shellfish, in spite of plentiful, accessible oyster beds, which were much appreciated by British colonists.

Could oral traditions sustaining taboos survive three millennia? Aboriginal Australia has many myths about Ancestral Beings turning peninsulas into islands (for example, Kangaroo Island, South Australia)—a probable reflection of a post-glacial sea level rise completed 6500 years ago. Detailed, localised accounts of volcanic eruptions lasted even longer. On the Atherton Tableland, the Ngadyandyi have stories apparently vividly explaining the origin of volcanic crater-lakes, although the last eruption occurred more than 10 000 years ago. They recount that two newly initiated men

» *West Point midden, northwest Tasmania, excavated in 1965. On the massive mound's surface were seven circular depressions—hut foundations. The site was occupied 1300–1800 years ago by a band exploiting a southern elephant seal colony for 3–4 months each summer. Hunters probably caused this seal's extinction in Tasmania, for it now comes no closer than uninhabited Macquarie Island. The midden contained stone tools, remains of young seals, shellfish, lizards, birds and wallabies, and three human cremation pits with bones broken and burnt after death along with grave-goods of a shell-necklace and eagle's claws.*

broke a taboo and angered the Rainbow Serpent. As a result, 'the camping-place began to change, the earth under the camp roaring like thunder. The wind started to blow down, as if a cyclone were coming. The camping-place began to twist and crack

. . . there was in the sky a red cloud, of a hue never seen before. The people tried to run from side to side but were swallowed by a crack which opened in the ground'.)[45]

» Survival

Demographers maintain that 500 is the critical size for a viable population. By 1802, when Flinders landed on Kangaroo Island, no people survived but only kangaroos so tame that 'the poor animals suffered themselves to be . . . knocked on the head with sticks'.[46] At contact, the much larger island of Tasmania was still inhabited. Controversially, Jones suggested that, because of 'the trauma which the severance of the Bassian bridge delivered to the society', Tasmanian culture was on a downward trajectory:

> slowly but surely there was a simplification in the tool kit, a diminution in the range of foods eaten, perhaps a squeezing of intellectuality . . . The world's longest isolation, the world's simplest technology. Were 4000 people enough to propel forever the cultural inheritance of Late Pleistocene Australia? . . . were they in fact doomed—doomed to a slow strangulation of the mind?[47]

The opposing, more popular view is that Tasmanian society was dynamic and branching out in new directions. The evidence for this is the invention of boats, the recolonisation of Hunter Island and the increasing use of new stone sources from distant quarries. The trigger for these new initiatives was probably the change to a drier climate 3500 years ago, which led to increased burning and expansion into previously unoccupied regions.

» Sealers and whalers

The first sustained foreign impact on Tasmania came from sealers, who from 1798 hunted each summer in Bass Strait and down the eastern coast. By 1800, British and American companies were dropping groups of 10–15 men on uninhabited islands for the sealing season from November till May. Soon these sealers began coming ashore on Tasmania's northern and eastern coasts for repairs and fresh food. A few hundred sealers came each year, their visits coinciding with Aboriginal migrations to the coast for seals, shellfish, birds and eggs in summer. At first Tasmanians were cautious of the newcomers but soon began to exchange kangaroo skins for tobacco, flour, tea and hunting dogs. Aborigines incorporated this unfamiliar animal into their society with extraordinary speed, even though building an affectionate relationship with a tame animal was something totally strange. Tasmanians proved outstanding at training dogs and used them effectively for hunting, besieging settlers' huts and guarding their own camps. The dogs were greyhounds and deerhounds that proved superb at chasing and bailing-up large kangaroos, significantly increasing Aboriginal hunting capabilities. Previously, catching a kangaroo often involved a foot-chase of 10 km (6 miles) or more.[48]

Desperate for one of these status symbols and hunting aids, a group of west coast Aborigines traded a 14-year-old girl to the Macquarie Harbour pilot in exchange for a dog.[49] Ironically, when the same people later had more dogs than women, they offered Robinson dogs in exchange for an Aboriginal woman in his party, but he refused.[50] By 1832, Aboriginal groups contained more dogs than people. When the remaining 26 members of the central tribes walked through the streets of Hobart to Government House to the strains of a brass band later that year, they had over a hundred dogs with them.[51]

Trade, raids and disputes over women

The first recorded Aboriginal raid for a 'white woman' ended in laughter. On Baudin's 1802 expedition,

> Thirteen natives attacked our gallant carpenters, Horville and Buron, and as the latter had a pretty face they mistook him for a woman. Eight of them led him away into the wood, while the rest hit Horville on the shoulders with their lances to prevent him from rescuing his companion, whom they examined and then released with great roars of laughter when they saw he was a man.[52]

Aboriginal men often lent or traded their women for white men's goods. Each spring, the northeast tribe gathered at strategic points along the coast. When the sealers arrived, a ceremonial dance was held and arrangements were made for women to accompany sealers to the islands for the season. Sometimes Aboriginal men also went along. Some women came from the host band, while others were abducted from other bands and exchanged with sealers for dogs and foreign food. Some women, such as Walyer, went willingly. Walyer, known as the Aboriginal 'Amazon', stood 1.8 m (6 feet) tall and is now regarded as a hero of the resistance, but as a girl her back was broken by an Aboriginal man who was trying to kill her with a club. To escape his threats, she later joined sealers in Bass Strait.[53] Other women were sold but strongly resisted. A woman called Mary told Robinson that she had been exchanged 'for a bag of flour and potatoes' but refused to go and had to be carried off bound hand and foot.[54]

At first, Aboriginal women were taken by sealers primarily because of their seal-hunting and food-providing skills—in the cold waters it was women who captured seals from the rocks, and crayfish, abalone and other shellfish from the ocean depths. Shellfish, crayfish and seals were major foods in Tasmania. Women were excellent swimmers and could stay underwater a long time. First they stood on a rock and sang a special song, then swam out to capture seals by lying on the rocks beside them, imitating their movements and eventually clubbing them to death. Women also dived to depths of 4 m (13 ft) to collect food. Fronds of giant kelp were used as underwater 'ropes' to get down to the ocean-floor, where they levered shells off the rocks with small wooden wedges and put them into rush-baskets suspended from their necks. Crayfish were grabbed from under rocks and thrown up onto shore.[55]

In the six years from 1800–06 sealers collected over 100 000 seal skins, but by 1810 seal numbers had been depleted so severely that companies moved elsewhere. About 30 independent sealers remained; most were renegade sailors, escaped convicts or ex-convicts and some had been there since the 1790s.

Sealers were known as 'banditti of the straits', but most treated Aboriginal women reasonably well because they valued their labour as well as sexual services.[56] When Robinson arrived in 1830 and tried to remove the women to his newly established Aboriginal settlement, he encountered strong resistance from the women as well as sealers. After he forcibly took fourteen women to marry his Aboriginal men, the sealers delegated James Munro to plead with the governor for their return. Munro's own wife had been taken and he was left alone on his island to care for their three children. Sealers argued that their Aboriginal wives wanted to stay with their husbands and children rather than marry strangers. Governor Arthur took the sealers' side and sent a letter ordering Robinson to return some of the women. He also suggested authorising sealers to become official 'conciliators' of the Aborigines.

This threat to his authority was too much for Robinson, who immediately began recording shocking stories he claimed Munro had told him of atrocities committed by sealers on Aboriginal women. The sudden appearance of such tales precisely when he wanted to blacken the sealers' reputation is highly suspicious and it seems inconceivable that Munro would have told Robinson such self-incriminating stories. The final reason for rejecting these lurid tales as untrue is their uncanny resemblance to a volume of horror stories by Bartolemé de las Casas, intended to condemn Spaniards in the Americas.[57] These stories made Spanish conquistadors a byword for cruelty but have now been discredited—Las Casas either invented the incidents or drew them from the Old Testament and other early sources.[58] They all have similar features— seizing children and killing them before their mothers' eyes, cutting flesh off living people and making them eat it, feeding people to dogs, cutting off victims' hands, cannibalism, emasculation, rape, ripping open pregnant women or burning people alive. Plomley, who edited Robinson's papers, expressed scepticism about these atrocities in lengthy annotations. It is also significant that no such tales were reported to Archdeacon Broughton's 1830 committee of inquiry into violence towards Tasmanians. Abduction and ill-treatment of Aborigines certainly occurred, but the extent of atrocities and 'massacres' has been grossly exaggerated.[59]

Raids by sealers for women severely depleted Aboriginal numbers—by 1830 only three women survived in northeast Tasmania among 72 men. Women also suffered frequent violence at the hands of their own people; as Péron observed in 1802: 'among the older women . . . one could see in all of them something of the apprehension and dejection which misfortune and slavery stamp on the faces of all those beings who wear the yoke. Moreover, nearly all were covered with scars, shameful evidence of the ill-treatment of their ferocious spouses.' (The context makes clear that Péron was describing scars caused by haphazard injury *not* by ritual scarification.) Similarly, in an 1820s history, Jeffreys wrote: 'The author had several opportunities of learning from the females that their husbands act towards them with considerable harshness and tyranny.'[60] No wonder that a 'young girl' and three 'young women' chose to swim across the icy Arthur River and join Robinson's party rather than stay with their own band.[61]

Another hazard for women was venereal disease. From 1804, whaling ships periodically visited southern Tasmania. In 1822 a temporary whaling station opened at Port Davey and others followed. At Bruny Island and elsewhere young Aboriginal women frequented the whaling camps, trading their favours for bread, flour, tea and tobacco. By 1820 there were sealing camps on Cape Barren, King, Hunter and Kangaroo islands, where about 50 sealers and a hundred Aboriginal women and their children lived.[62]

» The arrival of the colonists

In 1798, in the same year that sealers first arrived, George Bass and Matthew Flinders circumnavigated Tasmania, proving it to be separated from the mainland by a stormy channel 240 km (150 miles) wide. Whoever controlled Bass Strait effectively controlled the sea lane from Europe to Sydney, and so Governor King, worried about the intentions of French explorers such as Baudin, decided to place a settlement there. Their first attempt at establishing a colony on Bass Strait—in 1803 at Port Phillip Bay, now Melbourne—failed because of 'troublesome' Aborigines and the selection of a poor site. The commandant, David Collins, decided to establish a permanent colony in Tasmania instead. A small settlement had already been set up by Lieutenant John Bowen east of the Derwent River in the southeast in September 1803.[63]

When Bowen arrived in southern Tasmania, all was quiet initially. When the party landed, the local band vanished but later 'a solitary savage, armed with a spear . . . entered the camp, and was cordially greeted . . . By his gestures they inferred that he discharged them from their trespass. He then turned towards the woods, and when they attempted to follow, he placed himself in the attitude of menace, and poised his spear.'[64] Bowen's attitude was clear: 'I have not seen a single native yet, but some of the people found them . . . they appeared very shy and have since retired entirely from us . . . I have not made any search after them, thinking myself well off if I never see them again.'[65] However there was soon trouble over food, when Aborigines tried to prevent the settlers taking oysters and kangaroos, which were staples for Tasmanians and the newcomers alike.

At 2 p.m. on 3 May 1804 the new settlement under Collins at Sullivan's Cove (later Hobart) heard a cannon shot from Risdon Cove 10 km (6 miles) away. According to the testimony of former convict Edward White before Broughton's committee 26 years later:

> He was hoeing new ground near a creek; saw 300 of the Natives come down in a circular form, and a flock of kangaroos hemmed in between them, there were men, women and children; 'they looked at me with all their eyes', I went down to the creek, and reported them to some soldiers, and then went back to my work; the natives did not threaten me . . . the Natives did not attack the soldiers; . . . they had no spears with them, only waddies [clubs]; they were hunting; the soldiers came down from their own camp to the creek to attack the Natives; . . . the firing commenced about 11 o'clock; there were a great many of the Natives slaughtered and wounded; I don't know how many; some of their bones were sent in two casks to Port Jackson . . . they did not know there was a white man in the country when they came down to Risdon.[66]

The violent overreaction by Risdon's outnumbered defenders against peaceful kangaroo-hunters was deplored by the governor and contemporary historians. It was first called a 'massacre' by James Bonwick in 1870, while W.C. Wentworth in 1822 called it 'a murderous discharge of grapeshot' and John West in 1852 'a severe collision'. These nineteenth-century historians were under no illusions about its seriousness and significance.

It is unclear whether the cannon fired a blank to intimidate the Aborigines or if it was filled with grapeshot. A 1978 archaeological survey of the site with a metal detector turned up no grapeshot or bullets,[67] but it is a difficult terrain of small hills and valleys, as I saw for myself in the 1980s. Absence of evidence is not necessarily evidence of absence, but a similar survey of Pinjarra battlefield in Western Australia revealed both shot and some bones of the dead (see chapter 4). It is also unclear what the death toll was. Minimum estimates come from the young acting commandant, Lieutenant Moore, and David Collins, who put casualties at three killed and some wounded. Since then the number killed has grown to 50 or even 100 unarmed, bough-waving, singing hunters mown down by a drunken lieutenant.[68] Historian Phillip Tardif's account, based on a meticulous reading of the sources and a very detailed knowledge of the site, concludes that 'We will never know for sure how many were killed or wounded that day. Certainly it was more than two or three. Probably it was fewer than fifty. Somewhere in between lies the "great many" spoken of by Edward White, whose poignant testimony remains for me the most credible description of this sorry episode.'[69] The Risdon Cove massacre has become a founding story in Tasmanian history and the site is now Aboriginal land. Four days after the Risdon incident Aborigines made a reprisal attack on working convicts, and two months later Risdon was abandoned, as Hobart provided greater security.

Another settlement, under William Paterson, was established in the north in 1804, and Aboriginal resistance was encountered immediately, perhaps due to prior contact with sealers. Eighty armed Aborigines confronted Paterson's party and tried to throw a sentry into the sea. In retaliation one Aborigine was shot. Harassment of the newcomers continued, and they were driven up the Tamar River to the site of modern Launceston in 1806.

» Coexistence

In the south, Aborigines and settlers coexisted relatively peacefully until the arrival in 1807 of 700 new, mainly ex-convict settlers. This influx intensified the conflict over kangaroos and access to new provisions. Aboriginal craving for settlers' food and tobacco was 'regular and irresistible', according to Robinson, who described the Big River tribe of central Tasmania as 'passionately fond' of bread and sugar: 'flour is their object, also tea, sugar and blankets . . . they cannot do without these'. Similarly, when visiting the Port Davey people in the remote southwest, Robinson found their desire for tea was 'one of the chief sources of attraction in directing their migrations to those places or abodes where they think they can procure it'.

Apart from honey from native, stingless bees, Australian flora provides few sweet foods, so the craving for sugar is understandable. Western foods had the great advantages of being ready to use, easily carried and storable; Robinson came upon pits lined with bark ready to store plundered flour. Teapots and kettles were taken to make tea and clay pipes to smoke stolen tobacco. Although there was no shortage of native food, Tasmanian hunters closed in on the settlements and became dependent on British goods.[70] Inland resources were possums, wombats, echidnas, kangaroos and especially wallabies, which were caught by head-high nooses suspended across their trackways. (Red-necked wallabies provided 90 per cent of ice age Tasmanians' food.) Coasts furnished shellfish, seals, swans' eggs and muttonbirds. Tasmanians had enough meat and, in contrast to the mainland where the spearing of sheep and cattle was rife, raiders usually left introduced animals alone. What they lacked were any native tobacco or grains to grind into flour.[71]

Soon Aborigines were offering their women and it was 'well understood' that women would visit stockmen in exchange for provisions. Settlers were in great need of labourers, and if adult Aborigines had been prepared to work for wages or supplies, the two societies could have coexisted peacefully for a time. Aboriginal children were occasionally loaned as labour but this was rare. There is no evidence of the widespread 'kidnapping' claimed by some historians. Only 26 very young children lived in settlers' homes.[72] In 1819 the governor ordered all such children be sent to the Orphan School in Hobart. Twelve were there in 1820 but most went back to the bush on reaching puberty.[73]

» *Tasmanian Aboriginal Athol Burgess muttonbirding on Babel Island, Bass Strait in 1985. Each October, muttonbirds (short-tailed shearwaters) fly south from Siberia to Tasmania. The blossoming of lightwood trees was the signal for Aborigines to collect eggs and later feast on oil-rich fledglings. In late November, muttonbirds lay eggs in burrow-like nests in 'rookeries' on seaside dunes. The eggs hatch in February. Parent birds feed fledglings for 8–10 weeks and then migrate northwards, the young birds following in early May. Several hundred million muttonbirds arrive each year—in 1798 Flinders watched a continuous stream fly over Hunter Island for 90 minutes. Rookeries may be viewed near Strahan and at Carlton Beach near Hobart.*

By 1814, there were almost 2000 Europeans in Tasmania. Tasmanians tolerated the newcomers' presence and the few violent incidents were payback for the wrong-doing of individuals. Most violence towards Aborigines came from sealers, whalers and escaped convicts who became bushrangers—bandits who hid in the bush and stole from settlers at gunpoint. However, bushrangers never exceeded twenty in number and were no match for Aborigines, who befriended some and killed others.

Gradually, widespread exchange of goods developed. When Captain Kelly circumnavigated Tasmania in summer 1815–16, he saw a 'large mob' of natives on the northeast coast. He bartered with seal meat and in ten days acquired kangaroo and seal skins worth £180 in Hobart. Trade concluded with mass dancing.[74]

The *Hobart Town Gazette* of 25 April 1818 reported: 'Notwithstanding the hostility which has so long prevailed in the breasts of the natives of this island towards Europeans, we now perceive with heartfelt satisfaction the hatred in some measure gradually subsiding. Several of them are to be seen about this town and its environs, who obtain subsistence from the charitable and well-disposed.' There were so few

» Free settlers

Sadly, this period of relatively peaceful coexistence ended when the British government encouraged free settlers with capital to occupy 'empty' territory. Between 1817 and 1824, British numbers increased sixfold and all grassland and open forest in the central river valleys was settled, although very little of this land was enclosed. Prohibitively expensive wooden fences or hawthorn hedges were unnecessary on sheep farms and were uncommon until much later.

By 1824, 'settled districts' occupied 15 per cent of Tasmania. They included very little of the 1600 km (1000 miles) of coastline but many kangaroo hunting grounds.[75]

Pastoral expansion caused many problems. Foremost was the Aboriginal loss of land and game. One Aborigine recounted: 'When I returned to my country I went hunting but did not kill one head of game. The white men make their dogs wander, and kill all of the game, and they only want the skins.'[76]

Ever-increasing Aboriginal addiction to tobacco, tea, sugar, molasses, bread and flour also caused conflict. As a tribal Aborigine captured while robbing a hut and interviewed by Governor Arthur (with Robinson interpreting) explained: 'when the tribe attacked the hut it was in order to obtain food, and such articles as the whites had introduced amongst them, and which now instead of being luxuries as formerly, had become necessities, which they could not any other way procure'.[77]

The coveted goods were obtained by charity, cohabitation, prostitution or theft. 'Tame mobs' developed and in November 1824 about 60 Aborigines entered Hobart in search of provisions and blankets. The governor rapidly provided these and they settled on the riverbank opposite the town. Two years later the group decamped after two of their number were hanged for the murder of settlers. Violence had been instigated by a mainland Aborigine, Musquito, transported from Sydney to Norfolk Island in 1805 for murder and later freed to work as a stockman in Tasmania. Musquito spurned manual labour and when the authorities refused to repatriate him to Sydney, he and a Tasmanian Aborigine, Black Jack, killed seven settlers over nine months before they were captured, tried by jury and hanged.[78]

Conflict increased after 1824 and Aborigines used fire to destroy huts and crops. Tasmanian spears were only effective to 30 m (100 ft) and rarely delivered fatal wounds; clubs were used to finish victims off. Musket-balls were more lethal but until 1850 the only available guns were heavy, unreliable, slow, muzzle-loading muskets. Settlers could fire perhaps one round a minute, fully trained soldiers up to three. Muskets were accurate at 50 m (160 ft) but had only 50 per cent accuracy at 150 m (500 ft). British army tests in 1831 revealed a misfire rate of one in every six, usually due to wet powder or maladjusted flints. In wet conditions misfires increased to three in four.[79]

At first Tasmanians feared guns, believing them magic weapons that killed without visible missiles, akin to 'thunder and lightning'.[80] By the 1820s they had learnt to leap for cover in the second or two between the flash in the pan as gunpowder ignited and the actual discharge. Once a gun was fired, its owner was at their mercy while reloading, and misfiring caused much derision. Nonetheless, Aborigines valued guns for shooting birds and occasionally stole them.

Hostilities produced several black heroes, including Walyer, who learnt to shoot on Bass Strait islands. In 1828 she returned from the islands to lead the Emu Bay people. Robinson described Walyer standing on a hill ordering her band (seven men, a boy and another woman) to attack the whites, taunting them in English to come out of their huts and fight. Her opinion of them was not high—she once said that she liked a white man as much as she did a black snake.[81] Walyer died from influenza in 1831.

Aborigines would watch remote huts for days until the opportunity arose for a raid, then disappear into the bush without trace. It was not a regular or true guerilla war, but a series of hit-and-run attacks on stockmen's huts for food. As Governor Arthur lamented: 'The species of warfare which we are carrying on with them is of the most distressing nature; they suddenly appear, commit some act of outrage and then as suddenly vanish: if pursued it seems impossible to surround and capture them.' In Robinson's words, 'it was a futile battle with a shadow'.[82] Settlers, according to contemporary historian James Calder, were 'no match for the blacks in bush fighting, either in defensive or offensive operations'. Similarly, convict Jorgen Jorgensen, leader of one of the roving parties sent to capture Aborigines, wrote that blacks 'consider themselves our superiors in the art of warfare, save their fear of our firearms'.[83]

Both sides were on foot because horses were scarce in Tasmania and much of the country was too rough for them. Life for stockmen and shepherds was nearly as basic as for Aborigines. Almost total self-sufficiency was needed. Dwellings were simple one-roomed wooden huts with shingle or thatched roofs. There was constant fear of attack by Aborigines, who threw firesticks onto the roof and speared anyone emerging from the burning building. Help was non-existent; there were no police, soldiers or doctors outside the few towns. Food supplies came from far away so any losses were extremely serious. Because of the fear of attack, many settlers and shepherds in remote areas abandoned their holdings.

» The Cape Grim massacre

Initially, the European population was overwhelmingly made up of young males, leading to some conflict over Aboriginal women. The 1826 grant to the Van Diemen's Land Company to graze sheep in the remote, lawless northwest brought ex-convicts there. When shepherds lured Aboriginal women into a hut and tried to molest them, their menfolk retaliated by spearing a shepherd in the thigh, the whites shot a man dead, and Aborigines responded by driving 118 sheep over a cliff. In February 1828 a reprisal took place. Robinson was asked to investigate rumours of a mass killing and visited Cape Grim in mid-1830. He took evidence from two of the white perpetrators and some Aboriginal women living with sealers on Robbins Island and visited the site twice, once with one of the murderers. Robinson put the death toll at 30:

> On the occasion of the massacre a tribe of natives, consisting principally of women and children, had come to the [Doughboy] islands. Providence had favoured them with fine weather . . . They swam across, leaving their children at the rocks in the care of the elderly people. They had prepared their supply of [mutton] birds, had tied them with grass, had towed them on shore, and the whole tribe was seated round their fires partaking of their hard-earned fare, when down rushed the band of fierce barbarians thirsting for the blood of these unprotected and unoffending people. They fled, leaving their provision. Some rushed into the sea, others scrambled round the cliff and what remained the monsters put to death. Those poor creatures who had sought shelter in the cleft of the rock they forced to the brink of an awful precipice, massacred them all and threw their bodies down the precipice . . . I went to the foot of the cliff where the bodies had been thrown down and saw several human bones, some of which I brought with me, and a piece of the bloody cliff. As the tide was flowing I hastened from this Golgotha.[84]

Armed with this account, I went to see the site for myself in the 1980s and found Robinson's story plausible. The most reliable account of the Cape Grim massacre comes from historian Ian McFarlane, who has conducted detailed archival research, consulted with scholars and local observers, made many visits to the site and applied the most rigorous analysis of the evidence to reach his conclusion that Robinson's account is reasonably accurate. Robinson was no fabricator, although, as Plomley noted, he tended to exaggerate violence towards the 'poor, hapless souls' he was trying to save and to hide Aboriginal killing of whites. In 1831 Robinson made clear his expedition journals were for publication, which explains his lurid description of the 'Golgotha' of Cape Grim.[85]

» Reserves

As the white death toll mounted, pressure increased on the governor to keep Aborigines out of the settled districts. Arthur believed Tasmania could be shared between the two races. In 1827 he wrote that he intended 'to settle the Aborigines in some remote quarter of the island, which should be strictly reserved for them, and to supply them with food and clothing, and afford them protection from injuries by the stock-keepers'.[86] The northeastern coast was 'the best sheltered and warmest part of the island, and remote from the settled district'. It was also rich in native food but thinly inhabited. British settlement did not spread there till the 1860s and even today much of the northeast is thickly forested, wilderness country. Arthur understood that keeping Aborigines in even a large reserve was counter to their traditional life, but felt that 'it is but justice to make the attempt'.[87] After eight years in the Americas, Arthur's model was the reserves created there and in 1827 he sought a suitable 'ambassador' to explain his proposal.[88] The problem was that Aborigines fled at the sight of soldiers, making consultation difficult.

» Martial law and the 'Black Line'

During the first quarter of 1828, sixteen settlers were killed and twelve were wounded in 48 violent incidents. To try to prevent further bloodshed, Arthur issued a proclamation on 15 April aimed at achieving 'a temporary separation of the coloured from the British population of this territory' by keeping the 'formidable and troublesome' natives out of settled areas. Troops were stationed at five places around the perimeter of the settled districts, which Aborigines could only traverse if their leaders applied for a 'pass'. Trespassing natives were 'to be persuaded to retire beyond the prescribed limits' or captured 'without force' and 'treated with the utmost humanity and compassion'. Arthur had picture-boards explaining government policy placed on trees along the frontier. His proclamation included planning 'a negotiation with certain chiefs of aboriginal tribes', but he also wrote to the Colonial Office explaining that the 'spirit of dissension amongst the tribes' was such that his plan could not 'possibly be accomplished'.[89] Arthur's pessimism was justified—there was much intertribal feuding and many Aborigines were unwilling to move into the territory of a different tribe. Aboriginal women were more flexible, because on marriage they moved to their husband's country. On the later Friendly Mission, Aboriginal women were the main negotiators and succeeded in persuading remaining tribespeople to go to a single island reserve.

In spring 1828, Aboriginal attacks increased fourfold from the previous spring. The last straw was the murder of two British women and their two young children. The press greeted this with such outrage that Arthur was forced to take the extreme measure of declaring martial law—'law imposed upon an area by military forces when civil authority has broken down'. Martial law meant soldiers could arrest or shoot on sight any Aborigines found in settled districts. This measure had been used for six months in 1816 to rid Tasmania of bushrangers, but now it took over three years to achieve peace. The explicit aim was 'to inspire them with terror' as 'the only effectual means of security for the future'.[90] The goal was to make settled districts safe, not to annihilate all Aboriginal Tasmanians. Nor did the declaration of martial law herald a 'war'—the term 'Black War' for the period 1828–32 was coined by later, partisan historians.

The British thought there were about 2000 Aborigines in the settled districts, whereas the number was probably nearer 200. While soldiers scoured the region to capture them, the attacks on settlers intensified. Drastic measures were needed, and in

» *In April 1828, illustrative boards were nailed to trees around the settled districts. The upper two panels depict harmonious relations between black and white, who are on an equal footing; the lower ones show that the penalty for murder whether by black or white is hanging.*

February 1830 a bounty was introduced of £5 for every adult captured alive and £2 per child. When this also failed to halt British deaths, Arthur mounted a full-scale military offensive to end the conflict.[91] The result was the 'Black Line'—an attempt to drive all Aborigines out of the settled districts onto the narrow-necked Tasman Peninsula in the southeast. Every able-bodied white man was recruited, resulting in a line of 2200 moving abreast for seven weeks, but the sweep resulted only in the shooting of two Aborigines and the capture of an old man and a crippled boy. The white death rate exceeded the black, for five troopers were accidentally shot by 'friendly fire'.

The Black Line has usually been judged an expensive failure, but such a massive display of manpower and firearms achieved the desired effect. One Aboriginal woman, who found herself inside the line, described long rows of soldiers firing muskets, 'plenty of horsemen, plenty of soldiers, plenty of big fires on the hills'.[92] Aborigines did not know it was a unique operation, far too costly to repeat, and it convinced them to consider a negotiated peace.

In 39 months of martial law, 89 British were killed and twice that number injured. The Aboriginal death toll is uncertain but, as Reynolds says, 'there is a tendency among writers sympathetic to the Aborigines to exaggerate the numbers killed in order to emphasise the brutality of the colonial encounter. While this habit is under-standable, it greatly inflates the capacity of the colonists and generally underestimates the ability of the Aborigines'.[93] The much-quoted figure of 4:1 Aboriginal to white deaths in Tasmania is based on exceedingly shaky estimates of the Aboriginal popu-lation and unwarranted assumptions that all Aborigines subsequently 'unaccounted for' had been killed by white men rather than by other Aborigines or disease.[94]

Three detailed, independent casualty estimates have been made by Plomley, Windschuttle and lay scholar H.A. Willis. The latter has produced the most reliable tally, using plausibility criteria he believes are just as stringent as those employed by Windschuttle, but a wider set of sources of information. Willis found sixteen possible incidents in which more than five Aborigines lost their lives. During the first two decades of settlement, Europeans took more lives than did Aborigines. In the eight-year period from 1824 to 1831, the so-called Black War, Willis estimates about 163 Aboriginal and 172 settler casualties, whereas Windschuttle suggested that during the period more than twice as many whites were killed as blacks. Overall, Reynolds found in 1995 that approximately the same number of Aborigines and Europeans lost their lives in frontier conflict.[95] Similarly, Willis counted about the same number (188) of Aborigines and Europeans killed in the whole 1803–34 period, but when 'dubious' cases are added, his figures are 198 European casualties and 333 Aboriginal. In other words, during the first three decades of contact, one and a half times as many Aborigines died as Europeans.

What we don't know is how many Aboriginal deaths at white hands went unre-ported. Tasmania's difficult terrain and the superiority of spears over muskets makes

Aboriginal success in this frontier conflict believable, however. There are vast tracts of mountain and forest into which hunters could vanish and live well on plentiful native foods. In the 1820s and 1830s there was abundant game; Robinson's parties carried no guns but lived off the land. Europeans quickly realised pursuit was pointless because of the rugged Tasmanian bush, which presents a serious challenge to modern bush-walkers.

» The 'Friendly Mission'

Arthur regarded the conflict as a 'heavy calamity' and kept trying to achieve a negoti-ated settlement. In 1828 some Bruny Islanders visited Hobart, and Arthur set up a ration depot for them on their island. In March 1829 he advertised for 'a steady per-son of good character . . . who will take an interest in effecting an intercourse with this unfortunate race'. Robinson was appointed at the age of 41. He held evangelical beliefs and a 'missionary desire' to improve the Aboriginal lot, 'especially as [he] entertained an impression that this race would ultimately and at no distant period become extinct'. Robinson's motto was *amicus humani generis*—friend of the human race. He saw his mission as 'the cause of God': he must 'civilise the Aborigines', who had to be 'taught to labour'. They would have to 'hoe the ground, to plant potatoes, to catch fish, to assist in building their huts etc'. He planned to keep the children in a dormitory 'separate from the rest of the tribe'.[96] These ideas derived from mainland missions, but Robinson's first task was to bring Aborigines in from the bush.

On his seven expeditions Robinson collected 151 Aborigines. No force was used, but his Aboriginal guides persuaded people that 'coming in' was in their own best interest. On every expedition there were more Aborigines than white men. Three women, Truganini and Pagerly, both 18 year olds, and Drayduric (or Dray), aged 30, carried out most negotiations. Later, Truganini explained why she had helped the conciliation mission: 'Mr Robinson was a good man and could speak our language, and I said I would go with him and help him.' It was 'the best thing to do . . . I hoped we would save all my people that were left.' Living near Hobart, she said, 'I knew it was no use my people trying to kill all the white people now, there were so many of them always coming in big boats.' Truganini told Aborigines they met that 'our people were all being killed and it was no use fighting any more, and Mr Robinson was our friend, and would take us all to a good place'.[97] Tragically, what no one anticipated was the fatal impact of foreign germs. Half the captured Aborigines died from pulmonary complaints before reaching their island refuge, some within just a few days of first contact with whites.

One family, the Lanneys, continued living in the northwest but in 1841 began 'a remarkably persevering and daring system of attacks on an outlying shepherd's hut'. The hut was cleared out on 6 July, restocked, and robbed again on 13, 14, 19 and 20 July. Company men then set up a spring-loaded gun to go off when the door was opened. It fired on the next raid on 23 July but only scared the intruders, who dropped their booty. The gun was re-set on 24 July, and on 25 July the raiders 'carried off amongst other things the spring gun'![98] They later gave themselves up because they said they were lonely. They were taken to Flinders Island, where by 1847 five out of seven Lanneys had died from disease.

» Disease and depopulation

The attraction of regular supplies of food and tobacco was important in persuading Aborigines to 'come in'. By 1833 about 220 were on Flinders Island at the Aboriginal Establishment of Wybalenna (meaning Black Men's Houses). Promises of food, clothing and safety were kept, and Robinson turned it into the prototype of the multipurpose institution—welfare settlement, hospital, training centre, school, church, agricultural institution, ration-depot, pensioners' home and prison—that later proliferated on the mainland.[99]

By 1847, only 46 Tasmanians survived at Wybalenna. They were taken by ship to Oyster Cove ex-convict station 30 km (19 miles) south of Hobart. Truganini died in 1876, but others of mixed race survived on the Bass Strait islands and elsewhere, and in the 2001 census 17 442 people in Tasmania identified as indigenous.

Why was the Aboriginal death toll so high? Flinders Island's climate was not unhealthy and a doctor there said it was more salubrious than mainland Tasmania. Between 1833 and 1837 only one of 70 convicts died, but 40 Aborigines succumbed, although provided with the same food as the convicts and the services of a doctor. Change of diet led to some ill health; the daily adult ration was 1 lb (450 g) of salt-meat, 1.5 lb (675 g) of flour, plus cabbage, turnip, tea, sugar and tobacco. Fresh meat was regularly provided only after 1839 when the Mission acquired sheep and pigs. An 1839 Board of Inquiry identified as a major problem the refusal of Aborigines to do any gardening or other work to help grow food. At Wybalenna convicts, not Aborigines, worked the native garden as well as their own plots.

Cooking was also a problem, for Aborigines boiled salt meat and vegetables together, reducing the nutritional value. Imported supplies were supplemented by native food, for Flinders Island is 200 km (125 miles) in circumference and well-endowed with bush 'tucker'. Aborigines went on regular, long, hunting expeditions for wallabies, eggs, shellfish, muttonbirds and seals. Half the Aboriginal community was 'frequently absent on hunting excursions for weeks together', and during nine months in 1839 at least a quarter was continually absent.[100]

Robert Hughes described Wybalenna as 'a benign concentration camp' but Reynolds argued that it was the 'best equipped and most lavishly staffed Aboriginal institution in the Australian colonies in the nineteenth century'. Aborigines were free to roam the island. Their children were more regimented, being forced to wash and attend school and women were expected to attend sewing, cooking and literacy classes, but no Aborigines were forced to work or subjected to physical punishment, and the men spent their time playing marbles, cricket and rounders. Frequent corroborees were held and animated singing and dancing continued until midnight, the women dancing clothed but the men naked. Traditional dances included clever imitations of emus, kangaroos and crows and one in which 'the men represented the attack of a Tasmanian "tiger" [thylacine], wounded after being supposed to have destroyed some of their children'. Others such as the horse or bread-making dance were new inventions.[101]

Aborigines refused to 'work like prisoners', and would only erect fencing, shear sheep, clear forest land, harvest crops or build roads when paid to do so. Marriage was encouraged, but those Robinson arranged seldom lasted. When four Aboriginal 'sealing women' were wed, within a week all had 'separated from their husbands' and declared they 'intended taking dogs and going into the bush'. There 'nightly appointments' with convicts took place, rewarded with tea, sugar and tobacco. Women could charge highly for sexual favours, for convicts were in their power—one word to the commandant about such illegal 'fraternisation' and the offending convict was flogged and deported to a penal settlement. Jealousy and fighting caused frequent disruption.[102]

One criticism is that evangelical Christianity was 'rammed down their throats'. An unforeseen result was that Christian doctrine, with its message that all people are equal before God, was seized upon by young activists, who used it effectively. In 1846 they sent a petition to Queen Victoria from the 'free Aborigines Inhabitants of Van Diemen's Land now living upon Flinders Island', aimed at ridding themselves of an unpopular superintendent. The petition succeeded but also led to the less popular move back to mainland Tasmania. Exile caused severe loss of morale, but broken hearts were not the cause of Aboriginal mortality. Indeed, the Tasmanians were keen to move to Victoria, but when Robinson took fifteen for a visit to Melbourne in 1839, five absconded, looted shepherds' huts, wounded four stock-keepers and murdered two whalers. The two Aboriginal men involved confessed and were hanged in 1841 and Truganini and her female companions were sent back to Flinders Island.[103]

The catastrophic death rate was due to new diseases, particularly pulmonary and sexually transmitted ones. When Robinson reached Bruny Island in 1829 he found only nineteen Aborigines survived from the southeast tribe that six years earlier was 160-strong.[104]

The apparently low level of syphilis puzzled historian Lyndall Ryan, since it 'was noted among the stock-keepers and sealers'. An explanation comes from Baudin in 1802, who noticed that Aborigines 'seem to be subject to a type of yaws, for several had ulcerated legs. We discern no trace of smallpox on their faces or bodies, and they are possibly fortunate enough as well not to know syphilis.' This 'yaws' was the temperate form, treponarid, which gave Aborigines cross-immunity from venereal syphilis but not from gonorrhoea or chlamydia. Doctors attributed only two Aboriginal deaths at Wybalenna and Oyster Cove to syphilis. If treponarid was endemic in Tasmania, the disease must pre-date islanders' isolation 14 000 years ago.[105]

The effects of the disruption of traditional Aboriginal society, sterilisation by gonorrhoea, infanticide, abortion and the kidnapping of women were very clear by 1830—there were almost no Aboriginal children. The first band Robinson met in 1830 comprised 20 adults, 2 adolescents and only 4 children. By comparison, at the time of contact there would have been as many children as adults in a normal band. Only about 30 children were among the 200 Aborigines Robinson took to Wybalenna. By 1835 there were 56 men, 50 women and only 14 children, for there were very few births and most babies died in infancy. Of the 9 women at Oyster Cove in 1869, only 2 had ever given birth and all babies had died. Truganini, Dray and Pagerly had all been 'afflicted with a loathsome disorder which they had contracted during their cohabitation with the whalers at Adventure Bay'.[106]

Venereal disease sterilised and chest complaints—influenza, pneumonia and tuberculosis—killed. In 1829, nine of the southwest tribe died from respiratory disease, which also accounted for most of the 132 deaths during Wybalenna's sixteen-year existence. There were flu epidemics in 1837, 1839 and 1847. Sadly, Robinson's last 'gift' to the settlement was lethal Spanish influenza which he contracted in Melbourne in January 1839 and from which eight Aborigines at Wybalenna died. Flu is an airborne virus; once inhaled, it easily leads to pneumonia, the major cause of influenza deaths.[107]

Aboriginal mortality on Flinders Island was comparable to that during the first fifteen years at many mainland missions, such as Poonindie, South Australia, and Fraser Island, Queensland. Virulent new germs, the change to a largely Western diet, a sedentary life and wearing clothes without adopting Western hygiene proved fatal. The *coup de grâce* was delivered by alcohol, which became a major problem once survivors moved to Oyster Cove. Until the 1820s, alcohol was scarce in Tasmania and the first inebriated Aborigine was not seen till 1823. Some Aboriginal women living with sealers became alcoholics, but hunters who plundered stock-keepers' huts took the food but left the rum. Paradoxically, Central Tasmania was the one part of Australia with a ready source of alcohol—the sap of *Eucalyptus gunnii* or 'cider gum'. If fermented, this sweet, honey-like liquid is mildly intoxicating. Robinson saw Aborigines tapping the trees to make the sap run, sucking it up through reeds.[108]

» The question of treaties

No treaties were ever made between any government and Aboriginal Australians, but their feasibility is still under discussion. Governor Arthur, remorseful about Aboriginal dispossession, wrote: 'On the first occupation of Tasmania, it was a great oversight that a treaty was not . . . made with the natives and such compensation given to the chiefs as they would have deemed a fair equivalent for what they

« GRAVE-ROBBING »

Unfortunately, the fascination of early scientists with Tasmanian origins led to the shameful mutilation of the corpse of William Lanney—the last 'full-blood' Tasmanian man, who died of cholera in Hobart on 3 March 1869, aged 35. Born in 1834, he was the youngest of the Lanney brothers, survived Wybalenna, was repatriated to Oyster Cove and went to sea as a whaler in 1851. As soon as he died, Lanney's white friends persuaded the governor to save his remains from scientists' clutches. His corpse was placed in the hospital morgue under guard, but that evening Doctor Crowther, a member of the Royal College of Surgeons, tricked the guard, unlocked the morgue and removed Lanney's head. Chief hospital surgeon, Dr George Stokell, a leading member of the Royal Society of Tasmania, discovered the theft and cut off the hands and feet. Rumours spread and mourners at the funeral demanded the coffin be opened. Cries of horror greeted the sight of Lanney's mutilated body but nothing could be done. The coffin was sealed, covered with a Union Jack, some flowers and a possum skin, and escorted to the cemetery by a large crowd of Lanney's shipmates and other friends.

Incredibly, more was to follow. In the dead of night, Stokell and other Royal Society members crept to the grave, dug up the body, removed it to the morgue, mutilated it yet further and then reburied it in a different cemetery. Crowther was also bent on grave-robbing but found an empty coffin. Furious, he went to the morgue and broke down the door with an axe to find only a few particles of flesh. There was an outcry from the press and a public inquiry was held. Crowther lost his post but Stokell was supported by the governor and got away with his crime. He even flaunted a tobacco pouch made of Lanney's skin. The hands and feet were later found in the Royal Society's premises but Lanney's head was never located.

Truganini was terrified that she, too, would be 'cut up', but when she died in 1876, she was buried secretly by the government at midnight, only to suffer a different fate. Two years later her grave was dug up and her body acquired by the Royal Society Museum in Hobart, where it was displayed from 1904 to 1947. In 1974 the Tasmanian Aboriginal community successfully applied for the return of her remains. In spite of massive public support, the Tasmanian Museum trustees were reluctant to part with the body, and it took special legislation in 1975 to obtain it. The remains were then kept in Reserve Bank vaults until cremation on 30 April 1976 and the ashes scattered on D'Entrecasteaux Channel the following day. Truganini was finally at rest, a century after her death. More recently, Michael Mansell of the Tasmanian Aboriginal Centre has succeeded in repatriating Crowther's collection of Aboriginal remains from Britain.[a]

» *Truganini wearing a kangaroo-skin cloak. Truganini, or Trugernanner, was born in 1812, the daughter of Mangerner, the chief of the Bruny Island tribe. Her people suffered at the hands of sealers, whalers and timber-getters; her mother was stabbed by sealers, her sister was abducted to Bass Strait and there accidentally shot, her uncle was killed and her fiancé drowned while trying to save her from abduction by timber-getters. Truganini was known for her petite beauty, vivacity, intelligence and coquettishness. She had five husbands but no children, for she probably acquired gonorrhoea while frequenting Adventure Bay whaling station. From 1829 to 1834 she assisted Robinson. In 1835 she went to Flinders Island and later Oyster Cove. She died in Hobart on 8 May 1876. Another full-descent Tasmanian Aboriginal woman, Suke, survived on Kangaroo Island till 1888, but Truganini became known as 'the last Tasmanian', a title strongly rejected by today's Tasmanian Aborigines.*

»   «

surrendered.'[109] Similarly, the Executive Council wondered in 1831 whether, as in the United States, 'some treaty could not be made with these people, by which their chiefs should engage for the tribes not to pass certain lines of demarcation . . . and . . . allow a European agent to reside with or accompany each tribe'. The difficulty was to persuade each side to adhere to a treaty, for Arthur feared there was little likelihood of Aborigines or European 'riff-raff' abiding by the rules.[110]

Would treaties have worked? Realistically, no. First, Aborigines would not give up territory to newcomers. The concept of selling land was totally alien. Second, communication problems made real understanding impossible. Third, Aboriginal society did not include the idea of a chief representing one or more bands; instead decisions were reached through consensus. Thus a separate treaty would have been needed with each of Tasmania's bands. Finally, Aborigines would not have welcomed a white agent living among them.

» Batman's treaty

Were fair, meaningful treaties possible anywhere in Australia? The only treaty ever negotiated was in Victoria in 1835 by settler John Batman, possibly influenced by growing British humanitarian concern reflected in the abolition of slavery in 1833. Batman had a mixed record on race relations—he offered his services to Arthur as a conciliator, but earlier participated in bounty-hunting parties of settlers and police. In 1830 Batman used his 'tame' Sydney blacks to track Aborigines to their camp, where they fired at sleeping figures and captured two men, a woman and a child, but shot the men when their wounds held up the party's progress. In 1835 Batman sailed to the mainland to obtain land, and tried to legitimise his land acquisition by a private treaty.

Batman negotiated his 'treaty' in just one day.[111] On 6 June he set out 'to find the natives'. After walking 13 km (8 miles), Batman wrote, 'we fell in with . . . a family: one chief, his wife and three children'. After giving them presents, they were escorted a further 13 km to some huts, where they met 'eight men all armed with spears' and then the families. 'In all, the tribe consists of forty-five men, women and children . . . Each of the principal chiefs has two wives and several children.' By calling every adult man a 'chief', Batman identified eight 'chiefs' in this one band. Usually there was just one informal leader in each band. The two Sydney Aborigines negotiated and Batman tells how, 'After a full explanation of what my object was, I purchased two large tracts of land from them—about 600 000 acres [nearly 250 000 ha] . . . and delivered over to them blankets, knives, looking glasses, tomahawks, beads, scissors, flour etc. etc., as payment for the land; and also agreed to give them a tribute or rent yearly. The parchment the eight chiefs signed this afternoon . . . giving me full possession of the tracts of land.' The next day Batman handed over the remaining tribute, marks were made on a tree by a Sydney Aborigine and a 'principal chief', Batman was given two possum-skin 'cloaks or royal mantles' and departed.

The deeds granted land to Batman and his heirs 'for ever' to 'occupy and possess' and 'place thereon sheep and cattle'. There was no word about Aboriginal access or hunting rights. What did this Aboriginal clan think the treaty meant? Perhaps that Batman was initiating the 'tanderrum' ritual, in which temporary access to land was granted after a ritual exchange of gifts.[112]

Batman paid his tribute on the first anniversary, but Governor Bourke declared the treaty illegal. Constitutional lawyers in London agreed with its rejection because Australia belonged to Britain as vacant Crown land. Aborigines had a 'right of occupancy' but could not grant land to others. Nor did the government recognise 'in them any right to alienate to private adventurers the Land of the Colony'.

Effects of Batman's treaty

What Batman's treaty did achieve was relatively peaceful settlement in central Victoria. Gift exchange was continued through the governor and then by Aboriginal Protectors. Good relations were also aided by escaped convict William Buckley, who acted as interpreter. Buckley was a soldier transported to Port Phillip Bay in 1803 for receiving a roll of stolen cloth. He escaped and was starving when adopted by Wathaurong people, who regarded him as a reincarnated leader. In his reminiscences, Buckley recorded:

> They have a belief, that when they die, they go to some place or other, and are there made white men, and that they then return to this world again for another existence . . . In cases where they have killed white men, it has generally been because they imagined them to have been originally enemies, or belonging to tribes with whom they were hostile.[113]

These beliefs help to explain unpredictable Aboriginal reactions to white strangers; some shipwrecked sailors received great kindness, others were killed on sight. Buckley totally assimilated and lived as a hunter-gatherer for over 30 years before hearing of a ship's arrival and surrendering to a surveyor. He proved his identity from initials tattooed on his arm and his unusual height (193 cm or 6 ft 4 inches), was pardoned and had to relearn English. Significantly, Buckley said Batman's treaty 'could not have been, because . . . they have no chiefs claiming or possessing any superior right over the soil; theirs only being as the heads of families'.

At the founding of Melbourne in 1835, Buckley told 200 assembled Aborigines in their own language that the government would 'feed and clothe and care for them' as long as they stayed 'peaceable and well-behaved'. Unfortunately 1836 witnessed an influx of new settlers and foreign germs. The killers were a major flu epidemic, typhus and syphilis, which Buckley described as 'new to the natives', for previously 'they had no such disorder'. By 1840 the Medical Officer reported 'great Aboriginal mortality'.

《　》

Tragically, Victorians—like Tasmanians—had become victims of global colonisation. Even had effective treaties been negotiated, nothing could have saved the First Australians from the microbes European explorers, sealers and settlers inadvertently carried with them. Most deaths came not from guns but the new germs brought by the newcomers. Robinson's Friendly Mission, despite its benevolent intentions, spelt disaster for most of those he contacted. Aborigines with no prior immunity often succumbed to 'pulmonary disease' simply by standing downwind of a European. Tasmania's small population had withstood the rigours of the ice age and 14 000 years of total isolation from the outside world only to be struck down by invisible invaders.

The islanders with their spears and bush skills proved a good match for foreign soldiers but they had no defence against the new germs. Only gradually did the survivors build up some immunity and Tasmanians were only saved by a dozen or so mixed-race survivors primarily living on the Bass Strait islands. Mainlanders had more room to move to avoid contact with the strange newcomers, but, as in Tasmania, the lure of the new often proved an irresistible, but fatal, attraction.

DEPOPULATION

A century of struggle (1820s–1920s)

In Sydney in 1812, colonists were suffering the extremes of Australia's climate. Three 15 metre (50 ft) Hawkesbury River floods had swept away their crops, followed by severe drought. It was time to break out from the Sydney basin. The Blue Mountains dominated the western skyline, 65 km (40 miles) inland. Named for the blue haze of oil droplets from Eucalyptus trees, the sandstone range rises to 1360 m (4462 ft). The only options were to cross the mountain barrier or abandon the colony, but the latter was never seriously considered, even by later humanitarians deploring colonisation's dire effects on Aborigines. Had the British withdrawn, other colonists, such as the French, would have stepped into the vacuum straightaway.

The British still didn't know if the inland was inhabited. Was smoke on the ranges from Aboriginal burning or natural bushfires? Various exploratory expeditions followed streams up long mountain valleys but ended below waterfalls boxed in by high cliffs. Some escaping convicts optimistically believed China lay beyond the mountains but starved to death in a labyrinth of box canyons and dense scrub, unable to reach their goal.[1]

The mountain barrier was not finally breached until 1813, when explorers Blaxland, Lawson and Wentworth followed the ridges rather than the thickly wooded valleys and used packhorses to venture further than previous parties on foot. They did not take Aboriginal guides as Blaxland found 'very little information can be obtained from any tribe out of their own district'. After three weeks they reached the top and gazed over boundless, rolling grasslands. A road was built by the end of 1814, which the modern highway and railway still follow. Soon Aboriginal war parties were also using it for lightning raids on other tribes or government ration-depots.[2]

» Wiradjuri country

The move westwards began peacefully. In 1815 Governor Macquarie visited the new settlement of Bathurst on Macquarie River 150 km (93 miles) west of Sydney. Several local Aborigines visited his camp, 'very handsome, good looking young men

... clothed with mantles made of the skin of possums which were very neatly sewn together and the outside of the skins were carved in a remarkably neat manner'. Macquarie exchanged clothes, metal axes and 'yellow cloth' for a skin cloak. Those he met were Wiradjuri people. This large tribe numbered perhaps 3000 people, thinly spread over 97 000 km² (37 000 sq. miles) of central New South Wales. In the

» *Nahraminyeri, a Ngarrindjeri woman from Point Macleay, South Australia, photographed in c. 1880, is wearing a full-length possum-skin cloak with a pouch for her child and is carrying a digging stick. Cloaks made from as many as 80 possum skins were worn by Aborigines in the colder parts of mainland Australia.*

1820s, 500–600 Aborigines inhabited the Bathurst region—a density of one person to 35–41 km^2 (13–16 sq. miles), a similar population to that of other New South Wales tablelands.[3]

Unfortunately, settlement around Bathurst displaced a Wiradjuri group that adjacent groups were unable or unwilling to absorb. As other Aborigines explained: 'It was their country, and the water belonged to them, and if it was taken away they could not go to another country, for they would be killed.'[4]

Fear and amazement marked Aborigines' first encounters with horsemen, for no one had ridden an animal in Australia before colonisation. A horse with its huge teeth, feathery tail and shining feet striking sparks from the ground was bad enough, but when the rider dismounted and the creature seemed to split in half, they were terrified.[5]

Macquarie avoided too-rapid expansion. By 1820, he had let only 114 whites move west and neither side felt threatened. Harmony prevailed until his governorship ended, the British Colonial Office began encouraging emigration and settlers flooded inland. The number of whites grew tenfold and farmers spread across 20 000 km^2 (7700 sq. miles) of Wiradjuri country.

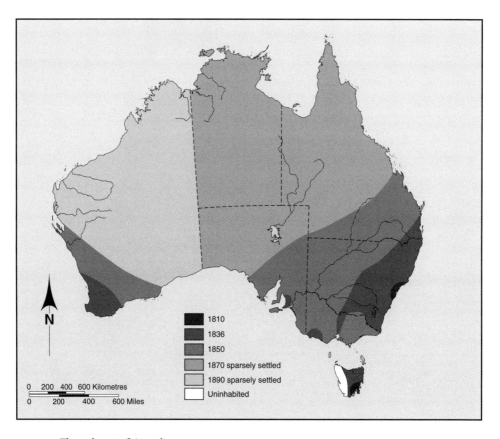

■	1810
■	1836
■	1850
▨	1870 sparsely settled
▨	1890 sparsely settled
□	Uninhabited

0 200 400 600 Kilometres
0   200   400   600 Miles

» *The settlement of Australia.*

The impact was serious. Native seed-bearing grasses were trampled by cloven hooves. Kangaroos and possums were shot for settlers' cooking pots. Prime river-bank locations were taken over and huts and stockyards built on flat, treeless areas, including sacred initiation grounds invisible to white eyes. Tension built during the drought of 1822–24. In 1822, Aborigines attacked a farm and later fatally speared a shepherd. Raids on flocks and homesteads increased and by 1824 some farms had been abandoned.[6]

A young, muscular Wiradjuri warrior, Windradyne or 'Saturday', 182 cm (6 ft) tall and 'of noble appearance and piercing eye', led a hundred fighters in raids to kill or disperse sheep and cattle, spear any shepherds that resisted, and rob the huts. Settlers responded by calling for military protection and arming their shepherds. On 8 January 1824 the *Sydney Gazette* reported Windradyne's capture, which involved six white men

» *This lithograph entitled 'A Native Chief of Bathurst' is thought to be of the Wiradjuri leader Windradyne.*

who 'had actually to break a musket over his body before he yielded, which he did at length with broken ribs'. The commandant of Bathurst military camp displayed Windradyne in chains to try to 'teach the natives a lesson', but, when released a month later, Windradyne moved freely around town. Ironically, a white man's gift to Windradyne precipitated open warfare. Settlers had established riverbank market gardens to grow vegetables for sale. When a gardener dug up some potatoes and showed Windradyne and his family how to cook them, they liked them so much that next day a large armed group returned for more. The gardener called for help, spears were thrown, shots were fired and several Aborigines were killed or wounded.

Revenge attacks followed. On 24 May, three shepherds were killed and the first hut was burnt—Millah-Murrah, inadvertently built on a ceremonial ground. Then four more shepherds were speared or incinerated in their huts. Seven deaths within three days were too much for the white community—they called for military help. Fear ruled the countryside and no one, black or white, was prepared to go out alone.

Windradyne and his 50 men continued their raids. Then, on 31 May, a stockman was speared through the arm but escaped to a neighbouring property, where the overseer formed a posse of six mounted stockmen. Frustrated by failure to find the perpetrators, when they came across an Aboriginal family group, they opened fire, killing three women.[7]

Reaction in Sydney, which regarded itself as a law-abiding, humane, Christian society, was outrage, the *Sydney Gazette*'s editor deploring the murder of 'poor inoffending creatures'. Eventually, five of the six murderers were charged with manslaughter and were sent to Sydney for trial but acquitted. Some of the issues were that contemporary British law did not admit evidence from non-Christians and required the names of the victims. Even if Aboriginal witnesses were available, there were strong taboos on naming the recently dead. The law was later changed to try to overcome these problems.

» Martial law

By August 1824, 15–20 stockmen had been killed and continuing violence led Governor Brisbane to declare martial law in the Bathurst region.[8] The garrison was increased to 75 foot-soldiers, but no mounted troops, as had been requested. Brisbane pointed out that 'infantry have no chance of success' against the Wiradjuri, but cavalry arrived only in mid-1825.[9] Brisbane declared his intention to protect innocent Aborigines, especially women and children, and wisely ensured that magistrates accompanied each military expedition. In early September 1824, four parties of foot-soldiers, each led by a magistrate, set out to try to arrest assailants of three stockmen. According to magistrate George Ranken's report, 'none of us succeeded in seeing the enemy'. They did succeed in keeping Aborigines 'in a constant state of alarm', and soon leaders came into Bathurst asking for peace. In December, martial law was repealed, and Brisbane reported 'during the four months that martial law prevailed, not one outrage was committed under it, neither was a life sacrificed or even blood spilt'.[10] However, in September sixteen men of a distant Mudgee clan were killed by stockmen in skirmishes following a Wiradjuri attack that killed two of their number.[11]

Three vague stories of 'massacres' surfaced many years later.[12] Reverend Threlkeld of Lake Macquarie Mission claimed in the 1850s that he was told by a visiting Bathurst magistrate that in 1824 'a large number' of Aborigines had been 'driven into a swamp . . . and mounted police rode round and round and shot them off indiscriminately until they were all destroyed'. This story is almost certainly untrue—there were no mounted police in Bathurst until 1825, when hostilities were long over. Threlkeld may have fabricated massacre stories to support his dire need of funds for his mission.[13]

In 1887, William Suttor, grandson of humanitarian settler, George Suttor, retold family stories, including one of a massacre when soldiers placed food 'within musket range' of an Aboriginal camp. 'Unsuspectingly they did come, principally women and children. As they gathered up the white man's presents they were shot down by a brutal volley.'[14] This also seems unlikely, since on their abortive 1824 expeditions soldiers found no Aboriginal camps. Both stories may have been white inventions to save face for the soldiers' failure even to see any Aborigines, who had plenty of rugged forest ranges in which to hide from the redcoats.

NATIVES ATTACKING SHEPHERDS' HUT.

» *Frontier violence: attack on a shepherds' hut, Port Lincoln, South Australia, 1864.*

Finally, in 1962, amateur historian Percy Gresser wrote in the *Bathurst Times* of a massacre at Bells Falls Gorge, a spectacular local landmark. Historian David Roberts decided to write his postgraduate thesis on this massacre, only to find no evidence it had ever happened. Roberts also discovered that Gresser had subsequently decided that *all* Aborigines escaped the soldiers in 1824.[15]

Nevertheless, Wiradjuri Mary Coe's book about these events is now used as a school textbook. Journalist Bruce Elder's account in his influential book *Blood on the Wattle* has been taken at face value by many Wiradjuri people, such as tennis champion Evonne Goolagong-Cawley, who recounts (in the second edition) her shock when she learnt for the first time of this massacre of her people. Similarly, a large display in the National Museum of Australia features it as a massacre site, quoting the words of a modern Wiradjuri elder: 'this is a place of great sadness. Our people still hear the echoes of the women and children who died here'.[16] Such myths hinder rather than help the cause of reconciliation, because they unnecessarily increase black anger about white brutality.

» Accommodation with settlers

Windradyne jauntily turned up at the governor's feast in Parramatta in December 1824 leading 260 Wiradjuri men, women and children. Martial law was lifted and Windradyne was presented with an olive branch and a straw hat labelled 'peace'. Unfortunately, in 1830 the Wiradjuri were hit by Australia's second smallpox epidemic. Mortality was terrible and one in three died, but some accepted the offer of vaccination and were saved.

Later Windradyne was wounded in the knee in an intertribal battle and taken to Bathurst hospital, only to cast off his bandages and return to his friend George Suttor's property Brucedale, where he succumbed to gangrene. In the 1950s a plaque to his memory was erected, describing him as 'first a terror but later a friend to the settlers'.[17]

The tragedy is that history would have been very different, had all settlers been as enlightened as 18-year-old Suttor, who established good relations with local tribesmen and learnt their language. (A major problem was that both sides found the other's language so difficult that it was extremely hard to learn unless you were a child or a gifted linguist.) The story is told that:

> In 1824 Suttor invited a Wiradjuri man named Penneegrah to help him find his way around the rough country between Bathurst and Mudgee. Suttor and Penneegrah were visiting an outlying hut when they encountered a war party led by Windradyne. Recognising him, Suttor addressed him as one leader to another. They spoke together in friendship and, despite his burning anger, Windradyne took a polite farewell and left them in peace. Although the war was pursued with a vengeance, Brucedale was spared.[18]

Suttor and other humanitarian settlers shared the land with the Aborigines. It was accommodation rather than confrontation. Aboriginal people in the settled regions were still effectively dispossessed of their land but in return for their labour were given medical help, food, shelter and security. Many settlers managed to build good relations with Aborigines, outstanding examples being the Wills family in Victoria, the Murrays of Yarralumla in the Canberra region, the Duracks in the Kimberley and the Gunns in the Northern Territory.[19]

» The rolling frontier

The frontier moved inexorably westwards. In almost every year of the 1830s an area the size of Ireland was taken over by pastoralists. By 1840, an arc of unfenced sheep-runs spread across a huge area of grasslands on the far side of the mountains. These stages of contact were reproduced all over the continent. At first there was Aboriginal 'shock of the new', curiosity, and a developing eagerness to taste new foods and possess new tools, then the inevitable misunderstandings. Aborigines regarded all native creatures as their property and thought the settlers' new animals were theirs to hunt.

Hostility grew as they realised the newcomers were there to stay; then came a few years of resistance and sporadic violence, the ravages of savage reprisals and introduced diseases and the final crumbling of traditional Aboriginal ways of life. Tribes were unable to retreat because of hostile neighbouring groups or to survive on the shrunken remains of their hunting grounds, and the only option was to 'come in' to new settlements. The best they could hope for was to live in their own tribal territory in a camp attached to the station of a friendly pastoralist who fed the whole group in return for labour; the worst was death or degradation in a camp on town fringes, exposed to alcohol, prostitution and disease.

The two societies were so different that clashes were almost inevitable, even when there was initial goodwill on both sides. Because of the Aboriginal system of delayed retribution for perceived wrongs, they acquired a reputation for 'treachery'. One incident in 1805 on a new farm on the Hawkesbury River illustrates the problem: 'A native, while in the act of eating with one of the settlers and his labouring man, had scarce ended his meal before he took an opportunity of seizing the settler's musket and powder, and by a yell summoning his companions, who instantly put the unfortunate settler to death.'[20]

A typical chain of events leading to frontier violence was:

A stockholder . . . erects his hut and stockyard. A day or two after his first arrival one or two blacks drop in, they are well received and entertained, get some meat and damper fare offered . . . in a week or so the whole tribe is domesticated with the squatter . . . Soon however they see an ox killed, cut up and prepared for eating and they eat part of him themselves. That evening out of curiosity they kill one for themselves . . . The blacks are remonstrated with, they then proceed to spear some every day. The squatter at length takes up arms, the blacks spear him or any of his stockmen when they find them with their backs turned and war commences and often continues for months and years.[21]

A succession of governors found it impossible to control the exodus of new settlers from Sydney and in 1840 Governor Gipps granted temporary leases to 'squatters', people who took sheep or cattle beyond the limits of land ownership and claimed a run on Crown land by dint of possession. It was likewise impossible to maintain the rule of law and curb squatters' excesses. The settlers encountered armed Aboriginal resistance of varying intensity and duration.

» Casualty rates

'It is now a popular (but not universal) conception that Australian frontiers were violent places where whites slaughtered Aborigines indiscriminately,' wrote respected historian Richard Broome in 1994. He was commenting on the 1990s Koorie Heritage Trust's exhibition in Melbourne. (Koorie or Koori is a name widely adopted by southeastern Aborigines, meaning 'people' in Eora.) I, too, saw this exhibition and was surprised to learn 'several thousand' Aborigines died in massacres in Victoria and 'many thousands more died beyond prying eyes'. This is patently untrue. Even figures on the exhibition's massacre map contradicted these extravagant claims, and the actions of missionaries, protectors and humanitarian settlers meant that unreported killings were few. [22]

In Broome's latest estimate, about 1000 blacks and 80 whites died in frontier conflict in Victoria between 1835 and 1850. This gives a ratio of twelve black to every one white death. It is a soundly based estimate, based on much detailed research by himself and others.[23] Historian Ian Clark counted 430 black casualties in the Western District, and in eastern Victoria there were only a few European but 450 or more Aboriginal casualties, many resulting from raids by Kulin troopers on their traditional enemies, the Kurnai of Gippsland. Add an unknown number of 'war dead' from the Murray Valley and the northeast, plus deaths of wounded Aborigines, and the figure of 1000 is realistic. The figure of 450 deaths in Gippsland comes from a private letter written in 1846 by young squatter Henry Meyrick home to his relatives in England:

> The blacks are very quiet here now, poor wretches. No wild beast of the forest was ever hunted down with such unsparing perseverance as they are. Men, women and children are shot whenever they can be met with . . . I have protested against it at every station I have been in Gippsland . . . but these things are kept very secret as the penalty would certainly be hanging . . . For myself, if I caught a black actually killing my sheep, I would shoot him with as little remorse as I would a wild dog, but no consideration on earth

would induce me to ride into a camp and fire on them indiscriminately, as is the custom whenever the smoke is seen. They [the Aborigines] will very shortly be extinct. It is impossible to say how many have been shot, but I am convinced that no less than 450 have been murdered altogether.[24]

Meyrick's estimate has great weight, as he admitted to the same base attitudes in himself and was privy to the secrets of other squatters.

Other southeastern regions were far more peaceful. Settler Edward Curr, a reliable observer and author of a major study on Aborigines, thought only 2 of 120 Bangerang deaths in a decade in the Murray River valley were due to white violence and none to alcohol. Yet Bangerang numbers dropped from 200 to 80 in that time due to new diseases.[25]

In the tablelands and highlands of the southeast, the subject of my doctorate, my thorough search of historical records revealed no loss of Aboriginal life from guns, but over 90 per cent mortality through new diseases, even excluding smallpox, which never penetrated the Canberra or Cooma regions.[26]

Reynolds estimates that continent-wide between 1788 and 1928 (the date of the last known massacre—Coniston, Northern Territory) a total of 2000–2500 non-indigenous people (Europeans, Chinese and Pacific Islanders) were killed in frontier conflict and 20 000 Aborigines. Precise numbers will never be known, because records are fragmentary and some deaths went unreported. The figure of 20 000 (averaging almost 150 Aboriginal casualties per year) is based on an estimated average ratio of black to white deaths of 10:1.[27]

Detailed regional studies in progress should clarify Reynolds' 'guesstimate'. The struggle was most intense in northern New South Wales in the 1840s and Queensland in the 1860s–1870s. Self-governing colonies came into being one-by-one—South Australia and Western Australia in 1836, Victoria in 1851, Tasmania and Queensland in 1859. Each colony had its own parliament, able to legislate concerning its indigenous people. As the parliaments of frontier colonies such as Queensland were settler-dominated, it was sometimes convenient to turn a blind eye towards violence against Aborigines. Historian Neville Green enumerated the deaths of 30 settlers and 121 Aborigines in Western Australia in violent encounters between 1826 and 1852, a rate of 4:1 black deaths.[28] Victoria's rate of 12:1 Aboriginal casualties may be due to intense competition for the rich lands in the west and the unbridled operations of its native police in the east. Ironically the colony with the lowest black death rate (3:2) is Tasmania, notorious for its supposed genocide.

After 1850, Aboriginal casualties increased when colonists acquired two efficient new weapons—breech-loading, multi-shot rifles and six-shot revolvers. The new guns were much faster firing and more accurate than their predecessors. This greater fire-power explains the much higher Aboriginal casualties in Queensland than elsewhere.

Young onto the land.

» *This picture shows two settlers who have built a small hut in the Clarence River region close to the Queensland border. The settlers are accompanied by an Aboriginal group and one has his arm possessively round the shoulders of a young woman.*

Most of Queensland was settled after the introduction of the new weapons and Queensland accounts for half of Reynolds' estimated Aboriginal 'war dead'. About a third of all Aborigines lived in Queensland, which covers almost a quarter of the continent. They lived mainly on the coastal fringes, and put up particularly strong resistance to white encroachment, perhaps because they were used to repelling foreign intruders from their shores. Until detailed research is done, the ratio of indigenous to non-indigenous deaths on the Queensland frontier will be unknown, but a tally of 5:1 is attested to by squatter G.S. Lang, who wrote in 1865:

> The blacks . . . driven to sheer desperation . . . kill far more white men than is generally imagined. I have known 32 killed, in one small district, in about two years . . . The blacks are mercilessly shot down in turn . . . 156 blacks having been killed in the same district in the same time; and the blacks take revenge upon all, murdering even those who are kindest to them, until the cruelties practised on both sides are so atrocious as to be almost incredible.[29]

» NATIVE POLICE «

Many Aboriginal deaths in Queensland were actually at black rather than white hands, because of the operation for 40 years of native mounted police, who took few, if any, prisoners. Conflict in Australia was always small-scale. There were no citizens' militias and colonists only prevailed when supported by 'native police'—armed and mounted Aboriginal trackers. It was a leading humanitarian, Alexander Maconochie, who in the 1830s suggested a native police force and recommended that Aborigines be recruited as constables, on the precedent of successful native Sepoy troops in India. The aims were to uphold law and order on the frontier and promote employment and discipline for Aboriginal troopers, whose families were to be established in villages and educated to become settled farmers. Native police came into being in Melbourne in 1842.[a]

The aim was for Aboriginal troopers to operate in districts far away from their own country, so that they had no kinship links with frontier tribes. The force was intended to combine skills of black and white and be impartial, treating Aborigines as British subjects who, like armed bushrangers, were defying the law. The original intake of 22 Aboriginal volunteers was made up of heads or sons of heads of clans around Melbourne. They joined to extend their black power by tapping into white power. Joining gave them access to rations, a uniform, a gun and a horse, and there was nothing Aboriginal men took to more enthusiastically than riding.

The Victorian force operated only from 1842 to 1853. In northern New South Wales a native police force was set up in 1848, with just fourteen Aboriginal men from the west of the colony. When Queensland became a separate colony in 1859, the force was transferred to the new colony's control and renamed the Native Mounted Police or, more familiarly, Black Police. Initially it had 22 white officers and sergeants and 120 Aboriginal troopers (200 by the 1870s). Until disbanded in 1900, this 'foreign legion' of armed and mounted native mercenaries terrorised their Aboriginal fellows in Queensland.

In Queensland, punishment expeditions were often carried out by unaccompanied armed black troopers who tracked a group into the bush, discarded their uniforms but not their rifles, crept up, surrounded the camp and 'dispersed' men, women and children in wholesale massacre. Killing Aboriginal women and children was justified, said a black policeman in 1857, because, 'Suppose you don't kill piccaninnies [children], in time they become warriors and kill you. If you kill the women no more piccaninnies are born.'[b]

A native police force was also formed in 1884 at Alice Springs in what later became the Northern Territory, but after several atrocities under its notorious commander William Willshire, who was tried for murder in 1891 but acquitted, the force was disarmed and used only for tracking. South Australia, Queensland (after 1900) and Western Australia used armed black trackers on occasion, particularly to help find and kill Aboriginal outlaws.

» *Aboriginal tracker of the Northern Territory police in the 1950s.*

» 《

» Massacres

From the early 1970s, most historians have portrayed Aborigines as victims of frontier conflict, while largely ignoring the impact of new diseases.[30] Passionate advocacy of the Aboriginal cause by Bill Stanner, Charles Rowley and Henry Reynolds deserves much credit for a marked increase in public sympathy towards Aborigines, but has led to overemphasis on violence in Australia's past. In the lead-up to the 1988 bicentenary,

several popular accounts of massacres appeared, full of lurid, invented details. An
even more sensational account was published in 2000 by expatriate journalist Philip
Knightley, who wrote: 'It remains one of the mysteries of history that Australia was
able to get away with a racist policy that included segregation and dispossession and
bordered on slavery and genocide.'[31]

Knightley's mystery is easily solved; Australia was able to get away with a policy
that 'bordered on slavery and genocide' because there was no such policy. This is not
to deny the terrible bloodshed on the frontier and the suffering and dispossession of
Australia's Aboriginal people. It is a tragic story that needs no exaggeration, as a recent
meticulously researched book about the Gulf country of northern Australia vividly
brings home. In this remote region the infamous coast track linking Queensland to
the Darwin region and Kimberley goldfields saw a devastating collision between
Aborigines and pastoralists, drovers and prospectors. In the first decade of contact this
lawless frontier was a perpetual hell, lacking police, missionaries or any effective protectors of Aborigines. Coupled with this lack of restraint, the Gulf region attracted
some of the dregs of colonial society, spelling disaster for many Aboriginal groups.
Until a police station was opened at Booroloola in 1886, on the coast track five
Europeans were killed by Aboriginal spears but the Aboriginal death toll was over 300.
This gives a ratio of 60:1 Aboriginal deaths. Many of those who were not gunned
down fell victim to starvation or kidnapping: 'Aboriginal people had to contend not
only with the abuse of their women, dispossession, and the prospect of being shot on
sight, but also with the kidnapping of young girls and boys.'[32]

Seven of Australia's most notorious and well-researched massacres are sum-
marised below, including the four Knightley described (Pinjarra, Waterloo Creek,
Forrest River and Coniston), to illustrate the range and character of such 'collisions'.
One is found to have been a myth, another to have been a battle rather than a massacre, but the rest are shameful events, where whites massacred defenceless
Aborigines or engaged in massive reprisals for the murder of whites. In only one case
were the murderers brought to justice.

Battle of Pinjarra, Western Australia (1834)

In Western Australia there was a tragic battle at Pinjarra in 1834, in which 15–35
Pinjarup were killed by an expedition of mounted police led by Governor Stirling,
whose aim was to arrest some Aborigines who had murdered a soldier. Military
historian John Connor sees Pinjarra as a battle rather than a massacre, since the
Pinjarup were armed and opened hostilities. The Aborigines got the better of the
initial encounter, for when five mounted police rode into their camp, three were
unhorsed and one later died of a spear wound to his head. The Pinjarup could then
have easily escaped, but chose to stay and fight, taking heavy casualties until Stirling
ordered a ceasefire.[33]

Waterloo Creek, New South Wales (1838)

By the late 1830s, young settlers had taken up all prime grazing land northwest of Sydney. Kamilaroi people retaliated by spearing five stockmen and stampeding cattle. Settlers appealed for protection and a mounted police force of five officers and twenty men was dispatched to the Gwydir region under the infamous Major Nunn, who had been instructed to 'use [his] utmost exertion to suppress these outrages'. This he did during a 53-day campaign in early 1838. Fifteen Aborigines were arrested but all were released, except one who was shot when escaping and one who was retained as a guide.

For the next three weeks, Nunn's party sighted no Aborigines, until they were suddenly attacked. A corporal was wounded and four or five fleeing Kamilaroi were shot dead in retaliation. The mounted police set off down the valley in pursuit, each armed with musket, sword and pistols. Two hours later they found their quarry at Waterloo Creek and massacred them. As the secretary of state for the colonies later wrote to Governor Gipps: 'The worst feature of the case was . . . the renewal of the pursuit of the Blacks . . . the object of capturing offenders was entirely lost sight of, and shots were fired at men, who were apparently only guilty of jumping into the water to escape an armed pursuit.'[34] Lyndall Ryan has recently re-examined the evidence and considers eyewitness Sergeant Lee's estimate of 40–50 killed in this massacre the most reliable.

Myall Creek, New South Wales (1838)

After Major Nunn left the Gwydir region in 1838, the Gwydir settlers felt unprotected from Aboriginal raids. A posse of nine ex-convict stockmen and one native-born station manager rode out to finish Nunn's reprisals by 'hunting some blacks'. On 9 June 1838, the vigilantes rode into Myall Creek station and forcibly removed the resident group of Kwaimbal Aborigines to a nearby stockyard, where they shot and hacked to death 28 people. Their victims were mainly women and children, as most of the men were away for the day cutting bark for a neighbouring property. The murderers tried to burn the bodies, but there was a white witness and when the station overseer returned, he was so sickened by the carnage that he wrote to the local magistrate. Governor Gipps ordered a full investigation, which resulted in eleven men being tried. Gipps saw himself as a bastion of British law in a regrettably lawless colonial society. Determined that justice should be done, when the jury took just fifteen minutes to acquit all eleven, he managed to get a second trial of seven of the men, who were finally found guilty and, in spite of many public protests, they were hanged on 18 December 1838. The men's defence was that they did not know it was illegal to kill Aborigines, as it was so common on the frontier. Prior to this, few settlers had been tried for killing Aborigines and only one had been hanged for the crime (John Kirkby at Newcastle in 1820).[35]

Hornet Bank, Queensland (1857)

Queensland black police under their young white officers carried out massive reprisal raids each time whites were killed. A notorious Aboriginal massacre of settlers took place at Hornet Bank Station, northwest of Brisbane, where eleven people were butchered—Mrs Fraser, seven of her nine children, the tutor and two shepherds. Mrs Fraser and her two eldest daughters were raped before being killed. Motives for the attack were revenge for the rape of Aboriginal women by the Fraser boys; Mrs Fraser had repeatedly asked the officer of the native police to reprove her sons 'for forcibly taking the young maidens'.

One 14 year old was badly injured but escaped, and the eldest son, Billy, mad with grief, returned, vowing to destroy the whole Yeeman tribe. Public outrage was such that frontier 'rough justice' took over, and within a year Billy, the native police and posses of squatters and non-local black hands had killed over 150 Aboriginal people.[36]

Cullinlaringo, Queensland (1861)

The worst massacre of whites in Australian frontier history occasioned similar punitive action, and again the number of those shot in retribution dwarfed the number of whites killed. The nineteen victims belonged to the family of humanitarian settler Horatio Wills, who only two weeks earlier had driven his flocks from Victoria to establish Cullinlaringo station west of Rockhampton. When their camp was attacked, all were slaughtered: eleven men, three women and five children, including babies, clubbed to death. The murders were not provoked by the Wills family—they were unarmed apart from one revolver and believed in befriending Aborigines—but they presented an easy target in revenge for earlier 'dispersal' raids by native police.[37]

Forrest River, Western Australia (1926)

In each area, violence usually lasted only a few years, for then the frontier moved on. The last regions to be settled by pastoralists were the Northern Territory and the Kimberley.

One of the most notorious massacres was the supposed mass killing of Aborigines by a police patrol near Forrest River in the Kimberley. It began when a police patrol was sent out to move Aborigines from Nulla Nulla station southwest of Wyndham, which was going broke through cattle-spearing. On 23 May 1926, they came across a ceremonial assembly at Durragee Hill, where about 250 Aborigines were gathered. Shots were fired by an Aboriginal police tracker and three Aboriginal men were slightly wounded. (One of those shot later testified at the Royal Commission and did not mention any fatalities.) As the Aborigines fled, they heard further shots when the constable shot 31 camp dogs involved in stock-killing. Two days later the police were shown the naked body of pastoralist Frederick Hay, who had been speared by an Aborigine named Lumbia in a dispute over cattle-killing. A large police party under

» *George 'Black' Murray with seven native police and two junior officers in the 1860s in Queensland.*

two young constables, Denis Regan and James St Jack, was sent out on 1 June to arrest Lumbia. They brought him in for trial on 4 July, along with 30 potential witnesses. Then, on 30 July, Reverend Gribble, superintendent of Forrest River Mission, reported rumours of murders by the police party. Gribble's widely publicised claims aroused outrage in national and international newspapers and led to the appointment of a Royal Commission—a government-appointed enquiry in which court rules of evidence do not apply.

Unfortunately, it was a deeply flawed affair. The sole Commissioner, George Wood, conceded that, 'If I cannot get direct evidence I shall have to depend on hearsay'. There was plenty of that, but no evidence anyone had been killed or was even missing. Wood formally admitted that 'no evidence had been adduced before the Commission that would justify a prosecution on a charge of murder', yet he made 'an unqualified finding of guilt'. His verdict was that the police patrol had murdered eleven Aborigines during their pursuit of Lumbia. The police were then supposed to have cremated the bodies at three separate locations. There was not a shred of evidence for this finding, but it was exactly what the outside world wanted to hear.[38]

The two policemen were arrested, charged with murder and jailed for two months, but at the committal hearing the prosecution could not make even a prima facie case that anyone had been murdered. The constables were released, and no evidence has surfaced in the 80 years since their discharge to give the accusations any further credibility.

The committal proceedings have been disregarded by influential writers such as Reynolds, Rowley, Elder, Knightley, Shaw and the *Encyclopaedia of Aboriginal Australia*, which presents as fact that 'eleven Aboriginal people had been shot and their bodies burnt (other estimates suggest 100 or more)'. The Encyclopaedia wrongly describes the police as being 'tried for murder but acquitted'—it never came to a trial for there was no case to answer. Nor were the police 'then promoted'.[39]

In his 1999 book *Massacre Myth*, Western Australian journalist Rod Moran argues that this alleged massacre never happened. Moran became involved from the Australian tradition of giving people a 'fair go', in this case the accused policemen's families. He also thinks that 'getting the story as accurate as possible is important for the coherence and integrity of the heritage of our Aboriginal fellow-citizens'.[40]

What Moran has found is that Gribble's list of missing Aborigines appears to be a complete fabrication—several turned up a week or two later and others on the mission's roll had not been seen at the mission for months or even years before the alleged killings. (Between mid-1926 and mid-1927 only 150 of the 800 listed on the roll had visited the mission—where were the other 650? Probably either dead from the flu epidemic raging locally in 1926–27 or simply 'gone bush'.)[41]

Moran's disassembly of evidence establishes that Wood's findings were a travesty. All forensic and ballistics evidence was negative. No human remains were found even though the number of Aborigines said to have been shot ranged from 1 to 1000.[42] Burning the bodies would have been physically impossible because of the lack of sufficient firewood in the sparsely vegetated, sandstone-range country. (From my personal experience of the Kimberley, this was my first reason for doubting mass cremations.) A surveyor working in the area in 1926 found the trees so slight that there were '[none] suitable for marking'.[43]

However, the myth of a Forrest River massacre lives on, although its historian Neville Green now sees it as neither proven nor unproven but merely as 'probable . . . given the violent history of the Kimberley'. The extent of the violence in this region is uncertain, pending detailed studies, but Moran's research on this and two other alleged massacres shows it may have been exaggerated.[44]

Coniston massacre, Northern Territory (1928)

The last known massacre in Australia was a punitive police raid in reprisal for the death of an old white dingo-trapper, Fred Brooks, on Coniston Station northwest of Alice Springs. While camping near an Aboriginal group, Brooks accepted an Aboriginal man's loan of his wife for the night in exchange for food but then failed to provide the promised items. It was the fourth year of the most severe drought ever recorded and desert Aborigines were almost starving. Early next day the irate husband and his uncle set upon Brooks, hacked him to death, stuffed his body down a large rabbit hole and quickly made their escape into the Western Desert.

Fearful retribution followed at the hands of settlers led by mounted Constable George Murray, who was the only active policeman in 650 000 km² (250 000 sq. miles) of Central Australia. Rumours had reached Coniston that the Walbiri were coming in to kill all whites and station blacks, so Murray was given a free hand. The first party shot at least sixteen Aboriginal men and one woman who intervened in a fight. Murray later bragged to police in Darwin that 'the number shot was nearer seventy than seventeen'. Murray then rode out again, this time with settler Nugget Morton, who was bent on revenge for an Aboriginal attack that almost took his life. They spent three weeks hunting Morton's attackers and admitted killing fourteen Aboriginal men but made no mention of two ceremonial gatherings they 'dispersed' with bloody slaughter well-remembered 50 years later. Amazingly, the subsequent Board of Enquiry exonerated Murray, who admitted 31 killings but claimed they were all in self-defence. The public outcry that followed ensured that Coniston was the last punitive expedition.[45]

» Oral history

The validity of oral history has become a controversial issue for those trying to find out what happened in the past. Most Australian museums' avowed policy is to 'give primacy to Aboriginal voices', even when such stories are factually incorrect.[46] Balancing oral and written history has long been a problem for historians; as Bain Attwood, a leading authority on Aboriginal history, has said, 'If the oral history is contradicted by written evidence, most of us are of the opinion that we have to reject Aboriginal memory. But there is a second way of proceeding . . . Can't we ask, if they are telling these stories . . . Isn't it faithful to what was generally happening?'[47]

Three stories from the rich, continuing oral history of Gurindji of Central Australia illustrate the deep gulf between Aboriginal and Western history. They concern bushranger Ned Kelly, Captain Cook and American President John F. Kennedy. One story tells us that Ned Kelly brought a billycan and damper and came to the Victoria River district before any other whitefellas. He taught them how to cook damper and make tea, and although there was only one small damper and one billy, all the Gurindji were fed. Captain Cook—known as 'Big England'—came to Sydney by boat and then travelled inland to shoot Aborigines. Then Kennedy visited and they told him how badly English whitefellas treated them. He promised to make a big war, and the Gurindji walked off Wave Hill Station in 1966 and started the land rights movement. This oral history is not to be taken as literal truth—Kelly, Cook and Kennedy were never in Central Australia. Instead, the stories are parables concerning the bringing of Christianity and law to the region, dispossession, shooting and finally international support for land rights.[48]

Reynolds and Broome agree that new germs rather than guns had by far the major impact.[49] It is difficult to quantify their relative contributions to depopulation, but in Central Australia historian Dick Kimber has rigorously pieced together written records and both white and black oral history to produce estimates of Aboriginal casualties within a 400 km (250 mile) radius of Alice Springs. This is dry country where there was strong competition for waterholes. It emerged that between 1860 and 1895 punitive patrols avenging the murder of whites and spearing of cattle shot 650–850 Aborigines—almost all men. This is a horrifyingly high casualty rate, averaging 18–24 murders per year, but introduced diseases, especially influenza and typhoid, accounted for even more deaths. Kimber estimates another 900 of an estimated original population of 4500 in the early 1860s died from the new germs.[50] The situation in the dry country of Western Australia was probably similar.

Traditional violence

Another significant factor in Aboriginal depopulation was black-on-black violence. Punishment duels, pitched battles and payback murders were witnessed at first contact in Sydney and elsewhere. In Victoria: 'Overall, at least 250 Aborigines are known to have been killed by other Aborigines in inter-tribal fights in the Port Phillip District between 1835 and 1850. If the number of Aborigines killed by Aboriginal troopers in this area is added to this, possibly 500 or more Aborigines were killed by other Aborigines in Victoria. This approached the number of Aborigines killed by Europeans in this area, and is an awesome number of deaths.'[51] Many of these black-on-black deaths derived from the dispossession and disruption that followed European arrival. These drove people into the territory of traditional enemies, who tended to kill strangers on sight.

A graphic account of traditional violence comes from William Buckley, an escaped convict who lived with Aborigines in Victoria from 1803 to 1835. He had fought in the French Revolutionary Wars but found Aboriginal warfare 'much more frightful'. How credible are Buckley's stories, which were told to a journalist 20 years after he emerged from the bush? Some consider them fanciful and sensationalised, but fortunately, shortly after coming back into colonial society he confided in Reverend George Langhorne, a missionary for whom Buckley worked as an interpreter. Langhorne wrote a four-page account of Buckley's answers to his questions, which has the ring of authenticity, but was not published for 80 years. Both it and the book fit well with data from other ethnographers, according to leading anthropologist Les Hiatt.[52]

Buckley witnessed 50 violent deaths during his three decades among the Wathaurong. His own clan's casualties included nine women, seven men and seven children, and ten enemies, including two children, were killed in revenge attacks. All but two of the conflicts were disputes over women. Buckley described his band being attacked by a war party of 300 men, shaking their spears and 'smeared all over with red and white clay':

> The fight began by a shower of spears . . . One of our men advanced singly, as a sort of champion; he then began to dance and sing . . . Seven or eight of the savages . . . threw their spears at him; but . . . he warded them off, or broke them every one . . . They then threw their boomerangs at him, but he warded them off also, with ease. After this, one man advanced, as a sort of champion from their party, to within three yards of him, and threw his boomerang, but the other avoided the blow by falling on his hands and knees, and instantly jumping up again he shook himself like a dog coming out of the water. At seeing this, the enemy shouted out in their language "enough", and the two men went and embraced each other.
>
> A general fight now commenced . . . spears and boomerangs flying in all directions . . . At length one of our tribe had a spear sent right through his body, and he fell. On this, our fellows raised a war cry; . . . the women threw off their rugs, and each armed with a short club, flew to the assistance of their husbands and brothers . . . Men and women were fighting furiously, and indiscriminately, covered with blood; two of the latter were killed in this affair, which lasted without intermission for two hours . . .
>
> Soon after dark the hostile tribe left . . . ours determined on following immediately . . . On approaching the enemy's quarters . . . and finding most of them asleep, . . . our party rushed upon them, killing three on the spot, and wounding several others. The enemy fled precipitately, leaving their . . . wounded to be beaten to death by boomerangs . . . The bodies of the dead they mutilated in a shocking manner, cutting the arms and legs off, with flints, and shells, and tomahawks.[53]

Most frequent were payback killings. A young woman was speared through the thigh because she had absconded with a man from another band; the man involved was seriously injured in single contest. Another dispute concerned a woman abducted by a man from another group four years earlier. When the two groups chanced to meet, the woman was forcibly returned to her original husband, but by night her jealous abductor crept up, pinned the man to the ground with a jagged death spear and took the woman away again. The avengers could not find the murderer, but on a later hunting excursion accidentally encountered his band. A bloody battle followed. The murderer escaped but Buckley's band killed the murderer's two young children, for 'when the parents cannot be punished for any wrong done, they inflict it upon the offspring'. Revenge came immediately, for that night the children's murderer was killed, most of his flesh was cut off and carried away on their spears and his mangled remains were roasted between heated stones and eaten, accompanied by a continual 'uproar of dancing and singing'.

The next fight concerned avenging broken betrothal agreements. Often a young girl was promised to one man but given to another, in which case her firstborn child was 'almost invariably killed at its birth'.[54]

The atrocities sickened Buckley. Eventually, he left the band after 60 hostile warriors killed all his 'relations'. The cause was a fatal snakebite that a man suffered when stepping over a fallen tree with Buckley's group. His 'brother-in-law' was blamed for this accident, because he 'carried about with him something that had occasioned his death . . . frequently they take a man's kidneys out after death, tie them up in something, and carry them round the neck, as a sort of protection and valuable charm, for either good or evil'. Buckley went and lived alone in a hut beside the River Barwon where he built weirs and lived on fish.

Corroboration for high death rates from black-on-black violence comes from Arnhem Land, where anthropologist Lloyd Warner estimated 200 men were killed in 20 years (between 1909 and 1929). Of these deaths, 35 resulted from avenging expeditions. Another 27 men were murdered in smaller raids. There were at least 72 pitched battles and in two of them two lines of men stood 20 paces apart and threw short spears; neither side was armed with shields and 35 men were killed. Formal pitched battles were intended to put an end to chains of revenge killings, but the death toll was horrendous. The region's population was then about 3000—an annual average casualty rate of 1:300.

Revenge attacks occur in all human societies. 'The fundamental principle underlying all the causes of warfare is that of reciprocity,' Warner wrote; 'if a harm has been done to an individual or a group, they must repay . . . by an injury that at least equals the one they have suffered'. Special factors contributing to high Aboriginal death rates were constant raiding for women, never-ending chains of payback killings, and the belief that most deaths (except for those of infants and elders) resulted from an enemy's sorcery and must be avenged.[55]

Infanticide and abortion

A survey of 350 preindustrial societies concluded that abortion was an 'absolutely universal' practice. Australian women achieved miscarriages by eating particular herbs or by applying heavy pressure to the stomach. Other methods included pounding the stomach with stones or tying cord round the belly and gradually tightening it.[56] Infanticide—the deliberate killing of a newborn infant—was similarly practised in virtually all early societies and has been reported for most regions of Australia. Anthropologist Gillian Cowlishaw found that two distinct main reasons emerged for infanticide—the deliberate postponement of motherhood or close succession of children. Early reports from South Australia, Victoria, western New South Wales, Queensland and the Northern Territory show the killing of the firstborn child or children was most frequent. The firstborn was often considered too immature to live, or the mother too

« CANNIBALISM »

Cannibalism in a general sense—the practice of eating one's own species for food—was rare among hunter-gatherer societies and never a regular part of Aboriginal Australia. In contrast, on islands where protein was scarce, such as New Zealand, cannibalism was practised for food value. Among the head-hunting highland tribes of New Guinea, cannibalism was widespread, again probably due to protein starvation. The fatal viral disease of 'kuru,' or laughing sickness, similar to mad cow disease, was transmitted by the consumption of human brains; when the Australian Government ended mortuary feasts in New Guinea in the 1950s it also ended the transmission of 'kuru'.[a]

In the nineteenth century, Europeans regarded cannibalism with both fascination and repulsion. It was seen as the greatest depravity by authors such as Daisy Bates, who included lurid accounts of 'rife baby cannibalism' in articles she sold to magazines and newspapers to finance her humanitarian work. (The word 'cannibalism' appears in the titles of 11 of her 20 published articles.) These may be based less on fact than on others' adventure stories, for in 1898 Bates visited London, where *Wide World Magazine* ran tales by Louis de Rougemont (real name Henri Grin) who claimed he was stranded for 30 years in the Kimberley among cannibals and reported that 'the women among the Australian Aborigines frequently eat their children'.[b]

While Bates and de Rougemont must be discounted as unreliable, respected Australian anthropologists Ronald and Catherine Berndt concluded that, in Australia, 'regarding cannibalism in a more general sense, there is no doubt that it was practised'. Killing and eating newborn babies did occur, often 'to feed a weakly but elder child who is supposed thereby to gain the strength of the killed one' but its prevalence has been 'grossly exaggerated', according to the Berndts.[c] Eating the flesh did not always follow infanticide, although this did happen. For example, when pastoralist Michael Durack was exploring the Kimberley in 1882, he came across a deserted Aboriginal camp:

> The camp had been left hurriedly, probably on his coming, and embers still glowed on a small cairn of stones. Hoping to find a bird or goanna . . . to appease his hunger, he moved the hot stones to uncover in horror the part-cooked body of a child.[d]

Aborigines generally abhorred cannibalism. Often an Aboriginal group would call their enemies cannibals and many myths were told of evil spirits that killed humans for food. Cannibalism was seldom the motive for murder, but when someone died, ritual cannibalism was occasionally practised, according to archaeologist Michael Pickering, who has reviewed all ethnographic references to cannibalism in Aboriginal Australia. It took two forms—mortuary cannibalism, in which parts of one's own dead were eaten, and consumption of the flesh of slain enemies.

Uniquely, Australia has authentic eyewitness accounts of cannibalism from a literate white man. William Buckley gave two eyewitness accounts of cannibalism in Victoria, the first not for publication so there was no reason to exaggerate. He described how flesh was taken from the long-bones of slain warriors for revenge or to acquire their strength. Ritual cannibalism also occurred for love: 'They eat also of the flesh of their own children to whom they have been much attached should they die a natural death.'[e]

'It seems clear', wrote the Berndts, 'that burial cannibalism was fairly wide-spread, and that in most cases . . . only parts of the body were eaten. The expressed aims were to absorb some of the dead person's qualities or attributes; to identify publicly with him and so ward off sorcery accusations; to show respect; or to give a child an opportunity to be reborn, from the same or a different mother.'[f]

Strict rules governed such rituals and the distribution of body parts. Some Europeans witnessed burial ceremonies where kidney-fat was shared out, and many observed Aborigines carrying around pieces of a corpse, such as a desiccated human hand strung from the neck. This practice doubtless gave them their undeserved reputation as cannibals. Michael Pickering concluded that cannibalism's frequency, form and nature have been wildly exaggerated and sensationalised: 'For most groups it was certainly never practised and was seen as socially unacceptable behaviour.'[g] Only in some areas was consumption of human flesh socially sanctioned, although still rare and infrequent. The regions where detailed, consistent accounts suggest cannibalism occurred are parts of Victoria, coastal Arnhem Land and northeastern Queensland.

《　》

young to begin rearing a child. This helps to explain why most traditional Aboriginal girls did not rear children until some years after puberty and marriage.[57]

Mothers also needed to limit the size of their family, for only one child-in-arms was manageable. A mother normally breastfed a child until the age of three, and even a few 5 year olds were partly breastfed. Such prolonged lactation inhibited ovulation, acting as a spacing mechanism between children. If one birth followed another too closely, mothers smothered the newborn, as the renewed milk supply benefited the unweaned older child. Likewise one of a pair of twins was killed at birth, as was a deformed child or Siamese twins—in oral tradition, two pairs were born in Arnhem Land. Infanticide increased in times of hardship. A newborn baby was strangled, had its head beaten against a rock or its mouth stuffed with sand. Some groups, such as the Kurnai, simply left unwanted babies behind when moving camp.

If the mother died in childbirth or of disease, the baby was also killed. When a woman died of 'consumption' (tuberculosis) in Sydney in early 1792, her body was put in a grave and then Colbee placed her infant daughter beside her, dropped a rock on the child's head and quickly filled in the grave. Europeans there 'had not time or presence of mind sufficient to prevent it', but Colbee justified it as a more humane death than starvation for lack of a nursing mother as there were almost no alternative native foods for infants.[58] Before colonisation there were neither domesticated animals, milk, containers in which to boil food nor soft native foods suitable for babies, so mothers' milk was all-important. Many women's traditional ceremonies aim to promote lactation, and circles found in women's art usually signify breasts.

Aboriginal women lost some babies in childbirth. Evidence from Ernabella Mission points to 'a higher infant mortality at birth than had been thought', for example, all four Pitjantjatjara babies born within four days in April 1965 suffered complications at birth, and survived 'due only to their mothers having come into the hospital for delivery'. Edward Curr recorded that Bangerang women gave birth to between six and eight children, but half these babies were killed or died at birth. Two ethnographers independently said 30–50 per cent of South Australian babies were killed.[59] Infanticide increased when the first mixed-race infants were born. At birth, all Aboriginal babies are pink in colour but those of unmixed descent soon become black. Bates, who lived with Aborigines at Ooldea, South Australia, from 1910 to 1934, recounted the fate of three newborn mixed-race children: 'One was taken to the German mission . . . The other two were destroyed in infancy.'[60]

» Pre-contact health

In 1788 most Aborigines were described as healthy; they were almost certainly in better shape than convicts and crew in the First Fleet. Although infant mortality was high and life expectancy extremely low, Aborigines who survived infancy were relatively fit and disease-free. The measurements of Yarraginny, a tribal leader from Goulburn, were taken in 1848 by a doctor, who said 'such a perfectly formed man would scarcely be found in the British army'. Australia's native foods supported a nutritious, balanced diet of protein and vegetables with adequate vitamins and minerals but little salt, sugar and fat. Life on the move kept people lean and fit, if sufficient resources were available.

In coastal environments, families raised strong children, whereas in arid regions, which cover 70 per cent (5.5 million km²/2 million sq. miles) of the continent, frequent long droughts led to malnutrition and even death. Malnutrition adversely affects women's fertility. In undernourished populations, wide birth-spacing is an ecological adaptation to reduced food intake in bad years. Throughout the natural world, connections between nutrition and fecundity are clear. Nomadic Aboriginal women became pregnant only in good years when food was plentiful. This direct association between the fertility of woman and nature was a powerful factor in Aboriginal blurring of the dichotomy between humans and their environment.[61]

What was Aboriginal life expectancy? Bates tells of tribal elders leading active lives into their eighties, but a more realistic picture of traditional life comes from early physical anthropologist, Andrew Abbie. After twenty years of fieldwork in remote regions with bush-born Aborigines he found:

> Aborigines born under native conditions used to face a poor prospect. Some thirteen per cent of all children were dead within their first year and twenty-five per cent by the end of the fifth year. The best possible average expectation of life at birth was barely forty years. The probable order of importance of causes of death was: injury (including warfare and murder), disease, magic, old age. Relatively few survived the dangers of youth and middle age to enjoy any old age.[63]

Native Australians could expect 'barely forty years' of life but an average life expectancy of 40 would have equalled that of Europe at the time. They suffered from trachoma (a disease of the eyes), intestinal parasites, skin diseases, hepatitis, arthritis, periodontal disease, tooth attrition, anaemia, famine-induced stress and yaws. However, remoteness from the outside world, low population density and nomadism impeded the spread of infectious diseases. Healers developed a great store of knowledge on natural medicine and remedies. Some could splint broken bones and successfully amputate injured limbs, cauterising with clay, leaves or fire. Prehistoric 'surgeons' also treated head wounds by performing trepanations; drilled holes have been found in skulls of three women, who all survived the operations.

Ancient disease

Prehistoric human remains reveal evidence of ancient trauma, infections and degenerative diseases. Palaeopathologist Stephen Webb analysed ancient skeletons, focusing on stress indicators that correlate with diet, dietary change, population growth, the degree of sedentism and crowding. The term 'stress' is here used to indicate serious, even life-threatening, physical conditions, not emotional stress.

Aboriginal health varied regionally, with certain common features. Childhood deprivation was frequent, for growth arrest lines were found in 60–80 per cent of individuals, indicating growth stopped up to three times during childhood. Australia's desert nomads were healthiest, because they avoided the infections that more sedentary, crowded groups suffered, although their high incidence (71 per cent) of growth arrest lines reveals periodic food shortages. Coastal people also suffered much less stress. Murrayians—people of the crowded, central Murray River region—were least healthy and more often than others died before their mid-thirties. Webb's explanation is:

> The Murray has always been an area of plenty but it is likely that in the late Holocene [the last 10 000 years] there were increasingly more people sharing it. Under such circumstances it seems that the diet of the central Murrayian was fast becoming one biased more towards a high carbohydrate than a high protein intake . . . while bulk vegetable food fills bellies and is largely always available, its quality and food value is not necessarily high. Further evidence for the ingestion of large amounts of sticky carbohydrates comes from the presence of thick calculus build-up around the teeth of these people. This is similar to the dental deposit on the teeth of New Guinean sago traders . . . It . . . is probably due to the widespread use of the cooked Typha root [bulrush] as a staple food.[63]

Murrayians lived close together on dense concentrations of mounds—artificial raised areas formed by the deliberate heaping-up of earth from the surrounding plain. Many such mounds have stone tools and fireplaces and some had huts built on them. The mounds were up to 48 m (60 ft) in diameter and rose 0.5–1.5 m (1½–5 ft) above ground level. Space was short—95 mounds lie within 1 km² (⅓ sq. mile). Some were communal cooking 'ovens' owned by a group of families, where early settlers saw 1000 kg (1 ton) of bulrush roots cooked at once.

This is the closest Australian hunter-gatherers came to sedentary life in a 'village', and archaeologist Elizabeth Williams has termed these mound-dwellers 'complex hunter-gatherers'.[64] Ethnographers suggest each extended family owned a particular mound and adjacent fish traps. One disadvantage of such close, continuous communal living was poorer sanitation, which created ideal breeding grounds for infections and parasites. By 1788 the lower Murray and Darling river valleys were probably the most densely populated parts of Australia, but overcrowding, a sedentary lifestyle and food shortages took a severe toll on Murrayian health.

Prehistoric trauma

Many prehistoric bone fractures resulted from violence; many forearms appear to have been broken deflecting blows from clubs. Most parrying fractures are on the left forearm held up to block blows to the left side of the body from a right-hander. Parrying fractures were detected on 10 per cent of desert men and 19 per cent of east coast women; for both these groups, they were the most common type of upper-limb fractures. Desert nomads also often broke their legs in the rocky terrain.

Fractured skulls were twice to four times as common among women as men. The fractures are typically oval, thumb-sized depressions caused by blows with a blunt instrument. Most are on the left side of the head, suggesting frontal attack by a right-hander. Most head injuries are thus the result of interpersonal violence, probably inflicted by men on women.[65]

Arthritis

Arthritis detected on prehistoric skeletons affected males more than females, elbows more than knees and Murrayians more than others. Particularly common was arthritis in the right elbow-joint of adult men, derived from throwing a spear, with or without a spear-thrower. Women of the Queensland coast had Australia's highest incidence (15 per cent) of arthritis of the knee because of their method of shellfish-gathering. Shellfish, especially pipis (*Plebidonax deltoides*), were collected by digging into soft, sticky mud and sand. Boring down with the toes to expose burrowing pipis produced strong, twisting, mechanical stresses on knee and ankle joints. Murrayian women suffered a different work-related arthritis; they used both arms wielding heavy digging sticks to gather bulrush roots and suffered chronic degeneration of both elbow-joints. Murrayian men were prone to arthritis in both elbows from harvesting bulrushes but also suffered from spear-throwing, as their right elbows are more affected than left.[66]

» New diseases

Traditional society was not disease-free but its endemic diseases were chronic, long-term ones, such as trachoma and yaws. Foreign microbes from Asia and Europe met no resistance. Most lethal was smallpox, but even in southern regions that smallpox didn't reach, other new diseases exacted a terrible toll. Both tuberculosis and syphilis survived the long voyage from England. From 1828 Australia instituted tight quarantine controls but, as faster ships were built, there were occasional outbreaks of measles and influenza at various ports, some with severe impact on previously unexposed Aborigines.

Smallpox

The first smallpox epidemic hit the new colony in April 1789 (see chapter 2). 'How a disease, to which our former observations had led us to suppose [the Aborigines] strangers, could at once have introduced itself, and have spread so widely, seemed inexplicable' to Watkin Tench, who asked:

1. 'Is it a disease indigenous to the country?'
2. 'Did the French ships under Monsieur La Perouse introduce it? Let it be remembered that they had now been departed more than a year and we had never heard of its existence on board of them.'

3.   'Had it travelled across the continent from its western shore, where Dampier . . . formerly landed?'

4.   'Was it introduced by Mr. Cook?'

5.   'Did we give it birth here? No person among us had been afflicted with the disorder since we had quitted the Cape of Good Hope, seventeen months before. It is true that our surgeons had brought out variolous matter in bottles, but to infer that it was produced from this cause were a supposition so wild as to be unworthy of consideration.'[67]

The answer to the first question is 'no'. All authorities agree that smallpox was never endemic in Australia. Smallpox is a crowd-infectious disease that evolved from animal diseases and arose with the growth of large, dense populations in Europe and Asia generated by the development of agriculture. A *concentrated* population of at least 200 000 was required for the smallpox virus to sustain itself and become endemic, as the normal incubation period was only 12–14 days.[68]

Among small or scattered societies, such as those in Australia, epidemics were caused by close contact with infectious visitors from the outside world. After smallpox had run its course, it died out until the next introduction, leaving a legacy of heavily scarred, sometimes blind survivors. Most victims' faces, especially the noses, were covered with large, depressed pockmarks. None of this distinctive pockmarking was seen on Aborigines before the epidemic, but Fowell 'conjectured that it [smallpox] was among them before any Europeans visited the country as they have a name for it'. King and Hunter reported the name as 'gall-gall', and Collins said: 'From the native who resided with us [Arabanoo] we understood that many families had been swept off by this scourge, and that others, to avoid it, had fled into the interior parts of the country . . . they gave it a name (galgalla), a circumstance that seemed to indicate a preacquaintance with it.'[69] This is not necessarily correct as 'gall-gall' may simply mean 'spots' or 'itch'. Across the continent, 28 names for smallpox are known, for example 'nguya' (pustule) in South Australia, 'boola' (poison) in Western Australia, and 'moo-nool-e-mindye' (dust of the Rainbow Serpent) in Victoria, where this Ancestral Being was blamed for the affliction.

Did the French bring the disease? No, despite stories recorded by Obed West, a friend of Kruwee, an elder who witnessed the First Fleet's arrival:

From conversations I have had with old blacks, some of whom were strongly pockmarked, I gathered that they contracted the disease [smallpox] from the men of La Perouse's ships. On the south side of the bay . . . there is . . . a cave. This was shown to me by the blacks as the place where all who had the disease went. The blacks had a great horror of the disease and were afraid to go near any who were suffering. The patients were made to go into the cave, and then at intervals supplies of food, principally fish, were laid on the ground some little distance from the cave. Those of the sufferers who were able, would crawl to the spot for the food and go back again.[70]

Remains of many smallpox victims were seen in caves at Botany Bay in September 1789, but there was no smallpox aboard Lapérouse's ships.[71] Even had there been, the virus could not have survived thirteen months between the departure of the French and the onset of the epidemic.

If not the French, were the British responsible? Cook's visit was too early but what about British arrivals in 1788? There was no smallpox among the First Fleet nor did any further ships (excepting that of Lapérouse) reach Sydney before the outbreak. The voyage to Australia took so long—eight months—that no ship from Europe reached Sydney carrying smallpox cases.

The only other possible European source was 'variolous matter in bottles' brought out by surgeons in case smallpox broke out on the voyage or proved endemic in Australia. In Europe, dried smallpox scabs were collected from mild cases, powdered and used to protect susceptible people against the disease. In 1983 the British were accused of germ warfare by the late Professor Noel Butlin, who claimed: 'it is possible and, in 1789, likely, that infection of the Aborigines was a deliberate extermination act'. Butlin was an economic historian writing about population rather than disease and was possibly unduly influenced by his reading of the fate of indigenous North Americans, caused by the accidental, and perhaps occasionally deliberate, spread of smallpox there.[72] Butlin had no evidence for his claim, but a headline on 7 January 1984 in *The Age* newspaper read 'How English settlers waged biological war on Aborigines'. Aboriginal activists took up the story. Even after several academic authorities published refutations, the myth was perpetuated by influential historians David Day and Henry Reynolds. In 2001 Reynolds wrote: 'one possibility is that the epidemic was deliberately or accidentally let loose by someone in the settlement at Sydney Cove. Not surprisingly this is a highly contentious proposition. If true, it would clearly fall within the ambit of the Genocide Convention.' Reynolds argued strongly for the theory of germ warfare, but produced no historical evidence and ignored voluminous scientific research disproving the possibility.[73]

When I began research for this book in 1997, I discovered that infection of Aborigines with bottled smallpox scabs was not merely implausible but impossible. The key work is *Smallpox and its Eradication* published in 1988 by the World Health Organisation, principally authored by Australian virologist Frank Fenner, an authority on the disease. After reading much of this 1400-page book, I went to see Professor Fenner in Canberra. My first question was—'Could the smallpox virus have come from an earlier European case, lying dormant for 15 months in human carriers or material from ships?' Fenner's answer was an unequivocal 'no'; smallpox does not lie dormant and all cases among unvaccinated, susceptible people are obvious. Even had contaminated material such as clothes or blankets from an active but undiagnosed smallpox case been left ashore from French ships, the virus would have been rapidly inactivated by heat, sunlight or rain. My second question concerned the 'shelf life' of variolous matter—'Could it have survived a long voyage through the tropics and two summers in Sydney's hot, relatively humid climate?' The answer again was no.[74]

My final query was: 'If, by some chance, the three-year-old English variolous matter was still active, is Butlin's scenario of accidental or deliberate infection possible?' Again Fenner's answer was no. People caught smallpox by inhaling airborne droplets of virus in face-to-face contact with an active case or by infection from contact with blankets a victim had recently used, but there had never been active smallpox among Europeans or on any ships in Sydney.[75]

What then was the source of Australia's smallpox? A northern, Asian origin was suggested in various books and articles published between 1911 and 1966 by medical scientists Sirs Edward Stirling and John Cleland. The 1829–32 epidemic evidently spread to eastern New South Wales from the northwest and Cleland wrote: 'From this wide extent and outbreaks . . . I believe the real solution lies in an introduction by Malays into Northern Australia'. Contemporary firsthand observers of the second epidemic in 1829–32, such as Dr Mair of Bathurst, agreed. George Clark (an escaped convict then living with Aborigines) reported: 'the disease proceeded from the north-west coast, and spared none of the tribes as far as the Liverpool Plains [near Bathurst], attacking 20 and 30 at a time, none escaping its fury'.[76] In 1829, explorer Charles Sturt saw active cases among Aborigines on the Darling River.[77] The epidemic travelled down to the mouth of the Murray River, where in 1831 Sturt came across a mass of skeletons too numerous to have been battle deaths, and unlike any other Aboriginal burial ground.

Historian Judy Campbell has made a compelling case that all Australia's smallpox epidemics originated in Indonesia, where the disease was endemic and outbreaks occurred in the 1780s, 1820s, 1860s and 1870s. Fenner agrees that 'origin from the Macassans is most likely', as does Campbell Macknight, an expert on the Macassans.[78] Some academics still find a smallpox epidemic 15 months after British arrival just too much of a coincidence, but in fact the outbreak of smallpox in Australia correlates with the beginning of Macassan visits to northern Australia in the eighteenth century. Although it is 2100 km (1300 miles) from the Gulf of Carpentaria to Sydney, a network of Aboriginal trading routes spanned Australia and in 4–6 years infection could have travelled across the continent. The country is so flat that speedy progress was possible along rivers and from waterhole to waterhole, even if people did not travel as far during summer (November–April) to avoid tropical rains and desert heat.

Makassar's population was too small to support endemic smallpox but outside contacts occasionally brought it to this busy port. Smallpox was increasingly prevalent in Indonesia in the nineteenth century. Severe epidemics affected Sumatra, the eastern archipelago and southern Sulawesi in 1780–83 and later. On the way to and from Makassar, there would have been frequent contact with areas where the disease was endemic. Some correlations have been suggested between smallpox epidemics in Sulawesi and the four great epidemics in Australia—in the 1780s, 1820s, 1860s and 1870s.[79]

The voyage from Makassar to Australia took 10–15 days. As the normal incubation period for smallpox was 12–14 days, it is very possible that Macassans brought smallpox to Australia, where they had close contact with Aboriginal people. Some of the Macassans Matthew Flinders met in 1803 bore tell-tale pockmarks, perhaps deriving from the 1780–83 Indonesian epidemic. Recollections of Jack Davis, an Arnhem Lander, suggest smallpox struck Cobourg Peninsula in Arnhem Land long before the second epidemic in 1829–32. Davis, who was born about 1830, told how very old people recalled that when they were children, smallpox 'killed plenty black-fellows'.[80] The name for smallpox in Arnhem Land is 'purrer-purrer', a clear derivation from its Macassan name 'puru-puru'.

In 1789 there were no European observers outside Sydney, but we know small-pox affected much of southeastern Australia, including the whole lower Murray River valley and Port Phillip (later Melbourne) region. Smallpox's impact often *preceded* European settlement, for colonists, including doctors, reported blindness and distinc-tive pockmarks on people with no previous contact with outsiders.

The only groups of tribes in southeastern Australia never affected by smallpox were the Kurnai of Gippsland and the Ngarigo of the Snowy Mountains; their languages thus lack any word for the disease. These two great confederacies were protected by their rugged terrain, a remote location in the extreme southeast and by enmity with their neighbours. The Kurnai were traditional enemies of the Kulin nation to their west, as were the Ngarigo of Ngunawal and the Wiradjuri to their north. When Robinson met these tribes on his journey from Melbourne through the Australian Alps in 1844, he found no pockmarked or blind people at Omeo in the Victorian Alps, Cooma on the high tablelands of the Monaro, or Yarralumla (now Canberra) on the upper Murrumbidgee River, but the signs were numerous among the Wiradjuri and Ngunawal at Yass only 50 km (30 miles) downstream. The Ngarigo suffered over 90 per cent mortality through other new diseases, however, beginning with a flu epidemic in the Monaro region in 1839.[81]

Smallpox frequently travelled ahead of the settlers. Adelaide was not established until 1836 but already the disease had struck the Kaurna. Missionaries wrote: 'They have no remedy against it, except the nguyapalti, the smallpox song, which they learnt from the eastern tribes, by the singing of which the disease is believed to be prevented or stopped in its progress'.[82]

In the third outbreak, Aboriginal numbers on the Cobourg Peninsula reduced from 200 to 28. This 1860–61 epidemic spread along Aboriginal trade routes into northern Queensland, Central Australia and 2000 km (1250 miles) across the continent to the Great Australian Bight, where active smallpox was recorded in 1867. A fourth epidemic began in the Kimberley in the late 1860s and spread westwards to the Pilbara and down the coast to Geraldton. Inland Northern Territory peoples were also affected. Indeed, the terrible death toll caused by smallpox on Victoria River Downs station in pre-contact times is well-remembered in oral history. Worst affected were the Karangpurru grasslands people, whose numbers dropped from 500 people to just two men.[83]

Allan Young, a Karangpurru man, said that a very long time ago a terrible sickness (smallpox) came upon the Karangpurru people. He identified the place of origin as a sickness site; neighbouring people knew of the sickness and erected brush walls in an attempt to inhibit the spread of the disease.[84]

The severe effects of smallpox, influenza, tuberculosis and venereal disease have been seriously underestimated by most historians, who instead overemphasise the role of conflict in the disintegration of Aboriginal society. Worldwide, the process of globalisation caused a drastic decline in indigenous populations from the unintentional spread of killer diseases to the new worlds of the Americas, Pacific and Australia. The impact of new germs on people with no prior immunity was horrendous. In the century after Columbus landed in America, smallpox evidently killed 95 per cent of the pre-Columbian population, the world's greatest human biological catastrophe. The New World was much more thickly populated than Australia, for the environment was richer and crop production widespread. Australia and North America are similar in size but much of Australia is desert. Densely inhabited islands were particularly vulnerable. Captain Cook's ship inadvertently carried syphilis, tuberculosis and influenza to Hawaii in 1779; typhoid epidemics followed and Hawaiian numbers fell from around 500 000 to 84 000 by 1853, when smallpox arrived and killed another 10 000. Even in modern Bangladesh and India, where smallpox was endemic for 2000 years, a quarter of unvaccinated people usually died in each epidemic.[85]

Each smallpox epidemic ended when there were no new people to infect, but their effects were severe. In Australia, Campbell estimates 60 per cent mortality in a 'virgin soil' epidemic, 50 per cent in the tropics where there was some prior exposure, and 25 per cent or less among small, scattered family groups of the arid interior. Both the first and second epidemics reached the Centre.[86]

Across southern Australia during the first 50 years of European settlement, smallpox virtually wiped out a whole generation. Smallpox was to Aboriginal Australia what the Black Death was to Europe in the Middle Ages.

Venereal disease

Both gonorrhoea and syphilis came to Australia with the First Fleet. Syphilis is a serious, sexually transmitted disease which first appears as open genital sores. The secondary stage is marked by lesions in skin and mucous membranes. Infection is transmitted from mothers to foetuses, leading to frequent miscarriages and infant deaths. About half the foetuses die and the rest are born with rashes, pneumonia and skeletal abnormalities. Its final stage comprises progressive dementia, generalised paralysis and in some cases blindness, deafness, severe tissue loss and facial disfigurement. Today syphilis develops slowly and is treatable with antibiotics, but in a previously unexposed population its effects were far more severe. Its impact on Aborigines resembled that when syphilis first hit Europe in 1495: 'its pustules often covered the body from the head to the knees, caused flesh to fall off people's faces, and led to death within a few months'.[87] Gonorrhoea was not identified as a separate venereal disease until the twentieth century, but is longer-lasting and twenty times as common as syphilis. It involves inflammation of mucous membranes of the genitals of both sexes, and often leads to sterility. If gonorrhoea in women is untreated, uterine infection becomes a chronic condition, sterilising and sometimes killing through abscesses or peritonitis.

Venereal disease was a major factor in Aboriginal depopulation, since it led to infertility. As settlement spread into areas beyond police control, many convicts and shepherds formed liaisons with Aboriginal women, who became carriers. Syphilis spread rapidly in Victoria with the influx of settlers from Tasmania; by 1837, as police magistrate Foster Fyans observed in Geelong, 'large families of natives—husband, wife, boys and girls—were eaten up with venereal disease. The disorder was an introduction from Van Diemen's Land, and I am of the opinion that two thirds of the natives of Port Philip have died from this infection'.[88]

In southeastern Australia, venereal disease was widespread by the 1840s. Butlin estimated that by 1855 its steady spread had caused a 40 per cent reduction in fertility among Aboriginal women. In Queensland, syphilis spread so rapidly that by the 1890s half the Aborigines in some regions were affected. There was no cure and little treatment, although Bates tells of victims treated by burial up to the neck in wet sand. Syphilis was rife in southern New South Wales in 1844 when Robinson, who was in Cooma on his journey through the Snowy Mountains, wrote: 'Syphilitic and other European Disease among the Natives is prevalent, and their numbers are rapidly decreasing'. White people only settled the Cooma district in the late 1820s and smallpox never reached Australia's mountainous southeast but by 1866 only two full-descent Aborigines remained of 500 Ngarigo people.[89] The Aborigines of southwestern Western Australia also escaped smallpox, but their numbers decreased rapidly, due to venereal disease, tuberculosis and measles.

By the 1890s, doctors sadly predicted that 'syphilis alone would probably suffice to exterminate the Aborigines'. British fears of this led to the establishment of isolation hospitals in Western Australia, the Northern Territory and Queensland. In 1908, the Western Australian government set up 'lock' hospitals on the northwest coast.[90]

Patients, often in neck chains, were marched by police to the nearest port and shipped to Carnarvon. Men were confined on Bernier Island, women on Dorre. Over a quarter died there, in what Bates called 'tombs of the living dead'. The lock hospitals were closed at the end of 1918, when treatment for those in the final stages of syphilis became available.

Herbert Basedow, a medical practitioner and anthropologist, concluded after visiting Darwin in 1911 that of all diseases, syphilis was 'the most formidable in bringing about the speedy decimation of Aboriginal tribes'.[91]

Yaws and treponarid

Two forms of endemic syphilis-like disease were widespread—yaws in hot, damp northern regions and treponarid in the arid centre and temperate south. Lesions on prehistoric crania identify both yaws and treponarid as pre-colonial diseases. Cross-immunity between introduced syphilis and endemic forms meant they did not occur together.

Yaws is a highly contagious, non-venereal disease, spread by close physical contact. It is usually acquired by children, who generally recover, leaving them immune from further attacks. Yaws neither kills nor sterilises but may enter a third stage—gangosa—leading to blindness and facial disfigurement, especially destruction of the nose and the roof of the mouth and deformity of long-bones, causing lameness and 'boomerang legs' (bowed in side-view). Blind people 'without noses' were seen in tropical Australia (for example, by Cadell in 1868 in Arnhem Land) and in the arid centre (for example, early twentieth-century photographs by Spencer, Basedow and Abbie). Arrernte (Arunta and Aranda) people in Central Australia call this treponarid 'erkincha' and have a myth explaining its origin. Ulcers were treated with bush medicines such as infusions of the inner tree bark of *Rhizopara stylosa* in Arnhem Land.[92]

Sturt's description of ulcerated, blind, lame and noseless people matches Abbie's photographs. The incidence of Aboriginal yaws rose steadily before the Second World War due to poor health and living conditions, and 1950s blood tests showed that up to 75 per cent in some settlements had suffered the disease. Subsequently, antibiotics proved effective and yaws has been largely eradicated. The presence of yaws in tropical and arid Australia restricted the early spread of syphilis to temperate regions. Syphilis was rare in Northern Territory Aborigines until the 1970s, when yaws almost disappeared and a generation reached adulthood without cross-immunity.

Other new diseases

Other serious new diseases were typhoid, tuberculosis, diphtheria, influenza and measles. These affected the whole Australian community but particularly previously unexposed Aborigines. Mumps struck in 1824, whooping cough in 1828, scarlet fever in 1833, diphtheria in 1858, and measles in 1850. In 1875 measles killed 20 per cent

›› *14. Rock painting of a turtle at Ubirr, Kakadu National Park, Northern Territory.*

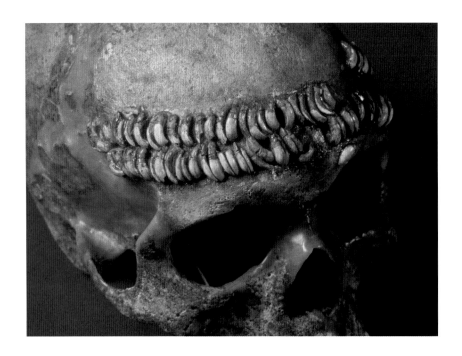

›› **15.** *A double-stranded band of notched wallaby teeth encircled the forehead of this man buried in Roonka cemetery on the Murray River, South Australia, over 4000 years ago. Headbands were made of fine twine covered by wax and painted white or decorated with teeth set in gum.*

›› **16.** *Australia's oldest known human remains were found in this crescentic sand-dune on the downwind side of extinct Lake Mungo in western New South Wales.*

›› **17.** *Pukumani poles or grave-posts on Melville Island, Northern Territory. In the Pukumani rituals, Tiwi dancers wear elaborate ornaments and body decorations and commemorate events in the life of the deceased through dance. Carved and decorated poles are erected around the grave during the rites.*

›› **18.** *Rock paintings of a kangaroo and men with guns in Wynbarra rock-shelter, Northern Territory.*

›› **19.** *Wandjina site north of Gibb River in the Kimberley region, Western Australia.*

›› **20.** *Wandjina and snakes panel, Mandangarri site near Gibb River homestead, Kimberley, Western Australia.*

» **21.** *Djingalo of tall, slim 'Carpentarian' build making a hand-stencil in a rock-shelter on Wessel Island, Northern Territory. Stencils are made by blowing pigment either directly or through a tube over the hand, leaving an outline.*

» *22. A dingo in Magnificent Gallery, Laura, Queensland. With a call resembling a howl, dingoes are much closer to wolves than dogs and have never been domesticated. They invariably return to the wild to mate.*

» *23. Panel of male Bradshaw figures with large headdresses, tassels, armbands and sashes, King Edward River crossing, northern group, Kimberley, Western Australia.*

›› **24.** *Nauwalabila rock-shelter during excavation. This is currently Australia's oldest known human occupation site. It has stone tools and ochre aged more than 50 000 years.*

›› **25.** *The marsupial thylacine or 'Tasmanian tiger', distinguished by its striped back and tapering hindquarters, has been extinct on the Australian mainland for about the last 4000 years. This rock painting in Kakadu National Park, Northern Territory, depicts a thylacine with its cub.*

›› **26.** *Fish trap built by Anchor Gulunba in 1978 on the Bulgai Plains between the Liverpool and Tomkinson Rivers, Arnhem Land, Northern Territory. The conical fish trap will be positioned in the gate when the tide turns and water begins to flow out.*

» *Aborigines in neck chains (c. 1890) in the Kimberley. Police used neck chains to bring in prisoners and witnesses, since, before roads or gaols existed, this was the only means of preventing agile hunters escaping during the long trek back to a police post. They were used in remote regions of Western Australia and the Northern Territory until after the Second World War, partly because many Aborigines preferred to sleep chained outside under the stars rather than locked in hot, stuffy rooms. Chains were also used to prevent sufferers from leprosy or syphilis running away and infecting others when they were being taken to leprosaria or lock hospitals. While neck chains seem the epitome of cruelty to us, apparently they chafed less than handcuffs or the leg irons worn by convict chain-gangs, which crippled some prisoners. The 1935 Royal Commission into the Condition and Treatment of Aborigines recommended neck chains as the most humane way of 'restraining native prisoners'. The 1937 Conference on Aboriginal Welfare agreed. Public opinion prevailed, however, and neck chains were banned from then on.*[93]

of Aboriginal residents at Coranderrk Mission, Victoria. When the 1948 measles epidemic reached Ernabella Mission, South Australia, all 300 Aboriginal people there contracted the disease, some also developed pneumonia, and at least 23 died. A second measles epidemic struck Ernabella in 1957 and 27 infants died. The first 'virgin soil' outbreaks of measles killed a quarter of the Aborigines who encountered it.[93]

Epidemics of influenza (called epidemic catarrh at the time) occurred in 1820, 1826–27 and 1838 but the worst was the Spanish flu. Indigenous historian Gordon Briscoe wrote, 'Spanish influenza lasted from early 1918 to late 1919 and was severe, killing more than 20 million people worldwide. Approximately 12 000 people died of influenza in Australia during this pandemic, of whom 1030 were Queenslanders. At least 30 per cent of the Queensland death toll (315 people) were known to be

Aborigines.' It also almost wiped out the Barkindji of the Darling River in New South Wales. Later, Asian flu caused further mortality, for instance at Ernabella in 1957.[94]

Tuberculosis was another killer. Tuberculosis is a highly infectious respiratory disease spread by sneezing, coughing or even just talking—and thrives in crowded conditions such as Aboriginal camps and missions. It was 'probably the leading cause of death in the late nineteenth century for Aborigines in many parts of the country', Dr Neil Thomson wrote in a review of Aboriginal health in 1991. At Point Pearce Aboriginal settlement, South Australia, in 1880–99, tuberculosis caused 20 per cent of all Aboriginal deaths. At first contact, Aboriginal mortality from tuberculosis was about 10 per cent.[95] A vaccine was developed in the 1940s and tuberculosis has been largely eradicated in Australia, except among Aborigines, where its incidence is 15 to 20 times that of non-indigenous people.

Macassans brought malaria to Port Essington, Northern Territory, in 1843 where it affected whites and blacks alike. (Aboriginal people in Cape York may also have been affected occasionally through Torres Strait Islanders who traded with malarial New Guinea.)[96] Further outbreaks of malaria followed as increasing numbers of Asians and South Sea islanders arrived. By the 1890s, malaria was rife in tropical Australia but was eradicated in the 1960s. In the 1870s, tropical Australia was also hit by the scourge of leprosy (Hansen's disease) brought from Asia by pearlers and gold prospectors. To control infection, leprosaria were established on offshore islands. By the 1950s leprosy had become the most serious Aboriginal medical problem in the tropics; its incidence among coastal Aborigines was one in twenty, the highest rate in the world. Aborigines called it the 'big sick'. Thankfully, modern medicine brought it under control and the last leprosarium closed in 1985. Among new cases, Aborigines account for a quarter, the rest being mainly asylum seekers from Asia.[97]

《　》

The small size of the original indigenous population and the subsequent drastic decrease allowed massive transplantation of whites into sparsely inhabited Australia. The Aboriginal population decreased until the 1930s, when it was as low as 60 000, a reduction of between 80 and 90 per cent from pre-contact times. It was modern medicine and the discovery of penicillin that finally made the breakthrough, although in Tasmania irretrievable damage had already been done. When effective treatment for venereal disease became available in the 1940s, Aboriginal numbers began to rise. Then, in the 1950s and 1960s, the development of antibiotics and immunisation gradually led to a significant improvement.

TRADITION

Indigenous life at first contact

Australian Aborigines have the oldest living culture in the world. The way of life their ancestors developed in the ice age was ideally suited to the continent's unpredictable climate and often harsh environment. It survived little-changed until disrupted by the impact of colonisation. One of the colonists' major mistakes was to assume that, because the Aborigines were nomadic, they could readily move out of the way of settlers. Only gradually did the newcomers learn more about traditional indigenous life, and begin to recognise the strong ties binding 'nomads' to particular areas. In 1798 Collins remarked: 'Each family has a particular place of residence, from which is derived its distinguishing name . . . they have also their real estates. Bennelong . . . often assured me that the island Memel, called by us Goat Island, close by Sydney Cove, was his own property; that it was his father's, and that he should give it to Bygone [Bigon], his particular friend and companion . . . He told us of other people who possessed this kind of hereditary property.'[1] In the 1830s, Reverend John Dunmore Lang wrote: 'Their wanderings are circumscribed by certain well-defined limits, beyond which they seldom pass, except for purposes of war or festivity. In short, every tribe has its own district, the boundaries of which are well known to the natives generally.' As distinguished anthropologist Bill Stanner expressed it in 1968:

No English words are good enough to give a sense of the links between an Aboriginal group and its homeland. Our word 'home', warm and suggestive though it may be, does not match the Aboriginal word that may mean 'camp', 'hearth', 'country', 'everlasting home', 'totem place', 'life source', 'spirit centre' and much else all in one. Our word 'land' is too spare and meagre . . . To put our words 'home' and 'land' together into 'homeland' is a little better but not much. A different tradition leaves us tongueless and earless towards this other world of meaning and significance.[2]

Nowadays the word 'country' has been adopted, and many public events commence with a 'welcome to country' by local traditional owners or custodians.

» *Big Bill Neidjie, one of the Gagudju people of western Arnhem Land. In 1979 he became a ranger in the newly created Kakadu National Park. He wrote a book,* Story about Feeling, *and in 1989 was awarded an OAM.*

Some regions, such as the Yolngu territory in Arnhem Land, were never settled by newcomers. Such tribal land provides physical and spiritual sustenance. To Aboriginal eyes, no 'natural' features exist; every hill, waterhole or cave was created by Ancestral Beings. Bill Neidjie, a Gagudju elder, described the land as 'like a history book': 'Our story is in the land . . . It is written in those sacred places, that's the law'. Similarly, Margaret-Mary Turner said: 'that land is our spirit, or soul itself . . . You aren't just related to people, you are related to the country. And you look after that country that you are related to, just as you look after the people.'[3]

Galarrwuy Yunupingu's view, that 'an Aboriginal deprived of his tribal land is like a leaf torn from its tree', has been widely quoted in the battle for land rights— indigenous people owning and living on their traditional land. Some anthropologists have found, however, that the pull of the new proved even stronger than attachment to traditional country. For instance, in the 1930s Stanner discovered that the rich environment of the Fitzmaurice River region in the Northern Territory had been deserted for 50 years, not through conflict or disease, but by a voluntary, permanent exodus to places where longed-for new stimulants of tea and tobacco could be obtained. 'Eventually, for every Aboriginal who, so to speak, had Europeans thrust upon him, at least one other had sought them out,' he wrote.

Nowhere, as far as I am aware, does one encounter Aborigines who want to return to the bush, even if their new circumstances are very miserable. They went because they wanted to, and stay because they want to . . . There is a real, and an intense, bond between an Aboriginal and the ancestral estate he shares with other clansmen. Country is a high interest with a high value; rich sentiments cluster around it; but there are other interests; all are relative, and any can be displaced. If the bond between persons and clan-estates were always in all circumstances of the all-absorbing kind it has sometimes been represented to be, then migrations of the kind I have described simply could not have occurred.[4]

» Spirituality

'Did traditional Aborigines have a religion?' Early ethnographers such as Collins believed they didn't, although he described initiation ceremonies and mortuary rites involving belief in an afterlife. The first anthropologists agreed. Anthropology—the study of the human species—arose as a scholarly discipline between the 1850s and 1890s. Ethnographers studied human societies through firsthand observation, but anthropology was seen as an exciting, new 'possible science of universal human custom'. In the 1890s, Walter Baldwin Spencer, an evolutionary biologist, and Frank Gillen, an Arrernte-speaking postmaster in Alice Springs, began research in Central Australia. They reported beliefs in reincarnation, spiritual conception and totems—religious emblems from nature that indigenous people see as part of their identity. In 1899, they published *The Native Tribes of Central Australia*, a book highly praised by Sir James Frazer, leading anthropologist of the time and author of *The Golden Bough*, a treatise on the 'evolution of the thoughts of man through the successive stages of magic, religion and science'. Frazer regarded Aboriginal Australians as lacking religion but possessing a belief-system based on 'magic'. This view was shared by Spencer and his 'band of brothers'—anthropologists Fison, Howitt, Gillen, Roth and Mathews—and later by Durkheim and Freud.[5] The idea of evolution from simple to complex forms dominated nineteenth-century intellectual thought. Religion was seen as having a progressive development, from primitive, non-rational, 'magical' belief-systems to the great world religions of Buddhism, Hinduism, Taoism, Judaism, Islam, and Christianity.

Bill Edwards, teacher, Uniting Church minister and fluent Pitjantjatjara-speaker, believes that Aboriginal beliefs constitute a religion because, 'Aboriginal systems of beliefs provide answers to the great universal religious questions of humankind, the questions about origins, meaning, purpose and destiny.'[6] Stanner's view was:

The Aborigines acknowledged that men's lives were under a power or force beyond themselves; that they venerated the places where such power or force was believed to concentrate; that they imposed a self-discipline to maintain a received tradition . . . we are dealing with lives of religious devotion.[7]

Aboriginal stories reveal a religious interpretation of the natural world focused on maintenance of fertility of humans and nature and the continuation of traditional society. Aborigines see traditional society as based on the spiritual. For example, there are several ingenious explanations for the moon's waxing and waning. The Iuwalarai of New South Wales told how there was a fertile green valley in the sky, peopled by round, shining moons which came out one by one, only to fall victim to the sun who cuts off thin slivers each night that become twinkling stars. Many myths explain the sun's setting and rising: the Wotjobaluk of northwest Victoria said that 'the sun was a woman, who, when she went to dig for yams, left her little son in the west. Wandering round the edge of the earth, she came back over the other side. When she dies she continued to do this.'[8] Throughout Aboriginal mythology the moon appears to be male and the sun female.

Ancestral Beings are the spirit powers who in the beginning emerged from the earth, sky or sea and journeyed across the land, creating its form and all living things. Some were able to transform themselves from human to animal form or animate to inanimate object and back again. Ancestral Beings interacted with human beings, gave birth to them, and gave them language and the 'Law'—correct social and religious practices. They are believed to be the source of the conception spirits that initiate pregnancy, their inherent power being released through rituals and ceremonies to ensure health, growth and to maintain and increase food supplies.

» Totemism and animism

Spencer saw Aboriginal rituals as pragmatic 'hunting magic'. In 'increase ceremonies' men mimed the actions of their totemic species in order to maintain and increase its numbers. The propagating powers of Ancestral Beings were concentrated in sacred increase sites, where ceremonies took place. Aboriginal beliefs are therefore totemist and animist. Animists maintain all natural objects possess a spirit or soul. Prime examples are Inuit societies, where every beach pebble contains its individual soul, or the Ainu of Japan, who regard every animal and plant as a spirit being. Tribal Australians believe in the presence of spiritual life-essence in the world and the interrelatedness of all living things, beliefs that are now called 'spirituality'.

Totemism is a relationship between an individual or group and an animal or plant or even such things as night, lust, itchiness or two women. Totems act as symbols in a belief system linking the human, natural and supernatural worlds. (The word 'totem' comes from a Native American language where it denotes group membership; its literal meaning is 'he/she/it is a relative of mine'.) Tribal Aborigines see themselves as associated with particular living or inanimate things and may share their names with their totems. It is often forbidden to kill, harm or eat your totem. Clan totems were conferred during the creation period and are inherited, symbolising the relationship of clan members to each other, their ancestors and to particular places.

» *Wandjina spirit figures painted inside a rock-shelter in the Kimberley. Wandjina (pronounced Wand-gin-a) are Ancestral Beings envisaged as having human form, but are often many times larger. They are spirits of the clouds and wear elaborate headdresses representing both hair and clouds. The rays that emanate from the headdress are feathers worn as decoration and the lightning they control. Wandjina are portrayed with eyes and nose but no mouth. Kimberley Aborigines have explained that the figures have no mouths because they control rain as well as thunder and lightning; if they had mouths, they might release unceasing rain upon the land. White in the paintings is associated with the towering white cumulonimbus clouds that herald the onset of the monsoon. These clouds are believed to be Wandjina spirits, who control fertility and regeneration of all life and punish people through lightning, cyclone or flood.*

Personal totems are conferred at conception or birth, when the spirit of the unborn child announces its identity.[9]

A person's totem is the essence of their spiritual past and is part of them from conception or birth. Leading Australian anthropologist Nicolas Peterson considers that Aboriginal religion is not strictly 'totemism' but it 'has many totems, and is probably unique in the degree of elaboration of its totemic forms and relationships. These symbols play a central role in religious ceremonies because they deal with people's relations to each other, to the landscape and to the ancestral past.'[10] Scholars of comparative religion agree.[11]

» Dreaming

Tribal Australians have a unique concept of the world that Spencer and Gillen immortalised as the 'Dreamtime' or 'Dreaming'—a literal translation of Arrernte 'alcheringa' or 'altyerrenge'. 'Alcheringa' means the 'Eternal' or 'Law' but 'Dreaming' is also appropriate—just as dreams are real to dreamers, so the doings of Ancestral Beings are real to believers. The Dreaming is the era of eternal beings, who existed in the past and still exist today.

Stanner preferred the term 'Dreaming' to 'Dreamtime' because the creative epoch is timeless and cyclic; western concepts of linear time are alien to Aboriginal thought. Through ritual, each generation experiences the present reality of the Dreaming.[12]

The Dreaming is a complex network of faith, knowledge and ritual that dominates all spiritual and practical aspects of Aboriginal life. The Dreaming lays down the structures of society, rules for social behaviour and ceremonies to maintain and increase the land's fertility. A totem is often described as 'my Dreaming'. The Dreaming comes from the land; it is a powerful living force that must be nurtured and maintained. Some Aboriginal views are:

- 'It's all linked up with people, land, religion. It's just like one big circle . . . The law is embedded in the stories.' (Emily Jane Walker, elder, Nambucca Heads, New South Wales, 1996)
- 'The Dreaming means our identity as people. It is the understanding of what we have around us.' (Merv Penrith, Wallaga Lake, New South Wales, 1996)
- 'By Dreaming, we mean the belief that long ago, these creatures started human society, they made all natural things . . . These Dreaming creatures were connected to special places and special roads or tracks or paths . . . the great creatures changed themselves into sites where their spirits stay . . . All the land is full of signs.' (Silas Roberts, Arnhem Land, Northern Territory, 1970s).[13]

The concept of the Dreaming does not suppose the world was created out of nothing, but assumes a pre-existing substance, such as mud or a featureless plain. Ancestral Beings lay dormant below the surface but then emerged, assuming the bodily forms of various humans, animals, birds and plants. They were neither wholly animal nor wholly human but in some sense both. They were shape-changing beings of immense power, who travelled across the land and sea, performing great deeds of creation, and now lie quiet in focal points of the landscape.

Imberombera, the great ancestress of Gagadju people, came across the sea to Arnhem Land. Her womb was filled with children and from her head were suspended woven grass or fibre bags called dillybags in which she carried yams, bulbs and tubers. She travelled far and wide, creating hills, creeks, plants and animals, and left behind her many spirit children, giving a different language to each group. In Central Australia, Kuniya, the carpet snake, camped by a waterhole on a large flat sandhill that turned to stone and became Uluru. Wilkuda the hunter threw down the skin of a giant kangaroo he had killed and it became Lake Eyre. In his canoe, powerful Ngurunderi chased the great codfish down the Murray River, where it swished its tail, creating wide bends. When Ngurunderi at last caught the cod in Lake Alexandrina, he sliced it into pieces and tossed them back into the lake where they became new species of fish.[14]

» Songlines

As Ancestral Beings travelled across the featureless land, they transformed it: a snake's meandering track became a river valley, eggs laid by the Rainbow Serpent became huge, round boulders, a group of sisters was chased up into the sky and became the constellation called the Pleiades. Routes taken by Ancestral Beings are called dreaming tracks or songlines, for the Ancestral Beings sang as they formed the land, laid down the Law and 'sang up' the country into life. They left songs as a record of their doings, teaching them to their human offspring. Each place where an event occurred was marked by a named, sacred site with its own story, called a story place. It is believed that performing the right songs and ceremonies at particular points along a ritual track gives people direct access to the Dreaming.

A songline is a long sequence of short verses that form a sung map of an Ancestral Being's creative journey. Song cycles have many verses that must be sung in the correct order. Each verse records the events of a particular site and is repeated several times. Aboriginal elders travelled along songlines with their young people, telling the stories and singing the songs of the sites, so that children acquired a mental map of their country. The words are often special song words in ceremonial language or from other tribal languages. All Aboriginal men were expected to learn them, and the process began at initiation. Elders took initiates to sacred sites at night and chanted the relevant lines over and over until they were word-perfect. After years of teaching, the man with the best memory became his clan's main 'songman'. Songmen also experienced new songs through dreams; this was seen as the 'finding' of a pre-existing dreaming song. Epic tribal songs were accurately preserved and knowledge of them conveyed great prestige and power. There are still songmen and women in Central Australia, where songlines commemorating the location of every waterhole were once vital to survival.[15]

Story places may be unmodified 'natural' features, such as waterholes, or can be marked by stone arrangements or rock art. Some dreaming tracks crossed hundreds of kilometres and several tribal territories. The final stopping place on a mythological path may be marked by a rock where the Creative Ancestor's body was transformed into stone or by a rock painting, where it painted its own image on to the wall. The ritual cycle ensured that sites were renewed through regular visits, when sacred paintings were touched up. Sadly, retouching has now virtually ceased, because the last specialist rock-painters have passed away.

» Oral traditions

Without written language, people relied on oral transmission to perpetuate culture. Globally, there are three forms of oral traditions—history, legends and myths— although they sometimes overlap. History is often based on genealogies, but Aboriginal Australians were remarkably ahistorical in outlook. Some Maori can recite their descent from the time their ancestors reached New Zealand 800 years ago. Similarly in Greece, records of actual events were passed down orally, as in Homer's *Iliad*. Legends are semi-historical narratives about the deeds of past heroes, for example King Arthur, while myths are stories relating the doings of supernatural beings or explaining the characteristics of living creatures.

Aboriginal stories and songs divide into secular and sacred, with a progression from one to the other. Children heard 'just so' stories of how the echidna (the porcupine of Australia) got his spines or why the crow is black, and also frightening, cautionary tales of monsters, such as the Bunyip, who lay in wait for children who dawdled or wandered off from camp. This 'just so' story from the Gunbalang in Arnhem Land tells how turtles got their shells and the echidnas their spines:

> In the beginning, Echidna Woman and Freshwater Tortoise were in human shape. But one day they quarrelled about a snail, for both wanted to eat it. At last Tortoise, in a rage, picked up a bundle of light bamboo spears and threw them at Echidna; they stuck in her back and became quills. Echidna retaliated by picking up a large flat stone and throwing it at Tortoise: it stuck to his back, like a shell. That is how they became what they are today.[16]

As children grew older, there were more serious stories that explained life and death, relations between people and the moral code, and the Dreaming. Lighter 'gossip' songs dealt with everyday incidents, particularly gossip about 'sweethearts'.

A public or 'outside' version of major myths was told to the whole community, but further, higher levels of meaning were revealed after initiation. Sacred songs enshrined special beliefs or instructions from Ancestral Beings, and some were acted out in ritual. The more important myths were 'owned' by certain tribal elders. Among the Arrernte people, only men who belonged to a certain stretch of country and owned the associated stories were entitled to repeat them and perform the associated rituals.

In Central Australia there is a tradition of group singing—men together or women together or both. Songs consist of a short phrase repeated over and over accompanied by boomerang clap sticks, the melodic lines being a series of descending patterns. Further north there is more individual singing. Most traditional songs are accompanied by clap sticks, the didgeridoo in Arnhem Land and, in part of Cape York, by skin drums.[17]

» DIDGERIDOOS «

The didgeridoo, a drone pipe, is the main musical instrument of indigenous Australia. Originally it was confined to tropical Australia, reflecting the availability of straight, hollow pieces of stringy-bark or ironwood, Darwin stringy-bark (*Eucalyptus tetrodonta*) being particularly commonly used. The interiors have been eaten out by termites, reducing them to tubes with thin walls that give out a ringing tone when flicked with a finger. Didgeridoos may have evolved from emu decoys—short, hollow wooden tubes used to lure emus and brush-turkeys by imitating their calls. The onomatopoeic name comes from a northeast Arnhem Land language. Didgeridoos are made from tubes that average 140 cm (55 inches) in length. Different lengths produce different sounds, and sometimes a resonator is used, the far end being placed in a big shell or, nowadays, a metal bucket.

The largest didgeridoos are 4.5 m (15 ft) long and need four men to carry them. Painted decorations are added for ceremonial use. Didgeridoos have mouthpieces made of gum or beeswax, and are traditionally played by a male performer encircling the mouthpiece with his lips and blowing directly into it. His tongue lies flat and his lips vibrate, producing two or three different notes. A continuous sound is generated by circular breathing, whereby air is inhaled through the nose by rapid sniffs while air held in the cheeks is simultaneously exhaled into the instrument. Didgeridoos were used in both sacred and secular contexts and have now become pan-Australian instruments.

» *Didgeridoo played by Wadamu on Elcho Island, Northern Territory.*

« »

One of the most widespread myths concerns the Rainbow Serpent—a powerful symbol of both the creative and destructive power of nature. The rainbow is thought of as a great snake or serpent, sometimes male and sometimes female. The Rainbow Serpent forms a link between earthly places such as waterfalls, where he manifests himself, and the sky above, to which he raises himself. His symbols are quartz crystals in the south and pearl shell in the north—both brilliant, shimmering, iridescent substances containing his power. Both are used in rain-making ceremonies, for the Rainbow Serpent appears in the sky with the showers and storms that bring the rain at the end of the dry season. In the Western Desert he guards waterholes where pearl shells are stored, and brings rain and life to a thirsty land. Whirlwinds are said to be the Rainbow Serpent's head looking above the earth as he crawls beneath. Everywhere the rainbow symbolises rain, water and fertility. In the monsoonal north, rain-making rites were conducted before the wet season. A whistling sound was heard before the Rainbow Snake's appearance—the noise of the storm whistling through his horns. Many tribes believed that without the Rainbow Serpent the earth would become parched and life would cease.[18]

» Language

The main groupings of Aboriginal languages were as different from each other as German and French or Hindi and Bengali (see chapter 6). There was no common language across the continent, but there was extensive contact between neighbouring language groups for trade, ceremonial life and the exchange of marriage partners. Often children would have parents who spoke different languages; they used their mother's tongue in the earliest years but most changed to their father's language before reaching puberty. Quite often they learnt three or four languages, and might be able to understand several more. Indeed the Original Australians were possibly the most multilingual people in the world.

Dialect chains enabled communication between different groups. Group A understood group B, group B understood C, who understood D, but A might not be able to understand C, or B understand D. Long dialect chains existed in central Queensland and the Western Desert, where dialect chains extending 3000 km (1850 miles) have been identified. Sadly, over a hundred Aboriginal languages have now disappeared, another hundred are almost dead and only about twenty are still being learnt by children.

All Aboriginal languages have a rich vocabulary and complex grammar. Linguistics professor Bob Dixon regards Australian languages as more similar in their grammatical organisation to the classical languages of Greek, Latin and Sanskrit than to modern ones such as English.[19] They have conjugation for verbs and declension for nouns, and many also have a gender system for nouns. The Dyirbal language of north Queensland has four genders—masculine, feminine, neuter and edible. The edible gender refers to food plants, a useful grammatical category in a rainforest environment with over 700 plant species, of which only one third are edible and many are poisonous. The edible gender was an ingenious way of teaching children the difference.

Aboriginal languages each contain up to 10 000 words, a similar number to spoken English. Special features are pronouns that distinguish not only 'you' singular and 'you' plural but also 'you-two', 'you-many', 'we-two', 'we-many-of-us', 'they two' and 'they many'.

The languages vary widely in vocabulary and grammatical structure but also generally resemble each other and usually employ a modest range of speech sounds of similar type. Words tend to be of two or more syllables and to end in a vowel. The main stress is usually on the first syllable. Some consonants such as 's' and 'v' are rarely used and 'ng' (as in singer) often occurs at the beginning of a word. There are frequently only three vowels. These are:

- 'a' as in 'mat' or 'but', or sometimes long as in 'far' (written 'aa')
- 'i' as in 'bit' (never as in 'bite') or sometimes long as in 'steel' (written 'ii')
- 'u' as in 'put' or 'boot' (never as in 'but').

Word meanings were extended to cover new items. Horses became known in the Sydney region as 'yaraman', meaning long-toothed one, and this name spread quickly with the colonists. Money was termed 'gadna', signifying pebble, by the Arabana of South Australia; telephone wires were known as 'yooroo', a spider's web, by the Gooniyandi of Western Australia. Aeroplanes were called 'kantyal', meaning eagle-hawk (wedge-tailed eagle) by the Wunambal in the Kimberley. The Andegerebinha people of the Northern Territory have also extended the meaning of their word for eaglehawk—they use it to mean 'policeman', because 'he swoops down and grabs you'.[20]

» Medicine men

Healers, 'clever men' or medicine men possessed spiritual powers derived from the Dreaming. Power came from an initiation ritual involving rebirth, symbolised by new 'insides' and magical substances.

The public account of rituals adopted by dreaming spirits in creating Arrernte medicine men was that the candidate:

goes to the mouth of their cave, and when they notice him there at daybreak, they throw an invisible lance which pierces his neck from behind, passes through his tongue, making a large hole in it, and comes out through his mouth . . . he drops dead and is carried into the cave. The spirits then remove his internal organs and provide him with a new set, together with a supply of magical stones on which his power will depend. He later comes to life again but is for a time insane. When he is partly recovered he is led back by the spirits to his own people.[21]

Photographs of Arrernte medicine men show the telltale, finger-sized round hole pierced through the tongue. Other rituals involved putting the initiate into a trance. Some healers had earlier suffered an extraordinary ordeal or near-death experience; there was no direct inheritance of healing powers, although in some regions sons and brothers of healers also became medicine men. Healers had special skills but were not full-time specialists and did not hold political power. Their role was to provide diagnosis, treatment, advice, explanation and reassurance, a role comparable to Western psychiatrists.

Techniques used included 'singing' patients into the desired state or 'extracting' harmful items from the body by rubbing, sucking or manipulation. The great value of such healers is their ability to provide culturally relevant, authoritative explanations and reassurance in an understandable, non-threatening way. The few healers who still exist have therefore sometimes been employed as health workers in medical services in outback Australia, but some preach strongly against injections, painkillers and evacuation of infants with chronic diarrhoea or other afflictions, and their employment by medical services is, as a result, controversial.

» Magic and sorcerers

There were three sorts of 'magic'—'productive magic' (fertility rites, increase ceremonies, rain-making and love magic), 'protective magic' (healing or counteracting the effects of accident or misfortune) and 'destructive magic' (sorcery intended to bring injury, illness or death to others).

The role of a medicine man was usually distinct from that of a sorcerer. Sorcerers were universally feared as causers of death and stealers of the soul but some tribes thought power for good or evil resided in the same person. Western Desert medicine men or 'Men of High Degree' both cured sorcery victims and used sorcery themselves.

'Pointing bones'—skewers made from the long-bones of men, emus or kangaroos—are perhaps the most famous of Aboriginal artefacts. The tip was sharply pointed and the butt covered with resin. String made from human hair was attached to the butt. Pointing the bone caused evil force to enter the victim's body and extract the life essence, which flowed back into the bone and was captured in the resin.

Bone-pointing was practised by sorcerers and other senior, initiated men and women, who made sure the victims became aware of the evil spell, sometimes by leaving the bone where they would find it. Given belief in its power, the victim often fell ill and died, for this was a psychological weapon. If it failed, it was explained that either the ritual was not performed properly or the counteracting magic was too strong.

In Central Australia when a plane first flew overhead medicine men attempted to drive away the monster by pointing bones at it. Belief in sorcery is so universal that most deaths apart from those caused by accidents and fighting are still attributed to it in traditional communities.[22]

Other objects associated with sorcery were kadaitja shoes, made from emu feathers, marsupial fur string and sacred blood. The shoes were worn by parties seeking to avenge an ill, as they disguised the identity of those who went kadaitja, for such are the tracking abilities of desert Aborigines that without emu-feather shoes the attackers' individual footprints could be identified. In Central Australia, the men who wore them first underwent the painful ordeal of having their little toes dislocated. The little toes then acted as 'eyes', seeing any roots or other obstacles in the way. In a typical kadaitja raid, the avengers would creep towards the victim's camp and the sorcerer would throw an invisible spear into the victim's back. Then the sorcerer would apply a magical stone to the wound, making it disappear without trace. The kadaitja party then hid and watched, and if the victim was not dead within two or three days, they went and killed him. Sometimes the victim was warned of his peril in a dream. Myths tell how dreams were made by birds, and when Willy-wagtail saw a bone being pointed, he told Cockatoo, who put a dream inside the victim's head, telling him who was pointing the bone so that he might ask his own medicine man to ward off the evil spell. Kadaitja raids were therefore usually performed at night to keep them secret from the birds.

» Shamans

Are there shamans in Aboriginal Australia? The word comes from Siberia, where 'saman' is 'one who is excited or raised'. Most writers use 'shaman' generically to describe a person who enters a trance-like state to gain spiritual inspiration or effect mystical cures. Among hunter-gatherers this is usually achieved through drumming, singing, dance and physical exhaustion, without the use of hallucinogenic substances. Anthropologist Matthias Guenther regards Australian medicine men as shamans and Australia as sharing in two key shamanic concepts: a multi-layered universe and two periods of existence, the Dreamtime and the present day. The tiers of the Australian universe are connected vertically by a rainbow, mountain or cosmic tree.[23]

Australian Aborigines also present the most thorough instance of 'world-enchantment', where the world of living people is strongly imbued with spiritual significance. Landscapes bear the all-pervasive marks of Ancestral Beings and totemic spirits, whose songlines cross the country.

» Women healers and bush medicine

Women played a major role in health care, for older women were the most knowledgeable practitioners of bush medicine, herbal remedies and midwifery. They also knew the properties of bush foods. Some plants are poisonous unless specially treated. For instance, nuts of *Macrozamia* and other cycads are toxic unless the poisons are removed by fermentation or lengthy leaching in water. Cycad kernels are safe to eat only if frothy or mouldy, when they are ground into a starchy 'flour' and baked into cycad 'bread'. Other fruits are known for their health-giving qualities—the wild plum (*Terminalia ferdinandiana*) is probably the world's richest source of vitamin C.

Many ailments, such as insect- or snakebites, wounds, boils, toothache, constipation and diarrhoea, were treated with barks, roots, leaves or minerals. A paste of ochre heals sores, rich goanna fat soothes burns, and eucalyptus gum salves toothache and dental cavities. Soaked wattlebark was drunk as cough medicine, gumleaves acted as poultices for snakebite, headaches and boils, and stringy-bark was used as bandages. A common treatment for snakebite was to suck the wound and bind the limb tightly. Cramped legs were cured by ant bite. Wounds were treated with clay or mud. A mixture of powdered white pipeclay, hot ashes and fat was sometimes applied as a poultice, and spider's web could be used to staunch a flow of blood.[24]

» Traditional life

Childhood

Aboriginal people realised the connection between sexual intercourse and pregnancy but believed a spiritual event had to be involved for conception to happen. Most thought a spirit child must enter the mother to give a baby life. Spirit babies were believed to live on the branches of certain trees so that women who walked underneath became mothers. In the Kimberley, spirit children were supposed to live in waterholes and to enter a woman's womb after her husband had seen one in a dream. When a woman became aware she was pregnant, she recalled the first signs of morning sickness and attributed conception to the totem of the place where that had occurred. Elsewhere, a woman who wanted a child would go to a spirit centre, such as a waterhole, and wait with legs apart, or hope that a spirit child might follow her back to camp.[25]

When birth was imminent, the mother and some other women left camp for a birthing place, generally a shady rock-shelter with a soft earth floor. There were special rituals to dispose of the afterbirth and to encourage lactation. At birth, the skin of Aboriginal babies is light in colour, so ashes and charcoal mixed with goanna fat or mother's milk were applied to prevent sunburn. After a few days, the skin darkens, except on the soles and palms. Babies were breastfed for an average of 2–4 years. Toddlers were fed eggs, bone marrow, grubs and cooked lizard tails. Babies slept in large wooden 'coolamons' (oval carrying-dishes) filled with sand that could easily be changed. On cold nights the mother scooped a shallow hole in sand or earth, lit a small fire in it, and, when it had burned down, placed the baby in the cradle in the fire-warmed hole and covered it with warm ashes. Babies were carried everywhere on the hip, under one arm or slung across the small of the back with feet through one arm and neck through the other, where they slept peacefully. (Childless women carried dingo pups slung the same way and used them for warmth on frosty, 'five-dog nights'.)

Babies were known by their relationship to others, such as 'little sister'. Later, nicknames were bestowed, some of which lasted a lifetime. Personal names were not given until children began to walk. Names given to boys during initiation remained secret and were never spoken aloud. When Aborigines first met white people, they often asked to be named. Surnames were frequently acquired by adopting the names of 'bosses' or cattle properties or those of white fathers, which is why many Aborigines have such English-sounding names. In tribal communities, traditional naming continues, except that nowadays Christian first names are bestowed at birth and totem, clan or 'skin names' may be used as surnames. 'Skin names' are ways of subdividing people in broad communities numbering, usually, thousands. I had the honour of receiving a 'skin name'—Nangari—after several years' fieldwork with a tribal group in the Territory. Classificatory family trees are exceedingly complicated but it only took elder Elsie Raymond a minute to work out in her head my relationship with every other person present. In fact, we all ended up in gales of laughter for I proved to be the mother of one of my fellow researchers.

» *Aboriginal children sleeping behind a windbreak and between little fires to keep warm in the 1930s in Central Australia, where winter temperatures can drop below freezing at night. They were surrounded by warm air from the low campfires of hot embers burning throughout the night and so were not cold, whereas Europeans sleeping on the ground with clothes and blankets were seldom warm at night.*

Traditional upbringing was reasonably carefree, but children learnt the moral code of caring and sharing and skills for later life. They were taught to recognise footprints in the sand, first those of their mother and then the tracks of every Australian creature. As Basedow related: 'One often has occasion to walk into a camp and find a . . . pitifully howling little urchin pleading to be taken to its mother. The only aid forthcoming from the blacks will be to direct the attention of the child to the footprints of the parent in the sand, and to urge it to follow them up.'[26] Toddlers stayed with grandparents in camp while their parents went out foraging, and soon began learning stories, songs and dance steps.

Toys were few. Games for young children imitated adult activities. Miniature spears were made for boys, who went out together hunting birds and lizards or engaging in mock battles. Later they learnt to throw spears at moving targets such as bark discs bowled along the ground. Cross-shaped pieces of wood with arms of unequal length bounced along when bowled, imitating a kangaroo's hopping gait. Girls were given little digging sticks, baskets, carrying-dishes or miniature grindstones and encouraged to help gather and process fruits and seeds. They also had 'dolls' in the form of twigs, twisted roots or pieces of clay, decorated for corroborees with red and white paint. Desert girls played a game called 'mani-mani', using leaves in the sand to re-enact incidents of camp life. String games (similar to cat's-cradle) were popular, using string made from natural fibre or human hair. Some girls could make 200 complicated patterns, representing crocodile nests with eggs or turtles on a log. Balls were made of grass or fur tied with vines or string and covered with beeswax. One ball game was a sort of aerial soccer; the ball was kicked into the air and the aim was to keep it aloft using only the feet. Another game, which was a bit more like rugby, involved two teams of about six players throwing the ball among themselves until their opponents intercepted. In a Queensland game that resembled hockey, stone balls were hit with bent-ended sticks. In Arnhem Land, boys would take a large, oblong bark slab, heat it, bend its tip upwards and polish the underside with resin and hot ashes. Then could then stand on the small sledge, propel it with one foot like a scooter and slide across soft mud at tremendous speed.[27]

Education involved children learning survival skills, appropriate ways to behave towards other family members, their obligations to each other, religion and kinship—the relationships that exist between relatives. By the time children reached puberty, they had learnt a great deal and knew what behaviour was expected of them. Boys and girls were treated much the same when young, but this changed as they went through their respective initiations into adulthood.

Social organisation

The smallest social unit was the family—a man, his wife or wives and his children. Families were often self-contained, self-supporting units, and in harsh environments might forage alone.[28] Most Aboriginal children grew up in an extended family, and a few such households camped and foraged together. A typical band comprised three to six households totalling about fifteen to fifty people, including three or even four generations. Often the men in one band were from different clans, because young husbands usually did bride service by going to live and hunt temporarily in the band of their wife's parents.

As they grew up, Aboriginal children learnt their family tree and how they should address and behave towards each relative. As well as biological relationships, there are 'classificatory' ones. Many Aboriginal children appear to have several mothers and fathers, because they also call their maternal aunts 'mother' and paternal uncles 'father'.

Initiation of girls

A girl at puberty went through certain rituals to mark her transition to womanhood, but because these were celebrated at the menarche, the timing of which was unpredictable, ceremonies were small in scale. Northern coastal tribes had the most elaborate rites, where a girl spent a few days away from camp with close female relations. As Catherine Berndt witnessed in Arnhem Land: 'The girl is a striking figure as she comes out of seclusion, smeared with red ochre and brightly decorated, her white forehead band shining. At the climax, all the women escort her at dawn to a freshwater stream or lagoon; and even the oldest among them forget their age as they splash and sing in the shallows.'[29] Afterwards the girl may participate in women's secret ceremonies relating to pregnancy, birth and lactation. During initiation some girls were purified by a smoking ceremony or ritual bathing. There was no tattooing but cicatrisation was widespread. In order to demonstrate their conquest of fear and pain, during mourning or simply as adornment, both boys and girls had cuts inflicted on their chests, stomachs, thighs or buttocks with stone or shell knives; the weals rose in pronounced ridges after ashes or clay were rubbed into the wounds. Body decoration in the Western Desert included patterned burns, made by holding hot coals against the skin. Some tribes removed two joints from the little finger of a female-initiate; on the Daly River, a ligature of spider's web was used to cut circulation until the end dropped off. A similar operation using cobweb was performed on girls of some east coast tribes and 'when the joint mortifies, the hand is held in an ant-bed for an hour or so, for the joint to be eaten off'.[30]

Male initiation

Boys were usually initiated at puberty, when the beard began to grow. The process involved lengthy separation from camp and the company of women. Senior men took boys off to seclusion in order to train and learn self-sufficiency. Women had an important role in the preparatory ceremonies and in providing food for celebrants, but were rigidly excluded from later sacred rituals. Initiation usually involved severe

The Original Australians

» *Aboriginal girls with decorative cicatrices in the Kimberley, Western Australia, in the 1930s. Body-scarring was practised throughout Australia. Scars were cut or burnt into the skin of the chest, abdomen, shoulders, arms, back, buttocks or thighs. Burns were made with hot coals, firesticks or heated stones and cuts were incised with sharp stones or shells and more recently with glass. Filling cuts with ashes or clay mixed with grease produced raised scars. Cicatrices were arranged in regular patterns of lines, dots or circles. Children usually received their first scars at puberty, with more added until adulthood. The patterns denoted identity and affiliations with a particular social group.*

tests, which caused fear and pain, and culminated in the ordeal of tooth avulsion, circumcision or depilation to mark the novitiates' passage out of women's control. It was a long period of physical and mental trial, testing and the gradual learning of tribal lore. Initiation transformed boys into men, allowing them to marry and father children, learn the sacred doctrines and on maturity take a full part in the secret sacred life of the group.[31]

Initiation is a symbolic enactment of death and rebirth. Some tribes believe the young boy is swallowed by an Ancestral Being, who eventually vomits him out as a man. Others see the initiate as returning to the Fertility Mother's womb to be reborn, his foreskin being cut to symbolise severing the umbilical cord. In some northern regions, circumcision was followed later by sub-incision. Circumcision seems to have originated inland in the Top End but it never reached the Darwin region and some coastal Kimberley Aborigines whom Dampier met in 1688 had their foreteeth missing but were not circumcised.

» An Aboriginal boy with his face painted for a ceremony, Central Australia, 1960s.

Special artefacts widely used in ceremonies were bullroarers—thin, oval pieces of wood, suspended from a string at one end. When whirled round at arm's length, bull-roarers make a weird, buzzing sound that becomes louder the faster they are swung. Aborigines interpreted the strange, high-pitched whine as the voice of an Ancestral Being. Bullroarers were used in many other countries and throughout Australia, except in the southwest and northwest corners and Tasmania. Bullroarers are no longer sacred and are sold in tourist shops. The most secret sacred Australian artefacts are 'tjuringa' or 'churinga'—elongated, flat pieces of wood or stone incised with pre-dominantly geometric designs, particularly spirals and circles. Most tjuringa are about 60 x 8 cm (24 x 3 inches) long. Traditionally, sacred boards and stones were stored in remote caves, but now some special 'keeping places' have been built for security.

Education of initiates continued throughout life, for knowledge meant power, responsibility and regular ceremonial duties. After initiation, usually at about the age of fourteen, the young man was welcomed back to his own group and was entitled to marry, although it might be many years before he obtained a wife.

Kinship laws were designed to avoid incest, and marriage partners were taken from outside the family group, although there were regions, such as the Mitchell River, Queensland, where first and second cousin marriages were preferred. Most Aboriginal regional communities were divided into two named, ritually distinct, intermarrying halves (moieties) and some were further subdivided. The divisions made it clear to everyone who they could marry. A spouse was selected from a different kinship group, usually the other half of their society.

Arrangements in many groups were made by the girl's maternal uncle. In some northern tribes it was virtually compulsory for a married man to see that his sister's daughter was married to his wife's mother's brother. In other words, there was an exchange of nieces between two men of succeeding generational levels, or in Western terms, his niece married her maternal great uncle. Not only did the bride have no say in the matter but she was forced to marry a much older man. On the other hand, widows were often given in marriage to younger men.

Strong taboos banned contact between a man and his mother-in-law, who were forbidden to converse or even look at each other. The reason for mother-in-law avoidance becomes clear in the context of the betrothal system. At the end of an initiation ceremony, when the whole intermarrying community was present, a meeting was held to arrange boys' betrothals. A woman in the correct relationship to a boy was chosen—*not* to be the man's wife but to be the *mother* of his wife. The young man might have to wait decades for her to produce a daughter, but meanwhile they could not even look at each other. This was to prevent the possibility of sexual intercourse between the two and the young man marrying his own daughter.

Girls were customarily promised as wives when they were babies, or even beforehand to men old enough to be their fathers or even grandfathers; a ten-year age gap was normal and sometimes it was twenty or even thirty years. Most Australian Aboriginal societies were polygamous, and many older men had at least two wives. A man's status depended on the number of his wives; the maximum recorded among the Tiwi was twenty-nine. In western Arnhem Land, two or three wives were the average, with the maximum about six, but in northeast Arnhem Land ten or twelve wives were not unusual. In desert regions, men usually had one or two wives, rarely three.

Polygamy still exists in Aboriginal society: about 40 per cent of marriages in some northern and central tribes still follow 'customary law' and polygamous tribal marriages still occur. Over a lifetime, most tribal Aborigines have more than one spouse, the difference between the sexes being that women are allowed only one husband at once. Traditionally, there were few or no unmarried women, for widows were usually remarried, often to a deceased husband's brother. This ensured that old people always had relatives responsible for feeding them.

Many girls were married before puberty. Groote Eylandt girls went to live with their 'promised' husband at the age of 8–9 years, Tiwi girls at 8–10 years, and Warlpiri girls at 9–12 years. However, girls of the central desert tribe did not marry until they reached puberty, which came later because of their strenuous lives and malnourishment (14–15 years).[32] Early marriage for girls is readily explained in economic terms. Females were economic commodities as well as sexual objects, valued both as active foragers and as producers of the next generation of food-producers. A girl therefore often married young, moved to her husband's clan territory and was 'apprenticed' to her older co-wives to learn the distribution of food in her new home. Prior to marriage, the future bridegroom, unless he already had one or more wives, might pay 'bride-price', living in the unmarried men's camp and hunting to support himself and provide some food for his future bride's parents. Sometimes after marriage the couple stayed for some years with the girl's parents so that the son-in-law could hunt for them, but later they moved back to the husband's traditional territory. As producers of the more reliable and larger part of food consumed, females were extremely valuable economically. Women reached peak efficiency as food collectors in middle age, when no longer tied down with pregnancy and child care, whereas men's greatest productivity as hunters came at about 25 years of age, when they had become fit, strong, experienced hunters. The system of marrying young girls to much older men meant that old men unable to hunt received plentiful food from their wives and younger relatives.

Aboriginal marriage was usually devoid of elaborate rites. Often the bride was simply handed over after she had been ritually deflowered. In some northern tribes, female kinsfolk pierced the girl's hymen with a digging stick and then led her to her promised husband. Fire symbolised marriage, and when the bride was to be handed over two firesticks were tapped and placed beside the man, the bride came to him and together they kindled a fire; the firestick and grooved timber symbolise male and female union. Elsewhere, as in Central Australia, a group of male elders would take a girl out into the desert and perform introcision—cutting the vulva—with a stone knife, and then all have forced intercourse with her.[33]

Aboriginal concepts of beauty stress youth. Sexual attraction was not so tied to appearance but was often 'ensured' by singing and 'love magic'. The most desirable man was a newly initiated youth, the most attractive girl one who had just reached puberty, a girl with small rounded breasts not yet drooping from years of suckling. Other attractive features are a healthy body, clear skin, a good crop of hair, a straight nose (in Arnhem Land), or a broad nose and long legs and arms (in the Western Desert). To call a woman 'bony' or 'skinny' was to use a term of abuse, implying she was no good at the food quest. (When Prince Charles and Princess Diana visited Uluru, local Aboriginal women commented on her thinness—'Poor lady, she can't afford to eat.') Traditional hunter-gatherers were so active, however, that most were very slim.[34]

Some couples eloped—a very dangerous undertaking, because once a girl was promised or married to a man she was his property, and at times the lovers were pursued and killed. On occasion, girls were captured and carried off by men of another clan; some young men became frustrated by the long wait for a wife and went on women-hunting raids, ignoring the danger of payback killings to avenge the loss. Wives were lent, shared and exchanged, pre-marital and extra-marital sex with 'sweethearts' was rife, and there were many 'affairs' between wives of old men and young bachelors. There was little or no homosexuality, but enthusiastic heterosexuality. In many Aboriginal societies, such as those in the Great Victoria Desert, intercourse before puberty and marriage was countenanced and even encouraged; in Western Arnhem Land in the 1960s, 'a girl may have her first full sexual association at the age of about nine, sometimes earlier, a boy not until twelve to fourteen or so'.[35] This early sexual activity continues and Aboriginal communities have extremely high rates of teenage pregnancy.

Sex even came into punishment, for if a woman transgressed customary law or some charge was trumped-up against her, she was offered a choice of forfeiting her life or, 'if she is willing to go out into the bush, making herself available to all the local men for as long as they wish, the episode will be overlooked and no more will be said.' Stanner recounted that on the Daly River in 1958 his friend Durmugam sadly told him that his second-youngest wife 'had been sexually abused, a traditional penalty, by a number of men, mainly Maringar [his enemies], on the ground that she had illicitly seen a bullroarer in Durmugam's camp—a pretext, he said vehemently, a lie. Would he, who knew the dangers, be likely to have a bullroarer there? They were all hidden in the bush.'[36]

Ceremonies

Apart from initiations, the major rituals are increase and rain-making ceremonies and funerals. Common elements are chanting, dancing, body-decoration and headdresses such as huge 'cones' decorated with bird-down in Central Australia or masks in the Torres Strait Islands.

One of the most elaborate increase ceremonies is the Kunapipi fertility cult. Kunapipi is a great Earth Mother, the living essence and symbol of fertility, and much of the ritual centres on procreation, pregnancy, childbirth and eternal renewal. During the fertility ceremonies, ordinary kinship taboos are ignored and a man may have sex with his tribal sister or mother-in-law. In eastern Arnhem Land and on the Roper River, young girls were deflowered with a specially shaped boomerang on the ceremonial ground, followed by ritual plural intercourse. The Kunapipi cult and some of the practices continue, for when I began fieldwork in the Northern Territory in 1988 I was strongly warned by the Sacred Sites Authority to beware of invitations to participate in any ceremonies.

Many increase ceremonies were simple rituals performed to nurture the creative powers of an Ancestral Being and thereby increase the population of the natural species associated with that Being. For example, in the Musgrave Ranges southeast of Uluru is a large, curiously eroded boulder believed to be the totemic body of the pink cockatoo woman, Tukalili. By pounding the boulder, Aborigines release the life essence of cockatoos, which rises into the air in the form of rock dust and fertilises living female cockatoos, causing them to lay more eggs.[37]

Equally important in the dry heart of the continent were rain-making ceremonies, which were aimed at invoking the help of the Rainbow Serpent or other Ancestral Beings. Procedures for making rain varied widely but often involved the use of crystals of quartz or calcite or pearl shells, which were sometimes placed in a waterhole. At Yiwarlarlay, the major rain-making site of the Lightning Brothers southwest of Katherine, Northern Territory, thousands of 'rain cuts' have been made in the soft sandstone of an imposing rock outcrop. It seems that there were singing and dancing and then each man present cut a groove in the rock to make 'Old Man Rain' bleed.[38]

All these ceremonies focus on continuance of life or life after death and Aboriginal funerals are long and elaborate. Death marks only the end of bodily existence, as the soul is indestructible. Spirits may have two forms, the soul itself and a potentially malignant spirit able to harm the living. When death comes, body and soul complete the life cycle by returning to their 'bone and soul country', whence the spirit may be reincarnated and again enter a woman's body to be reborn. Rituals enable undying spirits of the dead to return safely to a spirit home or totemic centre by way of the sky, a waterhole or an offshore island. A terrible fate in Aboriginal society was for one's corpse to be left for animals or birds to consume; interments were protected from dingoes by large stone cairns. Enemies were left unburied but never kinsfolk, except in extreme circumstances.

At funerals, close relatives wailed and injured themselves—the mother, daughters and wives of a dead man scratched their faces or hit their heads with sharp stones until blood flowed, and father, brothers and sons gashed their thighs. The dead person's possessions were ritually destroyed or buried in the grave and the place of death was avoided. Western Desert people burnt the deceased's shelter and belongings and moved their camp far away. These customs arose partly from grief and partly to keep evil, trickster spirits of the dead away from the living.

Burial methods included placement inside hollow trees, log coffins or bark cylinders, cremation (sometimes used when burial had to be quick, or one year after death as among the Wik, who used desiccation), interment or mummification on freestanding platforms—the skull and long-bones were then placed in a rock-shelter. When the body was interred, an aperture was left in the earth mound to allow the soul to escape and sometimes fires were lit to keep it warm until it departed.[39]

» *Carved trees surround the grave of Yuranigh, who guided Sir Thomas Mitchell on his last explorations and died about 1850. Nicking of outlines into the outer surface of trees was common in Australia, but the technique of removing a bark slab to carve the solid wood with geometric designs was confined to central and northern New South Wales. Carved trees were particularly associated with burials and ceremonial grounds and the patterns of spirals, circles, sinuous lines and concentric diamonds resemble those used to decorate skin cloaks and wooden artefacts. Eventually, bark regrowth tends to cover the carving. Very few living carved trees survive, and the group round Yuranigh's grave is Australia's largest still in existence. The site is open to the public and lies 5 km (3 miles) southeast of Molong and 30 km (20 miles) northwest of Orange in central New South Wales.*

Funerals of tribal elders continued for weeks. There are traditional prohibitions on uttering the name of the dead person. For instance, when I went to Uluru in the 1980s to help Aboriginal women record their dances and ceremonies, I found that another Josephine had recently died, and I was introduced as 'kunmanara'—'she whose name may not be spoken'. Fortunately, such taboos last only for a period. Words resembling the deceased's name are also banned and often replaced by a different word from a neighbouring tribe. Some Aboriginal organisations produce obituaries of leading Aborigines without mentioning their names.

Photographs can also cause problems. My first experience of this came in 1980 when I was working for the Australian Heritage Commission on site protection and visited Alice Springs to meet Aboriginal women about a sacred site threatened by a development proposal. They were camping near the site and asked me to take photographs in support of their campaign. Tragically, one night a tent caught fire and a child died, so they asked me to destroy all group photos. Nowadays, photographs of famous Aboriginal people are everywhere, and it is considered neither desirable nor practicable to withdraw those images when the person dies.

Elders

It took 30 or 40 years for Aborigines to be taught the whole encyclopedia of spiritual knowledge. Gradually they learnt the full song cycles and dances, visited all the sacred sites and were shown the sacred objects and designs belonging to each ritual performance. Most Australian societies, particularly in desert regions, were strictly segregated, and men's and women's ritual life or 'business' were kept well apart. Those who completed this long learning process were regarded with great respect as leaders of their community. They bridged past and present and provided guidance for the future by passing on their skills, knowledge and wisdom. Authority rested with these legitimate keepers of ritual knowledge, and tended to increase with age. This system has now generally broken down, but initiation ceremonies are again being held in some outback regions, having skipped a generation. Once initiation ceremonies ceased, the next generation was not considered qualified to receive sacred knowledge that then died with the elders, unless it was passed on to a non-Aboriginal. In my own experience, elders have sometimes asked me to 'book 'im', that is, write this information down before it is lost. Similarly, the only speakers of some Aboriginal languages are now non-indigenous linguists.

Traditional Aboriginal society was egalitarian. No adult man regarded himself as subordinate, because all had their Dreaming and 'country'. It was a classless, unstratified society, without any formal government. Unlike Melanesia or Polynesia, there were neither chiefs nor headmen. Although certain people might achieve prestige and power and build up a following, nowhere in Australia was there a regular system of hereditary leaders, chiefs, headmen or 'bosses' as they are now called.

(When I was running Earthwatch expeditions in the Northern Territory, I became known as 'little big boss'!) Decisions were made by consensus of male ruling elders. Not all older men were included in this decision-making process, for some were too old or ill or had transgressed tribal law. Typically there would be a meeting sitting down in the shade and, after much discussion, agreement would be reached on the right course of action. Such meetings have been called 'councils' by some anthropologists, who drew attention to an elaborate system of dispute-resolution recorded in mid- to late nineteenth century among Lower Murray River people, but the fact that women played a prominent role in such meetings may indicate post-contact influences. People of the Cape York peninsula were significantly more hierarchical and had a more developed system of individual authority than those of the Western Desert.[40]

Decision-making in Aboriginal communities is an extremely lengthy process—consultations with mining company executives have taken weeks, months or years before a decision is reached, which may well later be overturned by another meeting. Traditionally, women were excluded from the decision-making, but nowadays Aboriginal women have achieved a far greater voice in Aboriginal affairs.

Law and order

'Law' in a Western sense did not exist in Aboriginal Australia but there were principles of communal regulation and punishment for transgressors, now known as 'customary law'. Well-understood rules of proper behaviour were generally obeyed, because all children were taught that their infraction would result in supernatural, personal punishment. Trivial offences were dealt with by immediate family or kin, using ridicule or threats. Adultery and other transgressions of personal rights were, and still are, dealt with by the individuals concerned. This frequently brings those who mete out punishment into conflict with Western law, but nowadays exile to a distant community is often used as an alternative to imprisonment. Stealing (except of women) was rare in traditional times but now theft from non-indigenous people lands many Aboriginal youths in detention.

Punishments for serious offences were decided by ruling elders. Incest and breaking sacred laws were major crimes. Some offences were punishable by death or exile, with the alternative for women of mass rape. Other crimes received a sentence of spearing in the thigh; offenders stood and faced a squad of spearmen with only their dodging ability and perhaps a shield to protect them, and some lost a leg or even their lives in the process. Ruling elders also conducted inquests. Whether death came from snakebite, shark or crocodile attack, illness or accident, it was attributed to evil spirits working on behalf of an enemy. This belief also applies when a white person dies; for instance, when a Northern Territory researcher died of cancer in the 1980s, local Aboriginal people told me it was because he had visited sacred sites without their permission. Similarly, when Aborigines who accompanied us on fieldwork became ill, they attributed their illnesses to kicking a dangerous rock or taking ochre from a forbidden source.

Medicine men identified the person or group who had caused the death by sorcery, and revenge followed. Battles were formal 'set pieces' between two large groups of spearmen or single warriors at intertribal gatherings. In Central Australia in 1875, before the area was colonised, a great massacre occurred at Irbmangara (Running Creek) involving a Western Desert attack on the Arrernte, followed by much retribution. Between 80 and 100 Arrernte men, women and children were killed and infants' limbs were deliberately broken. Violence may have increased in contact times, due partly to the influence of alcohol but also to a shortage of women caused by the impact of new diseases. In southeastern Australia, raids to acquire more women were frequent in the nineteenth century.

The most common forms of violence were revenge attacks and payback killings. Some feuds continue down the generations but in northern Arnhem Land there was a special peace-making ceremony, the 'magarada'. The selected or self-confessed offender had to face a barrage of spears, but once blood was drawn his accusers were satisfied and the feud was over.

'Customary law' denotes 'right practice', rules and the proper way of doing things. Aboriginal law is believed to derive from the Dreaming and therefore to be unchangeable. Some Aborigines are now seeking Federal Government recognition of Aboriginal customary law, saying they would rather undergo a physical assault with spears and clubs from their peers than spend months or years in prison. They also complain that they are often punished twice for a crime—once by their tribal community and a second time under Western law. However, there are huge difficulties in encoding the many varying laws, which often survive in just a few regions. An even greater problem is reconciling Aboriginal traditions with Western law; human rights groups have denounced payback punishments as barbaric and the police have become suspicious of tribal law. It is also the case that some murders and sexual assaults have been labelled paybacks when in fact they are nothing of the sort.[41]

» Traditional economic life
Economy

Traditional economy was cooperative. Much food was shared. Staple food was collected by a woman and distributed among her and her husband's immediate family while large game brought back to camp by a hunter was divided among the whole foraging group—the same system as among Kalahari bushmen. Aboriginal Australia's economic system was relatively simple, with a remarkably uniform mode of production and division of labour across the continent. Digging was deemed to be women's work, hence men's reluctance to demean themselves by gardening in

« FISHING METHODS »

Aboriginal fishing was most advanced on the northern and eastern coasts, using over fifteen different methods Australia-wide. The largest sea creatures—turtles, sharks, codfish, dolphins and dugong—were usually taken by rope-tailed harpoons from canoes. Sometimes sea turtles were caught by men diving from a canoe, slipping a noose over the flippers and towing them ashore. Another method used was to turn the turtle on its back and hold it underwater to drown. Fish were taken in rock-walled traps that caught them as the tide ebbed.

Some hunters cleverly used one creature to catch another. In the tropics, a sucker-fish could be tethered to a long cord and released near a large turtle; it would attach to the turtle, which could then be towed ashore by means of the line. Elsewhere (in Moreton Bay, Queensland, and Proper Bay, South Australia) it was the practice to feed and 'tame' dolphins and use them to catch fish. When fishermen saw a shoal of fish, they ran to the shore and beat the water— their normal way of calling dolphins to come and feed. The dolphins headed for the shallows, driving the fish before them to be speared by waiting fishermen, and were rewarded for their efforts by a good meal.[a]

Australia has both the large, man-eating, saltwater *Crocodylus porosus* and the smaller, less dangerous freshwater *Crocodylus johnstoni*. 'Freshies' were caught by two men diving into deep water, one putting his hand underneath the crocodile's jaw and his thumbs over its eyes while the other grabbed the tail and kicked up to bring it to the surface. Those on land put a strong kapok vine round the snout, hauled it out hanging onto the hide, put a flat rock underneath its jaw and killed it by hammering the head with a large stone. The crocodile was then steamed in a ground oven.

Nets were widely used. Most were made from knotted vegetable fibre. In Queensland, strong nets were fashioned from vines and shaped into large bags, and men in canoes drove dolphins and dugongs into the nets and drowned them.

Aboriginal men used buoyant multi-pronged fishing spears from shore or canoe. Sometimes they dived underwater to transfix fish with a short spear; others stood motionless in their flimsy canoes or lay across them with their face in the water, ready to spear any fish venturing within range.

Small canoes were used by just one woman, often with a toddler on her shoulders clinging to her hair and a baby tucked between breast and raised knees.[b] The early colonists often saw canoes with smoke rising from within. The fire was kindled on a bed of clay, seaweed or sand, and fish were often cooked and eaten straightaway. Much fishing was done at night when firelight attracted prey. As they fished, women sang, 'inviting the fish beneath them to take their bait'.[c]

Women fished with lines. Shell fishhooks were introduced from Melanesia only 1000 years ago and line fishing is restricted to Australia's northern and eastern coast (with some gaps) as far south as the Victorian border. Eora women made two-ply lines by rolling long strips of inner *Kurrajong* bark on their thighs and twisting them securely together. The lines were then soaked in bloodwood tree sap to prevent fraying and could hold fish of up to 13 kg (30 lb).

» *Aborigines fishing from a canoe on the Hastings River in northern New South Wales in the late nineteenth century.*

《　》

colonial times.[42] Women gathered most of the carbohydrate and contributed on average 50 per cent to the diet in food-rich regions and 80 per cent in harsh environments. Carbohydrates were seasonally localised, so Aborigines were semi-nomadic even in the richest regions. Where food was scarce, as in the desert, people ate whatever was available, but in good years and more fertile regions they could afford to be more selective in their diet. Favourites were sweet native honey known as 'sugarbag' and 'honey ants'—ants with abdomens distended to the size of a grape by honey stored by worker ants. Other prized foods were sweet waterlily tubers, eggs, witchetty grubs (which were full of protein and fat), dingo puppies, goannas and echidnas.

Cooking methods were few and simple—the absence of pottery or metal containers meant nothing was boiled. Fish were sometimes steamed in large green leaves but in arid regions this was impossible. Most small game was covered in coals, lightly roasted and eaten half-raw. Earth ovens were used for large culls of small game such as flying foxes and for big creatures like kangaroos, emus or turtles. Entrails were removed, cooked and eaten separately. A hole was dug, a fire lit, green leaves placed on the embers, the game laid on top with hot stones or clay-balls inside the body cavity, then covered with more leaves or paperbark and a topping of earth or sand. An emu's neck might protrude from the top: when steam came out of the beak it was ready to eat. Similar but more elaborate ground ovens were used by Torres Strait and Pacific Islanders.

The complexity of cooking varied widely across different regions. Anthropologist Peter Sutton found that the Wik living in the wetlands of Cape York Peninsula 'used condiments such as native curry root to flavour oven-baked food, chose particular bark for its flavour in cooking, and separated raw liver from stingrays and sharks, then washed and shredded the flesh to remove the white liquid (usually only saltwater), lightly fried the liver in a baler shell, then packed the oily liver inside the dry flesh and bound the lot with bush string to cook slowly close to a fire, or give as a prized gift to a kinsperson.'[43]

The same basic hunting methods were used throughout Australia. Most game was stalked by a sole spearman, with mud plastered on his body to disguise his scent. Other techniques used were pitfalls, traps, nets, decoys, hunting-hides, communal drives, brushwood fences around waterholes to direct animals within spear-range, and poisoning of waterholes with pitcheri or other plants to stupefy fish and creatures that came to drink.

Birds were an important food source, especially the ostrich-sized emu. Although fleet of foot, emus are fatally curious and fall for such tricks as a hunter hiding behind a bush raising a feather-decorated stick—the emu comes to investigate and promptly has a noose slipped over its head. Other birds were taken by hand. A common strategy was to lie down in water and hold up a fish. When a hawk swooped to snatch the bait, the hunter grabbed it by the legs and wrung its neck. An ingenious way of catching waterfowl was for hunters to submerge themselves in a lagoon, breathing through hollow reeds, creep up to ducks or swans and drag them underwater by the legs so deftly that several birds were killed at once. Fowlers also threw a returning boomerang above a flock of ducks or parrots and imitated a hawk's cry, driving the bewildered birds down to water level, where several were decapitated at one blow from a well-aimed boomerang or caught in a net slung across a river. Cockatoos were trapped in Queensland by smearing viscous gum on tree branches so that, when the birds alighted, they could not escape.

Aboriginal people produced little above their day-to-day needs, so no specialisation of labour developed or any centralised authority to organise food distribution. Everyone was a hunter-gatherer. The only exception was during ceremonies, when women produced yam 'bread' or other stored food to feed participants. Such large gatherings necessitated a food surplus. Some were opportunistic get-togethers to feed on a beached whale, others were planned gatherings that exploited seasonally abundant food.

Each spring several hundred people from different friendly tribes journeyed to the Snowy Mountains to feast on the Bogong moth—a protein-rich food easily collected from rock crevices where millions of moths aestivate annually to escape the heat of their breeding-grounds on the inland plains. Timing of annual moth migrations is variable so the host tribe awaited the moths' arrival before sending out messengers to summon others to the feast. (Notched message sticks were carried by these emissaries as an *aide memoire* and to prove their credentials.) Corroborees were held on ceremonial grounds in mountain valleys and then, when they saw smoke-signals on the peaks, moth hunters climbed up, scooped drowsy moths from their resting places and consumed a kilogram or more of moths a day until the supply was exhausted. Ethnographers reported that emaciated Aboriginal men headed for the mountains each year and returned looking sleek and fat after weeks of feasting.[44]

Hunter-gatherer life alternated between feast and famine. Moth numbers varied cyclically and sometimes the moth hunters went hungry. In desert regions ten-year droughts were, and are, not uncommon; water became as scarce as food and desert nomads were reduced to digging up frogs and squeezing their bodies for water. (Before the water in desert pools dries up, frogs swallow it and bury themselves in the mud to await the next rains.)

Exchange networks

The shared features of Australian tribes owe much to exchange networks and regular contacts in what John Mulvaney has called 'a chain of connection'. Items, including food, were bartered between neighbouring groups. Many objects, ceremonies, songs and dances travelled right across the continent following chains of waterholes. Some resources such as ochre quarries were owned by particular families, who carefully

The Original Australians

« TORRES STRAIT ISLANDERS »

Torres Strait Islanders are Australian citizens, but have their own distinctive identity, culture and flag. In the 2001 census, 410 003 people in Australia identified as indigenous—366 429 (89 per cent) Aboriginal, 26 046 (6 per cent) Torres Strait Islanders and 17 528 (4 per cent) of both Aboriginal and Torres Strait Islander descent.[a] To be recognised as a Torres Strait Islander one must be a traditional inhabitant of the Torres Strait Islands or descended from a Torres Strait Islander. The Torres Strait Islanders living on the eighteen inhabited islands of the Torres Strait and the two communities (Seisia and Bamaga) on Cape York numbered 6764. The other 19 262 islanders live mainly in Queensland.

Torres Strait lies in latitudes 11–9 degrees south, between Cape York and southeastern New Guinea. More than 100 islands lie in the strait where the Coral and Arafura seas meet. Torres Strait only came into being 8000–6000 years ago, when the broad land bridge that previously joined New Guinea to mainland Australia was flooded. Sea levels stabilised around 3000 years ago, allowing extensive, food-rich coral reefs to develop and the islands to be occupied by people from the north.

In physical appearance and culture the Islanders resemble the Melanesian peoples of New Guinea rather than Australian Aborigines. They have strong cultural links with the Papuan region of New Guinea, but trade extensively with neighbours on both sides of Torres Strait. The language of the eastern group of islands, Meriam Mer, is closely related to Papuan languages, but Kala-Lagaw-Ya, which is spoken on the other islands, has Aboriginal as well as Papuan features. Now a common Torres Strait Creole language, Yumpla-Tok, is widely spoken. About 85 per cent of its vocabulary was borrowed from English and 14 per cent from indigenous languages.

Torres Strait Islanders have always been ocean voyagers. In the words of George Mye of Erub (Darnley Island), 'We are the mariners, the people who can navigate by the stars to small dots of islands beyond the horizon, reading the winds and tides, the reefs and skies.' The region was linked by vast trading networks, although there was no political unity. Each community was independent and often both at war and in fear of head-hunting raids from neighbouring islands or the Papuan mainland. (Head-hunting was practised widely in prehistoric New Guinea but not in Australia.) From the islands, Australia received turtle shells, harpoons and food, such as dried fish; from Papua, the Islanders received bows and arrows, drums and sailing canoes, while Australia's earliest exports to the Islands were spears and ochre.

» *Outrigger sailing canoe at Saibai Island. Traditional Torres Strait craft were double-outrigger, dugout sailing canoes equipped with two masts, rectangular pandanus-mat sails, a platform with storage containers and a fireplace made of sand on paperbark. Canoes ranged up to 20 m (65 ft) in length but averaged 14 m (45 ft), and could carry twelve people. Most were made to order in villages on the Fly River estuary in Papua that alone could furnish the massive tree trunks needed for dugout hulls.*

Only twenty islands have sufficient freshwater to support a resident population, but all were visited, primarily for fishing and gathering coconuts and wood. Marine turtles provide on average 130 kg (300 pounds) of meat. Dugong—large, herbivorous, tropical sea-mammals rich in oil—yield twice as much meat as turtles and are a favourite food. Hunters built observation platforms in shallow dugong breeding-grounds in western Torres Strait and harpooned them from outrigger canoes. This big-game hunting was extremely dangerous and hunting and feasting were accompanied by many rituals and taboos. Nowadays Islanders hunt from dinghies with motors, increasing success and reducing human fatalities. Dugong survival is a conservation issue and no commercial exploitation is now permitted, but small-scale traditional hunting continues.

Northern and eastern Islanders have gardens and grow yams, taro, sweet potatoes, bananas and coconuts. Pigs were imported from Papua but rarely bred and never became a major food as in New Guinea. Because of its dangerous, uncharted reefs and the inhabitants' fierce reputation, Torres Strait was little visited until 1868, when thick beds of pearl shell were discovered. Foreign pearlers thronged there, for pearl shell was in great demand worldwide for buttons. Islanders numbered 4000–5000 before this influx, but soon their population halved, due to new diseases brought by Europeans, Malays, Pacific Islanders, Filipinos, Chinese and Japanese.

'The results of the invasion might have been worse but for the arrival of the London Missionary Society in 1871', said anthropologist Jeremy Beckett;

» *Torres Strait Islanders dancing on Mer (Murray Island).*

'within a few years the Society had installed Pacific Islander teachers throughout the Strait . . . The missionaries suppressed warfare . . . and enforced Christian morality through island courts. The Islanders seemed to accept these changes, abandoning many of their customs and throwing themselves into the life of the church.'[b]

As George Mye recounted: 'We became Christians after 1871, because Christianity provided us with the opportunity of continuing the spirituality which our traditional religion, the zogo, embodied. Unlike some indigenous peoples elsewhere, we were able to adapt our beliefs and worships to Christianity, and so now we are committed Christians.'

In 1879, the colony of Queensland acquired legal responsibility for the Torres Strait Islands. Waiben, now Thursday Island, became the government and commercial centre and main port. The *Torres Strait Islanders Act 1939* sanctioned indirect rule through councils elected by each island community. During the Second World War some 800 from a population of 3000 Islanders served in the Torres Strait Defence Force, an invaluable contribution to Australia's defence.

A unique Australian initiative in international diplomacy was the 1978 Treaty between Australia and Papua New Guinea on maritime boundaries, which marked out a 'Protected Zone' in Torres Strait extending to the Papuan shore. Opportunities for employment decreased when plastic buttons largely replaced pearl, but a new industry of crayfishing developed. Nevertheless, many people had to leave to find work, and today four out of five islanders live and work in mainland Australia.

Modern transport and communications enable 'expatriates' to maintain their links with the islands and keep customs alive, especially the acclaimed dance and music festivals. Another unifying factor is Islanders' determination to control their own destiny. In 1988, the Islander Council's chairman demanded independence from Australia and a billion dollars' compensation for loss of land and resources. The Australian government delayed the decision, an anti-independence group arose and independence was shelved, for most islanders see regional autonomy within the Australian federation as a better option. Establishment of the Torres Strait Regional Authority in 1994 and granting of a separate federal budget allocation have helped move more swiftly in that direction. Torres Strait Islanders' national day is 'July One', the day on which the London Missionary Society brought 'the Light' of the gospel, but to this 'Coming of the Light' festival has been added Mabo Day on 3 June (see Chapter 8).

« »

The Original Australians

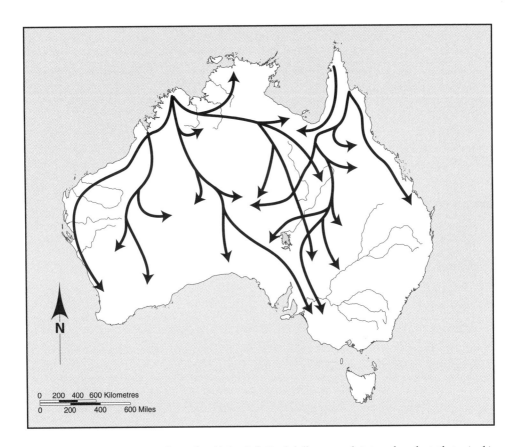

» *Major exchange routes for pearl and baler shell. Pearl shells were made into oval pendants that gained in sacredness the further they were transported. From the Gulf of Carpentaria, baler shell was transported over 1700 km (1050 miles) south. Pearl shell from the Kimberley was traded across up to eight tribal territories, reaching the Centre, Western Desert and Adelaide region.*

controlled the trade; at Mt William axe quarry in Victoria the rate of exchange was three pieces of axe-stone for one cured possum-skin rug.

There was also a roaring trade in pitcheri (a narcotic native tobacco), the young leaves of the two-metre-high shrub, *Duboisia hopwoodii*. The most prized variety comes from Bedourie in southwestern Queensland, which was traded north to the Gulf of Carpentaria and south to Port Augusta, South Australia. It was transported in special bags, ground into fragments and mixed with alkali ash derived from burnt wattle wood. Then it was chewed or made into a wad and carried behind the ear, where thin skin helped absorb the drug. Pitcheri has a higher nicotine content than a cigarette, and is an addictive, psychoactive drug that can be used as a painkiller and stimulant. One Aboriginal man walked 200 kilometres (125 miles) in two days sustained by nothing but 'a chew of *pituri*'. When explorers Burke and Wills were slowly dying in Central Australia in 1861, their one solace was pitcheri.[45]

《　》

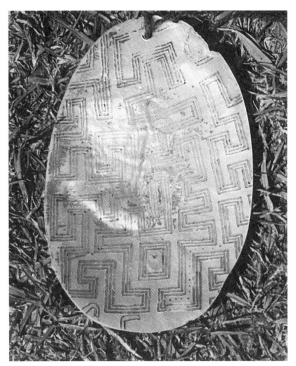

» *Pearl shell decorated with geometric designs found at Ross River in Central Australia. Shells were made into oval pendants up to 12 cm (5 inches) long and suspended on strings. Some were engraved with geometric designs and tracks and used as pubic ornaments and for ritual purposes.*

Aboriginal Australian society was remarkably homogeneous for a continent of such varying environments. Basic social and economic organisation was everywhere the same. The most striking contrast is between tropical 'high culture' and simpler southern societies. Some influences diffused southwards from the north, which was in contact with northern neighbours, but did not reach the extreme southwest or Tasmania, where basic hunter-gatherer life continued little changed since the arrival of the original Australians 2000 generations earlier.

ORIGINS
The last 50 000 years

We will never know when the first human footprint was made on an Australian beach. While some oral traditions tell of creation heroes arising from the land, others suggest overseas origins. Aboriginal elder Wandjuk Marika said of his people in Arnhem Land:

> The truth is . . . that my own people . . . are descended from the great Djankawu far across the sea . . . Djankawu came in his canoe with his two sisters, following the morning star . . . They walked far across the country following the rain clouds. When they wanted water they plunged their digging stick into the ground and freshwater flowed. From them we learnt the names of all creatures on the land and they taught us all our Law.[1]

To investigate the events related in these oral traditions, we first need to have a look at the environmental changes that made migration between continents possible. Global climate has been relatively stable for the last 10 000 years (the Holocene epoch) but we are living in a warm interglacial period that is due to relapse into another ice age after a further ten millennia or so. About 2.5 million years ago, the world began to get colder, as the warm, wet Pliocene era gave way to the Pleistocene ice epoch. Between 2 million and 15 000 years ago much of the world's water was frozen into ice sheets at the poles. Sea level fluctuated dramatically, producing about seventeen glaciations interspersed with shorter interglacial periods, which happen roughly every 100 000 years.[2]

During glaciations, the mean annual temperature was up to 10 degrees centigrade lower than today's and vast glaciers made a third of the northern hemisphere uninhabitable. Sea level dropped by as much as 120 m (395 ft), exposing vast continental shelves—portions of continents that are normally submerged under relatively shallow seas. The exposed shelves provided easy lines of movement along coasts but inland areas, now further from the sea, became drier. Global cooling also meant less evaporation from oceans and therefore less rainfall, and in Australia the central desert zone expanded significantly.

We know humanity's ancestors were African because the earliest hominins—members of the group of closely related species that includes modern humans, our ancestors and extinct 'cousins'—have been found only in Africa, and our closest living relatives, chimpanzees, are African.[3] To set Australian Aboriginal origins in context we must therefore begin our story in Africa, where the human lineage evolved.

The earliest move out of Africa was by *Homo erectus* (upright man) about 2 million years ago when present-day deserts were grassland. These early hunters needed to extend their home range to get enough meat, and followed migrating animal herds, gradually colonising the Middle East, southern Russia, India, the Far East and Southeast Asia. Human fossils have been dated in Georgia to c. 1.8 million years ago and in Java in Indonesia to c. 1.6 million years ago.[4]

» People on the move

When sea level was at its lowest, Southeast Asia grew in land size by over 2 million km² (775 000 sq. miles) of land. This area—now known as Sundaland—was added onto Southeast Asia, joining Java to the mainland. One could walk from Myanmar (Burma) to Bali, but not beyond. How do we know? Because very different animals are found in Asia and Australia. Had there not been a wide water barrier, tigers and monkeys would have been found in Australia and kangaroos in Asia. Biologist Alfred Wallace identified a line dividing Asian from Australian fauna. The only creatures to cross Wallace's line were those that could swim well, rats (which probably rafted across on flotsam), and humans.

Until 1998 it was thought that only *Homo sapiens* were smart enough to build watercraft and get across the straits. It was therefore a great surprise when Australian archaeologist Michael Morwood established that hominins travelled 600 km (375 miles) east from Bali along the Indonesian island chain to Flores. At the Meta Menge site, layers of volcanic debris above and below stone artefacts and associated extinct fauna were radiometrically dated to c. 840 kya (kya = thousand years ago). To reach Flores, people must have crossed two straits of 19 km (12 miles) and 9 km (6 miles) of open sea, although they were never out of sight of land. Almost certainly, the first crossing was from Bali towards the Rinjani volcano on Lombok, which was high enough to be seen from the Bali coast. Morwood maintains that deep-water straits have always separated Flores from mainland Southeast Asia. Some others argue volcanic activity may have created temporary land bridges, but if so, why didn't more Asian animals find their way across? Ancient fauna in Flores was confined to rats and good swimmers—pygmy elephants, komodo dragons and even bigger lizards.[5] It may be that people were fleeing a tsunami or violent volcanic eruptions in the Pacific 'rim of fire', desperately paddling out to sea on logs and accidentally being blown across to the next island. Such accidental voyages required no planning or use of language, which was probably a much later development.

Early stone tools found in Flores resemble Javan tools, and residues and use-wear marks on the edges of four Flores flakes—thin, sharp-edged pieces of stone struck off a larger lump or 'core'—show they were used for grinding food plants.[6] When the ocean was low, a series of stepping-stone islands led from Flores to Timor, the widest gap being 15 km (9 miles). Then only 60–90 km (37–55 miles) of open sea separated Timor from Australia's continental shelf, but hominins went no further than Flores, which lies about halfway between Asia and Australia. Sea voyages without a visible target destination were a massive advance that did not happen for another 700 000 years.

A joint Australian–Indonesian research team made an astounding find in 2004. *Homo floresiensis*, a new species of human, the smallest found on earth, was discovered in a large limestone cave in western Flores.[7] A fully grown *Homo floresiensis* had a brain the size of a grapefruit and was only 1 m (3 ft) tall. The little humans, nicknamed 'hobbits', seem to be descendants of a marooned, ancestral hominin population. Dwarfing of animals is commonplace on islands where food is in short supply and predators are few, but this is the world's most extreme example of human shrinking, which took place over perhaps a million years. They stood no taller than a three-year-old child, weighed about 25 kg (55 lb) and had arms almost reaching down to their knees. Their brains were smaller than most chimpanzees' and only a third the size of ours. Physical anthropologist Peter Brown has shown they were definitely human, and Mike Morwood claims they used stone tools and cooked their prey of juvenile pygmy elephants and other small animals. Others suggest the stone tools may have belonged to *Homo sapiens*, who colonised Flores between 55 000 and 35 000 years ago and may have been pygmy elephant and even hobbit hunters.[8]

Remarkably, the hobbits survived from 95 kya until 12 kya, when volcanic ash from an eruption poured into their cave. This probably wiped them out in the west of the island but dating expert Bert Roberts and archaeologist Doug Hobbs have found intriguing clues that they survived in central Flores until at least 500 years ago. Village elders told Roberts amazingly detailed tales of little, hairy, long-armed people called Ebu Gogo—'the grandmother who eats anything'.[9]

» Out of Africa

The discovery of *Homo floresiensis* bears on the debate over the origins of modern humans—whether *Homo sapiens* evolved in several different parts of the world from earlier populations, or as a recent, distinct African species. The multiregional theory maintains that human evolution has been continuous and parallel in Africa, Europe and Asia, but it has not gained wide acceptance because it requires an improbably high degree of parallel evolution among widely separated, large populations.[10] The hobbit puts perhaps the last nail in the multiregional coffin, for it is descended from earlier hominins but no one can argue that it contributed to our own species' genetic make-up.

According to the Out of Africa model, our ancestors, *Homo sapiens*, arose in Africa. Chris Stringer of London's Natural History Museum and most other scientists now hold that modern humans are the descendants of people who originated in northern Africa about 150 000 years ago and subsequently spread around the globe, replacing archaic human forms, with little or no genetic mixing.[11]

In 1987 the first human 'family tree' based on DNA (the molecule that carries the genetic blueprint of living things) was published. This showed that all living people descend from 'Eve', as our original maternal African ancestor was dubbed. She was not the only woman in Africa at that time (c. 80 kya) but is the only one to appear in everyone's genealogy because only her lineage survives to the present. The family tree was based on mitochondrial DNA (mtDNA), tiny structures in cells that provide energy. This mtDNA is a maternal 'bloodline' passing from mother to child each generation. Each time a woman has no daughters, her mtDNA vanishes. Occasional mutations allow identification of different strains of mtDNA, which geneticists trace back in time to reconstruct past human migrations.[12]

Evolutionary biologists have now improved their methodology and published many other trees, including some of the Y chromosome, the paternal line. In a sample of more than 12 000 contemporary East Asian men from 163 different populations, including Australian Aborigines, New Guinea highlanders and Pacific Islanders, 'no ancient non-African Y chromosome was found in the extant East Asian population'. The Chinese researchers concluded: 'modern humans of African origin completely replaced earlier populations in East Asia'. Then, in 2002, geneticist Spencer Wells produced a TV documentary and book entitled *The Journey of Man: A genetic odyssey*, tracing every living man to an ancestral 'Adam' living in Africa. 'There is more genetic diversity in a single African village than in the whole world outside Africa,' he says, 'indicating humans have lived there longest.'[13]

Humans were few and far between in pre-agricultural times. Geneticists estimate that, 'About 20 000 years ago there were probably only one or two million humans on earth, living in pockets quite isolated from each other . . . All people living today are descended from a population living in Africa some 150 000 years ago that may have numbered only 10 000 people.'[14] Global population was reduced even more when the Toba volcano in Sumatra erupted 74 000 years ago—the world's worst natural disaster of the last 2 million years. This enormous eruption spewed ash to the north-west, covering India, Pakistan and the Gulf region in a blanket 1–3 m (3–10 ft) deep and spread as far as Greenland where traces appear in the Greenland ice record. Wells thinks this catastrophe 'reduced the world population to between two and ten thousand'.[15]

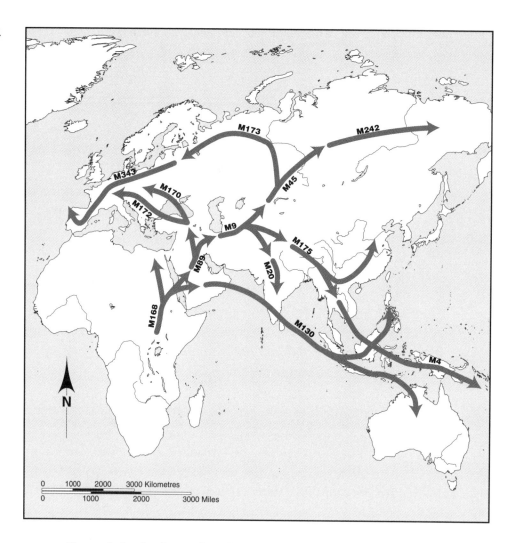

» The spread of modern humans from Africa to other continents based on genetic evidence. The DNA of all humans today points back to a common origin in east Africa about 150 000 years ago. By comparing mutations—or 'markers'—in the genes of people across the globe and mapping the results, scientists can see how people began to colonise the planet during the last ice age. This map traces the main Y-chromosome lineages around the world. The most ancient marker (M168) identifies the first modern journey out of Africa about 60 000 years ago. Australian Aborigines have the oldest lineage outside Africa. Their journey has been traced through marker genes M168 and M130. M130's descendants survive in low numbers (5 per cent) in southern India and Malaysia (10 per cent) but rise to 15 per cent in highland New Guinea and 60 per cent in Australian Aboriginal men.

The high proportion of a particular marker gene among Aboriginal men is explained by Wells as due to the emergence of prolific male breeders. 'The norm throughout evolution is for victorious males to create vast genetic legacies,' he noted in 2005. 'Until modern times men were often squeezed out of the mating game by stronger alpha males.'

Australian Senator Aden Ridgeway, who is of mixed Aboriginal and European descent, agreed to take a DNA test to trace his forefathers and proved to have the most ancient marker of all—M168—which tied him back to Africa. He also possessed a more recent 20 000-year-old marker—M170—from part of a migration that moved into central Europe and the Balkans. Spencer Wells of the National Geographic Society in Washington DC and Dr John Mitchell of La Trobe University, Melbourne, hope to encourage other indigenous people to tell their own stories through their own bloodlines under the recently launched five-year Genographic Project.

Before the discovery of DNA, blood groups were the main tool of genetics, the science of heredity. Blood samples from 10 000 Aborigines were analysed in the 1940s–1970s to make blood transfusion safer in remote areas. Uniquely, full-descent Aborigines lacked A2 and B of the ABO blood group system, S of the MNSs system and Rh negative genes r, r' and r''. Western Desert people show a distinctive genetic pattern, with the world's highest value in the N gene of the MNSs system, implying a very long period of isolation. Aborigines belong almost exclusively to A and O, with only a little B in the extreme north, where it is an import from New Guinea and Indonesia. Aboriginal Australians are possibly the world's only racial group completely lacking the S blood group antigen. Tellingly, in blood groups Aborigines resemble Caucasians; Europeans are mainly A and O whereas B is more characteristic of Asia. This evidence supports the Out of Africa scenario based on DNA.[16]

In the 1980s, molecular biology added a new tool to genetic research—DNA family trees. Sheila van Holst Pellekaan worked among indigenous people in the Darling River region of western New South Wales and the Yuendumu in the Central Australian desert. Leading by example, Pellekaan, a nurse, analysed her own blood and that of Aboriginal women interested in their own ancestry.[17] The results, published in academic articles and 'plain English' reports, were useful to both local Aborigines and researchers. The implied common ancestry for the riverine and desert groups was c. 51 500 years, an estimate that fits perfectly with archaeological evidence for first penetration of inland Australia.[18]

Several ensuing DNA studies have added to the picture. All support a common origin for New Guinea highlanders and Australians. Aborigines form an extremely ancient lineage, most different from black Africans and most similar to highland New Guineans. At that time, a land bridge connected New Guinea with Australia but it was submerged between 8 and 6 kya. New Guinea's highlanders were far more isolated than its coastal people or Australians and were relatively unaffected by later migrations. There was also very little contact between New Guineans and Australians across Torres Strait.[19]

Comparative studies of several thousand fossil skulls support the common origin hypothesis for the people of Greater Australia (Sahul), placing Aboriginal Australians and New Guineans together in an Australo-Melanesian group.[20] In short, skeletal, DNA and other genetic evidence indicates relative Australian homogeneity—initially, at least—characteristic of a population isolated for a long period.

» From Africa to Australia

Climatic change drove periodic migrations out of northeast Africa. Huge portions of the globe were uninhabited, so migrants possibly encountered few or no prior occupants. Hunters living by productive, shallow lakes in northern Tanzania were probably forced to the ocean shore by occasional prolonged droughts. On the coast they used food from the tidal zone, moving onward as each area was depleted.[21] The First Australians' ancestors probably left Africa by the coastal route when the sea level had dropped sufficiently to allow easy passage across the mouth of the Red Sea. Alternatively, they may well have come via Egypt. According to Wells, 'All modern human genetic diversity found around the world was in Africa around 60 kya. The mtDNA and Y chromosome give us the same dates for the earliest non-African genetic lineages, and it is now agreed by most geneticists that humans began to leave Africa around this time.'[22]

How fast did they move? Estimates range from 1 to 4 km (½ to 2½ miles) a year. The beach-hugging route, which may have been used by earlier hominins as well, is consistent with people who had adapted to a marine environment and were able to use simple watercraft. The beach-huggers took only a few thousand years to move along the shorelines of southern Arabia, India and the Bay of Bengal into Southeast Asia. Entry into the empty southern continent between 60 and 50 kya, a time of low sea level, is therefore eminently feasible.[23] Recent genetic studies of Andaman Islanders and the Orang Asli, the original people of Malaysia, have shown that 'mitochondrial DNA variation in isolated "relict" populations in southeast Asia supports the view that there was only a single dispersal [of modern humans] from Africa, most likely by a southern coastal route ... The primary dispersal process, at least from India to Australasia, was very rapid.' Vincent Macaulay, David Bulbeck, Stephen Oppenheimer and their colleagues estimated it took people only about 3000 years to disperse from India to Australia between 70–60 kya, a rate of 4 km (2½ miles) per year.[24] The shortest land route from northeast Africa to Australia is about 15 000 km (9300 miles). Later, other modern humans headed eastwards by a route north of the Himalaya. After 35 kya, Upper Palaeolithic (Stone Age) tools are found in southern Siberia, northern China, Korea and Japan. In northeast Asia, people eventually crossed the Bering land bridge into the Americas. While some researchers have argued for much earlier occupation of the Americas, the mass of archaeological, environmental and genetic evidence favours a relatively late initial human occupation, between about 15 000 and 12 000 years ago.[25]

» Culture of the First Australians

Behavioural changes accompanied physical developments. In Africa, innovations such as production of paint from ochre, blades (long, narrow, sharp fragments of stone struck from a core) and the use of grindstones for pulverising plant food go back to 280 kya.[26] Africans were collecting shellfish and trading artefacts at 140 kya and fishing at 110 kya. By 100 kya bone tools and 'art' (symbolic markings) in the form of patterns incised on ostrich eggshells were in evidence. By 80 kya some Africans were making backed-blades—small stone knives resembling penknives. At 75 kya South

Africans wore snail-shell necklaces, the world's oldest jewellery. Five millennia later, one group developed microliths, tiny blades mounted on shafts as barbs or projectile-points. They also buried their dead.

Many but not all of these developments are found in early Australia. Australia's earliest sites contain ochre, signifying painting. Some also show evidence of long-distance exchange networks, freshwater fishing, ritual burial and personal adornment such as shell necklaces.[27]

Australia's earliest stone artefacts are known as the Core Tool and Scraper Tradition. Scrapers are flakes with sharp edges used for chiselling, cutting or scraping, while core tools are hand-held, large choppers with flaked margins. Those made from river cobbles are known as pebble tools. These Australian tools vary regionally, but bear a general resemblance to stone industries of c. 100 kya, such as the Mousterian of Eurasia and the African Middle Stone Age.

The distinctive stone tool of ice age Australia is the 'horsehoof core'—a high-backed, flat-based core, dome-shaped like a horse's hoof. Cores resulted from removal of flakes from the circumference and often then became hand-held chopping tools. In regions lacking fast-flowing rivers and hence cobbles to use as pebble choppers, horse-hoof cores performed the same function. Both pebble tools and horsehoof choppers were still in use in nineteenth-century Tasmania, where they were employed to fell saplings for spears or hut-frames, prise off bark-sheets for canoes and cut notches when climbing trees.

» *Man demonstrating stone toolmaking at Yuendumu, Northern Territory, in 1965. Toolmakers first hit a stone core to detach sharp flakes. Unusually among stone toolmakers, Aborigines worked towards rather than away from the body.*

What the First Australians' did not share was the Upper Palaeolithic 'cultural revolution' of 50–40 kya, for their ancestors had left Eurasia long before.[28] Ice age Australia lacked the standardised, specialised artefacts of ice age Europe, and hafting (attaching a handle to an implement) and microliths did not become widespread until 5 kya. In Europe the earliest representational paintings of animals—at Chauvet Cave in the Ardèche region of France—date to 35 kya. Australia's oldest rock art is of similar antiquity. It consists of hand-prints and hand-stencils made with red ochre, cupules (small cup-shaped depressions) and engravings (petroglyphs) of circles, tracks (footprints), lines and other 'geometric' motifs hammered or abraded into the rock. Cupules are non-utilitarian, symbolic marks for they were pounded onto vertical walls and even the ceilings of rock-shelters. (A rock-shelter is a naturally formed overhang sheltering a floor area.) Ice age Australian art closely resembles the earliest art of Eurasia. Cupules are in caves in southern India in contexts older, possibly much older, than 100 kya, in Malaysian Sabah and in Myanmar.[29] Neanderthals also made cupules; in La Ferrassie cave in the Dordogne, an infant was buried under a 'tombstone' bearing cupules in pairs. European caves have many 'geometric' engravings such as the 'macaroni' of Peche Merle. In Cosquer cave near Marseilles the first phase of rock art was dominated by finger-markings and hand-stencils. European rock art gradually evolved from early pre-figurative markings to splendid representational paintings, and the sculptures in bone and stone of the Upper Palaeolithic.[30] Australian art also evolved and by c. 20 kya hunters were painting figures of humans and animals in tropical rock-shelters but Aboriginal material culture never attained the complexity of ice age Europe. In Australia, nomads instead put huge amounts of time and energy into 'hunting magic' and the development of incredibly elaborate ceremonies focused on the increase and maintenance of food supplies, as they fought for survival in the windswept deserts of the late ice age.

» The world's first intercontinental crossing

When the sea reached its lowest levels, the amount of habitable land around Australia grew by 2.5 million km² (950 000 sq. miles). Land bridges connected Tasmania and New Guinea to the mainland, forming the supercontinent known as Sahul. The probable time of first human entry is 60–50 kya, a time of significantly low sea level.[31]

How did people reach the new continent? The deep sea trough between Timor and Australia was around 70 km (43 miles) wide at lowest sea level and around 150 km (93 miles) at 63–70 kya. Passage from Timor was relatively easy because small islets acted as stepping stones and each summer northwest winds blow strongly from Timor to Australia. At 60 kya, this summer monsoon was at least as active as nowa-days. Another possible route was east to the Aru coast of New Guinea, but this demanded more directional skill in sailing.[32]

The first migrants may have known land lay to the south, as from Timor's moun-tains the horizon distance is 175 km (110 miles). They may have even been able to see

smoke from lightning-lit fires, as smoke from bushfires billows a long way into the
atmosphere. Or they could have been following the path of birds migrating south.

The first people to reach Australia may have been accidental castaways, blown out to sea in a flimsy craft or clinging to a log. It is probable that, throughout pre-history, a trickle of people made landfall on Australia's coasts, since recent mtDNA research has revealed 'high diversity within Australian and New Guinean populations' resulting from colonisation 'between 40 and 70 thousand years ago'. At present it is unclear whether this diversity resulted from a single migration with a heterogeneous source population or from multiple movements of smaller groups over many millen-nia. It is also possible that there was a joint initial colonisation of New Guinea and Australia, since: 'The sequences from New Guinea are somewhat more closely related to those from Australia than either of these populations are to the Asian sequences . . . Also, the sequences from the New Guinea highlands are on average more closely related to the Australian sequences than those from the New Guinea coast.' This is to be expected, as the highlanders have remained fairly isolated whereas coastal New Guinea was much affected by the later influx of new, Austronesian people.[33]

Were there deliberate migrations? Melbourne researcher Robert Bednarik has replicated a Stone Age voyage from Timor to Australia.[34] Using only stone tools, in three months eight boat-builders constructed an 18 m (60 ft) bamboo raft with wooden steering oar, vine ropes and a palm-leaf sail. With five men aboard, this experi-mental craft reached Australia's continental shelf in just six days. Greater Australia (Melville Island) was reached on day thirteen. Land remained invisible for nine-tenths of the voyage. Bednarik proved what earlier computer simulation models had sug-gested—bamboo rafts could sail from Asia to Australia using Stone Age technology.

» A one-way trip

What the First Australians did not know was that it was a one-way journey. They could not retrace their steps, as Australia lacked materials for buoyant watercraft. Native bamboo was too thin-stemmed for raft-building, and there were few trees large enough to be suitable for making dugout canoes. Only 30 km (19 miles) of sea separate Bathurst and Melville islands from the north coast, but when the sea reached its present level 6500 years ago, Tiwi people became almost completely isolated and now differ genetically, linguistically and culturally from mainland Aborigines.

» Settlement

Tantalising clues to the story of first human arrival in Australia emerge year by year. Any remaining traces of the very first Australians lie underwater on submerged continental shelves. The best evidence comes from two rock-shelters in Kakadu National Park in Arnhem Land. Stone tools are found throughout the earth floors of

« WATERCRAFT »

Rafts made from logs, bark, reeds or branches were common in Australia, but some coasts lacked any watercraft. Instead, people swam or used logs. The 10 km (6 miles) of sheltered water between Great Keppel Island and the Queensland shore were crossed by men alternately dog-paddling and resting on their 'swimming log'. Flimsy bark canoes were used on lakes, rivers and sheltered bays.[a] The most seaworthy Australian watercraft were sewn-bark canoes, built from two or three bark-sheets sewn together, plus stretchers and ribs. A replica was once paddled 60 km (37 miles) in sheltered water. Along the northwest coast dugout canoes gave way to sewn-bark ones, mangrove rafts and finally 'swimming logs' off the Pilbara. Thereafter there were no watercraft along 4000 km (2500 miles) of coast as far south as the Murray River with its simple bark canoes.

In the Sydney region, a canoe could be made in a day, the bark coming from *Casuarina* (a species of she-oak) or stringy-bark eucalypts. Bark was more easily stripped from trees after rain, so in winter to early spring Eora went upriver

» *A Worora youth paddles a triangular, mangrove-log, 'kahlua' raft on George Water, Kimberley, Western Australia. The logs are tied or pegged together so their broad ends form a stern and the thin ends a pointed bow. The Kimberley coast has 9 m (30 ft) tides, among the world's highest, and currents of 10 knots, but Aboriginal tide-riders accomplished journeys of 16 km (10 miles) before their rafts became waterlogged. The Gayardilt (Kaiadilt) of Bentinck Island used similar mangrove rafts but two recorded voyages of 13 km (8 miles) each resulted in 50 per cent mortality.*

to make new canoes. The bark was bunched at each end and tied with cords made from vines. These craft of 3–4 m (9–12 ft) long and 1 m (3 ft) wide could hold five people. They had only 15 cm (6 inches) of clearance from the water but performed amazingly well.[b] They were poled or propelled with paddles up to 60 cm (2 ft) in length. 'These they use one in each hand and go along very fast sitting with their legs under them and their bodies erect,' Bradley wrote. 'I have seen them paddle through a large surf without oversetting or taking in more water than if rowing in smooth seas.'[c]

» A canoe-tree in Blanchetown Reserve, River Murray, South Australia. The scar on this river red-gum resulted from Aborigines removing a large, oblong, naturally curved piece of bark to make a canoe.

《　》

Malakunanja and Nauwalabila shelters, which have very similar sequences, with the earliest human occupation dated to 53–61 kya. A later re-dating program at Malakunanja confirmed the previous ages but sceptics have suggested the sites may have been disturbed. Having visited the sites, talked to the excavators and examined the artefacts for myself, which become increasingly brittle with depth, I think there is every reason to believe that these two rock-shelters contain evidence of the earliest human occupation yet found in Australia.[35]

Claims for earlier human occupation (as at Jinmium) have not withstood scientific scrutiny, but some further 50 000-year-old sites are now accepted, such as Devil's Lair south of Perth, Western Australia.[36] Archaeologists Peter Veth and Sue O'Connor have shown that Australia's earliest dated sites lie inland rather than on the coast. It seems the first colonists headed inland and exploited big game on the plains.[37]

The world's oldest ground stone tools have also been found in tropical Australia. These are made of hard, volcanic rock and have a sharp, bevelled cutting edge produced by grinding. The blade is hafted into a wooden handle as an axe (with its cutting edge and handle in the same plane) rather than an adze (with an arched blade set at right angles to the handle). Adzes, typical of New Guinea and Polynesia, are absent from Australia. Ground-edge, hafted axes first appeared in tropical Australia 30 000 years ago, but became widespread only c. 4.5 kya. They were often used one-handed for chopping toeholds up trees in search of honey.[38]

» Lake Mungo

Almost all major archaeological discoveries in Australia have been accidental. In 1968 Jim Bowler, a young geomorphologist studying ancient sand dunes, was riding his motorbike on the lee shore of now dry Lake Mungo when he came across broken, burnt human bones exposed by erosion.[39] The remains proved to be that of a gracile girl or young woman, 148 cm (4ft 10 inches) tall. Importantly, this young woman had been accorded the formal ritual of cremation and her remains treated with care and respect.

In 1974 Bowler found another skeleton nearby. This time the body was buried, not cremated, and the remains were definitely adult, with an estimated height of 170 cm (5 ft 7 inches). The pelvis and large femur-head indicated a male. The right elbow was severely affected with osteoarthritis—an affliction of spearmen. Mungo Man had also lost his two lower canine teeth simultaneously when much younger, probably in the rite of tooth avulsion during initiation. Finally, the hands were placed in the lap, probably holding his penis—a common feature of historic Aboriginal burials.

These burials are of tremendous importance to Aboriginal people as well as scientists, and in 1981 the Willandra Lakes region was listed as a World Heritage Area for its cultural and natural significance to all humankind. As I wrote in the Australian Heritage Commission's nomination: 'The Willandra Lakes system stands in the same relation to the global documentation of the culture of early *Homo sapiens* as Olduvai Gorge relates to hominid origins.' After study, the human remains have been returned to a 'keeping place' controlled by local Aboriginal custodians. This concept of 're-burial' is that the ancient Mungo people will lie in peace and dark in their own country, but still be available for scientific study.

There has been much debate about the age of the Mungo remains; palaeo-anthropologist Alan Thorne claimed that they dated to 60 kya.[40] Bowler therefore reanalysed his original samples. It took three years' work, 25 new dates and four

» *Australia's oldest human burial. The grave of Mungo Man, who was buried on the shores of Lake Mungo about 40 000 years ago. Red ochre was scattered over the corpse, another indication of the antiquity of Aboriginal respect for the dead and use of ochre in ritual.*

separate laboratories, but in 2003 Bowler's team published revised ages for Mungo Man and Woman of about 40 kya in the prestigious British scientific journal *Nature*.[41]

The story began about 60 kya, when this inland region boasted thirteen large freshwater lakes, grasslands and woodlands. Lake Mungo filled due to a gradually cooling climate that meant less evaporation and greater river-flows from the highlands.[42] People reached the region and camped on sand dunes on the eastern side of Lake Mungo, where excavation revealed over 700 artefacts, charcoal from ancient campfires and burnt bone. Stone tools were horsehoof cores, steep-sided scrapers and flakes and Mungo shows classic features of the oldest Australian tradition of toolmaking. The earliest stone artefacts found—eleven silcrete flakes—are dated to 47–45 kya and the underlying deposits are culturally sterile. This means that humans first reached Lake Mungo between 50 and 45 kya, a timing that fits well with their earlier arrival in the north.

From 60–43 kya Lake Mungo was full of freshwater and the land greener and more lush than at any stage since. Freshwater fish, shellfish, small land animals, eggs and vegetable food were abundant. Analysis of otoliths (fish earbones) indicates the First Australians used traps and fixed gill-nets to catch fish of identical species and age in a single event, such as a spring spawning run. Most otoliths came from golden perch, which are difficult to catch by other means.[43]

For thousands of years people lived well at Lake Mungo, but then it began to dry. At about 40 kya the drying trend accelerated and severe dust storms blew from upwind sand dunes in the Red Centre. Evidence is the layer of windblown dust and desert sand deposited above the graves. Water level oscillated but was never as deep as before. People continued to live there intermittently until the height of the last glaciation around 19 kya, when the lake finally dried up. Thereafter occasional visits were made, but by then people had moved to permanent rivers elsewhere in this semi-arid region.

» Origins

In January 2001, Aboriginal origins again hit the headlines.[44] Thorne's team made startling claims that the world's oldest DNA had been successfully recovered from Mungo Man. Thorne's 'di-hybrid theory' suggested that a migration of gracile people from China preceded one of more robust people from Java, the two then merging to form the modern Aboriginal population. Mungo Man and Woman exemplified the gracile people, Kow Swamp in northern Victoria the robust. Kow Swamp is a burial site beside a lake where Thorne excavated 40 robust individuals, some buried with shells as 'grave goods'.[45]

However, the original C-14 dating of 9–13 kya has been revised to 19–22 kya by archaeologist Tim Stone, who sees the robust Kow Swamp people as ice age adapted relatives of the gracile people of Lake Mungo. As the height of the last ice age approached, drying of lakes fragmented the small human population, groups became isolated and skeletal diversity increased. A robust build was better adapted to the increasing cold, for bigger people are better at retaining body heat. Most Australian early prehistoric remains are robust rather than gracile, but there was a significant decrease in body proportion after the ice age. Compared with earlier populations, modern Aborigines are gracile.

» Tri-hybrid theory

In 1993, population geneticist Joseph Birdsell published detailed data from the 1930s on 3000 tribal Aborigines, showing a graded physical variation across Australia. In the north, skin colour is darker, baldness rare and greying of head hair earlier; in the colder southeast, bodies are stockier, beards abundant and balding pronounced.[46]

Birdsell explained this diversity with his 'tri-hybrid theory' of three waves of colonists—first came small, lightly built 'Barrineans', named after Lake Barrine in the north Queensland rainforest, where they lived. They were followed by 'Murrayians', of stocky build and abundant body hair, and finally tall, dark 'Carpentarians', whose racial affinities were with the tribes of southern India such as Dravidians.

Australian Aboriginal skin colour varies slightly. Human skin darkness depends on the pigment melanin and is controlled by both genetic and environmental factors. Colour has evolved to be dark enough to protect against ultraviolet radiation, sunburn and skin cancer, radiate excess heat efficiently and prevent sunlight destroying folic acid, a nutrient essential for fertility and foetal development.[47] In tropical and sub-tropical regions over many generations people with dark skin on average live longer and have more successful families. As people expanded from the equator into higher, less sunny latitudes, over many millennia their skin colour gradually became depigmented and light enough to foster vitamin D production and avoid rickets, a bone disease caused by lack of sunlight. A transect from South Africa to Norway shows a clear gradation from dark brown skin in equatorial Africa to medium brown (from 10 to 20 degrees north) and then light brown in North Africa and the Mediterranean countries, finally giving way to depigmented, 'white' people north of 50 degrees north latitude in Britain and Scandinavia.

Across Aboriginal Australia there is a gradation from dark-brown in the tropical north and central deserts to copper-coloured, medium-brown among Murrayians and around the southern coasts including Tasmania. These differences appear to result from adaptation to climate over an extremely long time period.[48] Tasmania lies between 40 and 45 degrees south, an equivalent latitude to Italy, but geneticist Stephen Oppenheimer deems Italians to be light-brown but Tasmanians medium-brown. Why the difference in skin colour in the same latitudes? The simplest explanation is that the original Australians were all dark brown but over 50 000 years those in the south gradually became slightly lighter coloured, but not as light as the inhabitants of Italy who had inhabited their peninsula for over twice as long. Similarly, the extreme slowness of skin colour change explains why Meso-Americans who have lived about the equator in the New World for at least ten millennia are not as dark as equatorial Africans, for their skin lightened over the much longer period they spent in temperate Eurasia en route from Africa.

Most scholars now regard Birdsell's Barrineans and Murrayians as part of the founding population, with subsequent variation resulting from environmental factors. The one consensus among palaeoanthropologists is that all Australia's prehistoric human remains are *Homo sapiens* and ancestral to modern Aborigines. There is variation over time and space but also a basic unity and long continuity in Australoid physical form.

» Genetics

DNA analysis has vindicated Birdsell's Carpentarian migration, although its timing seems to be mid-Holocene rather than earlier. Geneticists Alan Redd and Mark Stoneking, who studied mtDNA from present-day Aborigines in Arnhem Land and theKimberley–Sandy Desert region, found them to be ten times closer to Indians than

« PHYSICAL CHARACTERISTICS »

Many variations in appearance contribute to individuality but Australian Aborigines of unmixed ancestry are readily recognisable. Common features are exceptionally thin legs, a narrow face, broad noses depressed at the root and fairly wide at the nostrils, chocolate-brown skin, dark brown hair, an erect carriage, long, narrow head, retreating forehead and chin, pronounced brow ridges above deep-set, fairly large, brown eyes, large teeth but not especially thick lips and a projecting jaw.[a]

» *Australian Aboriginal man from Central Australia.*

The original Australians have very lean bodies with the most elongated legs found in humankind, a thermo-regulating adaptation to a hot, dry climate. Height and build differ markedly between male and female. At contact, Aboriginal men averaged 170 cm (5 ft 7 inches), and women 157 cm (5 ft 2 inches), but height varied regionally. The tallest people were in the Kimberley, the shortest in north Queensland rainforests, where men averaged only 155 cm (5 ft 1 inch), just 5 cm (2 inches) more than African pygmy populations.[b]

In tropical rainforests the usual build is lightweight and small. Palaeoanthropologist Colin Groves points out that the low ultraviolet light on the rainforest floor limits the skin's production of vitamin D for skeletal growth, leading to the evolution of small skeletons. Similarly, short, broad noses are adapted to warm, humid conditions. Australian Aborigines often have noses as wide as they are long while African 'pygmies' have the widest noses in the world. Rainforests are also poor in food resources, hence it is more efficient to be small and eat less.[c]

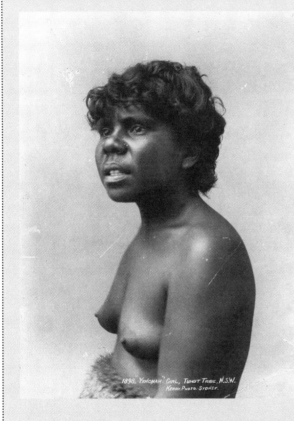

» *Yenomah, a girl from the Tumut tribe, New South Wales, taken in 1898.*

Aboriginal head hair is usually wavy to straight but Barrineans and Tasmanians have much crisper, springier, helically curled forms with oval rather than round hair shafts. Because of their distinctive hair, dark skin and small stature, Birdsell termed Barrineans and Tasmanians 'Oceanic Negritos' ('little blacks' in Spanish). Short, lightly built Negritos inhabited Southeast Asia before Mongoloid people arrived from the north. Negritos still survive, such as the Semang of the Malay Peninsula, the Aeta in the Philippines and Andaman Islanders in the Bay of Bengal. The latter have woolly, 'peppercorn' hair (disposed in tufts with bare areas) with a flattened cross-section typical of

Negritos. In height, Barrineans resemble Semang adult males but Tasmanians did not live in rainforests and were slightly taller. Australian Aborigines have more body hair than Negroid or Mongoloid people but less than Caucasian, except for Murrayians who had 'a heavy growth of hair on their faces, arms, chests and legs'. Curiously, Tasmanians lived in a much colder climate than Murrayians but were far less hirsute.[d]

Some physical anthropologists emphasise differences, others similarities, and, although there is an underlying homogeneity, both modern and ancient Aborigines are physically diverse.

《　》

to New Guineans. The time of separation of Aboriginal Australians from southern Indians was estimated at 3390 years (with 95 per cent certainty it lay between 1686 and 5093 years ago).[49] Pellekaan's earlier study linked two Aboriginal populations with southern Indians. The link was closer with desert Aborigines than the more southerly, Darling River group, who were more remote from points of entry. These studies of mtDNA and the Y chromosome produced patterns consistent with ancient separation between Australians and New Guinea highlanders and much more recent links between Aborigines and South Asians.[50] Who were these Holocene immigrants? 'Dravidians' from southern India was the answer I received from an Indian audience when showing slides of Aborigines at a Science Congress in Delhi. Birdsell's theory of a migration of 'Carpentarians'—tall, slim people originating in the sub-continent—was based on similar body build and hair-form and now DNA studies have proved him right.

The distribution of Aboriginal bio-genetic markers, such as blood groups, fits well with the DNA evidence.[51] Like indigenous people elsewhere, Australian Aborigines were the product of intermarriage between different populations originating in different parts of the world.

» Impact on the environment

Humans had two major accidental impacts on the virgin continent—transformation of the vegetation through burning and the extinction of megafauna. Human burning of fire-sensitive vegetation caused a dramatic decrease in trees and shrubs right across the arid zone, which covered 70 per cent of the continent during the ice age. When the first people moved inland, they encountered a totally unfamiliar, arid environment. Even stranger were the animals, including megafauna—giant species of marsupials, reptiles and birds. There were 3 m (10 ft) high kangaroos, rhinoceros-sized wombats (*Diprotodon*), huge flightless birds (*Genyornis*), land-crocodiles (*Quinkana*), the world's largest lizards—7 m (23 ft) long carnivorous *Megalania*—50 kg (110 lb) snakes

(*Wonambi*) and massive terrestrial horned-tortoises. These giants became extinct, together with all 19 species of Australia's marsupials that exceeded 100 kg (220 lb) and 22 of 38 medium-sized species over 10 kg (22 lb). In all, 94 per cent of Australia's large mammals were wiped out.[52]

Pleistocene animal extinctions happened worldwide. In North America, mammoths, mastodon, giant sloths and other megafauna became extinct 12.5–11 kya. There, this coincided both with human arrival and rapid post-glacial warming, whereas in Australia, human arrival and megafaunal extinction occurred well before the height of the last glaciation, which occurred between 30 and 15 kya.[53] A breakthrough in dating extinctions came in 1999 when earth scientists Gifford Miller and John Magee established that the giant flightless bird *Genyornis* died out c. 46 kya.[54] They obtained 700 dates on *Genyornis* eggshells, showing *Genyornis* were present continuously from long before 100 kya until 50–45 kya, when they became extinct relatively suddenly.

Relative ages were obtained on eggshell fragments and associated sediments from three widely separated study areas—the arid internal drainage basin of Lake Eyre and the cooler, wetter, semiarid Port Augusta and Lake Victoria regions. The similar patterns and timing of *Genyornis* extinction across three different environments but continuous occurrence of emu eggshells before, during and after *Genyornis'* disappearance show climatic change was *not* responsible. Why did *Genyornis* die but the emu survive? *Genyornis* carried twice the body mass of an emu, and a heavy body and short, thick legs made *Genyornis* a slower runner and therefore an easier target for hunters' spears. *Genyornis* was also a more specialised feeder. *Genyornis* targeted a specific set of food resources of mainly tropical and arid-adapted grasses, while emus also ate more non-grass herbs and desert scrub.

Emus survived and today graze from the tropics to the snows, whereas *Genyornis* did not outlast the change in its normal habitat between 50 and 45 kya. The carbon isotopic composition of the teeth of wombats mirrors the same vegetational transition. Miller and Magee see *Genyornis* as a victim of ecosystem disruption and 'speculate that human firing of landscapes rapidly converted a drought-adapted mosaic of trees, shrubs and nutritious grasslands to the modern fire-adapted desert scrub. Animals that could adapt survived; those that could not, became extinct.'[55] However, megafauna had previously survived even greater aridity (c. 140 kya). The only new factor in Australia 50 kya was human arrival.

Archaeologist Michael Smith has found one site with secure evidence of human predation on megafauna. It is a midden at Wood Point on eastern Spencer Gulf, South Australia. There *Genyornis* eggshell associated with stone tools gave an age of 47±5 kya.[56] This fits well with the date of 45 kya for the disappearance of megafauna in the Naracoorte Caves in temperate South Australia.[57]

The theory of a fairly sudden, widespread extinction event about 46 kya has gained wide currency. In both eastern and western Australia a remarkable correlation exists between first human arrival and megafaunal disappearance. (There are virtually no bone deposits and therefore no data from the north.) Slight cooling but no major climatic shifts marked the 51–40 kya period. In the Willandra region, megafauna also disappeared soon after human arrival and well before the lakes dried up in a regional climatic shift c. 40 kya.

One site shows a different picture, according to archaeologist Judith Field. At a campsite beside the shallow, ephemeral lake of Cuddie Springs in semiarid, north-western New South Wales, she excavated megafaunal bones associated with artefacts at 30–37 kya.[58] Field maintains that hunters occasionally camped there and scavenged carcasses of *Genyornis*, *Diprotodon* and other megafauna. The bones are typical of a waterhole assemblage where animals died as the lake dried up. Others have argued that the skeletons are not articulated, that is, they are not still lying in the sediments where the animal died or first came to rest, but are detached individual bones that may have been washed into a sediment differing in age from the bones. Bert Roberts found that optically stimulated luminescence (OSL) dating showed that sand grains in the crucial deposit are of different ages, perhaps caused by an ancient flood. The tooth of an ancient crocodile was also found out of place there. The jury is still out on Cuddie Springs but it is possible that some megafauna lasted longer in well-watered refuge areas in eastern and southern Australia, which hunters did not penetrate until later. Examples are Tasmania, Kangaroo Island in South Australia and Cloggs Cave in eastern Victoria where I excavated the jaw of a giant kangaroo, *Sthenurus*, in a basal layer dated to 22 kya.[59]

Australian megafauna vanished long before similar extinctions in the Americas, Madagascar and New Zealand. The only events with which all these extinctions correlate is the arrival of a new predator: man. Giant moas disappeared soon after the Maori arrived. In Mauritius the dodo survived only 80 years after the Dutch arrived with guns and pigs that ate the eggs.[60]

Clearly, human arrival rather than climate change foreshadows extinction, but was it by hunting or burning, or both? Extinction specialist Paul Martin saw humans' rapid spread and efficient hunting as the main cause. Australian ecologist B.W. Taylor agrees: 'The first Australians and the first Americans both brought fire with them and used it in hunting . . . man's use of spears to kill game being driven by fire was far more effective than simply trying to get close enough to spear game.'

Zoologists Tim Flannery and Peter Murray likewise attribute extinction to big-game hunters' arrival in virgin country with 'naïve' animals unafraid of humans. (African megafauna survived because it co-evolved with humans.) Even when animals had learnt to fear humans, Aborigines hunted them successfully, and it is significant that the animals that were lost were large and lumbering or, if middle-sized, were slow runners.[61]

'As hunters,' says Flannery, 'the Aborigines were the primary carnivore on the continent, taking the lion's share of animal protein. Through the use of fire they were

also the top herbivore, with their fire consuming more vegetation than any herbivorous species . . . So extensive and effective was Aboriginal hunting that the large
marsupials were rare at the time of European contact.'[62]

Peter Murray concluded that: 'A gradual attrition of these populations by
hunting . . . would seem to account for the differential nature of the extinction pattern
better than any drought or fire ecology argument . . . The cause of megafaunal
extinction . . . was probably due to a combination of all the above agencies, but without the influence of Aboriginal man, the megafauna would have survived until the
arrival of the Europeans.'[63]

'But where are the kill sites?' you may ask. There aren't any, for Aborigines
did not carry massive carcasses back to camp nor did they use stone-tipped spears
until much later, but they were accomplished hunters who employed fire, pit-traps
and ambushes to snare large prey. Red and grey kangaroos are swift and large—the
adult males stand 2 m (7 ft) high and weigh 90 kg (200 lb)—but have been successfully hunted by Aborigines using only wooden javelins or clubs. Tasmanians never
developed stone-tipped spears but still captured large kangaroos and emus. Arrival
of a new predator in a continent with an inherently low carrying capacity for
large mammals upset the fragile ecological balance and gradually wiped out the
megafauna by a combination of hunting and habitat alteration through burning.
Maori boast of their forebears' successful moa hunting, but Aborigines see themselves as conservationists and tend to deny their ancestors' big-game hunting.

» Impact of the firestick

Charcoal in the lowest layers of living sites shows that fire was used widely.
Aborigines used it to cook, smoke animals from burrows, drive game into ambushes
and make fresh grass spring up to attract herbivores. Ashes act like manure, and
sweet, new shoots and leaves appear at the first good rain after burning. In arid
Australia, light burning of vegetation, patch by patch, was done in early spring.
The aim was hunting, 'cleaning up the country', making travel easier and reducing
risk of snakebite. Fire was also used for signalling and clearing ground for camping.

Firesticks (slow-burning, smouldering torches of rotten wood or rolled bark)
were carried when travelling. Deliberate Aboriginal burning was termed 'firestick
farming' in 1969 by archaeologist Rhys Jones, based on his Tasmanian research.[64]
There modern vegetation can be explained only by prehistoric firing. In 1827 an
Englishman exploring mountainous northwest Tasmania climbed a high peak and
saw to his amazement open grasslands amid the rainforest. When Aboriginal firing
ceased, the grass became sour and rainforest reclaimed the area.

In Tasmania, fire was used to keep routes open along the west coast and extend
the narrow coastal strip of heathland, wet scrub and small grassy plains. Temperate
rainforest is not food-rich, whereas newly burnt forest is rapidly colonised by native

bracken fern, the roasted rhizomes of which formed a carbohydrate staple. Open heathland provided orchids, berries and starchy grass-tree trunks and a habitat rich in wallabies, possums, bandicoots, mice and birds. Skilful burning thus increased the food supply.

Systematic landscape burning was linked with orderly, seasonal exploitation of different environments, primarily to obtain game. In Arnhem Land at monsoon end:

> the main burning season began as [Gidjingali] people fanned out from the confinement of their camps eager to taste new foods . . . They burnt the tall grass as they went, both to clear the ground for easier walking and also as part of their hunting strategy. A fire lit late one morning in July 1972 on the grassy plains . . . crackled . . . across . . . six square km to die in a swamp. Behind the flames, women using their digging sticks prodded the burnt-out holes of goannas, fat after the rains, and dragged them out to break their necks by pressing their heads downwards against their chests. That afternoon, 50 kg of goanna (*Varanus* sp.) and 10 kg of long-necked turtle were obtained, and the following day a second party went over the same ground and got an equivalent haul.[65]

Most tropical ecologists agree that 'tropical savannahs are man-made by fire, and could not have existed before man used fire for hunting'.[66] In northeast Queensland, palynologist Peter Kershaw has shown that a dramatic increase in charcoal and the change from rainforest to eucalypt species about 46 kya can only be explained by Aboriginal arrival.[67]

In Arnhem Land early in the dry season Yolngu hunters burn fire-breaks around fire-sensitive monsoon forests to protect them from later more severe fires. Fruit trees are also burnt to ensure a good supply of berries. The result is a mosaic of burnt and unburnt patches. Such light, regular burning is considered the mark of conservation-minded people in harmony with their environment. Since the 1970s, controlled Aboriginal-style burning has been used to manage national parks like Kakadu. Annual firing there tends to be more efficient and therefore more severe than traditional fire regimes, leaving nothing but vast expanses of blackened tree-trunks. In contrast I have seen much greater biodiversity in the adjacent Mount Borradaile region that is owned by Aborigines but never deliberately burnt, the only fires being natural ones.[68]

Flannery sees Australian vegetation as a vast Aboriginal artefact, 'designed to provide maximal food and comfort to its inhabitants in the most sustainable manner'.[69] Captain Cook called Australia 'this continent of smoke'. In temperate Australia, firesticks produced the open 'park-like' country so admired by the colonists, but then pyrophobic Europeans, anxious to preserve their wooden houses and fences, banned Aboriginal firing. This led to increased fuel loads and the change from frequent low-intensity burns to occasional disastrous firestorms.

By 35 kya, people had spread all over Australia, including the Red Centre and alpine grasslands of Tasmania. Life was more than merely a battle for survival. In the earliest sites there are used pieces of ochre—evidence the First Australians painted their bodies, artefacts or cave walls. They cremated or buried their dead with some ceremony and possibly initiated their young men by tooth avulsion. They practised art in the form of engraving, painting, stencils and hand-prints. The ice age art-style known as 'Panaramittee', after the South Australian site where it was first recognised, is found Australia-wide.[70] It is a largely 'geometric' style, the main subjects being circles and lines. Figurative motifs are almost confined to human footprints and the tracks of animals, birds and reptiles. Ice age Australians also wore ornaments, such as shell necklaces and bone beads.

Stone artefacts were mainly 'maintenance tools' to fashion others of wood, bone or shell. At Mungo we see an ice age craftsman's toolkit, prehistoric equivalents of our axe, chisel and knife. This same basic toolkit for chopping, scraping and cutting remained in use throughout Australian prehistory. Some specialised tools also developed, as in ice age Tasmania, where wallaby hunters used small sharp scrapers, the size and shape of a thumbnail, to cut up carcasses.

Gradually, stone tools became less massive and more efficient. Early Australians also used wooden spears and digging sticks. Organic items rarely survive in archaeological sites, so what is preserved is only a fragment of the whole material culture. I was fortunate enough to find ice age bone tools in limestone Cloggs Cave.[71] Most common were sturdy awls made from kangaroo fibulae. A glossy sheen on the tips shows they were used to pierce holes through animal skins, presumably to make skin cloaks with kangaroo sinew as thread, as was still done in recent times. Awls were also used to 'sew' canoes, for instance by the Wik people in Cape York.

» Climate change

When humans first arrived in Australia, the climate was wetter and rather cooler than now, with more surface water. Conditions deteriorated during the last glaciation (c. 28–19 kya), when sea level dropped to minus 120 m (395 ft), exposing wide continental shelves.[72] This meant drier air masses and less rainfall for the interior. Inland Australia became a dustbowl, combining the harshest aspects of present-day Tierra del Fuego and Inner Mongolia. At the peak of the last ice age, temperatures were at least six degrees centigrade colder than today. Most inland lakes dried up, deserts expanded and sand-dunes covered a third of the continent. The Kimberley and Mungo regions were abandoned for many millennia, people taking refuge in the narrow, green, coastal strip. Only Tasmania was heavily glaciated, but small glaciers capped the Snowy Mountains in the southeast and treeless plains replaced earlier woodlands.

Nevertheless, human occupation continued on the coasts, and the end of the ice age at c. 14 kya saw only minor changes to traditional life. The climate became milder when continental shelves were flooded. As the coastline moved inland, rainfall increased, and this became more rapid after 10 kya. The new coastline gave richer opportunities for human settlement. Stabilisation of sea level about 6500 years ago extended tidal reefs and estuaries, with their accessible fish and shellfish resources. At river-mouths sandy barriers now formed lagoons. Food-rich small bays developed in drowned river valleys such as Sydney Harbour. Many regions became more favourable for human exploitation, and population increased.

The most drastic post-glacial change was the flooding of one seventh of Sahul. On the gently sloping northern plains, at times the sea inundated 5 km (3 miles) of land annually. Even in the Great Australian Bight, 1 km (⅔ mile) of coast disappeared every fifteen years. This dramatic loss of habitable land drove people inland, causing greater competition for resources. At the same time, as rainfall increased, population levels went up. Rainfall and population size were closely correlated in most of pre-historic Australia.

Displacement and population growth apparently led to increasing warfare and territoriality, changes reflected in rock paintings. The earliest great battle scenes belong to the time of rising seas. Anthropologist Bob Layton and others have argued that distinctive regional rock art styles also developed as visual markers of clan identity, and territorial organisation changed from flexible, cooperative and bonding to the bounding type, with clear boundaries separating groups. They suggest clan totemism—the use of inherited emblems to represent a group of people related by descent from shared Ancestral Beings—developed as a more effective means of local organisation, with groups firmly anchored in the landscape and focused on the defence of local territories.[73]

Paintings of yams first appeared in post-glacial times, when tropical rainfall increased to an annual average of more than 1200 mm (47 inches), the critical threshold for their growth. The encroaching ocean may also have engendered the myth of the Rainbow Serpent, which is believed to have emerged from the sea to create the landscape and give birth to many babies. Some became humans, others the first animals. The Rainbow Serpent then created food, shelter and freshwater springs and became a peacemaker, promoting alliance among local clans.[74]

» Appearance of the dingo and new artefacts

New, specialised, composite artefacts known as the 'Small Tool Tradition' proliferated in post-glacial times.[75] Typically, small blades were hafted onto wooden handles, comprising stone points used as spear-tips and backed-blades. Microlithic backed-blades occur in huge numbers—20 000 were found in one small, arid area (Arcoona) near Lake Torrens, South Australia. Functional analyses have shown that backed-blades served as spear-barbs and teeth on saw-knives. They probably armed prehistoric death spears, which have as many as 40 sharp stone flakes set into two grooves on the shaft.

Backed-blades and stone points were alternative methods of arming a spear for greater penetrating power. Both were weapons. Stone-armed spears were effective, portable new projectiles that maximised hunting success in unfamiliar environments. They were ideal for mobile hunters combating high ecological risks while spreading into previously uninhabited or little-used regions, such as sandy deserts. The two varieties of stone-armed spear have different but overlapping distributions that correlate with different raw materials, for stone-tipped spears were made only where long reeds or other lightweight shafts were available.

Australian backed-blades and points closely resemble those of the Mesolithic (Middle Stone Age) of the far south of India and Sri Lanka, another link to the Dravidians. The antiquity of geometric microliths in Sri Lanka is as early as 28 000 years. Similar microlithic tools have been found in the Andaman Islands, Java, Sulawesi and mainland Southeast Asia in 9000-year-old contexts.[76] Diffusion from outside Australia therefore seemed a possibility but recently, indisputable backed artefacts (of the type known as geometric microliths) have been excavated from a 15 000-year-old layer at Riversleigh in northwest Queensland.[77] Backed-blades also appear in Mussel Shelter in the Sydney region at 9000 years. Archaeologists Michael Slack, Peter Hiscock and Val Attenbrow suggest backing of artefacts was a technological strategy in operation at various times in the past rather than the product of diffusion by a particular ethnic group from overseas, but more data are needed to resolve this question.[78]

Australia's stone points may tell a similar story of independent invention followed by widespread proliferation in the mid-Holocene. The earliest come from Kakadu about 7000 years ago, but further excavation and a larger sample size may change the picture. The earliest stone points found in the Kimberley are in coastal sites dating to around 5000 years ago and inland 1500 years later.[79] The renowned, pressure-flaked, bifacially worked Kimberley points are a much later development.

Another artefact to appear in the Holocene was the multipurpose spear-thrower. A stone tool was usually mounted with resin on the distal end opposite the hook. In arid regions, this was a 'tula' flake for working hard desert timbers. The Tiwi of Bathurst and Melville Islands, who were cut off from the mainland about 6500 years ago, have no spear-throwers. Significantly, simple javelin-type spears with barbs cut in solid wood are typical of these islands and other regions that lack spear-throwers. Javelins were too heavy to use with spear-throwers and seem an earlier type. This was confirmed by the chance discovery of plain and single-barbed wooden javelins in Wyrie Swamp peat bog, South Australia, where they lay in a 10 000-year-old campsite with boomerangs and digging sticks. Everywhere javelins preceded spear-throwers.[80]

The appearance of spear-throwers in late Bradshaw paintings allows us to date their presence in the Kimberley to between 4500 and 8000 years ago, and the Tiwi evidence indicates introduction into Australia after 6500 years ago. Linguist Patrick McConvell has discovered significant similarities in words used in various Aboriginal languages for spear-thrower, pointing to its rapid diffusion from Cape York Peninsula.

One indisputable import into Australia was the dingo or wild dog (*Canis familiaris dingo*), which was not part of the continent's native fauna.[81] Dingoes were in Australia by 4000 years ago.[82] They closely resemble the Asian pariah dogs that are widespread in Indonesia, Bangladesh and India. The mtDNA of all dingoes has proved to be extremely similar, indicating all descend from a very small founding population, possibly a single pregnant female, brought from Indonesia 5000–4000 years ago.[83]

» New developments in rock art

Intriguingly, the equipment used by animated hunters painted on rock-shelter walls in northern Australia mirrors the 10 000-year-old excavated artefacts of Wyrie Swamp. Both the Dynamic figures of Arnhem Land and the Bradshaws of the Kimberley hold boomerangs and plain or multi-barbed javelins. Hunters are small, finely drawn figures painted in red ochre, often of purple-red or mulberry hue. They are shown in profile view, unlike virtually all other human representations in Australian rock art. Bradshaws (which were named after the first European Australian to describe them and are also known as 'gwion gwion'), average only 20–30 cm (10–12 inches) in height. Later the two styles diverge markedly, profile figures continuing in Arnhem Land but not in the Kimberley, where huge, frontal Wandjina spirits succeeded Bradshaws.

Both Dynamics and Bradshaws appear suddenly with no obvious precursors. Rock art expert Grahame Walsh therefore suggested that Bradshaws mark 'the possible arrival of a different group'. He has compared Dynamic and Bradshaw style figures with overseas rock art and demonstrated remarkably close similarities with North Africa.[84] Walsh established a rock art sequence by examining hundreds of superimposed paintings. The Bradshaw style ended about 5000 years ago when hunters with spear-throwers and stone-tipped spears first appear in paintings and the first stone points occur in occupation deposits. Bradshaw paintings also depict extinct thylacines but not dingoes. The Bradshaw style therefore lasted until 5000–4000 years ago, but the Dynamic style finished rather earlier as it doesn't show dingoes, spear-throwers or stone points.

Walsh argues for ice age antiquity for Bradshaw paintings and Bert Roberts obtained age-determinations on wasps' nests overlying paintings by dating pollen and quartz grains from deep inside. This gave a minimum age of 19.6±1.7 kya for a Bradshaw figure overlain by a wasp nest.[85] Roberts has produced preliminary dates of up to 35 kya for traces of earlier art comprising hand and grass prints and hand-stencils. Early engravings are circles, tracks and cupules. The huge, naturalistic figures painted in outline, known as the 'Irregular Infill Animal Style', may be of similar antiquity, for shell associated with large engraved figures in the Pilbara gave an age of 21 kya.[86] It seems that tropical Australia was inhabited early, but mostly abandoned during the arid peak of the last glaciation. Then as sea level rose, people moved back again.

» Languages

The 250 distinct Aboriginal languages divide into a number of different language families. Each family comprises languages related to each other in pronunciation, grammar and shared vocabulary, which probably derive from a common ancestral language. One of these language families covers almost 90 per cent of the continent and some words occur right across this vast region, for example, 'mara' or 'mala' for 'hand' and 'pina' for 'ear'. This homogeneous family is termed Pama-Nyungan (PN) (pronounced pahma-nyoongan), after the words for 'person' at the northeastern and southwestern ends of the linguistic region. The PN group contains 'suffixing languages': suffixes are added to the end of words to indicate grammatical functions. The more complex non-PN varieties consist of 60 languages in nine language groups, spoken in the Kimberley, Top End and Gulf of Carpentaria region. Non-PN languages have undergone grammatical innovations and are profoundly dissimilar in lexicon to PN. In particular, prefixes are added to verbs to indicate subject and object, using elements that were formerly separate pronouns to make incredibly long words.

Dixon attributes the underlying similarity of Australian languages to descent from an ancient proto-Australian language and the differences between PN and non-PN as due to elaboration in the tropical north. Others such as Patrick McConvell suggest PN expanded only about 6000 years ago from a homeland near the Gulf of Carpentaria.[87] Vocabularies for Tasmania, which was separated from the mainland for 14 000 years, are fragmentary but also indicate suffixes, and some words and the sound system are very similar to those of Victorian languages.[88]

Have Australian indigenous languages any affinities with the outside world? Dravidian of southern India is the only connection that deserves any consideration, according to Dixon. Similarities between Australian and Dravidian languages were noticed as far back as 1856 by Bishop Caldwell. There are remarkable superficial resemblances, especially in sound systems, but languages change so rapidly that after a few millennia, linguistic connections are almost impossible to prove. Research has shown that in Australia about 15 per cent of basic word stock changes after every 1000 years.[89]

» New foods in the diet

In the last 4000 years, some new food management techniques were adopted and people began to utilise new foods, such as starchy cycad seeds that were highly toxic until poisons were leached out by prolonged soaking or burial in soil. Others began to climb the Snowy Mountains each summer to feast on huge aestivating masses of migratory Bogong moths, an easily caught source of protein that taste like roast chestnuts when grilled on a stone 'hotplate'. Archaeological evidence shows that moth hunting is at least 1000 years old.[90]

Stone-built traps were widely used to catch fish, both coastally and inland. Large eels, *Anguilla australis occidentalis*, were particularly abundant in western Victoria, where traps were built from basalt blocks. At Toolondo in the western district, Aborigines excavated an artificial channel 2.5 km (1½ miles) long to join two swamps, cutting through a low divide to let water flow in either direction. This drainage system operated as a form of swamp-management, retaining water in times of drought and coping with excess during floods.[91] Archaeologist Harry Lourandos calculates the Toolondo system would have taken 13 000 hours of labour, and 3000 m³ (3924 cubic yards) of earth would have been excavated. Stone tools indicate the channels were Aboriginal-built and prehistoric.

A thousand people gathered for a month or two's eeling and ceremonies at places such as the Lake Bolac outlet in western Victoria. Each family built its own stone-walled trap and in the opening placed an eel-pot made from strips of bark or plaited rushes with willow-hoop at its mouth. Men standing behind the trap grabbed eels emerging through the narrow end of the tapered pot. They killed the eels by biting them on the back of the head and then threaded them onto a stick to take back to camp and roast on the fire.

Large, stone-built eel-traps at nearby Lake Condah are less than 2000 years old for they could operate only during present-day lake-levels, not lower or higher levels as existed earlier. At the beginning of the wet season each autumn, increased water-flow triggers migration of eels that metamorphose from the yellow-brown to the silver stage, enabling them to adapt from fresh- to saltwater and swim down to the sea and their tropical breeding grounds. Eel hunters spent March and April operating their traps and smoking the eels in hollow trees. They traded the surplus with other groups and buried some in the ground. Similarly, Wik people dried native plums for later consumption—rare examples of short-term food storage.

» Stone houses in villages?

Southwestern Victoria is littered with rough, football-sized lumps of basalt from local extinct volcanoes. Aborigines heaped these small boulders into low, horseshoe-shaped walls roofed with sticks and bark-sheets. No mortar was used and the irregular rocks were not modified in any way. I have seen dozens of these hut-bases and none exceeds 30 cm (1 ft) high. Most huts occurred singly and were 2–3 m (7–10 ft) wide, housing a family of four to seven, averaging five. Hut size was proportional to the number of occupants. One hut with a diameter of 4–5 m (13–16 ft) housed eleven people.[92]

The inhabitants of this fertile region, later known as *Australia Felix*, were more sedentary than most other hunter-gatherers, but still moved camp several times each year. In autumn, several hundred people assembled to exploit eels and each family built itself a temporary hut. Such hut-groups were not permanent and to describe them as some have done as 'villages of stone houses' is an exaggeration. The term 'village' implies permanent residents living in a cluster of permanent homes in the country. Nowhere in Aboriginal Australia did this happen; even in the richest environments people moved camp several times a year as local food supplies were exhausted. Even eel fishermen moved every month or so.[93] In poorer coastal regions, such as Australia's southwest, the Nyungar seldom stayed longer than two or three days in one place, almost never more than a week and usually only one day. The main reasons for such frequent moves were to obtain varied, fresh food and avoid the rubbish that built up and the insect pests that were attracted when they camped for too long.[94]

» Continuity and change

Australian Aborigines have been described as 'an unchanging people living in an unchanging environment'. However, change did occur even if it was less revolutionary than on other continents.[95] Over 50 millennia, Australians adapted to significant climatic shifts. Between 30 and 20 kya Central Australia became a waterless dustbowl and people were forced out to the coastal fringe, only later to be driven inland again by rising glacial melt-water. The sea's advance was erratic, but at times it inundated significant areas. On the shrunken landmass there were more mouths to feed, and population also rose as food resources increased in favourable warm, wet, post-glacial conditions. This led to greater competition for resources and intensification of food collection strategies, such as communal fish traps. Increased territoriality and regionalisation are clear from the development of more distinctive rock art styles that feature scenes of warfare. About 3500 years ago, further environmental stress began, and continues today, with frequent severe droughts or floods, each occurring once every 3–7 years. This led to the development of other survival strategies, such as long-distance kinship networks that help desert people migrate into other tribal territories during lengthy droughts.[96]

« »

Why did food production, pottery, metallurgy, architecture or towns not develop in prehistoric Australia? One reason was its isolation, but another more telling factor was that Australians had no need to change; Australia experienced far less drastic environmental change than the northern hemisphere, where vast ice sheets made much of northern America and Eurasia almost uninhabitable and only those who adapted by developing new items such as clothing could survive. Unlike humans trapped in ice age France and Spain, nomadic Australians could adapt to climate change by moving elsewhere in their vast island continent. Whereas most other populations became food-producers of necessity, Australians were able to continue opportunistic hunter-gathering to the present day. Their fundamental adaptation to this driest of continents had been made over 50 000 years ago by ancestors who developed a way of life ideally suited to Australia's harsh, unpredictable climate.

ASSIMILATION

A time of trouble (1930s–1970s)

Before the 1970s, government policy towards Aborigines went through three broad phases—protection, assimilation and integration. From 1788, the main thrust was protection from harmful colonial influences. Protection varied over time and space; at its best it eased the transition from traditional to modern Western society, at its worst it was coercive and racist. Then, in the late 1930s, both humanitarians and Aboriginal leaders such as William Cooper proposed the then radical policy of assimilation—the cultural process of making similar. Assimilation aimed to enable indigenous people to have the same levels of education, health, employment and material comfort as the dominant society. The ends were held to justify the means, which were the removal and education of mixed-race children for intermarriage and absorption into Anglo-Australia. By the late 1960s, assimilation had fallen into disrepute, because it involved forcible child removal, institutionalisation and loss of racial identity.

» Protection

In new colonies, missionaries were usually foremost in protecting indigenous people, but not in Australia. Conversion of 'heathens' was not among the motives for sailing to Botany Bay. Only one clergyman, Protestant Reverend Richard Johnson, sailed with the First Fleet and it wasn't until 1815 that the first 'native institution' or mission was set up. Christianity aimed to raise Aborigines from 'barbarism' to 'civilisation' by education. Missionaries hoped that if 'they were taught to think as we think, to feel as we feel, to live as we live, then the Aborigines would be blended with the general population'. They argued that 'humanity and Christian mercy constrained them to raise the Aborigines from their abject wretchedness. They should also make some recompense for depriving them of their lands. The best recompense, as they saw it, was to teach the Aborigines to appreciate the advantages of Christian civilisation. The difficulty was that . . . the Aborigines spurned the gift.'[1] Missionaries recognised colonial society's terrible effects on those Aboriginal people who had become urban fringe-dwellers. They sought government land grants to provide refuges from alcoholism, violence, disease, prostitution and begging, and offered rations, medical aid, education and training for employment. However, very few missions were established. Tasmania had none until Wybalenna in 1833 and missions in other states were too few, too impoverished and too late. New South Wales had only seven missions in over 800 000 km² (300 000 sq. miles).

The first mission outside Sydney was founded in 1824 by Reverend Lancelot Threlkeld near Port Macquarie (now Newcastle). High costs forced him to open a coal-mine nearby to support the initiative. Threlkeld made few converts but mastered the now-extinct Awabakal language and published a grammar in 1834—the earliest published systematic study of an Australian language. He also translated some of the Anglican prayerbook and New Testament. The mission closed in 1841, for its congregation had vanished 'from the Aborigines becoming extinct in these districts'. Depopulation was caused by disease, conflict and voluntary movement to towns for white men's goods. Soon few Awabakal remained. Even Threlkeld's main assistant, Biraban, deserted the mission for urban attractions and died an alcoholic.[2] The second New South Wales mission, founded at Wellington in 1825, closed in 1842 because of alcoholism and depopulation. The death toll at missions was often high because measles, tuberculosis and other infectious diseases affected *all* resident Aborigines plus incomers seeking medical help, but mortality among the untreated was even greater.

Why were Australia's early missions so unsuccessful compared with those on Pacific and Torres Strait islands? The Pacific crusaders were often indigenous Christian converts who risked their lives to go and convert their fellows, but Aboriginal Australia didn't have fixed communities or a social order readily able to adapt to new ways. Nomadic Aborigines were unwilling to settle in one place and frequently deserted the missions, as attendance was voluntary. Missionaries saw indigenous people as 'children of God' in need of salvation, education and training, whereas Aborigines saw no point in white men's drudgery and little in education, although white medicine and hospitals were appreciated. The gulf was too wide, even though both Christians and southeastern Aborigines believed in an afterlife and an all-powerful Father in the sky. Once their traditional culture was undermined, tribal Aborigines became 'the people in-between'—they couldn't continue to live their old life and didn't fit readily into white society.

In 1838 the Aborigines Protection Society was founded in London. A British government report from the same period recommended the appointment of missionaries, reservation of hunting grounds, schooling for the young and special laws to keep them safe. 'No expenditure should be withheld which can be incurred judiciously for the maintenance of missionaries, who should be employed to instruct the tribes, and of protectors, whose duty it should be to protect them.' The committee was well

›› *27. Albert Namatjira painting near Burgundy Mountain, Alice Springs, Northern Territory, c. 1940–50.*

›› *28. Dick Roughsey (Goobalathaldin), 1920–85, from Mornington Island, Queensland. He won major prizes for his children's books,* Giant Devil Dingo *and* The Rainbow Serpent, *and published his autobiography in 1971.*

›› **29.** *Camp at Papunya, Northern Territory, 1980, with dot-painting. Papunya was established by the federal government in 1959 to provide a home for desert people.*

›› **30.** *Witchetty grubs in the centre of a large dot painting by Billy Stockman Tjapaltjarri.*

›› **31.** *Woman collecting grubs from the roots of witchetty bushes* (Acacia kempeana) *near Uluru, Northern Territory.*

›› **32.** *Aborigines setting the scrub alight in the Balgo region, Western Australia.*

›› **33.** *Close-up of a line painting on bark being created by an Aboriginal artist in 1978. He uses a fine brush made of bark fibre to cross-hatch the body of a goose.*

›› **34.** *An Aboriginal woman demonstrating bush foods. Many indigenous people now earn their living on their traditional lands, passing on their bush skills in tourism and eco-tourism projects.*

›› **35.** *Aboriginal protest on Sydney Harbour during the bicentenary celebrations in 1988.*

›› **36.** *Aboriginal children on swings at Papunya, Northern Territory.*

›› **37.** 'Sorry; written in kilometre-high letters during the Reconciliation march, 28 May 2000. The aerial message was a grassroots initiative of a group of non-indigenous Sydneysiders, who 'just wanted to send a really strong message that we were sorry'.

›› **38.** Reconciliation march across Sydney Harbour Bridge, 28 May 2000. About 200 000 people walked across the bridge in an expression of goodwill and support for the Aboriginal cause, probably the largest turnout on a single day for a particular cause in Australian history.

» **39.** These woven containers were made in 1972 by Burarra women, Blyth River, central coastal Arnhem Land. When carried, the handles are suspended from the forehead and the containers hang down the back.

» **40.** An indigenous artist with the silk fabric she designed. Since the 1970s, Aboriginal design and production of batik and other textiles has become internationally renowned, and provides a cash income in remote communities.

» **41.** *Bill Harney (left) applying white pipeclay body decoration to fellow Wardaman people for a corroboree at the rain-making site of the Lightning Brothers, Yiwarlarlay, Northern Territory.*

aware of the problems of colonisation *without* missionaries: 'the intercourse of Europeans in general . . . has been, unless when attended by missionary exertions, a source of many calamities to uncivilised nations'.[3]

Nonetheless, missions were given little else but land until the 1950s. Many of the 211 missions established in Australia survived only a few years, but others like the Benedictine mission at New Norcia, Western Australia (1847–1970s), and the Lutheran mission of Hermannsburg, Northern Territory (1877–1982), were long-term successes.[4] Hermannsburg effectively prevented the destruction of the western Arrernte people in the face of the advancing cattle industry, whereas eastern Arrernte, unprotected by any mission, almost disappeared. Aborigines found missions useful sanctuaries from black enemies and trigger-happy whites. Old people and children could stay there in safety and medical help was available. Missions provided a reliable food supply and a place to leave children temporarily when going out bush. They kept kinsfolk together and became a home for dispossessed people, establishing many communities that still survive.

Further mission stations were set up in southern Australia, such as Point McLeay, South Australia (1859), Maloga, Victoria (1874), and Warangesda, New South Wales (1879). Later, the mission years were seen as a golden age when protection, land, food, health care, work, houses, schools, churches, law and order were provided. Strength in numbers and shared identity promoted Aboriginal solidarity. Missions fostered health, education and the Christian moral code of non-violence. The downside was that some Aboriginal men's authority was usurped by European missionaries and superintendents. Senior men's role as educators was diminished by Western education, and their status declined while women's tended to increase. Aboriginal women now often dominate the family and have become community leaders, whereas many men have lost both status and self-respect.

The best missions, such as Hermannsburg and Kunmunya in the Kimberley, helped to preserve Aboriginal culture, but many tried to stamp out Aboriginal customs and beliefs and treated Aborigines like children. As late as 1977 at Kalumburu a Spanish Benedictine monk's daily greeting to a group of middle-aged Aborigines was 'good morning boys and girls'. Missionary Robert Love of Kunmunya, however, declared: 'In this mission we will never tolerate paternalism. These people are our equals in intelligence, and our superiors in physique. The only differences are in the colours of our skins and the fact that we have had centuries more practice at becoming civilised.'[5]

During his 28 years at Hermannsburg (now Ntaria) from 1894, missionary Carl Strehlow became fluent in Arrernte and translated the scriptures. His son, Ted Strehlow, collected sacred artefacts for safekeeping, now housed in a special 'keeping place' in Alice Springs. Christianity was forcefully promoted—only Christians could eat in the communal kitchen. This Lutheran policy led to 172 converts in 28 years.

Some were equivalent to 'rice Christians' in India but others were genuine believers and a few became pastors. Aboriginal painter Albert Namatjira was born there in 1902, educated in the boys' dormitory and became both a baptised Christian and an initiated elder, yet his sad story shows the immense problems of trying to bridge two such different worlds (see Chapter 8). Many missionaries tried to prevent initiation ceremonies that they deemed 'barbarous'. Many also opposed polygyny, to which Bishop Gsell on Bathurst Island developed a pragmatic solution—he bought the infant brides. In his book *The Bishop with 150 Wives*, he recounts how between 1921 and 1938 he used tobacco and metal axes to buy little girls from the old men to whom they were betrothed, raised them as Christians in the mission dormitory and then found them husbands among young men who would otherwise have waited much longer for a wife. While this satisfied Western objections to child brides, it disastrously disrupted Aboriginal marriage systems.[6]

Not all missions were unhappy places: I well remember Dick Roughsey (Goobalathaldin, which means 'rough sea') fondly reminiscing by our campfire in north Queensland about his days at the Scottish Presbyterian mission on Mornington Island, where he learnt to read, write a beautiful copperplate hand and sing hymns and folk songs in a Scottish brogue! He trained as a stockman, but later became an artist, children's book author, chairman of the Australia Council's Aboriginal Arts Board and won an OBE. He also won major prizes for his children's books, *Giant Devil Dingo* and *The Rainbow Serpent*, and in 1971 published *Moon and Rainbow: The Autobiography of an Aboriginal*.[7]

In northern Australia, twenty more Christian missions were founded between the 1880s and 1920s, mainly on islands or the coast, where supplies could be brought in by boat. The main attraction of the missions was food and tobacco, provided as reward for labour and church attendance. The response of the Njul Njul people of Beagle Bay in the Kimberley to this moral blackmail was—'no more tobacco, no more h'Allelulia'![8]

Twentieth-century pressure to shut down missions was intended to help Aborigines but has achieved the opposite. Frequent criticisms were that missionaries were too authoritarian, suppressed indigenous culture, customs and language and undermined families by separating children from their parents and making them sleep in single-sex dormitories. While these criticisms have some validity, what has replaced missions is infinitely worse. Outback communities may have achieved land ownership but there has been a huge increase in substance abuse, domestic violence and crime and a sharp decline in health, education and jobs. Missions still functioning today are confined to the Torres Strait Islands and remote parts of the Northern Territory and Western Australia, especially the Kimberley, where they provide a superb service in very difficult conditions. Now only 40 'missions' remain in remote regions (17 in Northern Territory, 14 in Queensland and 9 in Western Australia).

» *The Aboriginal village at Yarrabah Mission south of Cairns, Queensland, c. 1900. This Anglican mission was founded in 1892. Initially benign, an increasingly harsh regime developed and all traditional activities were banned. In 1960 the church handed over Yarrabah to the Queensland government, which continued to control every detail of the lives of Yarrabah people. In 1986 Yarrabah became self-managing with limited rights to the reserve land under the Deed of Grant in Trust system. It is now home to 3000 people.*

» A dying race?

Missionaries aimed both to convert the 'pagan savages' and to ease their passing. In 1837 Bishop Broughton made a comment that was to be extremely influential: 'They appear . . . gradually to decay; they diminish in numbers; . . . within a very limited period . . . they will be extinct.' Churchman J.D. Lang thought rapid population decline might be due to 'Divine Providence', others to 'some unknown force'.[9] Colonisation's terrible impact was known by 1858, when the editor of the *Melbourne Age* newspaper told readers to try to 'smooth the pillow of a dying race'.

In 1836, the young Charles Darwin visited Australia on his round-the-world voyage in the *Beagle*. His fascinating observations clearly strongly influenced his later theories, but seem almost unknown among writers on Aboriginal Australia. In the Bathurst region on the tablelands west of Sydney, Darwin met 'a party of a score of the black aborigines . . . each carrying, in their accustomed manner, a bundle of spears and other weapons . . . they were all partly clothed and several could speak a little English: their countenances were good-humoured and pleasant, and they appeared far from being such utterly degraded beings as they have usually been

« ERNABELLA/PUKATJA »

Ernabella Mission (1937–74) in Central Australia was a model of what the best missions should be. It resulted from the vision of a Presbyterian surgeon from Adelaide, Charles Duguid, who understood that tribal Aborigines' survival depended upon being given freedom and adequate opportunity to adapt to the inevitable changes they would experience. They needed time to absorb new ways, assess new values and choose new directions. There was to be no compulsion, no imposition of Western ways and no interference with tribal customs. They would need a new faith to sustain them as old beliefs disappeared, but Ernabella's firm policy was that Aborigines should be free to accept or reject Christianity. In fact, some did become Christians, the concept of the Dreaming or Law—'tjukurpa'—providing a ready link with the Bible's teaching of 'In the beginning was the Word'.

Duguid believed that immediate medical help should be offered, mission staff should be trained in particular skills and obliged to learn the language, and responsibility should be quickly passed to the Aborigines.[a] Teaching was in Pitjantjatjara for the first five years of a child's schooling, so that they could read and write their own tongue. (Although there is very limited literature available in Aboriginal languages, this literacy in Pitjantjatjara enabled them to write each other letters in later years when away from the mission.) Arithmetic was rudimentary, since in Pitjantjatjara there are no numbers beyond four. There was no compulsion to wear clothes, which harbour germs unless washed frequently, not easy in the desert. Schoolchildren had fun each morning hosing each other down before settling to lessons under the shade of paperbark trees in the sandy creek bed. Babies were looked after in the traditional way. No nappies were used, but Duguid recalls:

> I remember seeing an Aboriginal tribal mother hold out her baby for a bowel
> motion, and then clean its buttocks by scraping them gently with a flat stone.
> After that she powdered them with fine sand. By contrast to this, my wife has
> told me of the expression of disgust on one Aboriginal mother's face when she
> was staying in our home and was shown how a white mother used nappies for
> a baby and washed them clean after use.

Teacher Winifred Hilliard described Ernabella's early days and the reaction of a Pitjantjatjara group when they came out of the desert in 1951 and saw their first whites: 'They had their first sight of strange people with fair skins, long noses and "weak" blue eyes, and were not impressed.'[b]

Only a few changes were made to traditional ways. Aborigines regarded it as a waste to give food to somebody near death when there were others in greater need. The superintendent found one such case in camp and undertook to supervise feeding the patient. The man recovered and was 'most grateful'. Infanticide was also banned. When the first set of twins was born at the mission in 1961, it took a week for the mother to agree to keep both babies and her husband uttered some threats, believing that there must have been two fathers.

The mission provided employment opportunities for both men and women and introduced them to wages, and a cash economy. There was a shop, where they learnt to buy food to cook in their camp. They found white people's routine and the long hours of labour incomprehensible; there is no word for work in any Aboriginal language. Nevertheless, men learnt fence-building, well-sinking, carpentry, sheep-shearing and brick-making, and proudly built their own houses of mud brick. One young man who had lost his leg after being speared in a tribal fight was taught to touch-type and earned his living preparing school materials. The women's craft centre, Ernabella Arts, produced a wide range of goods for sale and became renowned for batik-dyed fabrics featuring Aboriginal designs.

Then came the 1970s and pressure for land rights, self-determination and self-management. The result was that in 1974 administration of Ernabella was transferred to a local Aboriginal council and subsequently the land was handed back under the *Pitjantjatjara Land Rights Act* of 1981. Under its new name, Pukatja, Ernabella still exists and the craft centre continues but now Pukatja suffers the problems of so many outback Aboriginal communities. Standards of nutrition, hygiene, health and education have declined horrendously, petrol-sniffing and drunkenness are rife and dedicated missionaries have been replaced by short-term employees, who tend to 'burn out' in a couple of years.

Paul Toohey, a well-respected journalist, visited Pukatja, one of a dozen communities of the Anangu-Pitjatjantjara Lands, in 2001. He paints a horrifying picture of a community in crisis in 'a shabby desert town of filthy tin houses and office buildings that look more like jail blocks':

In the town of Pukatja, population 400, there are 60 petrol sniffers. They control the town and everyone is frightened . . . there is no sense of community . . . Liquor is banned but there are drunks. Petrol-sniffing is illegal but is now fully accepted as a part of life. Sniffers roam town, all day, cans stuck to their faces . . . Petrol . . . is sold to children by greedy relatives or even given by parents in order to protect themselves from their children's violent demands . . . White people work behind iron doors or grilles because sniffers and drunks pull knives or star-pickets when they don't get their way . . . The Aborigines are almost entirely welfare-dependent . . . There is no police presence on the Lands, apart from Aboriginal police aides. Inevitably, these men have petrol-sniffing children or relatives . . . Relatives use the powerful obligations inherent in the skin-family system to persuade aides not to prosecute their own . . . The physical effect of petrol-sniffing is described by doctors as 'similar to an electrical short', whereby fatty tissue on brain nerve-endings wastes away, causing the 'wires' to flail about in the brain. Many sniffers eventually lose the ability to stand upright. Those who manage to cheat death are likely to find themselves wheelchair-bound and in full-time care. The Ngaanyatjarra Council, representing remote communities in Western Australia, has identified 40 young people from its area either dead or permanently intellectually or physically disabled from petrol-sniffing in a 15-year period. It also reports a prevalence of sexual violence and 'an acutely high risk of exposure to HIV' among sniffers, who tend to have 'multiple sexual partners with similarly poor sexual health' . . .

'In the worst cases,' says Peter Morrison, a white community development officer in the Lands for eight years, there are 'nine-year-old girls sniffing petrol and being pack-raped. That's the reality of the Lands . . . I've got no love for the Christians, but when they were here there were butcher shops, vegetable gardens and people's health was better. They had something.' . . . Nyaningu, a Pukatja elder and church minister, says, 'We want the work to come back, horses, cattle, fencing, gardens, welding. We used to be busy. But whitefellas are like a cloud. They come and go.'[c]

« »

represented. In their own arts they are admirable . . . In tracking animals or men they show most wonderful sagacity; and I heard of several of their remarks which manifested considerable acuteness.'

Yet Darwin's favourable first impression was outweighed by pessimism about their future:

It is very curious thus to see in the midst of a civilised people, a set of harmless savages wandering about without knowing where they will sleep at night, and gaining their livelihood by hunting in the woods . . . The number of aborigines is rapidly decreasing . . . This decrease, no doubt, must be partly owing to the introduction of spirits, to European diseases . . . and to the gradual extinction of the wild animals . . . Besides the several evident causes of destruction, there appears to be some more mysterious agency generally at work. Wherever the European has trod, death seems to pursue the   209

aboriginal . . . The varieties of man seem to act on each other in the same way as differ-

ent species of animals—the stronger always extirpating the weaker . . . It was melancholy
at New Zealand to hear the fine energetic natives saying that they knew the land was
doomed to pass from their children.[10]

This belief in the stronger always destroying the weaker, whether animal or human, was expounded in Darwin's books, especially *The Descent of Man* published in 1871. Darwin's ideas were developed by others into the later disastrous theory of social Darwinism and the belief that Aborigines were less evolved than Europeans and therefore doomed to extinction. The inevitability of their disappearance became common doctrine, exemplified in Daisy Bates' 1937 book, *The Passing of the Aborigines*. What none then understood was that Darwin's 'mysterious agency' was nothing but the devastating impact of new diseases, which he had significantly underestimated. It was only the development of antibiotics and preventative modern medicine that saved the situation. Only in 1939 was the decline in tribal numbers halted and a slight increase recorded.

» Jobs

The earliest jobs for Aboriginal men came from the pastoral and whaling industries. By 1844, 300 Aboriginal whalers were employed in South Australia and Eden, New South Wales, where two whaleboats were successfully manned by all-Aboriginal crews.[11] The adventure and variety of whaling life appealed to Aboriginal hunters and they could go home for a break each year in the off-season.

Most Aboriginal people were prepared to negotiate with the newcomers, and were sufficiently wily to exploit them. They traded goods or did odd jobs to fulfil their immediate needs. Fish, animal skins and feathers were exchanged for food, tobacco and alcohol. In towns easy food was to be had from bakers and butchers by hewing wood or fetching water, Aboriginal women's sexual services were always in demand and children became adept at begging. By these strategies Aborigines could usually satisfy their hunger for white men's food, which acted like a magnet. For example, Protector William Thomas set up Nerre-Nerre-Warren reserve 65 km (40 miles) from Melbourne to keep Aborigines away from white men's vices and disease, only to find them always in town. Aborigines had 'strong motives' for begging, he wrote in 1843:

> On one day . . . in the public road [in Melbourne], I went up to four groups who had fires
> at midday enjoying themselves; I counted their mendicant fare . . . there were 21 good
> white loaves, besides abundance of meat from the shambles [slaughter yards]; one of
> them holding up two loaves exclaimed, 'no good Nerre-Nerre-Warren, "marnameek"
> (very good) Melbourne'.[12]

» The pastoral industry

Indigenous bush skills and local knowledge have always been highly valued, and Aboriginal stockmen formed the backbone of the vast new pastoral industry that developed between 1820 and 1900. Aboriginal men outnumbered white stockmen by five or six to one on the cattle and sheep properties or ranches known as stations, and Aboriginal women worked in homesteads and tended vegetable gardens, goats and chickens. Frontier districts always suffered from a severe shortage of labour, exacerbated from the 1850s by goldrushes that drew white labour away. On northern cattle stations Aborigines worked as drovers, stockmen and desert shepherds, for example at Ernabella (including pre-mission Ernabella). Further south in cooler, better-watered sheep country, they were needed as shepherds and shearers.

Mary Durack vividly describes pastoral life in her book *Kings in Grass Castles*, telling of generally good race relations in the outback during the opening-up of western Queensland and the Kimberley to cattle. Accounts by other pastoralists in the early phases of the cattle industry in north Queensland and the Northern Territory paint a similar picture, once the frontier phase was over.[13] Most managers had good

» *Aboriginal stockmen ride out from the stockyards to muster cattle on Beswick Station, Northern Territory, 1954.*

reputations among both blacks and whites. 'Bosses' were viewed by Aboriginal employees as their protectors. A good 'boss' or 'missus' was given a 'skin name'. Often Aborigines asked the 'boss' to give them a European first name and some also adopted the 'boss's' surname. Mutual respect, loyalty and trust developed. 'Bosses' intervened to protect their stockmen from police charges relating to tribal murders; the 'missus' entrusted her young children to Aboriginal women's care and white children learnt to speak the local Aboriginal language.

Many rural Aboriginal people have fond memories of living in a station community under a 'good boss', of horsemanship, corroborees each night in the camp and three months' wet season 'walkabout' when cattle-work was slack and they reverted to hunting and visiting sites in their own 'country'. It was a rough life and some bosses were violent but, because of the shortage of labour, it was in the manager's interest to treat his Aboriginal stockmen fairly well and look after their extended families. The highest praise for a 'boss' was that a camp 'never went hungry'. 'Tucker'—the bush term for food—was Aborigines' top priority; often it was European 'fast food'—bread, flour and beef—that first attracted them to come in from the bush. At a station the Aboriginal 'mob', as it was known, often numbered between 50 and 100 kinsfolk, in effect a whole residential group. In return for their labour and land, they expected enough food for the whole camp, including the old and sick. When supplemented with bush food, the diet was adequate and station Aborigines were much healthier than urban fringe-dwellers, particularly because on stations alcohol and opium were both banned and unavailable. Housing was usually 'humpies'—shelters made of corrugated-iron and hessian sacking—appalling to European eyes, but Aborigines considered their living conditions 'soft' by bush standards.[14]

At first pastoral workers were paid in food, clothing and tobacco. Cash was seldom used on stations—most European stockmen drew wages only once a year before leaving for their annual holiday. Most Aborigines had never seen money and didn't want it nor did they want European-style housing. What they did want was 'plenty tucker'. This situation was described as 'workin' longa tucker', an expression identifying their workplace with a food-gathering site. 'Workin' longa tucker' was a strategy that allowed Aborigines to fulfil their material and spiritual needs, to keep relatives together and continue sharing among kinsfolk. It also gave them a sense of pride. As historian Ann McGrath put it in her book *Born in the Cattle* (the name by which station-dwelling Aborigines are known): 'The mobility and status provided by horse-riding, stockwork and mustering allowed stockmen and women as individuals, and the station community as a whole, a certain feeling of pride. The vastness of most cattle runs and the outdoor nature of the work allowed a sense of space and liberty.'[15]

The period of paternalism but relative stability between 1910 and 1940 was generally considered a happy time—'after the wild times, before grog, before wages, before the Japanese war'. Initially Aboriginal pastoral communities considered cash-wages a problem rather than an asset. This was because payment in kind—rations, clothes, blankets and equipment—fitted well the Aboriginal sharing ethic, whereas cash paid to a few individuals did not. Nevertheless, without any consultation regarding their wants or needs, various Aboriginal Acts were passed (in Queensland in 1897, Western Australia in 1905 and the Northern Territory in 1911) laying down wage-rates for Aborigines in the pastoral industry. Inevitably Aboriginal women received far less than men and all were paid less than white workers; the best rate was two-thirds, in Queensland.

Pastoralists persuaded legislators that Aboriginal stockmen were less competent and reliable than white ones, but this was far from the truth. Aboriginal men, and some women, developed great skill at horsemanship and station work, especially finding lost cattle. As a white ringer (an Australian stock-worker or drover) pointed out: 'A white man rides around all day looking for cattle; an Aborigine rides around all day looking for cattle tracks. When he finds the tracks he will find the beast; a white man might wander for days and not see a beast.'[16]

Money was such a new phenomenon to Aboriginal pastoral workers that many did not actually claim their due wages. Those who did immediately shared with kinsfolk, for sharing is the most deeply ingrained of all Aboriginal traditions. Thrift and savings are totally alien concepts to people who did not even store food. In order, therefore, to provide a cushion against unemployment or sickness, up to two-thirds of Aboriginal adults' earnings (if clothing was provided) were held in trust by the state. By 1934, unclaimed Aboriginal trust funds amounted to £2400 in Western Australia, £3000 in the Northern Territory and a massive £293 549 in Queensland. Some protectors used trust funds to buy land for Aborigines, but most unclaimed money, with interest, reverted to consolidated government revenue. Aboriginal groups continue to lobby for the full return of these funds and accrued interest.[17]

» Changing times

The Australian Aborigines Progressive Association was formed in 1925 by New South Wales part-Aboriginal Fred Maynard, who campaigned for the right for Aborigines to be fully assimilated and left in control of their children.[18] The next year William Harris, a mixed-race farmer brought up in an orphanage, founded a similar body in Western Australia. The 1930s saw growing support for the Aboriginal cause from humanitarians, liberals and anthropologists such as A.P. Elkin, Bill Stanner and Donald Thomson, who sought to persuade the public that Aborigines were their intellectual equals. Aboriginal affairs hit the headlines in 1933 when three Arnhem Land tribesmen were gaoled for 20 years for killing five Japanese crewmen at Caledon Bay and another, Tuckiar, received the death penalty for murdering a white policeman. The federal government successfully appealed to the High Court and in 1934 the four were released, although Tuckiar disappeared while returning home. The government agreed to Thomson's request to send him alone into Arnhem Land to try to stop the killings; he emerged unscathed and recommended that tribal Aborigines be protected by strict segregation on large, inviolate reserves.

By the 1930s, tribal Aborigines were no longer living in southeastern Australia but some articulate men of mixed descent were campaigning for assimilation. At the time, assimilation was a radical policy that was not yet accepted by most white Australians. In 1937, John Patten and William Ferguson launched the Aborigines Progressive Association in New South Wales. Patten was an itinerant labourer and professional boxer and became a forceful public speaker. Ferguson left his mission school aged fourteen to become a sheep-shearer. Both spent their later lives campaigning for citizenship and better conditions on Aboriginal reserves. In Victoria, William Cooper established the Australian Aborigines League in 1932 and later sent a petition to King George V seeking federal control of Aboriginal administration and special Aboriginal electorates in federal parliament. The latter is contrary to the Australian constitution but the desire for federal rather than state responsibility for Aboriginal affairs led to the successful 1967 referendum (see Chapter 8). Cooper achieved worldwide publicity when he orchestrated an Aboriginal 'Day of Mourning' on 26 January 1938, when white Australia was celebrating the 150th anniversary of settlement. The 1938 protest influenced public opinion but the Second World War destroyed its momentum, and the impetus was not regained until the 1960s.

During the Second World War there were several changes to outback employment when Darwin, Port Hedland, Broome and other northern towns were bombed, and Australia faced a possible Japanese invasion. Over 3000 Aborigines joined the Volunteer Defence Corps for service within Australia. About 200 became de facto military personnel, patrolling northern coasts and rescuing stranded airmen, while others worked as civilian labourers on defence projects. They were fed army rations, housed and clothed and paid cash wages, the first cash some had ever received. They related well to regular troops and performed creditably. Another thousand mixed-race Aborigines enlisted in the army and served overseas, and one, Reg Saunders, became a commissioned officer. All were literate and of substantial European descent, as were the 300 or so from New South Wales, Victoria, South Australia and Queensland who served in the First World War. In 1945 a grateful nation revised its ideas about Aboriginal people, and in 1949 all Aboriginal ex-servicemen were given the vote in national elections, together with *all* Aborigines in New South Wales, Victoria, South Australia and Tasmania. Aborigines in these states had never been formally excluded from voting, but few did so. Then in 1961 a Senate committee on Aboriginal voting rights recommended that all Aborigines in all states and territories be immediately given the vote in federal elections, and by 1965 all indigenous people of Australia, whether literate or not, were enfranchised.[19]

The Original Australians

» First Aboriginal strikes

After the Second World War, attention turned to raising Aboriginal pastoral workers' pay and in 1947 the Northern Territory rate went up to 20 shillings a week—a big rise but still below white rates. Meanwhile in Western Australia the strike weapon came into play. In 1945 Aboriginal stockmen gathered in the Pilbara for both sacred and secular 'business'. They invited locally born white well-digger, mineral prospector and Aboriginal champion, Don McLeod, to attend the rituals and discuss how Aboriginal wages and living conditions could be improved and traditional life protected. McLeod suggested going on strike, as 30 stockmen from De Grey station had done the previous year for better food. Aboriginal decision-making involves long discussions until consensus is reached; after six weeks a strike was planned and sacred boards were sent out to inform all local Aboriginal communities. Co-organisers were McLeod, Dooley-Bin-Bin, a 'travelling Law man' and Clancy McKenna, an Aboriginal contractor. McLeod suggested they delay the strike until the Second World War ended. Just before sheep-shearing seemed a good time and MacLeod symbolically chose May Day. The problem of getting isolated, illiterate station-hands to act in unison was solved by making special calendars on which they marked off the days.

On 1 May 1946, Aboriginal stockmen on 20 out of 22 Pilbara properties went on strike, asking for 30 shillings a week plus keep. They survived by hunting kangaroos and prospecting for minerals, but the leaders were arrested and sentenced to three months' hard labour for 'enticing' Aborigines from their place of employment. Bail for McLeod was set at £300 (a year's wages) but through his contacts in Perth, a Committee for the Defence of Native Rights was formed and a protest meeting in Perth Town Hall was well-attended by churchmen, women's groups, academics, humanitarians, trade unionists and communists. A lawyer was employed, appeals lodged and the gaol sentences overturned. Aborigines learnt the useful lesson that, unlike their own immutable Law, white men's law could be altered. Little wonder that the first Aboriginal tertiary students chose to become lawyers!

In spite of harassment from police, pastoralists and government officials, industrial action lasted until the 1949 award of £3 per week plus keep, twice their original demand. However, only one in four Aboriginal stockmen returned to pastoral work. The rest had a vision of 'Narawuda', a land of promise and freedom, 'a station of our own' where they could make a living off their own land by running cattle and prospecting, 'a place for the old people to stay' and 'a school for the kids'.[20]

'The Group', as the strikers became known, formed a cooperative mining company. There was little equipment, money or even food, but lucrative finds of wolfram and tin were made, 700 starving Aboriginal men and women got picks and shovels and worked so hard that by 1951 they had saved £9000 and purchased a cattle station, Yandeyarra. That year they grossed £50 000! A new company, Pindan Proprietary Limited, was formed in 1955 and the group became the 'Pindan Mob'.

Success continued until 1960, when falling metal prices and other problems sent the company bankrupt and it acrimoniously split into two. One group set up Mugarinya Pastoral Company and later regained Yandeyarra under lease from the Aboriginal Lands Trust (set up in Western Australia in 1972). The other group formed Nomads Pty Ltd mining company and in 1971 acquired the 76 000 ha (190 000 acre) Strelley Station in northeastern Pilbara. The Nomad Strelley Aboriginal community is fiercely autonomous. An independent body handles outside grants and most individuals contribute their social-security benefits to a group fund. Fighting and traditional pay-back attacks are banned and rules on marriage and mother-in-law avoidance have been relaxed. Traditional law and culture are strong and initiations continue, but now circumcision is performed in hospital to avoid infection.[21]

» Equal pay

The worst abuses of Aboriginal employment ended after the Pilbara strike but there was still no equal pay. The cause was taken up by a new pressure group, the Federal Council for Advancement of Aborigines and Torres Strait Islanders (FCAATSI). This began in 1958, with 30 members drawn mainly from churches and trade unions, including just four Aborigines, but Aboriginal membership grew to 200 in the next decade. FCAATSI lobbied each Trade Union Congress until the 1963 Congress adopted a policy of ending discrimination against Aboriginal labour. A test case on equal pay for Northern Territory Aborigines was brought by the North Australian Workers Union (NAWU) in 1965. The Commonwealth Arbitration Commission visited cattle stations and heard pastoralists express grave concerns about the problems equal pay would cause Aborigines, who would lose their jobs because it would become impossibly expensive to pay them equal wages and also feed their many dependants. To a large extent, this is exactly what happened. However, the Commission believed it had no choice, declaring that 'there must be one industrial law, similarly applied to all Australians, Aboriginal or not'.

The dilemma policy-makers faced was that Australian law could not discriminate against Aboriginal stock-workers but 'it was clear to everyone that the institution of equal wages would result in the whole-scale removal of Aboriginal people from cattle station work to social security on the settlements—and the latter path was chosen. Of course, with hindsight this choice has had tragic consequences,' judges modern Cape York Aboriginal leader, Noel Pearson. Equal pay led to loss of contact with traditional lands, massive cultural and social impacts, long-term welfare dependency, passivity and disempowerment, leading to much of the present 'dysfunction' in Aboriginal communities. Pearson believes that a third option was available to 1960s policy-makers—'My own regret is that the resources that were made available by the federal government, through the social security system when people were removed to the settlements, were not instead used to subsidise wages for continued work in the cattle industry . . . I believe the social results would have been much better.'

The result of equal pay was that the Aboriginal communities of Cape York and elsewhere went from almost nil reliance on government welfare in 1970 to almost 100 per cent in 2005. This lack of work has been the foremost cause of the unravelling and near-destruction of Aboriginal society. There is a saying that for happiness in life you need only two things—love and work. And as another saying goes: 'The road to hell is paved with good intentions.'

In order to cushion the impact, the Commission decided to ease the award in over three years. This delay angered some people and there were further strikes, the focus of demands gradually changing from money to land rights—owning and living on one's traditional land.

The land rights movement had begun in 1963 when Yolngu tribesmen from Yirrkala Reserve, Northern Territory, sent a bark petition to Parliament protesting against excision of 390 km² (150 sq. miles) of their land for bauxite mining (see Chapter 8). Then in June 1966 Dexter Daniels from Roper River, an Aboriginal NAWU organiser, encouraged Gurindji stockman, Lupnga Giari or 'Captain Major', to bring Aborigines at Newcastle Waters station, Northern Territory, out on strike for equal pay. Twenty Aboriginal workers and 80 camp dependants left their rations and living-quarters and walked off to the nearest small town, Elliott, where trade union and welfare authorities provided food. Two months later they organised another walk-off, this time of 200 fellow Gurindji from Wave Hill station. Vincent Lingiari, a Gurindji elder, became their spokesman and they moved to Wattie Creek in the heart of 'their own country', set up camp in the dry bed of the Victoria River and began to live off the land.[22]

The Gurindji protest against poor pay and conditions rapidly turned into a claim for return of their traditional land, which was Crown Land leased by the huge British company, Vesteys. This strike was of tremendous symbolic and political significance. It marked a turning point in Aboriginal protest politics from workers' demands for better pay to an oppressed people campaigning for land. The Gurindji won widespread support. After two years of pressure, the federal government agreed to give them 26 km² (10 sq. miles) of land around Wattie Creek out of the 15 540 km² (6000 sq. miles) of Wave Hill station, where Vesteys retained their lease. This was the first real government recognition of an Aboriginal land claim, although very small. The Waterside Workers' Federation placed a $1 levy on its members and in 1970 presented the Gurindji with $10 000 to cover the costs of fencing. Lord Vestey offered a further 90 km², the cattle station Daguragu was established and 2500 km² of land was formally handed over in 1975 by the prime minister, Gough Whitlam. Finally, Gurindji were granted inalienable freehold title under the new *Aboriginal Land Rights (Northern Territory) Act* of 1976. A sad footnote to this story is that since 1991

Daguragu has been deserted, along with some other leases that were supposed to have provided various Aboriginal groups with an economic base.[23]

Aborigines who walked off stations kept their dignity but lost their jobs. The new award required both equal pay and good-quality housing to be provided for Aboriginal employees and their families—too expensive a package for cattle stations in such dry, rugged, unprofitable country. In some regions a third lost their jobs when it became uneconomical for pastoralists to employ Aborigines and support all their dependants, who averaged four per employee whereas most white stockmen were single. The Wave Hill drama had also raised fears of land rights claims, discouraging pastoralists from having a large black 'mob' in residence. Station managers reacted with more mechanisation, fencing and cattle-mustering by helicopter rather than on horseback to reduce employee numbers. Many Aborigines were evicted or simply walked off and set up fringe-camps around the nearest towns. A Kimberley hospital administrator commented in 1969: 'The Award created a multitude of problems affecting the [Aborigines] . . . as the stock work declined, more people drifted in . . . and by the end of December there were some 500 people in Fitzroy Crossing . . . Local names for this were and are the "ghetto" or "refugee camp".' Conditions there were inevitably much worse than on the worst station, and fringe-dwellers were exposed to all the dangers of 'grog' (cheap port and rum), gambling and prostitution.[24]

» Employment to unemployment

'Aboriginal employment history . . . was one few other Australians could match' was the wry comment of Richard Broome. 'They moved from no wages to small wages to "equal" wages and then to unemployment.'[25] This was in the 1960s and 1970s, a time of relative prosperity and full employment for other Australians, including the huge post-war migrant intake of displaced people from Europe. Yet Aborigines had become 'refugees' in their own land, existing on government handouts. Most of their supporters then and now are urban-dwellers with little understanding or experience of bush life and the policies they advocated were, and still are, idealistic but at times misguided. These 'bleeding hearts', as they are known, relentlessly promoted Aboriginal causes; as early as 1946 representations were made to the United Nations over the Pilbara strike. This pressured Australian governments to avoid international censure and the racist tag by going too far too fast with hasty, ill-conceived legislation. The result of equal pay was not what anyone intended, neither pastoralists, who valued their Aboriginal employees, nor Aborigines, whose 'golden age' was replaced by payment of 'sit-down money'—life on the dole. A hard, active but enjoyable life riding horses and working stock in their own 'country' turned into a lifetime of living on the fringes of Western society, waiting for pension day. Since the 1970s, 50–60 per cent of the Aboriginal workforce has been unemployed, a rate ten times that of the general Australian population and the 1950s Aboriginal rate (5 per cent) *before* strikes for equal pay. In remote areas typically at least half of all indigenous employment is provided by the government-funded Community Development Employment Program (CDEP), a work-for-the-dole scheme.

During my 40 years in Australia and much travelling in the Northern Territory and all six states, I have been struck by how seldom one sees Aboriginal people performing ordinary jobs apart from reserved positions in Aboriginal organisations, visitor centres or settlements. Travel writer Bill Bryson made the same comment in 2000 after several weeks touring the continent, including such outback centres as Alice Springs:

> What is perhaps oddest to the outsider is that Aborigines just aren't there. You don't see them performing on TV; you don't find them assisting you in shops . . . you would expect to see them sometimes—working in a bank, delivering mail, writing parking tickets, fixing a telephone line, participating in some productive capacity in the normal workaday world. I never have; not once. Clearly some connection is not being made . . . I didn't have the faintest idea what the solution to all this was; what was required to spread the fruits of general Australian prosperity to those who seemed so signally unable to find their way to it.[26]

Many Aboriginal people are unable find their way to prosperity because they have different values and many choose not to work at ordinary Western-style jobs. Certainly, Aborigines may encounter some racial discrimination if they search for a job, but Australia is now such a multiracial society that there is no room for official discrimination, particularly in view of the country's tough, strictly enforced human rights legislation enacted in 1975. There is a real scarcity of labour in the outback. I have met New Zealanders who have saved enough to buy a house by finding unskilled work in the mining industry; innumerable back-packers and immigrants of all colours and ethnic groups—but few Aborigines—work in cafes, shops, hotels, garages, farms and abattoirs. Some people have assumed that Aboriginal people are naturally lazy, but this assumption is incorrect; they work extremely hard and effectively at a task of their own choosing. The problem is that they see no reason to do the more menial Western-style tasks when they can live indefinitely on government pensions, unemployment benefit, child-support allowance and so on; unless they have completed an education, many better-paid jobs are closed to them, leaving only the menial. Most Aboriginal people see no 'shame' in living off government benefits, which they think of as their due as victims of dispossession. This means that dependency on government welfare services has become the norm in Aboriginal communities. The result is a continuing cycle of poverty.

A few Aborigines have managed to avoid the problems of the Western world by continuing to live a traditional life out in the desert. In 1984, the discovery of a 'lost tribe' caused much media excitement. Walimpirrnga Tjapaljarri and his group of eight people lived a traditional life in the Western Desert until 1984, when they walked out to the government settlement of Papunya. No one may go there without a permit from the Central Land Council, so it was possible to control media attention effectively. Fortunately, the group was reunited with some relatives and went with them to the remote outstation of Kiwirrkura over the Western Australian border.

There are still believed to be one or two other isolated small groups or individuals in the outback who still practise the nomadic lifestyle and eschew settlements. Only their footsteps have been seen and one is thought to live alone with only a dingo for company.[27]

» The 'coming of the grog'

The 'coming of the grog', like the 'Japanese War', is a marker event for Aboriginal elders in northern Australia when they talk about the past. As a protective measure, Aboriginal drinking of alcohol was banned Australia-wide in the 1840s. A common belief is that Aborigines are more susceptible to the effect of alcohol than Europeans, but there is no physiological proof of this. The problems lie rather in binge drinking, which increases the toxicity of alcohol. Urban Aborigines drank quickly to avoid detection and a third of Melbourne's Native Police died from alcohol abuse. By the 1940s, Australian citizenship and the right to consume alcohol were granted to Aborigines who held 'exemption certificates' complete with photograph. These were given only to those 'of good character and industrious habits' who spoke English, had 'adopted the manner and habits of civilised life', forsaken Aboriginal ways and were free from alcoholism, venereal disease or yaws. Aborigines derisively called them 'dog licences' or 'beer tickets', but they did help to confine Aboriginal alcohol consumption to those well-motivated to avoid drunkenness, which could lead to loss of the derided, but useful, certificate. This system of gradual introduction of alcohol to well-educated and integrated Aborigines ended prematurely in the 1950s, when Australia bowed to humanitarian pressure to grant all its indigenous people full equal rights immediately.[28]

By 1964, bans on Aboriginal drinking were lifted everywhere except northwestern Western Australia, where they lasted until 1971. Suddenly Aborigines gained equality, unlimited access to alcohol and the power to self-destruct. 'The coming of the grog' was a disaster. For example, in Katherine the Commonwealth Scientific and Industrial Research Organisation (CSIRO) successfully employed in its agricultural research many Aborigines, who lived within the CSIRO camp, but when the *Social Welfare Ordinance* of 1964 legalised Aboriginal consumption of alcohol, all hell broke loose. Anthropologist Francesca Merlan reported that, 'Levels of violence within the CSIRO camp increased . . . there was a marked escalation in levels of violence toward women . . . most men who worked there had died five years after grog came in.' Similarly, Duguid observed the new law's effect in Alice Springs: 'In 1934 I used to see drunken white men lying in the gutters; now [1964] it was the Aborigines. The white man's privilege had become the black man's curse.'[29] Alcohol abuse has destroyed innumerable indigenous lives, and continues to do so.

» Segregation or assimilation?

In the 1840s, Aborigines were still sole occupants of the northern half of Australia. If at that time large, permanent reserves had been set aside where they could pursue traditional life without interference, would long-term segregation have been successful? Northern Queensland was not settled until the 1860s, central Australia in the 1870s and the Kimberley in the 1880s. Even after the arrival of the first pastoralists and mineral prospectors, these inaccessible, rugged areas were only very sparsely occupied by non-indigenous people. Many northern regions, including three-fifths of the Northern Territory, remained unoccupied by colonists and in the early twentieth century huge reserves were declared.[30] It was hoped that Aborigines could be isolated from Western temptations and maintain a traditional lifestyle on reserves that were, and still are, out of bounds to non-Aborigines without special permits.

Nevertheless, the lure of the new was just too strong—Aborigines left the reserves and drifted into towns. In 1937 anthropologist Donald Thomson recommended Arnhem Land and other reserves be made into Aboriginal sanctuaries, like those in New Guinea, but the suggestion won neither black nor white support. By 1951 Arnhem Land still had 2000–3000 tribal Aborigines, but more and more young people went to Darwin every year. Drift is still occurring. The difficulty of keeping Aboriginal youths in remote northeast Arnhem Land away from substance abuse was vividly portrayed in the film *Yolngu Boy*, which tells the story of three youths' departure for Darwin, alcohol and freedom from elders' authority. It is the same inevitable process that emptied crofts in remote Scottish highlands and causes labour shortages in the American southwest, where ranchers have a saying, 'If you want to keep the boys on the ranch, don't let them go to town'.

Aborigines do not want to be protected in 'anthropological museums' far from Western food, technology, medicine, transport and entertainment. This issue has arisen in the management of Kakadu National Park, where indigenous people want to hunt with rifles, dogs and vehicles. The park is jointly managed by Parks Australia and local Aborigines, who have a majority on the board of management.[31] A compromise solution permits rifles and off-road vehicles, but bans European dogs in the interests of conservation of endangered native fauna.

The concept of several kin groups amicably sharing land was unrealistic. Now smaller, clan-based reserves have been created, primarily in the Northern Territory, where Aborigines form a third of the population and possess almost half the land. There, many local groups inhabit outstations—small, de-centralised, self-managing Aboriginal communities—and allegiance to clan is still strong.

In the 1830s, the concept of protective segregation on large reserves was attacked by
humanitarians, who argued that keeping Aborigines 'out of harm's way, as children' was
paternalistic and implied inferior status.[32] These early arguments for integration rather
than segregation were successful and paved the way for later government policies.

The British Government tried to alleviate the problems of Aboriginal dispossession in southern Australia by four measures—establishment of small reserves,
Aboriginal education, compensation from land-revenue funds and recognition of
continuing rights to hunt and occupy *un*cultivated land where blacks and whites
would be joint occupiers. Many small reserves were set up after the *Imperial Crown
Land Sale Act* of 1842. Secretary of State Earl Grey instructed all Australian Governors
to spend up to 15 per cent of land-revenue 'for the benefit, civilisation and protection
of the Aborigines', and to create more Aboriginal schools and small reserves, roughly
2.5 km² (1 sq. mile) in size. Reserves were seen primarily as 'central depots for the
distribution of rations'. About 40 reserves were established in 1850 in New South
Wales, 59 in South Australia by 1860 and six mission stations and a few government
settlements in Victoria by 1867.

Grey assumed *large* Aboriginal reserves were impracticable because of squatters'
needs to spread their flocks widely and move them during droughts. He therefore
issued an *Order of Council* in 1846 that pastoral leases 'give the grantees only an exclu-
sive right of pasturage for their cattle, and of cultivating such land as they require . . .
but that these leases are not intended to deprive the natives of their former right to hunt
over these districts, or to wander over them in search of sustenance . . . except over land
actually cultivated or fenced in for that purpose.'[33] Aboriginal customary, 'usufructuary'
rights were to continue on land leased to pastoralists; on all except cultivated land
Aborigines could still hunt and reside. (This imperial recognition of Aboriginal rights of
occupancy or communal native title to land was crucial to the High Court's recognition
of native title in the Mabo case; see Chapter 8.) Unfortunately, Grey's enlightened policies were never fully implemented, because British responsibility for Aboriginal Affairs
was almost at an end in all Australian colonies except Western Australia, and they gave
way to state governments more sympathetic to pastoralists than Aborigines.[34]

Most reserves thrived. By 1880 those at Coranderrk and Framlingham, Victoria,
and Point Mcleay (renamed Raukkan) and Poonindie, South Australia, were prosperous, stable, relatively happy havens of protection, independence and initiative.
Coranderrk Aborigines built their own cottages, erected picket-fences around neat
gardens of flowers and fruit-trees, and furnished their homes with sofas, rugs, rocking-
chairs, dressers, clocks, pictures and even a harmonium. One visitor to Framlingham
in the 1870s remarked their cottages were 'equal to those of English workingmen
and superior to those of many selectors in the district', and their young people had
'a better education than most of the farmers' children'.[35] (Between 1850 and 1900

government-funded primary education—free, compulsory and secular—became well established in settled regions, but half of Victoria's Aborigines did not live on missions or settlements and so tended to miss out, as did tribespeople in the outback.) Mission Aborigines dressed smartly in European clothing and became virtually self-supporting through selling farm produce and craft-work. Despite outward appearances, they continued to forage for bush food and retained Aboriginal values of sharing, kinship ties and obligations, dreaming stories, burial rituals and fear of sorcery.

A major problem of communal living on reserves was high mortality from new diseases. Tuberculosis caused 40 per cent of deaths on Victorian reserves between 1876 and 1912, and pneumonia, bronchitis, influenza, gastric complaints, hydatids, whooping-cough and measles took a high toll. Aboriginal numbers in Victoria dropped by 80 per cent (from c. 10 000 in 1835 to c. 1907 in 1853). New diseases accounted for 90 per cent of these deaths. By 1921 Victoria's Aboriginal population had declined to only 586. Half the children born before 1900 on Victoria's reserves died in infancy, some from congenital syphilis. (Pre-contact infant mortality has been estimated at 300–500 per 1000 live births.)[36] The advent of modern medicine wrought miracles and by 1960 only 5 per cent of children born to Victorian Aboriginal mothers were lost in infancy, a huge reduction but still twice Anglo-Australian rates.

Reserves were havens for mixed-race orphans; most Victorian reserves contained 8–40 per cent mixed-race Aborigines and by 1877 Coranderrk had 62 per cent. By then Coranderrk was the only Aboriginal reserve to pay its way and when funds were tight on the eve of the 1890s economic depression, the Victorian Government decided 'it was unreasonable that the state should continue to support able-bodied [mixed-race] men who were well able to earn their own living'. *The Victorian Aborigines Act* of 1886 laid down that only 'half-castes' aged over 34 years and 'full-bloods' were entitled to live on reserves and receive government aid; the rest were pushed into white society to fend for themselves. By 1920 only one reserve, Lake Tyers, still existed in Victoria, under a blend of old segregationist and new inclusionist thinking aiming to merge Aborigines of mixed race into the general community. The 1886 Act first formalised assimilation of people of mixed race, and virtually identical legislation was adopted in all other mainland states by 1911.[37]

» Aborigines of mixed race

The number of Aborigines on reserves, almost all of part-descent, had grown markedly by the 1880s due to better diet and resistance to disease. Anthropologists noted that 'physically the Aborigines absorb readily and rapidly into the white population. Indeed, three successive generations of mating with full whites can suffice to eliminate all distinctive Aboriginal traits.'[38] The tendency of Aboriginal characteristics to disappear has led to the present confusing situation where many people who identify as Aboriginal have white skin, blue eyes, narrow noses and blond, brown or red hair. Others resemble Japanese, Chinese, Melanesians, Polynesians or Afghans, for in the nineteenth century many different ethnic groups came to Australia to exploit gold and pearl shell or fulfil particular roles, such as camel-driving.

At the time of Federation in 1901, Australian governments sought to avoid the racial divisions engulfing South Africa with its three warring races, blacks, whites and coloureds, or formation of an Australian 'coloured north' equivalent to the 'Deep South' of North America. (Australia never had slaves, but many impoverished coloured people of mixed parentage lived in the tropics.) What became known as the White Australia Policy had three main elements—a belief that 'mixed-blood' Aborigines should be absorbed into the white population, that further non-European immigrants should be excluded and that suitable white colonists should be encouraged to settle. Although a very discriminatory policy, it was conceived as a chance to create a brave new world in Australia, free from the inequalities and interracial conflict that marred South Africa and North America.

After federation, Macassan fishermen's visits were terminated and 'Kanakas', or New Caledonians and other Pacific Islanders, were deported. Over 62 000 Melanesians had come to Australia between 1863 and 1904 to work in sugarcane and cotton plantations. Some returned home but many more stayed. Islanders' entry was prohibited in 1904 and within a decade over 7000 were forcibly repatriated. Many Pacific Islanders merged into Aboriginal communities or were repatriated no further than the Torres Strait Islands, and about 2000 remained in mainland Australia. Their descendants, now known as South Sea Islanders, number around 20 000 and mostly live in coastal Queensland.[39]

» Absorption

Absorption is the process whereby a dominant cultural group takes a minority group into their society, although cultural assimilation can occur without full social integration. For example, western European Jews before the Second World War adopted the languages and cultural mores of the countries in which they lived while remaining socially rather distinct. Such policies were in force in Australia from the 1860s to 1960s. From about 1910 to 1940 the federal government's policy was to protect 'full-bloods' and absorb those of mixed race. It aimed to preserve the Aboriginal race and ensure nomadic tribes had sufficient land to pursue their traditional life undisturbed but to 'collect half-castes and train them in institutions'. In 1935 it assured the Anti-Slavery and Aborigines Protection Society: 'In the Northern Territory half-castes are collected at an early age from the Aboriginal camps and taken to institutions where they are educated.'[40]

This policy of segregation/absorption was endorsed at the 1937 Native Welfare Conference to try to cope with the rapidly increasing mixed-race population. The increase was especially marked in the north, as Chief Protectors of Aborigines,

C. Cook (Northern Territory), J.W. Bleakley (Queensland) and A.O. Neville (Western Australia) reported. As *The Telegraph* noted in May 1937:

> Mr Neville holds the view that within one hundred years the pure black will be extinct. But the half-caste problem was increasing every year. Therefore their idea was to keep the pure blacks segregated and absorb the half-castes into the white population. Sixty years ago, he said, there were over 60 000 full-blooded natives in Western Australia. Today, there are only 20 000. In time there would be none . . . The pure-blooded Aborigine was not a quick breeder. On the other hand the half-caste was. In Western Australia there were half-caste families of twenty and upwards.

Although usually termed in past eras 'half-castes', by the 1930s many Aborigines claiming government rations on reserves had a quarter, an eighth or less Aboriginal ancestry.

Neville's policy was: 'If the coloured people of this country are to be absorbed into the general community, they must be thoroughly fit and educated at least to the extent of the three R's . . . To achieve this end, however, we must have charge of the children at the age of six years; it is useless to wait until they are twelve or thirteen.' Most, like Neville, saw primary schooling as the key to assimilation, and some missionaries felt that the younger the children, the better. They may have had in mind the Jesuit saying—'Give me the boy to the age of seven and I will give you the man.'

The 1937 conference formally adopted a policy of absorption: 'The destiny of the natives of Aboriginal origin, but not of the full-blood, lies in their ultimate absorption by the people of the Commonwealth.'[41]

Contemporary administrators, anthropologists, doctors and scientists regarded this 1937 policy of biological absorption as '"progressive" in relation to the prevailing racism of the times, and indeed . . . the only solution to rampant white prejudice'. We forget the terrible stigma then attached to illegitimacy, the emphasis on female moral purity and the widespread sexual exploitation of Aboriginal girls by both white men and their own people. Welfare was always part of the rationale for indigenous child removal policies, which is why throughout the program most institutionalised children were illegitimate, fatherless, young mixed-race girls.[42]

After the Second World War the emphasis changed to assimilation based on welfare considerations. In 1951 Commonwealth Minister for Territories Paul Hasluck called a Native Welfare Conference, which for the first time extended the assimilation policy to all Aborigines. 'Assimilation means, in practical terms,' Hasluck reported, 'that in the course of time, it is expected that all persons of aboriginal blood or mixed blood in Australia will live like other white Australians do . . . Assimilation does not mean the suppression of the aboriginal culture but rather that, for generation after generation, cultural adjustment will take place.' Hasluck saw assimilation as 'a policy of opportunity. It gives to the aboriginal and the person of mixed blood a chance to shape his own life.'[43]

Hasluck aimed to uplift Aboriginal people in a crude forerunner of equal opportunity policies. A 1965 conference redefined assimilation yet again: 'The policy of assimilation seeks that all persons of Aboriginal descent will choose to attain a *similar* manner of living to that of other Australians and live as members of a single community.'[44]

Was the assimilation policy racist? Racism is discrimination on the basis of perceived genetic superiority, so racists do *not* promote assimilation since inferior genes of the minority group might pollute superior genes of the 'master race'. Thus to keep the Aryan race pure, Hitler determined to exterminate, *not* assimilate, Europe's Jews. Second, Australia's assimilation policy assumed cultural, not biological, superiority. It was not so much racist as ethnocentric and paternalistic—its authors believed their own culture was superior. Also the policy disregarded Aboriginal values and feelings because it was assumed that Anglo-Australian ways were superior and that Aborigines would want to adopt these ways.[45]

The main problem with assimilation was that it led to wholesale intervention—the management, control and institutionalisation of mixed-race Aborigines, who were removed from their families, educated and employed in the general workforce, with consequent loss of language, identity and culture. This intensive social engineering resulted in constant intervention in Aboriginal lives. By 1911, every state (except Tasmania where Aborigines were thought to be extinct) had passed special Aboriginal laws; by 1987 more than 700 pieces of state and federal legislation had been enacted, incorporating over 70 definitions of Aboriginality.[46]

Extensive powers were given to missionaries, reserve managers and police. These 'bosses' controlled Aboriginal child care, education, marriage, employment, wages, travel, compulsory hospitalisation in cases of syphilis and leprosy and suppression of 'injurious customs' such as infanticide.

» The stolen generations

The foremost Aboriginal issue of the twentieth century was the policy of removing mixed-race Aboriginal children from their families to be educated and assimilated into mainstream society, the so-called 'stolen generations'.

Child removal officially ended in 1970, but two decades later the issue hit the headlines when part-Aboriginal James Savage was convicted of the rape and murder of an American woman in Florida. James was adopted in Australia by an American couple after his 15-year-old Aboriginal mother gave him to the Welfare Board at four days old. His later antisocial behaviour, drug addiction and crimes were explained at his trial as resulting from his removal as a child and subsequent confusion over identity.

Following the recommendations of the 1991 Royal Commission into Aboriginal Deaths in Custody (see chapter 8), a national inquiry into child removal was set up. Its 1997 report, *Bringing Them Home*, makes horrific reading. It contains the stories told by 535 Aborigines of mixed race who were removed. So harrowing are these tales that when tabled in federal parliament, it reduced the Leader of the Opposition to tears. One example from Western Australia in 1935 gives the flavour:

> I was at the post office with my Mum and Auntie. They put us in the police ute and said they were taking us to Broome . . . But when we'd gone [about ten miles] they stopped, and threw the mothers out of the car. We jumped on our mothers' backs, crying, trying not to be left behind. But the policemen pulled us off and threw us back in the car. They pushed the mothers away and drove off, while our mothers were chasing the car, running and crying after us. We were screaming in the back of that car. When we got to Broome they put me and my cousin in the Broome lock-up. We were only ten years old. We were in the lock-up for two days waiting for the boat to Perth.

» *The film* Rabbit-Proof Fence *vividly tells the story of the forced removal in 1931 of three part-Aboriginal girls, aged 8, 10 and 14, for schooling at the distant Moore Creek Native Settlement. The youngest girl had been promised to a much older tribesman, a practice abhorred by Christian authorities. Chief Protector Neville's notion of happy, self-sufficient, prosperous Aboriginal farming communities had already dwindled and died and Moore Creek proved to be overcrowded and underfunded. Remarkably, the girls managed to abscond, follow the rabbit-proof fence that extends north–south across inland Western Australia and walk 1600 kilometres (1000 miles) back home to Jigalong.*

These girls were removed solely because of their mixed parentage and were placed in Sister Kate's Orphanage in Perth, a school for 'lighter-skinned' children.[47]

Bringing Them Home gives the impression that poor living conditions, hunger and abuse typified all institutional life, but some people's experience was far more positive. For example, in 1996 Maureen Young, a Gnadu elder of Norseman, Western Australia, recalled: 'I was able to combine Aboriginal traditional-way spirituality, as well as the Christian spirituality. And I believe I really had a balance. And that's what made me a leader today . . . And I was really thankful that I did have the white man education as well as the Aboriginal education.' In similar vein, Beryl Carmichael, an elder of Broken Hill, New South Wales, said: 'The Aboriginal people were willing to go forward and you know, I can honestly say that a lot of them said the happiest times of their lives were on old Menindee mission.'[48]

The label 'stolen' for removed children is emotive but incorrect, since it implies forcible removal—often but by no means always the case—and illegality. In fact, the removals were in accordance with contemporary Australian laws, although not with basic human rights. It must always be wrong to take children from their families, except in the most dire cases of abuse or neglect or, in the case of orphans, when no other relatives can care for them. Some children were given to missionaries to save them from starvation or death. In the 1930s Australia was in the grip of the Great Depression and Central Australia was stricken by prolonged drought. As settler Doug Fuller said, 'even lizards were starving to death'. The desert could not sustain many people, so when Aboriginal women discovered that missionaries would look after children, they 'would wait on the side of the road for the mail truck to come along, to hand the kids over to the mail driver. They couldn't feed them, you see.'[49]

It was in such extreme circumstances in 1934 that two-year-old Lowitja O'Donoghue was removed from her mother, along with her two older sisters.[50] Seven years earlier two other siblings had been removed. Her Irish father with his brother had obtained leaseholds on two South Australian stations of red earth and spinifex, which local Aborigines describe as 'rubbish country'. Her father, Tom O'Donoghue, eked out a meagre living trading with Aborigines for dingo scalps. He built a tiny mud-brick cottage where he lived with Lowitja's Yankunytjatjara mother, Lily. Between 1924 and 1935 they had six children but could not feed them all, and Tom gave all but the youngest to missionaries at Oodnadatta. This small town was just a staging-post; the children were sent 1000 km (600 miles) away to a mission home in Adelaide. When Lowitja returned and asked 'Why was I taken away?' the response from her older relations was, 'Things were rough before'. Fuller's testimony bears this out; he took over the station from Tom O'Donoghue, whom he described as 'a good Catholic' and not a man to let his children starve to death. There was no Australian social security system (and no contraceptive pill) until after the Second World War;

previously, in hard times only the churches and charities were there to save children from the spectre of hunger and death.

In 1940 Tom O'Donoghue sold up and left Lily after being prosecuted and fined for 'habitually consorting' with an Aboriginal woman. (Mixed marriages were legal but not *de facto*, common law relationships.) Lily then moved to Oodnadatta where she was known as 'a fine old lady and well regarded in the town'. Sadly she became a heavy drinker after prohibition was lifted.

Lowitja was brought up in Colebrook Home along with her older siblings. She never saw her father again and was not reunited with her grief-stricken mother for 33 years. Communication when they finally met was difficult because she knew no Yankunytjatjara and her mother spoke no English. Lowitja found Colebrook 'stultifying' and 'joyless' but a classmate told the Inquiry: 'We were all happy together, us kids. We had two very wonderful old ladies that looked after us. It wasn't like an institution really. It was just a big happy family. Y'know they gave us good teaching, they encouraged us to be no different to anybody else.'[51] When Lowitja left at sixteen to become a domestic servant—the normal lot of mission girls—'Matron had told me that "I'd get into trouble" (that is, get pregnant) and that "I'd never make anything of my life". I decided to prove her wrong.'

This she did. She overcame prejudice to become a trainee nurse and graduate at Royal Adelaide Hospital, and joined the Aboriginal Advancement League to fight for Aboriginal eligibility to take up professions and apprenticeships. She also decided never to have children: 'More than anything I think I felt inadequate—I couldn't remember being mothered myself and I was frightened of doing it badly.' Lack of parenting skills is a serious problem for institutionalised children, the effect extending down the generations. Lowitja suffered another ordeal in 2001 when her explanation that she was 'removed' rather than 'stolen' was 'distorted' by a journalist and published as 'Aboriginal leader's shock admission'. In a dignified press release she made clear that, even if she had not been 'stolen' (forcibly removed), 'I know that my Aboriginal mother would have had no legal recourse, nor any moral support, in resisting our removal. I also know that her grief was unbearable.'[52]

Some Aboriginal mothers wanted a better life for their children and asked missionaries to care for and educate them. Benevolent intentions were mentioned, but only briefly, by the *Bringing Them Home* authors Sir Ronald Wilson, humanitarian and retired High Court judge, and Aboriginal lawyer Mick Dodson, Social Justice Commissioner. The latter, after being orphaned at the age of ten, 'agreed to go to boarding school in western Victoria' to be educated along with his older brother, Patrick, who was ordained as a priest. Both have since held many public positions.[53]

The *Bringing Them Home* report presented a surprisingly one-sided account of welfare policy from the 1930s to 1960s, for its authors failed to cross-examine witnesses or call evidence from those who administered the policy. For instance, Sister Eileen

Heath, who devoted her life to caring for part-Aboriginal children in missions in Western Australia, South Australia and the Northern Territory, wrote a detailed submission to the inquiry but was not called as a witness. A recent biography includes many tributes to her. Rosalie Kunoth-Monks of Utopia Station, Northern Territory, daughter of a traditional mother and mixed-descent father, testified that, 'Sister Eileen gave dignity to people of mixed heritage, and she did it in the most positive way . . . instilled into us, that we were worthwhile and that we could do exactly what we wanted to do with our lives.' (At the age of 16 Rosalie was chosen to play Jedda in Australia's first full-length colour film of the same name.) Likewise, Freda Glynn of Alice Springs said 'Saint Mary's was my saviour and I want that to be in the book'.[54] Kunoth Monks also personally witnessed in the 1940s the deaths of several mixed-race babies who were not rescued by welfare patrol officers in time and explained:

> In a lot of situations not even the Aboriginal people wanted half-castes. Up this way, if they had half-castes, they killed them . . . The children killed were from white man passing through, abusing an Aboriginal woman for one night stands . . . and usually these young ladies were promised to a husband, so they couldn't have a half-caste child and then go into a relationship with their promised husband . . . Grandmothers stepped on [the babies'] chests and smothered them, crushed their chests . . .[55]

Part-Aboriginal children removed from their families suffered emotional trauma but did learn to read and write, whereas those in the camps remained illiterate. Almost all today's national Aboriginal leaders are people of mixed descent, and either they or their parents were educated in an Anglo-Australian institution away from their families. The few leaders of full-descent such as Galarrwuy Yunupingu of the Yolngu people did some of their secondary education in distant boarding schools. His younger brother, Mandawuy Yunupingu, received a similar education and became principal of Yirrkala school, introducing 'both ways' learning there. In 1986 Galarrwuy founded the acclaimed Aboriginal band, Yothu Yindi. His vision is to develop a positive black-white relationship through the language of music. 'Through our music we are trying to bring you into our mainstream . . . Our music is as strong as yours . . . It passes on knowledge. We are trying to create music that will suggest a way for you to come and be part of our world.' Both brothers have been named Australian of the Year (in 1979 and 1993).

Illiteracy was, and often still is, the price that 'tribal' Aborigines pay to remain in their community. A classic example is Yidumduma Bill Harney, born of a Wardaman mother and white father, William E. Harney, about 1936, when 'Old Bill' was building roads in the Territory. When the project ended, his father left and young Bill and his sister, Dulcie, were cared for by his mother and Aboriginal stepfather on Willeroo cattle-station in their traditional country. There was no school so Bill never learnt to read or write. When Bill was four, his seven-year-old sister Dulcie was taken away by 'the Welfare' but the policeman told his mother they couldn't take Bill—'he's too small'. Thereafter Bill was kept 'undercover', as he recounts:

> My mum was very strict and careful that I didn't get taken away. She used to get this blackcurrant plum from the bush, and it makes your hair go black. My mum always used to crush the black plum together with a big heap of charcoal and put it all over my skin to make me go black, and when the Welfare would come along I'd be sitting right in the middle of those other blacks, and the Welfare bloke would call out, 'Any yella kids? Any half-caste kids around here?'
>
> 'No, nothing 'ere,' but I'd be sitting there with them all painted up black.[56]

Dulcie was taken to Croker Island Mission off Darwin, but came back at the age of ten to the Katherine horseraces in search of her family. She identified her mother by her footprint, put her foot alongside and exclaimed 'See my foot like yours! Look at the toes!' There was a joyful reunion. Dulcie returned to the Mission to complete her schooling but thereafter kept in touch and often brought her children to see their grandmother. After a traditional upbringing but no schooling Bill worked as a stock-man and eventually head-stockman, mailman, saddler, well-sinker, windmill-rigger, crocodile-hunter and fencer. Later he became an artist, tour-operator and Chairman of Wardaman Aboriginal Corporation. He prides himself in not drinking alcohol and never having been on the dole, has his own house in Katherine, and, last time I saw him, had been foster-father to more than 70 Aboriginal children allocated to his care by local magistrates. He summed up his life in his book, *Born under the Paperbark Tree*: 'First was the blackfella way . . . then I saw the different lifestyle of the European . . . Now today I put the Aboriginal lifestyle and the European lifestyle together, and I know both laws . . . There's only a few old fellas left like me now . . . I haven't been to school, but I went to the university of the bush, under the tree, under the stars . . . I come out top all round.'

Among those removed from their families, there was triumph as well as tragedy. Bob Randall was born to a Yankunytjatjara mother and white father in 1934 on Angas Downs station, Northern Territory. When Bob was seven, a policeman rode into their camp on a camel. The light-skinned boy was offered a ride and was so excited he didn't realise that he was being 'rescued' and would never see his mother again. Bob was taken to Alice Springs and then Croker Island. There he was educated and later established a career as a teacher. He also became a renowned singer and performer, and his song 'My Brown Skin Baby They Take Him Away' became the theme song for the stolen generations. He has now gone back to his roots and is a registered traditional owner of Uluru and a Yankunytjatjara elder.[57]

» Was it cultural genocide?

Modern activists have described child removal as cultural genocide, yet few contemporary voices were raised against it. Anthropologists such as Donald Thomson and Bill Stanner were well aware of the assimilation policy and seemed to approve it for mixed-race people but they were strongly in favour of remote reserves for those of full descent. It seems they considered that only Aborigines of full descent should be encouraged to retain their culture.

During the 1950s and 1960s more and more mixed-race children were removed for protection from alleged neglect, to be adopted out at birth, to attend school in distant places, to receive medical treatment or to work as maids in cities. By the late 1960s, institutions could no longer cope with the increasing numbers and new welfare practice discouraged use of institutions, so Aboriginal children at risk were placed with non-Aboriginal foster families. However, in recent years cross-cultural adoption has also become anathema to welfare authorities, who are now extremely reluctant to remove any Aboriginal children, whatever the problems of the home environment. In the past, cross-cultural adoption gave removed, abandoned or orphaned Aboriginal children the chance of a loving home and good education although they, like other adoptees, often experienced serious identity problems.[58] All lost their 'culture'—the way of life built up by a human group. Those removed from the outback also often forgot their language. The mother tongue of most urban Aborigines was already English.

Many hard-hitting submissions were made to the Inquiry into 'the stolen generations', the dramatic term coined in 1981 by historian Peter Read of Link-Up (New South Wales) Aboriginal Corporation, whose submission was liberally sprinkled with allegations of 'holocaust, atrocities, ethnic cleansing and genocide'.[59] *Bringing Them Home* suggested: 'The policy of forcible removal of children from Indigenous Australians to other groups for the purpose of raising them separately from and ignorant of their culture and people could properly be labelled "genocidal".'[60] Wilson later said he regretted including the genocide accusation in the report. 'We included it to step up the pressure for reparation . . . [but] it gave people who were opposed to the report an argument for objecting to it.'[61]

Others have termed child removal 'cultural genocide'—a policy that aims at rapid and complete disappearance of the cultural, moral and religious life of a human group. This is in spite of its deliberate exclusion from the 1948 Genocide Convention because Raphael Lemkin, who coined the word 'genocide', convincingly argued that cultural genocide was much more than 'just a policy of forced assimilation by moderate coercion'. At that time assimilation was approved by Lemkin, his colleagues and most others, including Australia's earliest Aboriginal activists.[62] However, by the 1960s, forced assimilation was becoming anathema to indigenous and non-indigenous people alike, because of the terrible emotional trauma it caused, together with the loss of culture, language and identity.

» Numbers removed

How many were removed? The guide to the *Bringing Them Home* report stated in bold type that 'not one Indigenous family has escaped the effects of forcible removal . . . Those affected include the children who were forcibly removed, their families, communities, children and grandchildren.'[63]

Wilson and Dodd wrote 'we can conclude with confidence that between one in three and one in ten Indigenous children were forcibly removed from their families and communities in the period from approximately 1910 until 1970', but these figures have not withstood scrutiny. 'The one in three upper limit for child removal suggested by *Bringing them Home* is certainly wrong', said respected political science academic Robert Manne. 'The lower estimate of one in ten is far more soundly based.' The total number of children removed was far lower than the 100 000 initially claimed by Read. On the basis of a 1994 ABS survey of self-identified indigenous people, Manne considers likely a figure of 20 000–25 000 over six decades (averaging about 390 per year).[64]

All three test cases and two appeals for compensation brought by stolen generations members failed. The first, by Joy Williams, failed because her mother had asked the New South Wales Aborigines Welfare Board to declare baby Joy a ward of the state, had remained her legal guardian and approved arrangements for her fostering. In the Cubillo-Gunner case in 2000 Justice O'Loughlin (in a 470-page judgment) dismissed their claims primarily because of lack of any evidence of a policy of forced removal of part-Aboriginal children against their families' wishes. Both Lorna Cubillo and Peter Gunner were deserted by their white fathers. Lorna was removed in 1947, after her Aboriginal mother died, to a mixed-race institution in Darwin, where she was so savagely beaten that a nipple was torn off. A document with his mother's thumbprint authorised Peter's removal in 1956 and there was evidence of his earlier neglect. O'Loughlin accepted that the station-owner, Mrs Dora McLeod, had found Peter as a one-year-old 'unconscious' and 'totally neglected' and only saved his life with medical help. She also claimed that soon after his birth, his mother had left him in a rabbit-hole to die.

The stakes were huge. In 2001 when the appeal to the High Court also failed, there were 700 similar claims pending in the Territory alone, which could have cost the federal government several billion dollars.[65]

The *Bringing Them Home* inquiry concluded that 'all Australian parliaments' should make a formal apology, 'there is an international legal obligation' to make reparation, 'this obligation passes from the violating government to its successors until satisfaction has been made', and that 'reparation be made to all who suffered because of forcible removal policies'.

All state premiers have apologised. In May 1997, Prime Minister John Howard (1996–) expressed his personal 'deep sorrow for those of my fellow Australians who suffered injustices under the practices of past generations towards indigenous peoples', though he has consistently refused to make a formal apology, despite considerable public pressure. The minister for Aboriginal Affairs explained, 'The government does not support an official national apology. Such an apology could imply that present generations are in some way responsible and accountable for the actions of earlier generations, actions that were sanctioned by the laws of the time, and that were believed to be in the best interests of the children concerned.'[66]

Although there has been no official reparation, there has been an outpouring of compassion from the general public and the government in 1997 allocated $63 million to Link-Up—state-based organisations providing counselling, family-tracing, reunions, language-maintenance and archival and oral history programs.

《 》

In the nineteenth century, the policy of paternalistic protection of Aborigines at missions and government settlements provided some degree of security, health, education and employment but ended in institutionalisation, erosion of traditional culture and loss of control over their own lives. The twentieth century saw an enlightened movement towards equality for all Australians, which led to equal pay and equal access to alcohol, 'advances' that resulted in unemployment and social degradation. Similarly, the 1930s campaign for assimilation into mainstream society was considered progressive and was supported by black and white alike, but gave rise to the horrors of the stolen generations. The well-meaning but ill-conceived policy of forced assimilation of mixed-race Aborigines is now universally condemned for the trauma and loss of language and culture it brought to the stolen children and their families.

RESILIENCE

The story continues

During the 1950s and 1960s the concept of a multiracial society developed. Gradually the policy of assimilation was replaced by a policy of integration, whereby Aborigines could maintain a distinct cultural identity while pursuing equality of living standards and opportunity. Integration is still Australian Government policy, for it enables indigenous people to retain their identity in a pluralist society. Integration also provides a choice between Western urban society and the more traditional but less comfortable life in remote area communities.

Various new Aboriginal organisations sought revival of separate cultural identity but also full equality, civil rights and integration. In the 1950s most Aboriginal organisations were managed by whites but this gradually changed as Aboriginal leaders came under international influences. In 1969 Queenslander Kath Walker attended an overseas conference on indigenous people and came back convinced that Aborigines must control their own organisations and distinguish themselves from the dominant white society by cultural revival and assuming Aboriginal names. She adopted the name Oodgeroo Noonuccal and went on to become an acclaimed poet, writer, environmentalist, teacher and campaigner for Aboriginal affairs.

In the 1970s, the additional goal of self-determination was adopted—the right of indigenous people to 'decide within the broader context of Australian society the priorities and directions of their own lives, and to freely determine their own affairs'.[1] Self-determination was intended to enable indigenous people to set the course of change and agenda for action in their communities and to control policy implementation. After 1975 a policy of self-management was established to assist indigenous people and communities to be self-managing in all aspects of their lives. It involved the creation of over 3000 land and tribal councils, housing cooperatives and other indigenous federal, state and community organisations. Unfortunately, these desirable objectives of self-determination and self-management brought some problems in their wake, particularly a 'hands-off' policy by government authorities that sometimes bordered on neglect.

» THE DEVELOPMENT OF ABORIGINAL ART «

A major factor in Aboriginal advancement in the mid-twentieth century was the growing public recognition and appreciation of indigenous art.[a] In 1944, the first Aborigine was listed in *Who's Who in Australia*. Although he died in 1959 he is still one of Australia's best-known Aboriginal artists. Albert Namatjira was born at Hermannsburg Mission in 1902, and was educated there, but was also initiated into Western Arrernte tribal lore. His traditional name was Elea but he was baptised as Albert and later took his father's name, Namatjira, as a sur-name. At the age of eighteen he fell in love with a young woman named Ilkalita, but she belonged to a kinship group forbidden to him by tribal law. They eloped, travelling into the desert, but three years later met some fellow tribesmen, who told them they had been forgiven. They returned to the mission with their three young children and Ilkalita was baptised Rubena.[b]

Albert worked as a stockman, blacksmith and camel driver, but his true talent lay in art. He could draw animals well and decorated wooden artefacts with pokerwork, using a heated wire or hot metal tool, for the mission's fledgling craft industry. In 1934, by one of life's lucky chances, he saw at the mission an exhibition of watercolours by Rex Batterbee and John Gardner, and watched Gardner painting a local landscape. He was fascinated and asked

» *Watercolour of Mount Sonder and the Macdonnell Ranges, Northern Territory, by Albert Namatjira, 1945.*

Pastor Albrecht for paint and brushes, who in turn relayed the request to Rex Batterbee.

Two years later, Rex invited Albert on a two-month painting expedition in Central Australia. He quickly learnt the skills of brushwork, handling colour and portraying perspective, and, amazingly, in 1938 held his first solo exhibition in Melbourne, where his 41 landscape paintings sold out in just three days. The public loved and still love his rich varied vision, warm colours and pictorial realism. His paintings portray the dramatic landforms and vivid purples, mauves, reds and blues of Central Australia.

Namatjira expanded the vision of our sunburnt country and gave us new ways of seeing it. Rapidly he became a celebrated artist. In 1953 he was awarded the Queen's Coronation Medal, and the following year was flown from Alice Springs to Canberra to meet her in person. He bore his celebrity status with dignity and composure, aided by his wife. They had ten children, two of whom died in infancy, and all their five sons became painters. However, the burden of fame took its toll. In particular, the Northern Territory Administration made him and his wife full citizens in 1957.[c] This was done with the best of intentions but proved a disaster for it conferred the privilege of drinking liquor. Now Albert could drink in hotels and take bottled liquor home but his family could not. This anomalous situation caused much stress and led to Albert's arrest the following year for sharing alcohol with a fellow tribesman. His sentence of six months' imprisonment was later reduced to two months spent in 'open arrest' at Papunya reserve. Shortly afterwards, the angina that had troubled him since 1947 resurfaced and he died from a heart attack and pneumonia in Alice Springs hospital in 1959.

Before Namatjira, public knowledge of Aboriginal art was virtually confined to traditional paintings on rock and sheets of bark in tropical Australia. Bark paintings derived from the custom of decorating the ceilings of bark shelters in the wet season. The overhead sheets of bark were painted with finely drawn figures illustrating traditional stories. Style, technique and subject matter resembled those of rock art and the only major changes initiated by European collectors were to commission artists to paint non-sacred subjects for sale, first using portable rectangles of bark and more recently artists' paper.[d]

The legacy of Albert Namatjira is immense: he paved the way for acceptance of indigenous art by mainstream Australia. Importantly, all Namatjira's paintings are of landscape. He was using a modern medium to portray places—mountain ranges, rocks and trees—to which he or his fellow countrymen had ancestral connections. Multilayered meanings are embedded in the scenes he painted. As Galarrwuy Yunupingu, a senior Arnhem Land bark painter, later explained:

> When we paint—whether it is on our bodies for ceremony or on bark or on canvas for the market—we are not just painting for fun or profit. We are painting as we have always done to demonstrate our continuing link with our country and the rights and responsibilities we have to it.[e]

This deep feeling for land gives Namatjira's work a special quality. Similarly, it inspires the dot painters, who later illustrated traditional stories of their own country in a different medium. Their distinctive style of modern art also developed through a fortunate chance. In 1971, Geoffrey Bardon, a school-teacher at Papunya, encouraged his pupils to paint a mural on the school walls featuring traditional Aboriginal motifs. When elders saw it they were dis-satisfied and proceeded to paint a large Honey Ant Dreaming mural there themselves. This aroused intense interest and over the next year 50 men produced more than 600 paintings, using acrylic paint on hardboard and, later, synthetic polymer paint or acrylic on canvas. Like Namatjira, dot painters use modern media, but their style of art is very different from Western paintings and symbolic and 'abstract' rather than realistic.

Dot painters use the imagery of circles and lines to tell their stories and many paintings are 'maps' of their country and Dreaming sites.[f] The images are a development from ceremonial ground mosaics made from pellets of white clay or black charcoal, feathers, pebbles and chopped leaves and flowers of the native daisy and other plants coloured with powdered red or yellow ochre. A piece of ground is prepared, the mosaic made and danced over during a ceremony, being destroyed in the process. Some but not all ground mosaics are sacred, and canvases may be painted by a man or woman, husband and wife team or by men and women from one kinship group.

A few artists have achieved international acclaim for the quality and complexity of their work, which often has a three-dimensional quality through multilayering of dots on dots. Some of the most prominent are Billy Stockman Tjapaltjarri, Emily Kame Kngwarreye, Clifford Possum Tjapaltjarri and his daughter Gabriella, Jimmy Pike and Rover Thomas. Dot painting has revitalised Aboriginal traditions and also provided a profitable 'cottage industry' that enables artists to earn a good income while staying on their traditional land. Beginning with Namatjira, Aboriginal art has won worldwide fame and become one of Australia's best-known icons.

« »

» Freedom Riders and the 1967 referendum

The 1960s were a watershed in Aboriginal affairs. Perhaps the greatest catalyst for indigenous advancement was the student movement, which first brought discrimination against Aborigines to public attention. Then, as now, most non-indigenous Australians lived in southern coastal cities. It was possible to see Aborigines in films and occasionally on television but I had been in Canberra on and off for a decade before I met one. Equally rarely were Aborigines mentioned in the press, but all this changed in February 1965, when 30 students set off from Sydney on a 3200 km (2000 mile) 'Freedom Ride' bus tour of New South Wales country towns to investigate discrimination. The leader, one of only two Aborigines in the group, was Charles Perkins, a charismatic, articulate 29 year old. Perkins was born in Alice Springs of mixed parentage, educated by Anglican missionaries and later completed an apprenticeship as a fitter and turner. He excelled at soccer, was spotted by a talent scout from English club Everton and played for them in 1959. Later he played for South Australia and in 1961 joined the Federal Council for Advancement of Aborigines and Torres Strait Islanders (FCAATSI), becoming vice-president and completing a degree in law and government at the University of Sydney in 1964.

Perkins and his fellow 'Freedom Riders' found an informal colour bar entrenched in some country towns—Aborigines were confined to separate sections of cinemas, refused service in hotels and barred from clubs. In Moree, Aboriginal children were excluded from the public swimming pool unless with a school group. Witnessed by national media, students argued with the pool manager and the mayor until they were allowed to escort six Aboriginal children into the pool. Perkins took similar direct action in Walgett. Soon atrocious Aboriginal living conditions were headlines in the world press. The 1960s was the time of the Civil Rights campaign in the United States and of growing enlightenment, multiculturalism and prosperity in Australia, which has long seen itself as the land of 'a fair go', a pluralist society where all deserve equality.

One major problem was that the federal government had responsibility *only* for Northern Territory Aborigines. Only a referendum could change the Australian constitution to give it power to coordinate national policy and legislation in Aboriginal affairs. Perkins, FCAATSI and their supporters campaigned for this constitutional change and the government agreed to hold a referendum in 1967. This is the only referendum in which a 'No' case was not presented, and it passed with a considerable majority.

After the referendum, the federal government set up an advisory body called the Council for Aboriginal Affairs. Existing definitions of 'Aborigine' were abandoned in favour of self-identification combined with biological descent and Aboriginal community acceptance, an important policy change that enabled people of part-descent to assert their Aboriginality. The Council also influenced a change in official policy from

RIGHT WRONGS
WRITE

YES

for

ABORIGINES!

On May 27

Authorised by J. McGuinness, 9 Gough Street, Cairns. Issued by Federal Council for the Advancement of Aborigines and Torres Strait Islanders.

» *The massive 90.8 per cent pro-Aboriginal rights vote in 1967 remains the highest in any Australian constitutional referendum. The vote cut across party political lines, although rural Australia was far from wholehearted in its support. It amended two clauses in the Constitution. First, all Aborigines could now be counted in the census. In 1901 Aborigines were excluded from the census because it was (correctly) believed that it would not be possible to achieve an accurate population count. (Without an accurate total population figure for each state, it would have been impossible to allocate the number of seats in the House of Representatives between the states. By the 1960s, any inaccuracies in counting Aborigines in the outback would not have been significant.) Second, the federal government could now enact legislation for Aborigines in the states. However, this is a concurrent power and state governments can still legislate for Aborigines, causing considerable disagreement at times between state and federal authorities.*

assimilation to integration, which recognises that Aborigines have the right to live their own lifestyle rather than expecting them to merge into Anglo-Australia. The Council wanted tribal groups to have time and scope to adjust to the dominant society.

To achieve a gradual adjustment and to be able to maintain cultural traditions, land under assured title was needed. Land rights—owning and living on one's own land—became the principal rallying cry of the Aboriginal cause, yet, as Perkins wrote

The Original Australians

in 1988—'Although the land rights issue has wide support from Aboriginal people across the nation, for political reasons it has had limited support from Aboriginal and Islander people living in urban areas. To them the issues of compensation and adequate programs to restore a level of equity with non-Aboriginal Australians take precedence.'[2] This urban/bush divide is even more pronounced today. Tribal Aborigines are relatively few, inhabit the north and centre and are deeply involved in claiming land, while urban and most other regional Aboriginal populations are not in a position to engage in land rights claims.

The land rights movement began in 1963 at Yirrkala when the Yolngu agitated for the return of their traditional land (see chapter 7). Although Justice Blackburn's 1971 decision rejected the Yolngu claim because land held by tenure was not recognised as private property, he recommended compensation, protection of sacred sites and preservation of hunting rights. On Australia Day 1972, the Liberal prime minister, Sir William McMahon, confirmed Blackburn's judgment and ruled out land rights based on traditional association. Aborigines' patience snapped and they set up an 'Aboriginal Tent Embassy' (initially one beach umbrella) on the lawn in front of Parliament House to symbolise Aboriginal disadvantage and their desire to be treated as a separate political entity. The encampment grew, a 'Minister for Caucasian Affairs' was appointed and the media had a field day. For six months, Aboriginal campers severely embarrassed the government, who eventually sent police to demolish the 'embassy'. McMahon lost the next election in December 1972, and Gough Whitlam swept into office, heading Australia's first Labor government for 22 years.[3]

The Aboriginal flag was first flown on National Aboriginal and Islander Day in July 1971 in Adelaide but became a strong, unifying symbol of Aboriginal identity when flown at the Aboriginal 'embassy' in 1972. It was designed by Harold Thomas of the Arrernte. Black symbolises Aboriginal people past, present and future, red the earth, red ochre and Aboriginal spiritual relationship to the land, and yellow the sun, bringer of life.

» Self-determination and self-management

Whitlam was elected partly on a platform that included human rights and Aboriginal self-determination—the right to determine and control one's own destiny. The goal was for Aboriginal communities to decide the pace and nature of their future development as a significant group within the dominant society. The 'White Australia' Policy had been abandoned in 1969 and now the war against racism continued with the passing of the *Racial Discrimination Act 1975*, which banned discrimination on grounds of race, colour or ethnic origin in matters of employment, access to housing or public places and provision of goods and services.

Whitlam established a federal Department of Aboriginal Affairs (DAA), a National Aboriginal Consultative Committee (NACC) of elected Aboriginal members and the Woodward Aboriginal Land Rights Commission. He also froze uranium mining, which was often on contested ground. After wide consultation, Justice Woodward recommended setting up Aboriginal Land Councils and land claims mechanisms and the vesting of inalienable, freehold, communal title in Aboriginal Land Trusts in the Northern Territory. In May 1975 an Aboriginal Land Fund Commission was established to buy land and in August traditional land was purchased and returned to the Gurindji in a moving ceremony, where Whitlam poured sand into Vincent Lingiari's hands. A land rights bill was drafted but in November, only hours after its second reading, came Whitlam's dramatic, controversial dismissal by the Governor-General. (Whitlam had refused to call a general election after the Leader of the Opposition, Malcolm Fraser, blocked government finance bills.)

Fraser won the ensuing election and, to his credit, passed Whitlam's *Aboriginal Land Rights (Northern Territory) Act 1976*. Importantly, Northern Territory Aborigines were given a unique right of veto to prevent mining on their land, although they must consent to mineral exploration. Dealings between mining companies and Aborigines are mediated through land councils, and miners have to negotiate and pay royalties to traditional owners. Aboriginal mineral-rights campaigners still hold up this legislation as a model that all state governments should adopt.

Whitlam's policy had aimed 'to restore to the Aboriginal people of Australia their lost power of self-determination in economic, social and political affairs'.[4] This 'new deal' involved massive spending. Federal expenditure on Aboriginal advancement doubled in 1973 and doubled again the following year. The Aboriginal budget continued increasing under Labor and only decreased slightly under succeeding conservative governments (1975–83), because Fraser, a humanitarian, prosecuted a vigorous program to improve Aboriginal living conditions, health, education and housing, and also initiated a limited form of self-management for indigenous communities. The federal government funded indigenous national, regional and local community organisations such as FCAATSI, land councils and housing cooperatives, many of which were formed through indigenous people's own initiative. By 2001, the federal budget allocation for indigenous-specific programs had risen to $2.3 billion, three quarters of which was earmarked for programs aimed at improving the Aboriginal standard of living.[5]

In 1980 the Aboriginal Development Commission (ADC) was set up to fund Aboriginal land purchases, housing or business enterprises. 'Freedom Rider' Charles Perkins ran the ADC until 1984, when he became head of the DAA. Predictably, there were teething troubles and frequent questioning of shaky Aboriginal financial management and accounting. In 1988 Perkins was asked to stand aside and later resigned, although cleared of any actual wrongdoing. In 1990 the DAA was replaced by the Aboriginal and Torres Strait Islander Commission (ATSIC), which combined ADC and DAA functions. The chairperson, Lowitja O'Donoghue, and two commissioners were government appointments, the other seventeen board members were indigenous people elected by 388 regional councillors, themselves elected by about 40 000 voters in a special indigenous election. Voting in triennial elections was optional and voter turnout very low. Many candidates had no widespread support; in the 2002 elections one regional councillor was elected with a primary vote of only twelve. Some candidates relied on patronage to maintain their power. Nevertheless, ATSIC enabled indigenous decision-making and enjoyed a substantial budget ($1.2 billion in 2003 to spend on 2.4 per cent of Australians).

Finally, in 2004 a dysfunctional ATSIC foundered on the rocks of financial mismanagement, lack of accountability, nepotism and cronyism. Bipartisan political support died and ATSIC is now seen as an experiment that failed. The concept of elected individuals representing more than their own extended family or clan seems too alien to work in a fragmented indigenous society where decision-making is by consensus. This is the first hiatus in 32 years of elected indigenous representation and the majority of Aboriginal people, while critical of ATSIC, have been left voiceless. In November 2004, ATSIC was replaced by a National Indigenous Council of fourteen indigenous members, unelected but hand-picked by the prime minister to consult with the government on indigenous issues in an advisory capacity only.[6] Responsibility for provision of services to Aboriginal communities reverted to regular government departments, amid anxiety that this would put at risk culturally appropriate services.

» Land rights

Support for land rights peaked during the late 1970s, when the public saw it as a quality-of-life issue. The *Pitjantjatjara Land Rights Act* of 1981 gave to the corporate body Anangu Pitjantjatjara inalienable freehold title to 103 000 km² (40 000 sq. miles) of South Australian land, plus control of entry and a share of mining royalties. This gave Aborigines control of 19 per cent of South Australia, but all in the dry north. In more closely settled New South Wales, the *Aboriginal Land Rights Act 1983* established land councils and gave them title to existing reserves, the means to claim unused Crown land and to purchase other land on the open market. A fund (7.5 per cent of gross state land tax revenue for 15 years) was set up to fund land purchases and land council administration.

When Labor won back federal office in 1983, the new prime minister, Bob Hawke, did much for Aborigines but gradually electors became disillusioned with alleged Aboriginal waste of taxpayers' money. Land rights were thought to contribute to the 1980s economic downturn and threaten Australia's prosperity, which is based on agriculture, mining and tourism. Aborigines can prohibit all access to their land, roads or waters, locking up vast areas from tourism and productive use. They can also veto mining. In Australia the Crown owns *all* minerals, oil, gas and other subsurface deposits and retains mining rights even on privately owned land. But Aborigines,

» *The Governor-General, Minister for Aboriginal Affairs, Clyde Holding, Peter Bulla, Peter Kanari, Nipper Winmarti, Barbara Tjirkadu and Barry Cohen (left to right) at the handover of inalienable freehold title for Uluru and Kata Tjuta (the Olgas), which became a national park in 1958 and was granted to the Uluru Kata Tjuta Land Trust in 1985. The park is jointly managed by traditional owners and Parks Australia.*

unlike other Australians, can prevent or delay mining on their land—a right exercised in the cases of Coronation Hill, Jabiluka and Koongarra in Arnhem Land.

In 1982 nearly 10 per cent of Australia was held by Aborigines. By 2004, 15.7 per cent was under indigenous ownership, management or control. (Two-thirds of this area is desert, and the rest is made up of tropical coasts and islands.) A 1985 opinion poll revealed that only 18 per cent of Australians were in favour of land rights (24 per cent were 'firmly' and 52 per cent 'softly' opposed), so Hawke's promise of national land rights was quietly shelved.

» Bicentenary protest

Australia's Bicentenary celebrations in 1988 acted as a catalyst for Aboriginal protest and in June, at the Barunga (Northern Territory) Festival, Galarrwuy Yunupingu, Chairman of the Northern Land Council, presented the prime minister, Bob Hawke, with the Barunga Statement. This set the Aboriginal agenda for negotiations towards a treaty between black and white Australians. This claim of Aboriginal rights, framed by a bark painting, called for 'a national system of land rights; permanent control and enjoyment of our ancestral lands; compensation for the loss of use of our lands; protection of and control of access to our sacred sites, sacred objects, artefacts, designs, knowledge and works of art; the return of the remains of our ancestors for burial in accordance with our traditions'.

Most of these rights have now been more or less achieved. Australia has strong legal protection for Aboriginal sites, human remains, artefacts, designs and works of art. Much of this protection dates from archaeologists' efforts in the 1960s. All Aboriginal stone tools now belong to the Crown so, unlike in the United States, private collecting is illegal, even on one's own land. Permits (from state heritage authorities after Aboriginal consultation) are required for any collection or excavation, and excavated artefacts must be lodged in the regional museum. There is 'blanket' protection for all Aboriginal 'relics', such as rock art or burial places. Unmodified mythological sites are more problematic but can be protected by registration. These 'invisible' story places are under increasing pressure from new highways, pipelines, housing, mines and reservoirs. Aborigines are often accused of 'inventing' sacred sites in front of the bulldozers. The situation has improved with better legislation requiring site surveys before development begins. Ideally, significant sites are registered long before any threats arise. During my 13 years working on inclusion of Aboriginal sites in the Register of the National Estate, registration provided 100 per cent protection—none of the more than 2000 Aboriginal sites registered by the Australian Heritage Commission in 1979–91 was damaged or destroyed.[7]

The 1990s witnessed several Aboriginal attempts to halt major development projects. The first battle was over a mining proposal affecting southern Kakadu National Park where Coronation Hill contains gold, platinum and palladium worth over $1.5 billion—perhaps the world's richest mineral deposit. The Jawoyn people were divided between elders, for whom the area still held the ancestral spirit of Bula, and those who valued the jobs and royalties mining would bring. Hawke prevented mining at Coronation Hill.

Another major struggle began in 1992 over the development of a bridge to link Hindmarsh Island with the town of Goolwa, South Australia. Twenty-five Ngarrindjeri women claimed a bridge would desecrate secret-sacred sites. Under the *ATSI Heritage Protection Act* 1984 the federal minister banned the development, but this was overturned on a legal technicality. Then five other Ngarrindjeri women called the custodians 'liars' and the 'women's secret business' a complete fabrication. A South Australian Royal Commission was appointed, enquired and agreed the alleged evidence was fabricated. Four years of acrimonious public debate, formal inquiries and court cases ensued until the High Court upheld the developers' case and the bridge was finally opened in 2001. Ngarrindjeri and anthropologists remain divided. The cost of the case was tens of millions from the public purse and irreparable harm to the credibility of detribalised Aborigines.[8]

Opposition from state governments meant little progress towards national land rights until the Mabo decision in 1992, when Australia's High Court ruled that Eddie Mabo and two other Torres Strait Islanders should be granted 'native title' to Murray Island. 'Native title' was defined by Justice Gerard Brennan as 'indigenous inhabitants' interests and rights in land, whether communal, group or individual, under their traditional laws and customs'.[9]

The case took ten years and sadly Eddie Mabo died of cancer a few months before his victory, but this recognition of indigenous title to land is perhaps the most significant legal decision in Australian history. The Torres Strait Islands are inhabited by people of mainly Melanesian stock with a language, culture and lifestyle different from those of Aboriginal Australians, but in the 1870s the islands were annexed to Queensland and now form part of the Federation of Australia. The judges' decision therefore also applied to mainland Aborigines and determined that the common law of Australia recognises a form of native land title and that indigenous Australians have rights to land based on prior occupation. Where they remain on their land, these rights or 'native title' almost certainly survive.

Six out of seven judges agreed that, where it had not been extinguished, communal native title should be recognised as part of Australian common law. The response was immediate anger and fear from pastoralists and mining interests, fuelled by Aboriginal ambit claims to vast regions, including most of the Kimberley and Pilbara, half of Tasmania, the whole Australian Capital Territory and Brisbane's Central Business District. In response, the Keating Labor government passed the *Native Title Act 1993* and all states later introduced legislation consistent with the federal Act. Native title rights were recognised, but only vacant Crown land could be claimed by indigenous Australians able to prove *continuous* links to that area.

» The Wik decision

In 1996, the High Court's revolutionary Wik decision apparently opened *all* Australian land to native title claims. In *Wik Peoples v Queensland*, High Court judges ruled that native title was *not* automatically extinguished by leasehold grants of land and that pastoral leases (covering 42 per cent of Australia) do not necessarily extinguish native title. Vigorous, sometimes bitter public debate followed. Liberal Prime Minister John Howard put forward a 'ten point plan' of changes to what was now seen as the unworkable 1993 Act, while his deputy toured the outback promising 'buckets full of extinguishment'. By 1998 only two determinations of native title had been made, 678 often conflicting applications covering half the continent awaited attention and administration of the Act had cost $210 million.

The House of Representatives voted in favour of Howard's ten points, but some were rejected by the Senate. Finally, after 109 hours of Senate debate and

314 amendments, the bill was passed. 'Legislation by exhaustion' is how Frank Brennan, Jesuit priest and lawyer, described it, while expressing confidence that 'the major political parties will live with the detailed compromise':

> There will be greater emphasis on negotiated agreements. Pastoralists' . . . rights prevail over any conflicting rights of native title holders . . . Native title claimants will have access to an independent tribunal to put their case. The majority of Aborigines who could never establish a native title claim will still have access to the Indigenous Land Fund, which enjoys bipartisan support and which will reach $1.289 billion by June 2004, permitting annual payments of $45 million for land purchases and land administration.[10]

By 2002, only 32 claims had been determined in court and 38 by agreement. A huge backlog remains and many claims overlap, particularly on the Western Australia goldfields, pitting clan against clan. One WA pastoral station is subject to fourteen claims. Meanwhile, all states and territories have enacted some form of native title legislation. But land rights have proved no panacea. At their heart is the doctrine of communal rather than individual ownership and this tends to trap Aborigines in remote communities in poverty, where they cannot aspire to earn a good income, or own their own car, house or business. A 2005 paper by development economist Helen Hughes strongly asserts that communal title impedes economic development.[11]

» Aboriginal deaths in custody

In 1987 an inquiry was set up to investigate allegations against police and prison officers in relation to high rates of Aboriginal deaths while in custody. This proved a watershed, the government response setting in train new policies across Australia. The Royal Commission into Aboriginal Deaths in Custody (RCIADIC) spent four years and $30 million inquiring into 99 Aboriginal deaths in police custody, youth detention centres or prison in 1980–89. The Commission found 46 per cent of deaths resulted from natural causes (especially alcoholism and drug overdoses), 34 per cent from suicides, 15 per cent from injuries inflicted by non-custodians and only 5 per cent from custodians' actions, but 'no person had deliberately caused a death or deliberately inflicted harm'. The profile of Aborigines who died in custody is that 88 per cent were men (average age 32), 83 per cent unemployed, 77 per cent unskilled, 40 per cent not educated beyond primary level, 43 per cent had been removed from their families and 74 per cent had a criminal record before the age of twenty. Most deaths occurred in Western Australia (32), Queensland (27) and New South Wales (15); 60 per cent were urban-dwellers and 21 per cent from rural Aboriginal communities. RCIADIC made 339 recommendations, mainly aimed at lowering detention rates. A surprise finding was that Aboriginal men's survival rates were better in prison than outside. Keating's government devoted $400 million to the report's implementation, but a decade later only one in five recommendations, on matters such as suicide prevention, had been addressed, a further 115 Aborigines had died in custody, and even more had committed suicide outside prison.

Although indigenous people make up only 2.4 per cent of Australia's population, they comprise 19 per cent of adult prison inmates and a startling 41 per cent of the juvenile prison population. A contributing factor is the relative youthfulness of the indigenous population, whose median age is fourteen years less than that of the general population.

Over four times as many Aborigines die young, aged 15–34. Some of these deaths are as a result of car crashes, in which Aborigines are seriously injured or killed at up to four times the rate of non-indigenous people. Alcohol, overloaded cars, non-use of seat-belts and riding unrestrained in the trays of open-backed utility vehicles are the main causes.[12]

» Reconciliation

In 1990 a Council for Aboriginal Reconciliation (CAR) was created and given a decade to achieve reconciliation between indigenous and non-indigenous Australians. Within the 25-member council there was bipartisan agreement that Australians needed to know more about both sides of the country's history, to apologise to indigenous people for past wrongs and demand a better way forward. Ten years were spent on nationwide consultation to promote cross-cultural understanding. A strong grass-roots movement arose of 'Australians for Reconciliation', 'sorry books' were signed, 'seas of hands' planted, 'journeys of healing' begun and over a million people participated in bridge-walks for reconciliation. The culmination was Corroboree 2000 held in the Sydney Opera House. There the prime minister was presented with an 'Australian Declaration and Roadmap towards Reconciliation'. Key points were:

- We, the peoples of Australia, . . . make a commitment to go on together in a spirit of reconciliation.
- Reaffirming the human rights of all Australians, we respect and recognise continuing customary laws, beliefs and traditions.
- As we walk the journey of healing, one part of the nation apologises and expresses its sorrow and sincere regret for the injustices of the past, so the other part accepts the apologies and forgives.
- We pledge ourselves to stop injustice, overcome disadvantage, and respect that Aboriginal and Torres Strait Islander peoples have the right to self-determination within the life of the nation.[13]

The first controversial item here is recognition of 'customary laws', since some traditional practices conflict with Anglo-Australian law and with the 1948 United

The Original Australians

» *Founded in 1989, Bangarra Dance Theatre, Sydney, is one of Australia's leading dance companies. It fuses traditional Aboriginal and contemporary styles, values and stories. Two of its most nationally and internationally acclaimed works have been Ochres and Fish, which explore human relationships to the natural world through dance. Other productions, for example Praying Mantis Dreaming, have dealt with modern issues such as dislocation through the process of colonisation. Bangarra has been part of the indigenous artistic renaissance that began in the 1970s and like much of Aboriginal painting and drama, successfully combines creative art and activism. Its innovative dance style appeals to indigenous and non-indigenous audiences alike, and in spite of its small size and youth, Bangarra has been hailed as a strong force for reconciliation.*

Nations' Universal Declaration of Human Rights.[14] The Declaration also called for an apology from 'one part of the nation', meaning an official federal government apology, although Howard had already expressed his *personal* regret and sorrow at the 1997 Australian Reconciliation Convention in Melbourne. There, when the prime minister refused to utter the actual word 'sorry', the Aborigines in the audience turned their backs. Howard maintained that one generation cannot assume moral responsibility for its forebears' mistakes.[15] Populist opinion agreed. A major Newspoll survey in 2000 showed a clear majority supported reconciliation but opposed an apology or reparations.[16] Although Howard's refusal to say an official 'sorry' denied the desired closure on the past, the choice of outstanding Aboriginal athlete Cathy Freeman to light the flame at the Sydney 2000 Olympic Games and indigenous themes in the opening ceremony provided a fitting, inspirational end to the decade of reconciliation.

The 'fundamental bottom line', wrote Evelyn Scott, last CAR chairperson, is 'equality, respect and social justice'.[17] Social justice is so open-ended a concept as to be almost meaningless, but Mick Dodson, the first Aboriginal and Torres Strait Islander Social Justice Commissioner, wrote: 'Social justice . . . is awakening in a house with an adequate water supply, cooking facilities and sanitation. It is the ability to nourish your children and send them to a school where their education not only equips them for employment but reinforces their knowledge and appreciation of their cultural inheritance. It is the prospect of genuine employment and good health: a life of choices and opportunity, free from discrimination.'[18] In a political sense, much of this has already been achieved. There is total equality under the law and strictly enforced legislation bans discrimination. Aboriginal studies is now part of the school curriculum and education is free and available to all, although the remoteness of many Aboriginal communities makes access difficult. Health care is free to indigenous people and numerous affirmative-action programs are in place. Respect has grown for indigenous culture, which has a high profile and many outstanding proponents, such as actor David Gulpilil, broadcaster Ernie Dingo, Senator Aden Ridgeway, academic Marcia Langton, magistrate Pat O'Shane and innumerable brilliant artists and sportspeople. Racism is officially unacceptable in Australian society or politics. When Australia was under world media spotlight at the Olympics, commentators such as the BBC were agreeably surprised at the relative absence of racism in modern Australia's multicultural society.

How do we know when we have achieved reconciliation? Michael Dodson sees the way forward as resting in human understanding:

It is my belief that when the Aboriginal and Torres Strait Islander story of Australia is heard and understood then there will be a true reconciliation. The abstract language of human rights and justice will settle down on the realities of the lives and aspirations of individual men, women and children who wish simply to have their humanity respected and their distinctive identity recognised.[19]

After a successful decade of promoting the idea of reconciliation, the most pressing needs now are to improve Aboriginal health, living conditions and participation in education, but the agenda has been somewhat sidetracked by demand for a treaty.

» Treaty?

The last ATSIC chairman, Geoff Clark, insisted: 'A commitment from government to negotiate a treaty is essential.'[20] Clark was also deputy chairman of the Aboriginal Provisional Government campaigning for constitutional recognition of Aboriginal sovereignty and rights. The secretary was Michael Mansell, a radical lawyer from Tasmania, who in 1988 caused public outrage by leading an Aboriginal delegation to Libya seeking Colonel Gaddafi's support for trade sanctions against Australia.[21] Both Clark and Mansell see Australia as 'two nations', indigenous people and 'others', who can only be reconciled through a treaty. However, Evelyn Scott and others regard it as a divisive issue, liable to undo the goodwill generated by a decade of reconciliation.[22] It is also a practical and legal impossibility, for, as former Chief Justice Harry Gibbs said, 'a treaty is between two different nations and we regard the Aboriginal people as one people with us'.[23]

Treaties made elsewhere were either negotiated between two separate peoples before they merged (for example, in the United States and New Zealand) or with indigenous people still living in their own territory (such as the Inuit in Canada). Canada's small number of self-governing native reserves are often held up as a model for Australia but very few live in them because strict rules of eligibility apply. The Australian Government could certainly make domestic agreements with large Australian tribal groups such as the Tiwi, Yolngu, Pitjantjatjara or Wik. However, Canada does not have a national treaty with its 'first peoples' because most are no longer identifiable as a separate group.[24]

Aspirations for separate sovereignty and self-government are even less realistic in modern Australia, where most Aborigines have lost their language, religion and traditional lifestyle and 70 per cent now live in towns and cities. (Almost half live in Sydney, Brisbane and seven other coastal cities.) Nearly 80 per cent of urban 'Aborigines' have 'married out' or have non-Aboriginal partners, and nationally, the Aboriginal out-marriage figure in 2001 was 68 per cent.[25] Ethnicity is now simply self-identification as 'a person of Aboriginal or Torres Strait Islander descent who is accepted as such by the community in which he or she lives'.[26]

Indigenous population increased by 88 per cent in 1966–76 and 41 per cent in 1976–86. In the 2001 census the increase was 16 per cent, of which 4 per cent cannot be explained by natural factors such as a higher birthrate or better health but was

caused by increased self-identification.[27] Indigenous status has become not only some-thing to be proud of but also brings certain benefits in the fields of health care, legal aid, educational grants, tertiary scholarships and 'indigenous-preferred' jobs. This leads to some strange anomalies. In Tasmania almost 16 000 people claimed to be Aboriginal in the 2001 census but fewer than 7000 are acknowledged as such by the peak Tasmanian Aboriginal organisation. The issue of identity reached its nadir in 2002, dividing Aboriginal organisations and pitting families against each other. Of the 1297 Tasmanians who registered for the first indigenous electoral roll, 1100 (including the Tasmanian ATSIC commissioner) were formally challenged to prove their Aboriginality. After at least seven generations, the blood quantum of genuine descendants of Tasmanian Aborigines is only about 1/64th, so physical appearance is no guide to ethnicity. The row continued in 2005 with the Palawa people led by Michael Mansell dismissing a rival group called Lia Pootah or Little River as 'fakes' with a made-up Aboriginal name, who 'don't have a drop of Aboriginal blood in their veins'.[28]

» A long way to go

Meanwhile, over the last 30 years of self-determination and improvements in the polit-ical and legal spheres, a measureless human tragedy has unfolded in many Aboriginal communities.[29] Tackling Aboriginal disadvantage is the major challenge of the new millennium. Infant mortality, health and life expectancy are appalling, educational standards abysmal, unemployment astronomical, substance-abuse and crime horrific.

The statistics remain 'a hideous blot on the nation's report-card', as a 2004 editorial in *The Australian* expressed it. 'Aborigines die 20 years earlier than non-indigenous Australians, are 15 times more likely to be in jail and 10 times more likely to be murdered. By the time young Aborigines are 10 years old, only 65 per cent of them can read to the required benchmark, compared with a national figure of 90 per cent. In remote communities, domestic violence and sexual abuse of children are occurring on a scale that makes Pitcairn Island look like a model of civilised behaviour. And substance abuse in those communities—including children as young as five addicted to petrol-sniffing—is rife.'[30]

In 1788, Aboriginal life expectancy resembled European, averaging 40 years. Since then both indigenous and non-indigenous rates have increased significantly but now Aboriginal life expectancy is twenty years less than non-indigenous, stuck at levels not seen in the rest of the Australian population for a century. Indigenous men's life expectancy was estimated in 2002 at 59 years and women's at 65, in contrast with 78 for males and 83 for females in the general population. Infant mortality is twice the non-indigenous rate. Half the indigenous population smokes (twice the non-indigenous rate), and 61 per cent of adults are overweight or obese compared with 48 per cent non-indigenous. Aborigines are twice as likely to be hospitalised as others

A contributing factor here is streptococcal infections arising from unwashed clothes and bedding.[31]

Health standards are appalling, in spite of billions of dollars spent on health and housing, successful use of the army to install water supplies, power, sewers and other infrastructure in outback settlements and effective individual initiatives such as Dr Fred Hollows' trachoma and eye health program, which began in the 1970s. Trachoma is an endemic fly-borne, viral eye disease that increased in incidence (to twenty times the non-indigenous rate) as desert nomads moved into crowded, permanent settlements. A significant reduction (20–40 per cent) in avoidable blindness has resulted from this program and others involving improved hygiene in communities.[32] Previously nomadism had avoided many of these ills.

Sexually transmitted diseases are also a major indigenous problem. A 2000 survey of communicable diseases in Western Australia, South Australia and the Northern Territory found indigenous rates of chlamydia, gonorrhoea and syphilis respectively 8, 18 and 20 times higher than those for the total population.[33] In 2001 the Western Australia Sexual Health Centre revealed the rate of gonorrhoea infection in Aboriginal children aged 10–14 was 186 times the non-Aboriginal rate. This emerged at an inquest on the 1999 suicide of a 15-year-old Aboriginal girl who hanged herself with a garden hose in Swan River Nyungah Camp after being sexually abused, abuse that she had reported to the police. Three years earlier her 13-year-old cousin hanged herself at the same camp; child-welfare workers and the local Aboriginal medical service had been banned from the camp for years by a powerful elder.[34] The camp has now closed.

The latest threat is AIDS. Statistics are few, but in 1992 the transmission rate of HIV/AIDS among indigenous people was five times that of other Australians, and one Aboriginal community recorded one of the world's highest rates of infection.[35] Now 28 per cent of indigenous HIV/AIDS sufferers are women against only 6 per cent in the total population, that is, indigenous women are four times as likely to be infected. More than a third of indigenous cases were attributed to heterosexual contact, whereas in the total population the vast majority resulted from male homosexuality and injecting drug use. This alarming heterosexual spread is comparable to the dire situation in Africa and higher indigenous rates of STDs increase the likelihood of HIV/AIDS transmission.[36]

Former nomads have great difficulty in adapting their health practices to the dangerous environment of permanent settlements and housing. I will never forget the children with oozing ears, noses and eyes I saw in 1980 at the government settlement of Papunya, in the desert west of Alice Springs. The hospital had been vandalised. The school was no longer allowed to give children showers, milk or healthy school lunches, because such practices were considered 'paternalistic'. Many played truant and I met children who after six years of school could barely write their names, but most distressing were those with black, rotted teeth and 'glue ear'—untreated middle-ear infections leading to severe hearing loss. Many children were deaf by the time they started school at five. (Health clinics were provided but attendance was optional.) Papunya children were in worse health than children in refugee camps in Bangladesh where I had worked. I was so ashamed of this government settlement that I took my concerns to the federal minister, Fred Chaney, only to be told 'Australia has dozens of Papunyas but there is almost nothing we can do to improve things'. White paternalistic help was out. Nor were charities allowed to enter such settlements, although now World Vision has an office in Papunya and Mother Teresa's Sisters of Mercy provide a home in Katherine for elderly, homeless Aboriginal women.

» Petrol-sniffing, alcohol and drugs

Papunya has now succumbed to the petrol-sniffing epidemic devastating outback Aboriginal communities. Children walk around like zombies sniffing petrol from jam-tins round their necks and mothers even use petrol-soaked rags to soothe babies to sleep. Heavy sniffing leads to lead-induced brain damage, causing hallucinations, violent behaviour and death through respiratory failure. By 2000, Central Australia had 500 full-time sniffers and 20–30 teenage boys confined to wheelchairs.[37]

Petrol sniffing was first seen in Alice Springs in the 1940s and on the Cobourg Peninsula in 1950. Why do youngsters start sniffing? Among 42 Yolngu boys aged 12–16 from Ramingining, the surprising cause was a 1981 school visit to Singapore. The trip had backfired, turning the children against their own familes. They returned hating the fact that they were Yolngu, black and 'unlucky' because their fathers could not give them beds, cars or fashionable clothes. They were sniffing to forget who they were. Fortunately, their elders asked Richard Trudgen, a Yolngu-speaking development officer, for help. He spent 18 months teaching the community the dangers of sniffing and the realities of Western economic life, law and health. His masterstroke was to ask elders how they would have solved such a problem without him. Their answer was to bring back a particular ceremony that missionaries had stopped them holding. 'Well, no one here is going to stop you now,' Trudgen assured them. They held the ceremony, taught both their ancient law and the new Western knowledge in a 'university of the bush' and after three months petrol-sniffing stopped and has never really started again. The community had discovered real answers to their questions and so were empowered to take action to bring the problem under control. Sadly, petrol-sniffing continues to be a major problem in many other Arnhem Land communities, many elders have lost their authority and Yolngu-speaking Western educators are almost non-existent. Some communities elsewhere such as Yuendumu, Northern Territory, have instituted prevention programs, but the problem needs massive human and financial resources.[38]

In January 2005, a positive step towards eliminating petrol-sniffing was taken by the company BP, which has developed Opal, a low-aromatic, unleaded fuel, to combat the problem. Sniffers say it 'gives them nothing'. It is more expensive than other fuel but the federal government is spending $1 million a year to introduce it to remote communities in South Australia, the Northern Territory and Western Australia at the same price as ordinary petrol, although the implementation of this needs to be much faster.[39]

An even worse problem is alcoholism. As Noel Pearson said, 'Ours is one of the most dysfunctional societies on the planet today; surely the fact that the per capita consumption of alcohol in Cape York is the highest in the world says something about our dysfunction.'[40] The number of indigenous men 'at high risk' from alcohol through binge-drinking is almost treble the national number.

Boni Robertson, leader of an indigenous women's task force on violence in Queensland, found 'alcohol and drug abuse were reported to be primary factors in the level of violence and abuse being witnessed' and 'sexual, child abuse, physical, verbal, emotional, violent abuse happens especially on pay nights when people get full of grog and smoking marijuana'.[41] The Queensland Government lifted the ban on sale of alcohol to Aborigines in the 1950s, allowed alcohol consumption on reserves in the 1960s and erected reserve canteens in the 1970s under indigenous management. Today public drunkenness is condoned there. 'Aboriginal children today are the first and second generation legal drinkers, many of whom have grown up in communities saturated and ruled by both alcohol and violence.'[42]

Alcoholism is clearly the major cause of the horrific levels of sickness, mortality and violence in many Aboriginal communities, but drugs play an increasing role. Heroin seems largely responsible for the violent riot that erupted in the suburb of Redfern in inner Sydney on 15 February 2004. The riot, in which 40 police were injured by petrol bombs, bottles and rocks, was sparked by the death of 17-year-old T. J. Hickey, who died after becoming impaled on a fence while riding his bicycle at high speed, when he (mistakenly) thought he was being chased by police. The subsequent parliamentary inquiry learnt violence was 'regularly unleashed' there on police, with missiles thrown at them every week. Redfern was seen as a 'one-stop shop for heroin with a ready supply of robbery victims, heroin and injecting facilities . . . Criminals instead of elders now held control over the Aboriginal community . . . The real enemy of the young Aboriginal people are not the police but their Aboriginal kin who peddle heroin and by doing so commit them to a life of unemployment, poverty, misery and crime . . . Antagonism to the police has little to do with race and everything to do with . . . protection of a lucrative heroin trade.'

A sad postscript is that 'at 15, T.J.'s girlfriend is now on heroin'. Other problems afflicting both Redfern and T.J.'s home town of Walgett, in far western New South Wales, are constant truancy, absenteeism due to frequent lengthy family visits to relations far away and leaving school at the minimum age of 15 with poor prospects for employment or job training.[43]

ATSIC described the violence that is occurring in indigenous families as: 'The beating of a wife or other family members, homicide, suicide and other self-inflicted injury, rape, child abuse and child sexual abuse, incest and the sale of younger family members for misuse by others as a way of obtaining funds for drink or gambling . . . also verbal harassment, psychological and emotional abuse and economic deprivation.'[44]

The statistics are appalling. Aborigines are now 45 times more likely than other Australians to be victims of domestic violence, while their risk of being murdered is ten times greater. In Queensland, indigenous people are twenty times more likely to commit murder and fifteen times more likely to be a murder victim. One in three Northern Territory Aboriginal females is assaulted every year. Aboriginal women in the Kimberley are 33 times more likely to die through domestic violence than other women in Western Australia. Nearly four times more very young indigenous children are abused and neglected than non-indigenous. In New South Wales, eight times as many indigenous children are on care-and-protection orders.[45]

In 1999, Boni Robertson reported, 'Eyewitness accounts of horrific injuries, scarred bodies, stabbings, bashings, sexual assaults and mentally traumatised victims resembled reports from war zones. The researchers heard accounts of extreme brutality and depravity previously unknown to indigenous communities.'[46] A few specific examples of this black-on-black violence will bring this home:

- In a Cairns hospital there were twelve children who had been physically or sexually abused from one Aboriginal community of 450 people. One of these children had four different sexually transmitted diseases. She was seven years old.[47]
- For its extraordinary rate of suicides, homicides and domestic violence, the *Guinness Book of Records* in the 1990s identified Queensland's Palm Island indigenous community as the most violent place on earth outside a war zone.[48]
- High rates of indigenous pornography viewing are associated with violent crime. Each week $4000–$5000 worth of pornographic videos are ordered by Cape York communities. One indigenous community with a history of high pornographic video usage has the highest rate of men imprisoned for sexual offences in Queensland.[49]

Anthropologist Paul Memmott in a 2001 report found 'rates of violence are increasing, and the types of violence are worsening in some indigenous communities and regions'. He identified the most violent communities as those where alcohol was legally available and the population was relatively large. Tribal disharmony, considerable mobility and lack of cohesion characterise such communities.[50] As a result of the Queensland government's earlier ill-conceived policy of moving Aborigines to settlements far from their homelands, it has more disharmony within many of its indigenous communities than other states.

The Original Australians

The current level of violence is not traditional. As Trudgen recounts: 'I lived for eleven years in . . . Arnhem Land among kind, gentle people who looked after each other . . . It was only when alcohol came into the communities in the middle to late 1970s that we saw the first real acts of violence.'[51] At the same time, many people lost their own religion through the disruption of traditional education and initiation into tribal law. Aboriginal religion is localised to particular sacred sites so when people leave their own region, they tend to lose their religion as well. Many have also rejected missions and missionaries, and those who cooperate with white people are often accused of being 'coconuts'—white on the inside. However, Christian revival movements still sweep remote communities from time to time and Torres Strait Islanders, as well as many Aborigines, gain great strength from their Christianity. In the 2001 census, nearly 70 per cent of the total indigenous population said they were Christian. Of these, a third was Anglican, a third Catholic, and the rest belonged to the Uniting, Evangelical, Lutheran, Pentecostal or other churches.

» Pearson says the unsayable

Until the late 1990s, indigenous problems were a taboo subject. A powerful deterrent to publicising the indigenous 'culture of alcohol, substance abuse, violence and anarchy' was fear of promoting negative stereotypes or being called racist. In 1999 Robertson wrote:

> Indigenous women's groups, concerned about their disintegrating world, have been calling for assistance for more than a decade . . . At times, government representatives appeared to regard violence as a normal aspect of indigenous life, like the high rate of alcohol consumption. Interventions were dismissed as politically and culturally intrusive in the newly acquired autonomy of indigenous communities . . . the broader Australian community . . . seemed oblivious to the mayhem that was happening.[52]

It was Queensland Aboriginal leader Noel Pearson who finally broke the code of silence in 1999: 'Our life expectancy is decreasing and the young generation is illiterate'; 'progressive' thinking about substance abuse holds it is 'only a symptom of underlying social and psychological problems . . . But addiction is a condition in its own right, not a symptom. It must therefore be addressed as a problem in itself.' The 'symptom theory' absolves people from their responsibility to deal with addiction. 'Worse, it leaves communities to think that nothing can be done to confront substance abuse.'[53]

Pearson sees much 'progressive' thinking on Aboriginal issues as 'destructive'. The 'progressive' response to the appalling level of Aboriginal imprisonment has been to provide more legal aid, 'with no real belief that the outrageous statistics will ever be overcome', whereas 'the real need is for the restoration of social order and the enforcement of law. You ask the grandmothers and the wives . . . The only thing that

happens when crimes are committed is that the offenders are defended as victims [of
dispossession].' Further, the 'poison' of passive welfare dependency needs replacing
with integration into the real economy.[54]

> We have to be as forthright and unequivocal about our responsibilities as we are about our
> rights—otherwise our society will fall apart while we are still fighting for our rights . . . We
> have to struggle to restore our traditional values of responsibility. Our traditional economy
> was real and demanded responsibility (you don't work, you starve), the white fella market
> economy is real (you don't work, you don't get paid)—but there is no responsibility and
> reciprocity built into welfare (something for nothing). This something for nothing economy
> goes against our traditional principles of reciprocity and undermines these principles.[55]

In 2004, Pearson proposed a positive political program with five measures:

1. Replacement of the service-delivery perspective on Aboriginal affairs with social
    enterprise. Install real economic activity in Aboriginal communities, with welfare
    payments made to communities rather than individuals. The aim is for 'indigenous
    people to become self-sufficient and take control of their own destiny'. In 2000
    Pearson, with the backing of the Queensland Government, set up the Cape York
    Partnership Plan (CYPP), which has now established productive partnerships with
    big business and non-government organisations. CYPP is developing an indigenous
    business training institute and enterprises in ecotourism, fishing, horticulture, arts
    and crafts, and consultancy work.
2. Aborigines need to form a strong movement for the restoration of social and cul-
    tural order. 'Dysfunction, violence and substance abuse can be defeated only by
    conscious promotion of personal and collective responsibility.'
3. 'We must create a demand for the best available primary education for our children
    . . . Educational improvement . . . is driven by parental and community demand.'
4. 'We need to encourage geographic mobility among people in remote and regional
    areas, leading to secondary and tertiary education, other training and working careers
    in urban areas. Aboriginal social and economic integration is necessary, but the best
    way to achieve this is to give young people the security of socially functional home-
    lands to which they can return for longer or shorter periods and make a contribution.
    This is not an assimilationist program. Complete command of English and knowl-
    edge of European culture can be combined with an Aboriginal cultural identity.'[56]
5. Sending indigenous high school students out of their communities to attend board-
    ing schools in the cities in order to train local leaders and prevent another generation
    being trapped in the poverty that follows an absence of education.[57] This is similar to
    non-Aboriginal children who go away from farms and remote settlements to board-
    ing school and go home for the holidays.

This blueprint for social rescue by excising the poison of welfare dependency has been widely accepted. While still supporting symbolic reconciliation and recognition of indigenous rights, Pearson emphasises that 'Australians do not have an inalienable right to dependency; they have an inalienable right to a fair place in the real economy.'[58] As Fred Chaney, co-chairperson of Reconciliation Australia, puts it: 'The maintenance of cultural identity, which is so important to Aboriginal people's sense of self-worth, has to be accompanied by the skills and capacity to experience that same self-worth when they are operating in the mainstream culture.'[59]

How can these goals be achieved? A wealth of additional measures beckons. Greater use of the army to improve outback infrastructure; better training, pay and conditions for teachers and health professionals on long-term contracts in indigenous communities; a volunteer civic corps of reconciliation supporters; 'twinning' of indigenous with non-indigenous settlements; and treating depressed Aboriginal communities along the lines of AusAID development projects (as suggested by Wesley Aird, the first indigenous graduate from the Royal Military College, Duntroon). Another suggestion is integration, and thousands of Aboriginal people have already voted with their feet, heading for the cities and marrying out.

Above all, as a top priority, alcoholism, petrol-sniffing and drug addiction must be removed from the indigenous world at any cost. Tools to tackle these afflictions are law enforcement, zero tolerance, rehabilitation and education of both young and old. The Queensland Government is already tackling the problem of indigenous alcoholism and in South Australia a 'pro-consul' is addressing the petrol-sniffing epidemic. A breakthrough here has been development of Opal petrol.

The government could also assist by raising the tax and decreasing alcohol content in cheap cask wine, which only costs about the same per litre as lemonade, despite its role in the worst alcohol abuse in the nation. (Regions with high consumption of cask wine and regular-strength beer suffer the most alcohol-related violence and illness.) During the four years when cask wine was taxed in the Northern Territory before the High Court declared the tax illegal in 1997, road fatalities dropped 35 per cent, alcohol-related deaths fell by 20 per cent and hospital admissions for alcohol-related illness were down by 23 per cent. The amount of cheap wine sold in Alice Springs almost doubled by 7000 5-litre casks a week after the High Court decision. Cheap alcohol is clearly linked to higher levels of violence, illness and injury, but although the federal government could act, pleas from Aboriginal women, church groups and health groups, including the Aboriginal-run National Indigenous Substance Misuse Council, have so far fallen on deaf ears.[60]

As Robertson has written:[61]

We must commit ourselves to ongoing collaboration with non-indigenous people to achieve the true principles of self-determination, reconciliation and reciprocity . . . We must no longer allow ourselves to be portrayed as victims, but as proud and strong people. In our unique ability to endure all odds, we have stood tall and we have survived. Through our collective efforts, we can break the cycle of violence and we can work toward a future that allows our children to be proud of their cultural identity and to live a life free of fear . . . These are the goals to which we must all aspire.

» A new consensus

A breakthrough came on 26–27 November 2004 at a meeting of a dozen Aboriginal leaders held in northern Queensland. What emerged was the non-partisan Port Douglas Accord, with the Dodson brothers, Noel Pearson, Marcia Langton and others agreeing to move beyond the past and fuse the rights and responsibilities agendas in order to tackle Aboriginal disadvantage head-on through a dialogue with government on reform and mutual obligation or shared responsibility. Patrick Dodson pointed out that 'the mutual obligation stuff has a lot of resonance within Aboriginal culture and within Aboriginal notions of kinship. This concept has a grounding within our culture and society.' Mutual obligation programs should not be trivialised, but may be simple yet effective incentives to school attendance, such as 'no school, no swimming pool'.[62]

Similarly, Pearson said, 'There is no argument with the principle of mutual obligation if we are going to get things fixed. The mistake we made in the past was to think indigenous salvation came from legal and political acts. This is part of it, but we must assume responsibility and recognise these things are achieved through social and economic progress. You don't need to tell a parent who works that they need to wash their kid's face or feed their stomach.'

'The romantic savage myth that white intellectuals have imposed on the Aboriginal story—they lived in a paradise until cruel capitalism came along and destroyed it—is false and damaging,' Pearson says. 'Aborigines want the same things we all want—a job, a decent house and a good education for our kids.'

Meanwhile, Aboriginal Australian football legend Michael Long commenced a 'Long Walk' from Melbourne to Canberra to try to achieve a 'laying down of spears and guns'. As a result, Prime Minister John Howard met with three of his fiercest critics—Michael Long, Patrick and Mick Dodson—on 3 December 2004. The meeting ended with an agreement to tackle indigenous social and economic problems together. As Long said, 'the state of Aboriginal Australia was everyone's problem, everyone's disaster'.

Five days later, the new National Indigenous Council met for the first time. Its fourteen indigenous members include lawyers, business managers, a football star, a carpenter and a designer. Five members are women—a nurse, a school principal, a university professor and two lawyers. Its inspiring chairperson, magistrate Sue Gordon, was one of the 'stolen generation'—she was taken away from her mother as a four year old and told her mother was dead. Thirty years later, her mother found her again when Gordon was forging an impressive career. At eighteen, Gordon joined the army, then completed a law degree, became head of a Western Australia government department and in 1988 became Western Australia's first Aboriginal magistrate. In 2000 she headed an inquiry into indigenous domestic violence following the suicide of an abused teenage girl at the Swan Valley community in Perth (mentioned earlier in this chapter). She says the council's focus will be on stamping out 'monstrous' violence in Aboriginal families and reducing welfare dependency. Gordon believes the council's priorities should be on practical solutions to well-known problems. 'I have ongoing concerns about child abuse and family violence and see them as national issues of grave concern.' She sees a formal apology to the 'stolen generations' as a much lower priority: 'I personally don't want an apology. My mother was the one who should've got the apology. It's symbolic, whereas child abuse is happening every single day. That needs to be resolved.'

The council is not representative, but can operate without fear or favour. Most wish it well but even with all the goodwill and help in the world, it may take a generation to achieve practical results.

All agree that indigenous and non-indigenous must now 'walk the talk' and work together to make a real difference. What is needed is not more bureaucracy but empowerment of communities so that the necessary programs—zero tolerance of violence, substance abuse and truancy, plentiful scholarships and business partnerships with private enterprise—can be realised. 'There has got to be one goal,' Gordon says, 'and that is to make life better for Aboriginal people right across Australia.'[63]

» Resilience

Some Western Desert communities have managed to keep their customary way of life and culture intact on their own land while adopting the comforts of modern materialism and benefits of Western technology. The Spinifex people, as archaeologist Scott Cane calls them in his recent book, have changed only when change serves to enhance operation of their existing traditions. Communities such as the 130 people at Tjuntjuntjara, Western Australia, now use electricity, water-bores, modern medicine, four-wheel-drive vehicles and satellite communications. Babies are born in distant Kalgoorlie hospital, children attend Tjuntjuntjara bilingual school and adults live on payments from work with government and mining companies, the Community Development Employment Program (CDEP) federal work-for-the-dole scheme, pensions and family allowances. Western-style houses are provided, but 'a three-bedroom house with running water, satellite TV and a fence does not, to the distress of many people in government agencies, turn the Spinifex recipient into a happy, hygienic Western nuclear family'. The house will be used like a traditional wiltja (windbreak): 'People will camp outside, no lawn will be planted . . . cooking will be done on an open

« SCHOOLING »

Education is generally thought to be the key to a better future and quality of life. Strelley, Australia's first Aboriginal-controlled school, opened in 1976 in the Kimberley. Nowadays the 'Strelley Mob' own several cattle stations. Their schools are government-funded but teach children traditional culture in the Nyangumarta language, using textbooks prepared by elders assisted by non-Aboriginal teachers. Adults are taught to read before their children, thus avoiding erosion of their authority. Parents are committed to children 'growing up Aboriginal'. They believe that survival depends on isolation, both physical and philosophical, from dominant white society. Children are taught in Nyangumarta about their own history, spiritual beliefs, sacredness of the land, customary law and kinship, together with the value of Western-style work and English language, literacy and mathematics. The School Board's charter to non-Aboriginal teachers is 'Teach good Nyangumarta and good English'. Neither Christianity nor social studies is taught but children are encouraged to avoid alcohol and crime.

Stephen Harris and other educationalists hold Strelley up as an inspirational example of bi-cultural or 'two-way' schooling, enabling learning of a second culture without destroying or demeaning the first. The technique used is 'cultural domain separation'—a culturally compartmentalised 'two-way' school in which pupils learn 'to adopt appropriate roles in each cultural context, while maintaining personal and primary identity in the home culture'.

Nonetheless, Strelley has had its problems; some teenagers, as young as thirteen, have rejected their parents' conservative utopia in favour of the bright lights, alcohol and entertainment of Port Hedland. The Strelley Mob have reacted pragmatically by doubling the distance between their headquarters and town, but isolation is ever harder to maintain, given easier travel and the encroachment of electronic media and the internet.[a]

Strelley continues, but successful two-way schooling is now extremely rare. Until the 1970s, missionaries dedicated their lives to learning the local language to teach Aborigines to live in two cultures. Then outside pressures towards land rights and self-determination closed the missions, even though elders said they were not yet ready to go it alone. Richard Trudgen vividly portrays the catastrophic descent into illiteracy, unemployment, ill-health, substance-abuse and crime of the Yolngu of Arnhem Land in the three decades since the closure of the missions.[b] Teachers no longer learn local languages, and on average stay less than two years. Overall, Northern Territory school attendance has declined; employer bodies advise that 'more than ever before, they are unable to find

[Aboriginal] people who meet basic literacy and numeracy entry criteria for employment and training'; Aboriginal elders repeatedly state that 'their children and grandchildren have lesser literacy skills than they do'.[c]

Aboriginal Australia has suffered a general decline in educational standards, participation and retention rates since the 1970s, due to loss of mission schools, growing substance-abuse and mayhem in communities leading to epidemic truancy. Nationwide, less than half as many indigenous pupils stay at school to the end of year 12 as non-indigenous (32 per cent/73 per cent). Less than 20 per cent of indigenous pupils meet year 3 reading standards against 70 per cent of non-indigenous. Only 14 per cent of indigenous people have post-school qualifications against 34 per cent of non-indigenous. Only 2 per cent of indigenous people have university degrees against 11 per cent of non-indigenous.[d] Even in New South Wales, where Aboriginal languages are very rarely spoken, only half as many Aboriginal pupils finish year 12 as non-Aboriginal, including many Asian migrants whose mother tongue is not English.[e] The main problem is truancy. Why? Many Aboriginal youngsters find school an alien place, parental discipline is often weak and police cannot or do not enforce attendance of Aboriginal children as they do all others, for fear of the 'racist' label. The Yolngu have all the same problems as New South Wales Aborigines, although they have never lost their land, language or culture.

Provision of bilingual, two-way schooling is often impossible because of too few staff and the presence of different languages in the same community, for example, the school in Katherine has Aboriginal pupils from twelve different language groups. In such situations, children speak Creole and Aboriginal languages die out. The Yolngu and the Strelley Mob are among only 13 per cent of indigenous Australians who speak their own language at home. Today only 20 Aboriginal languages are spoken fluently by children and half these surviving languages have fewer than a hundred fluent speakers.[f]

Happily, the last few years have seen a turnaround in indigenous schooling, as Aboriginal leaders and parents have come to see that education is the all-important means for their children to overcome the problems of chronic poverty and unemployment. For example, after Aboriginal Chris Sarra became principal of Cherbourg State School in rural Queensland in 1998, the level of regular attendance rose from 50 to 95 per cent, literacy was boosted by 63 per cent, the progression of students from year 1 to 7 increased from 52 to 75 per cent and school morale soared. Chris said the secret of his success, as with all good educators, was simply believing in his students. 'I put in place a new team, who actually believed they could make the children in our school stronger and smarter. We also convinced the children that they could be stronger and smarter by making them feel great about being Aboriginal. Importantly, we got them to understand that they can be successful and they can still be Aboriginal.'[g]

The Strong and Smart program has now spread nationwide and Cherbourg School continues on its journey towards more positive approaches to learning. Chris Sarra has moved on to become director of the Indigenous Education Leadership Institute but his legacy endures. As the new principal, Jo Ross, explains on their website:

> For us when we say 'Strong' we mean being proud to be Aboriginal. When we say 'Smart' we mean working hard enough so we can 'mix it' with any other student from any other school.
>
> We are an almost completely Aboriginal school and so we embrace Aboriginality every day in a true and positive sense. We are extremely proud to know that Aboriginal people are connected to the very first Australians. As we warmly embrace Aboriginality, we make sure that we do not reject other people's whiteness.
>
> The key to our success in the past few years is having teachers, Indigenous and non-Indigenous, who believe that our children can learn, and are prepared to get on with the job of effective learning and teaching. This is greatly enhanced by the presence of Aboriginal teacher aides from the local community who are valued and respected for the knowledge they bring to the school.[h]

» Pupils at Cherbourg School, Queensland, putting into action the Strong and Smart program initiated by former principal Chris Sarra.

« »

fire, hardware will be damaged and left unrepaired.'[64] Yet Tjuntjuntjara 'conveys a sense of peace and companionship', of a happy community that has successfully adapted the dominant culture of non-Aboriginal Australia to their unchanging primary traditions.

Remoteness has helped. Tjuntjuntjara is a 'dry' (alcohol-free) settlement with little violence or crime. Communities are sufficiently small, closely knit and egalitarian for anti-social behaviour, violence and crime to be rare, the sanctions being shaming, reproach, ostracism, revenge, ritual spearing and fear of sorcery.

« »

For most indigenous people, leading a traditional life is no longer feasible, but many living in less remote regions have accomplished the difficult transition into the modern world equally successfully. Integration involves choice of lifestyle and of pace of change. Its aim is to attain equality of living standards and opportunity while retaining cultural identity. Many problems remain and much more government assistance is needed, but there are numerous outstanding cultural and economic ventures and indigenous people have distinguished themselves in every walk of life. High-achievers have become role models and are inspiring youngsters to be 'strong and smart' in all walks of life.

A great cultural renaissance has taken place in Australia over the last four decades and now Aboriginal people are proudly introducing others to their land, way of life and arts. When the world came to Sydney in 2000, the moment when leading Aboriginal athlete Cathy Freeman lit the Olympic flame symbolised this renaissance and, at the least, the beginnings of reconciliation. Cathy sees herself as a 'proud Aboriginal Australian' and runs her victory laps draped in both the Aboriginal and Australian flags.

It has been a long journey from that first footprint on an Australian beach more than 50 000 years ago to the present day, but the Original Australians have shown outstanding courage and resilience throughout. Thankfully, the world's oldest living culture has survived the disruption of colonisation and lives proudly on.

ABBREVIATIONS
TO THE NOTES

AA	*Australian Archaeology*
AAH	Australian Academy of the Humanities, Canberra
AAS	*Australian Aboriginal Studies*
ABS	Australian Bureau of Statistics, Canberra
AGPS	Australian Government Publishing Service, Canberra
AH	*Aboriginal History*
AHC	Australian Heritage Commission, Canberra
AIAS	Australian Institute of Aboriginal Studies, Canberra
AIATSIS	Australian Institute of Aboriginal & Torres Strait Islander Studies, Canberra
ANCA	Australian Nature Conservation Agency
ANH	Archaeology & Natural History publications, Canberra
ANU	Australian National University, Canberra
AO	*Archaeology in Oceania*
APAO	*Archaeology & Physical Anthropology in Oceania*
A&R	Angus & Robertson, Sydney
ASP	Aboriginal Studies Press, AIATSIS, Canberra
ATSIC	Aboriginal & Torres Strait Islander Commission, Canberra
A&U	Allen & Unwin, Sydney
BAR	*British Archaeological Reports*
CAJ	*Cambridge Archaeological Journal*
C. of A.	Commonwealth of Australia
CUP	Cambridge University Press, Cambridge
DAA	Department of Aboriginal Affairs
HRA	*Historical Records of Australia*
HREOC	Human Rights & Equal Opportunity Commission
HRNSW	*Historical Records of New South Wales*
HUP	Harvard University Press, Cambridge, MA
JAS	*Journal of Australian Studies*
JCU	James Cook University, Townsville
JHE	*Journal of Human Evolution*
ML	Mitchell Library, State Library of New South Wales, Sydney
MUP	Melbourne University Press, Melbourne
NARU	North Australia Research Unit, ANU, Darwin

NLA	National Library of Australia, Canberra
NMA	National Museum of Australia, Canberra
NPWS	National Parks & Wildlife Service
OUP	Oxford University Press, Oxford
Sci. Am.	*Scientific American*
SMH	*Sydney Morning Herald*
SUP	Sydney University Press, Sydney
Trans. and Proc. Roy. Soc. SA	*Transcripts and Proceedings of the Royal Society of South Australia*
UCP	University of California Press, Berkeley
UNE	University of New England, Armidale
UNSW	University of New South Wales, Sydney
UOS	University of Sydney
UQP	University of Queensland Press, St Lucia, Brisbane
UWA	University of Western Australia, Perth
WHO	World Health Organisation

NOTES

Footnotes to the boxed text can be found at the end
of the chapter in which they appear.

PREFACE

1   Blainey, G., 'Drawing up the balance sheet of our history', *Quadrant*, 1993, 37(7–8): 11, 15.

CHAPTER 1—EXPLORATION

1   It has been suggested that the Chinese were the first non-Aboriginal people to reach Australia, but there is no firm evidence for the claims made by Gavin Menzies in his book, *1421: The Year China Discovered the World*, Bantam Press, London, 2002.

2   Sharp, A., *The Discovery of Australia*, Clarendon, Oxford, 1963; Kenny, J., *Before the First Fleet: Europeans in Australia 1606–1777*, Kangaroo Press, Sydney, 1995; Ward, R., *Australia Since the Coming of Man*, Macmillan, Melbourne, 1987, pp. 22–5; Williams, G. and Frost, A. (eds), *Terra Australis to Australia*, OUP, 1988, pp. 1–38, re. Portuguese pp. 39–82; Smith, B., *European Vision and the South Pacific 1768–1850: A study in the history of arts and ideas*, OUP, 1960.

3   Kenneth McIntyre put forward the case for Portuguese 'discovery' of Australia in 1977 in *The Secret Discovery of Australia: Portuguese ventures 200 years before Captain Cook*, Souvenir Press, Adelaide and Pan Books, Sydney, 1982, but W.A.R. (Bill) Richardson has strongly disputed these claims in *The Portuguese Discovery of Australia: Fact or fiction?* NLA, 1989.

4   Hardy, J. and Frost, A. (eds), *European Voyaging Towards Australia*, AAH, 1990, p. 128; Heeres, J.E., *The Part Borne by the Dutch in the Discovery of Australia 1606–1765*, Leiden, London, 1899, pp. 18–44; Schilder, G., 'New Holland: The Dutch discoveries', in Williams and Frost, *Terra Australis*, pp. 83–116. 'New Guinea' is used to indicate the whole island—now divided into Irian Jaya in the west and Papua New Guinea in the east. The Spice Islands are the Maluku Islands, previously called the Moluccas, and the Banda Islands: Milton, G., *Nathaniel's Nutmeg: How one man's courage changed the course of history*, Hodder and Stoughton, London, 1999.

5   Hercus, L. and Sutton, P. (eds), *This Is What Happened: Historical narratives by Aborigines*, AIAS, 1986, p. 89; Heeres, *The Part Borne By the Dutch*, p. 37.

6   Carstenz [1623] quoted in T. Flannery (ed.), *The Explorers*, Text, Melbourne, 1998, pp. 19–20.

7   Sharp, A., *The Voyages of Abel Janszoon Tasman*, Clarendon, Oxford, 1968, p. 110; Tasman, A., *Journal of a Voyage to the Unknown Southland in the Year 1642*, presented in translated extracts in E. Duyker, *The Discovery of Tasmania*, St David's Park Publishing, Hobart, 1992, p. 15; Mulvaney, D.J., *Encounters in Place: Outsiders and Aboriginal Australians 1606–1985*, UQP, 1989, pp. 29–37; Major, R.H. (ed.), *Early Voyages to Terra Australis, Now Called Australia . . .* Hakluyt Society, London, 1859; re. smoke see Flinders, M., *A Voyage to Terra Australis*, London, 1814, vol. I, p. v.

8   Dampier, W. [1697] (ed. A.E.M. Bayliss), *Dampier's Voyages*, Sydney, 1945, quoted in Flannery, *The Explorers*, p. 27; Mulvaney, *Encounters in Place*, pp. 18–21; Dampier, W. [1697] (ed. M. Beken), *A New Voyage Round the World: The journal of an English buccaneer*, Hummingbird Press, London, 1998, pp. 220, 218–19, 222; Dampier, W. [1703], *A Voyage to New Holland in the Year 1699*.

9   Dampier (ed. Beken), p. 219; Dampier (ed. Bayliss), pp. 143–4; Mulvaney, *Encounters in Place*, pp. 18–21.

10 Dampier (ed. Beken), pp. 220–1.

11 Van Delft [1705] quoted in Kenny, *Before the First Fleet*; Schilder, G., 'New Holland: The Dutch discoveries', in Williams and Frost, *Terra Australis*, pp. 83–115.

12 Gonzal, J.E., report, quoted in Kenny, *Before the First Fleet*, pp. 112–13.

13 Macknight, C.C., *The Voyage to Marege: Macassan trepangers in northern Australia*, MUP, 1976; Macknight, C.C., *The Farthest Coast: A selection of writings relating to the history of the northern coast of Australia*, MUP, 1969; Macknight, C.C., 'Macassans and Aborigines', *Oceania*, 1972, 42: 283–321; Macknight, C.C., 'Macassans and the Aboriginal past', *AO*, 1986, 21(1): 69–75; Macknight, C.C., personal communication,

2005; Mulvaney, *Encounters in Place*, pp. 22–8; Macknight, C.C., 'Pre-1770 external contact', in S. Bambrick (ed.), *The Cambridge Encyclopedia of Australia*, CUP, 1994, pp. 82–6.

14　The town is Makassar but the name of the people and language is Makasar. Australian historian Campbell Macknight has made an exhaustive study of the Macassans' contracts and sailing passes, and my account is based on his work.

15　Flinders, *A Voyage to Terra Australis*, vol. II, pp. 228–33; Flannery, T. (ed.), *Terra Australis: Matthew Flinders' great adventures in the circumnavigation of Australia*, Text, Melbourne, 2000, pp. 203–7; Fox, J.J., 'Maritime communities in the Timor and Arafura region', in S. O'Connor and P. Veth (eds), *East of Wallace's Line: Studies of past and present maritime cultures of the Indo-Pacific region*, Balkema, Rotterdam, Brookfield, USA, 2000, pp. 344–54, esp. pp. 348–9.

16　Wallace, A.R. [1872], *The Malay Archipelago*, 4th edn, London, reprinted Gloucester, MA, 1962, p. 431.

17　Keen, I., *Aboriginal Economy and Society: Australia at the threshold of colonisation*, OUP, 2004, p. 167.

18　The inhabitants of Tahiti and New Zealand were separated by over 2500 kilometres (1550 miles) of ocean but spoke dialects of the same Polynesian language. Archaeological evidence and Maori oral traditions show that 800 years ago New Zealand was settled by Polynesians in a series of remarkable voyages from Ra'iatea in the Society Islands 200 kilometres (125 miles) west of Tahiti: Pritchett, N., *Maori Origins: From Asia to Aotearoa*, Auckland Museum, 2001; Evans, J., *The Discovery of Aotearoa*, Reed, Auckland, 1998, pp. 21–3; Irwin, G., *The Prehistoric Exploration and Colonisation of the Pacific*, CUP, 1992.

19　Cook, J. [1768–1779] (ed. J.C. Beaglehole), *The Journals of Captain James Cook on His Voyages of Discovery*, Hakluyt Society, Cambridge, 1955–67, vol. 1, p. 273; Cook, J. (ed. P. Edwards), *The Journals of Captain Cook*, Penguin, London, 1999, p. 117. At this time it was still unclear if the land Vanuatu (New Hebrides) that Spaniard Pedro de Quiros discovered in 1606 and named *Australia del Espiritu Santo* was the northern tip of *Terra Australis*, a separate island group or part of New Holland's eastern coast.

20　A modern myth is that the fires Cook saw were signals warning of his arrival. Aboriginal Australians did use smoke signals to communicate but not to the same degree as Indigenous North Americans. Smoke was used to signify the presence of water, game or a kill, to warn of intruders or to announce one's own imminent arrival at a camp or ceremony. By using dry or green fuel, pale or dark smoke was produced and thin or thick smoke columns created by varying the amount of fuel, spirals by whirling a burning branch around and puffs by passing a bark-sheet across the fire: Magarey, A.T., 'Smoke signals of Australian Aborigines', *Reports of Australasian Association for Advancement of Science*, 1893, vol. 5, pp. 498–513.

21　Cook (ed. Beaglehole), vol. I, p. 305; Cook (ed. Edwards), pp. 123–30.

22　Re. poison see McCarthy, F.D., *Australia's Aborigines: Their life and culture*, Colorgravure Publications, Melbourne, 1957, p. 87, and Howitt, A.W. [1904], *The Native Tribes of South-East Australia*, ASP, 1996, pp. 362–3; Banks, J. [1771] (ed. J.C. Beaglehole), *The Endeavour Journals of Joseph Banks, 1768–1771*, A&R, 1972, vol. II, pp. 122–37, quoted in Kenny, *Before the First Fleet*, pp. 127–32; re. spears see Cundy, B.J., *Formal Variation in Australian Spear and Spear-thrower Technology*, S546, British Archaeological Reports, Oxford, 1989.

23　Cook (ed. Beaglehole), vol. I, p. 312.

24　Banks, vol. II, pp. 91–137; Cook (ed. Beaglehole), vol. I, pp. 357–63, 395–9.

25　Parkinson, S., *A Journal of a Voyage to the South Seas*, London, 1773, p. 144.

26　Dixon, R.M.W., *The Languages of Australia*, CUP, 1980, pp. 8–9; Cook (ed. Beaglehole), vol. I, pp. 398, 411; Banks, vol. II, p. 137.

27　Banks, vol. II, p. 130; Cook (ed. Beaglehole), vol. I, pp. 399, 509; Smith, *European Vision*, pp. 6–7, 25, 72, 251.

28　Cook, J. [1768–71] (ed. W.J.L. Wharton), *Captain Cook's Journal During his First Voyage Round the World: Made in H.M.S. Endeavour 1768–71*, Elliot Stock, London, 1893, p. 38; Cook (ed. Edwards), pp. 403–4 (25 and 26 December 1774); Darwin, C., *Journal of Researches into the Natural History and Geology of the Countries Visited During the Voyage of H.M.S. Beagle Round the World*, T Nelson & Sons, London, 1890, pp. 259, 260, 264, 280; Jones, P., 'Ideas linking Aborigines and Fuegians: From Cook to the Kulturkreis school', *AAS*, 1989 (2): 2–13. Fuegians are now known as Yahgan.

29　Cook (ed. Beaglehole), vol. I, p. 387; Reynolds, H. [1987], *The Law of the Land*, Penguin, Melbourne, 1992, pp. 7–54.

30　*HRA*, series I, vol. I, pp. 13–14.

31　Pritchett, *Maori Origins*; Cook (ed. Beaglehole), vol. I, p. 305.

32　Banks, vol. II, p. 122.

33　*Ibid.*, p. 128.

34　*Ibid.*, pp. 122–3.

35　Service, E., *Primitive Social Organization*, Random House, New York, 1962; Service, E., *Origins of the State and Civilization*, Norton, New York, 1975; Diamond, J., *Guns, Germs and Steel: A short history of everybody for the last 13 000 years*, Chatto & Windus, London, 1997, pp. 265–70; Rowley, C.D., *The Destruction of Aboriginal Society*, Penguin, Melbourne, 1970, pp. 14–15.

36　Keen, *Aboriginal Economy*, pp. 106, 307–8, 427.

37 *Ibid.*, pp. 276–7, 421, 425–6. Most clans were 'patrifilial' (members gaining their identity from their father or father's father), but matrifilial clans existed in southeastern Australia.

38 Peterson, N. and Long, J., *Australian Territorial Organization: A Band Perspective*, Oceania Monograph 30, UOS, 1986; Peterson, N., 'Introduction: Australia', in R.B. Lee and R. Daly (eds), *The Cambridge Encyclopedia of Hunters and Gatherers*, CUP, 1999, pp. 317–23; Tindale, N.B., *Aboriginal Tribes of Australia*, UCP, 1974, pp. 4, 11, 30–3; Rumsey, A., 'Language and territoriality in Aboriginal Australia', in M. Walsh and C. Yallop (eds), *Language and Culture in Aboriginal Australia*, ASP, 1993, pp. 191–206, esp. pp. 199–204.

39 Under the Waitangi treaty's terms Maori people ceded their governorship and the sole right of purchasing their land to the British monarch in return for numerous 'presents', the full rights and privileges of British subjects and guaranteed possession of their lands, forests and fisheries. The treaty document in English and Maori was signed by 46 chiefs on 6 February 1840 at Waitangi in the Bay of Islands, and then carried around both islands so that over 500 Maori leaders could add their mark.

40 Locke, J. [1690] (ed. P. Laslett), *Two Treatises of Government*, New American Library, New York, 1965, pp. 327–41.

41 Vattel, E. de, *The Law of Nations or the Principles of Natural Law*, J. Newbury, London (trans. from the French), 1760, p. 91.

42 Re. *terra nullius*, see Reynolds, *The Law of the Land*, *passim* but Reynolds' work relies on his own definition of *terra nullius* that, without justification, adds a second meaning of 'a territory where nobody owns any land at all, where no tenure of any sort existed'. See Connor, M., 'Error nullius', *The Bulletin* (26 August 2003) and Dawson, J., 'The nullius ideal', *Quadrant*, 2004, XLVIII: 24–33; Connor, M., *The Invention of Terra Nullius: Historical and legal fiction on the foundation of Australia*, Macleay Press, Sydney, 2005; Connor, M. 'High Court challenged', *Weekend Australian*, 4–5 February 2006, pp. 17, 22.

43 Macknight, C.C., personal communication, 2005.

44 Butler, K., Cameron, K. and Percival, R., *The Myth of Terra Nullius: Invasion and resistance—the early years*, Aboriginal Curriculum Unit (Pt 4), Board of Studies NSW, Sydney, 1995; Frost, A., *Botany Bay Mirages: Illusions of Australia's convict beginnings*, MUP, 1994, p. 187.

45 Reynolds, *The Law of the Land*, p. 21.

46 Frost, *Botany Bay Mirages*, pp. 188–9.

47 Cook (ed. Beaglehole), vol. I, p. 397.

48 Plants domesticated in Southeast Asia and endemic in northern or central Australia include roots of taro (*Colocasia esculenta*) and Polynesian arrowroot (*Tacca leontopetaloides*), potato-like tubers of round and parsnip yams (*Dioscorea bulbifera rotunda* and *elongata*), seeds of wild rice (*Oryza rufipogon*) and native millet (*Panicum decompositum*), at least two fruit trees—Bloomfield cherry (*Antidesma bunius*) and *Manilkara kauki*—and three nut trees: country almonds (*Terminalia catappa*), candlenut trees (*Aleurites moluccana*) and macadamia (*Macadamia*).

49 Tindale, *Aboriginal Tribes*, p. 109.

50 Altman, J.C., 'Hunter-gatherer subsistence production in Arnhem Land: The original affluence hypothesis re-examined', *Mankind*, 1984, 14(3): 179–90; Meehan, B., *Shell Bed to Shell Midden*, AIAS, 1974.

51 Berndt, R.M. and C.H., *The World of the First Australians*, ASP, 1988, p. 108.

52 Mitchell, T.L., *Three Expeditions into the Interior of Eastern Australia*, Boone, London, 1839, vol. I, pp. 290–1.

53 Allen, H., 'The Bagundji of the Darling Basin: Cereal gatherers in an uncertain environment', *World Archaeology*, 1974, 5(3): 309–22, esp. p. 314.

54 See Flood, J. [1983], *Archaeology of the Dreamtime*, A&R, 2001, pp. 59–61.

55 Tindale, *Aboriginal Tribes*, pp. 96–7.

56 Globally, crop production arose in several different regions—wheat, barley, peas, lentils and melons in the fertile crescent of the Middle East; maize, beans and squashes in Mexico; potatoes, beans and squashes in South America; rice, millet and soybeans in China; sorghum, millet, groundnuts, yams and watermelon in equatorial Africa; taro and yams in New Guinea. Gradually animals, too, were domesticated. First was the dog (c. 10 000 BC in Southwest Asia, China and North America), then sheep and goats (c. 8000 BC in Southwest Asia), pigs (c. 8000 BC in Southwest Asia and China) and cows (c. 6000 BC in Southwest Asia and India); Diamond, *Guns, Germs and Steel*, pp. 125–8, 167; Cavalli Sforza, L.L. and F., *The Great Human Diasporas: The history of diversity and evolution*, Addison-Wesley, Reading, MA, 1995, pp. 140, 144.

57 *Macmillan Encyclopedia*, Macmillan, London, 1981.

58 Tindale, *Aboriginal Tribes*, pp. 110–11; Reynolds, H., *The Other Side of the Frontier*, JCU, 1981, pp. 98–9; Reynolds, H., *Frontier: Aborigines, settlers and land*, A&U, 1987, pp. 29–30, 53.

59 Butlin, N.G., *Our Original Aggression: Aboriginal populations of southeastern Australia 1788–1850*, A&U, 1983; White, J.P. and Mulvaney, D.J., 'How many people?' in D.J. Mulvaney and J.P. White (eds), *Australians: A Historical Library, Australians to 1788*, Fairfax, Syme & Weldon, Sydney, 1987, pp. 114–7; Mulvaney, D.J. and Kamminga, J., *Prehistory of Australia*, A&U, 1999, pp. 68–9; Kefous, K., 'Butlin's bootstraps: Aboriginal population in the pre-contact Murray-Darling region', in B. Meehan and R. Jones (eds), *Archaeology with Ethnography: An Australian perspective*, ANU, 1988, pp. 225–37.

60 Re. desert population, see Cane, S., 'Desert demography: A case study of pre-contact Aboriginal densities in the Western Desert of Australia', in B. Meehan and N. White (eds), *Hunter-Gatherer Demography*, Oceania Monograph no. 9, UOS, 1990, pp. 149–59; Diamond, *Guns, Germs and Steel*, p. 306.

Box—A lack of coconut trees (p. 25)

a   Foale, M., *The Coconut Odyssey: The bounteous possibilities of the tree of life*, Australian Centre for International Agricultural Research, ANU, 2003, pp. 23–32; Smith, J., *Australian Driftseeds*, UNE, 1999, p. 27; Hynes, R. and Chase, A., 'Plants, sites and domiculture', *AO*, 1982, 17: 38–50.

CHAPTER 2—COLONISATION

1   *HRA*, series I, vol. I, p. 1.
2   The name Eora (or Iyora) is the Sydney language term for 'person' and since c. 1950 has been used by linguists as a name for speakers of the Sydney language. Eora is used here for people of the Sydney coastal region. To their west Darug speakers occupied the forested Cumberland Plains and were known by the British as 'woods people': Troy, J., 'The Sydney Language', in *Macquarie Aboriginal Words* (eds N. Thieberger and W. McGregor), Macquarie Library, Sydney, 1994, pp. 61–78. Attenbrow, V., *Sydney's Aboriginal Past: Investigating the archaeological and historical records*, UNSW Press, 2002, pp. 30–6; Smith, K.V., *Bennelong*, Kangaroo Press, Sydney, 2001, pp. 74, 109–12.
3   Tench, W. (ed. T. Flannery), *1788 Watkin Tench: A narrative of the expedition to Botany Bay and a complete account of the settlement at Port Jackson*, Text, Melbourne, 1996, pp. 40–1; Egan, J., *Buried Alive: Sydney 1788–1792, Eyewitness Accounts of the Making of a Nation*, A&U, 1999; Flannery, T. (ed.), *The Birth of Sydney*, Text, Melbourne, 1999. The name Australia was not used until 1814, when navigator Matthew Flinders published a map of the continent entitled 'Terra Australis', or Australia.
4   Collins, D. [1798] (ed. B.H. Fletcher), *An Account of the English Colony in New South Wales*, Reed, Sydney, 1975, vol. I, p. 2.
5   Tench (ed. Flannery), pp. 42–3; White, J. [1790] (ed. A.R. Chisholm), *Journal of a Voyage to New South Wales by John White Esq.*, Royal Australian Historical Society, A&R, 1962, pp. 110–1, 152–4.
6   Tench, W. (ed. L.F. Fitzhardinge), *Sydney's First Four Years . . .*, Library of Australian History, Sydney, 1979, pp. 82–3.
7   King. P. [1790] (eds P.J. Fidlou and R.J. Ryan), *The Journal of Philip Gidley King, Lieutenant R.N. 1787–1790*, Australian Documents Library, Sydney, 1989.
8   *HRA*, series I, vol. I, p. 25.
9   Hunter, J. [1793], *An Historical Journal of Events at Sydney and at Sea, 1787–1792*, Bach, London, A&R, 1968, p. 77; Cobley, J., *Sydney Cove 1788*, Hodder & Stoughton, London, 1962.
10 Aboriginal views are from Mahroot, *NSW Legislative Council Votes and Proceedings*, in *Report from the Select Committee on the Condition of the Aborigines*, Sydney, 1845.
11 Eliade, M., *Australian Religions*, Ithaca, 1973, pp. 60–1.
12 Stockdale, J. (compiler) [1789], *The Voyage of Governor Phillip to Botany Bay, with an Account of the Establishment of the Colonies of Port Jackson and Norfolk Island . . .* (facsimile), Australiana Society, Adelaide, 1950.
13 Bradley, W. [1792], *A Voyage to New South Wales: The Journal of Lieutenant William Bradley RN of HMS Sirius 1786–1792* (facsimile), Ure Smith, Sydney, 1969.
14 Fowell, N. [1790], *The Sirius Letters 1786–90* (ed. N. Irvine), Fairfax Library, quoted in K. Butler *et al.*, *The Myth of Terra Nullius: Invasion and resistance—the early years*, Board of Studies NSW, Sydney, 1995, p. 52.
15 Collins, vol. I, pp. 13–14; Lapérouse's story is vividly told in Lapérouse Museum, Botany Bay.
16 Bradley [1788], quoted in Flannery, *Birth of Sydney*, pp. 53–8; Clendinnen, I., *Dancing with Strangers*, Text, Melbourne, 2003.
17 Bradley, *A Voyage*, pp. 84–5; *HRA*, series I, vol. I, p. 293; Connor, J., *The Australian Frontier Wars 1788–1838*, UNSW Press, 2002, p. 26.
18 Anon. [1790–1], 'Vocabulary of the language of New South Wales in the neighbourhood of Sydney', MS 41645, School of Oriental and African Studies, London.
19 Worgan, G. B. [1788], *Journal of a First Fleet Surgeon*, Library of Australian History, Sydney, 1978, pp. 28–9.
20 White, *Journal*, p. 118.
21 Collins, vol. I, p. 29.
22 Hilliard, W.M., *The People in Between: The Pitjantjatjara People of Ernabella*, Hodder & Stoughton, London, 1968.
23 Governor Phillip to Lord Sydney, 10 July 1788, *HRNSW* vol. 1(2), pp. 179–80.
24 Attenbrow, *Sydney's Aboriginal Past*, p. 17.
25 Tench (ed. Flannery), p. 242; Worgan, p. 22; Re. winter fish scarcity personal communication in 2005 from Robert Williams and Charles Gray of Cronulla Fisheries Centre, NSW Department of Primary Industries. Gray 'believes there is a movement to deeper water of estuarine fish in winter'. This is based on natural phenomena described by Williams as: '(1) Radiative transfer of heat out of the shallows during winter and hence what we assume to be a movement of fish into offshore and/or deeper and warmer water;

(2) Increase in water clarity during winter and hence a reduction in ambush efficiency by spearing or trapping.'

26   Collins, vol. I, p. 27; Poiner, G., 'The process of the year among Aborigines of the central and south coast of New South Wales', *APAO*, 1976, 9(3): 186–206; Attenbrow, *Sydney's Aboriginal Past*, pp. 63–6. The fern is from *Blechnum* spp.

27   Mahroot [1845].

28   Tench (ed. Flannery), p. 244.

29   Bradley, *A Voyage*, pp. 84–5; Stanner, W.E.H., *White Man Got No Dreaming: Essays 1938–1973*, ANU Press, 1979, p. 175; Convict's letter of 11 November 1791 published in *Ayre's Sunday London Gazette*, 15 July 1792, ms F980/A, ML.

30   Collins, vol. I, pp. 35–6.

31   *Ibid.*, p. 53.

32   Campbell, J., *Invisible Invaders: Smallpox and other diseases in Aboriginal Australia, 1780–1880*, MUP, 2002; re. Boorong see Smith, *Bennelong*, pp. 60–2, 65–8; information on the number of victims of smallpox is from Bennelong, quoted in Governor Phillip to Lord Sydney, 13 February 1790, *HRNSW*, vol. 1(2), pp. 304–10; Collins, vol. I, pp. 496–7; Hunter, p. 134.

33   Hopkins, D.R., *Princes and Peasants: Smallpox in history*, University of Chicago Press, 1983, pp. 3–13, 47–50, 58–61, 74–81; Collins, vol. I, p. 54.

34   Variolation gave inoculees a mild case of smallpox (*Variola major*). Some died, but the death rate in England of 1 in 48 to 60 cases of inoculated smallpox compared very favourably with that of 1 in 6 cases of natural smallpox, and all survivors acquired long-term protection. Variolation was introduced into England in 1721 and became accepted medical practice; in 1746 the London Small-Pox and Inoculation Hospital was established and, with the Foundling Hospital, offered free variolation. It was ten years *after* the first settlers arrived in Australia that Edward Jenner introduced in England much safer, simpler, cheaper, life-long protection against smallpox by vaccination with cowpox (*Vaccinia*), a relatively mild disease of cattle. *Vaccinia* virus proved much more stable and heat-resistant than that derived from *Variola* cases, and was successfully transported to NSW in 1804 where children were immediately vaccinated: Goldsmid, J., *The Deadly Legacy: Australian history and transmissible disease*, UNSW Press, 1988; Stearn, E.W. and Stearn, A.E., *The Effect of Smallpox on the Destiny of the Amerindian*, Bruce Humphries, Boston, 1945, p. 53; Fenner, F. *et al.*, *Smallpox and its Eradication*, WHO, Geneva, 1988, pp. 115–16, 255, 209–44, 253–62.

35   Tench (ed. Flannery), pp. 125–6.

36   *Ibid.*, pp. 134–9.

37   Collins, vol. I, pp. 110–11; Smith, *Bennelong*, pp. 53–9; Clendinnen, *Dancing with Strangers*, pp. 110–32.

38   Collins, vol. I, pp. 249, 263, re. Norfolk Island p. 317, re. language p. 506; Macarthur, E., letter of 7 March 1791 to Miss Kingston, quoted in F. Crowley, *A Documentary History of Australia: Volume 1, Colonial Australia 1788–1840*, Thomas Nelson, Melbourne, 1980, pp. 39–40.

39   Collins, vol. I, p. 495; Tench (ed. Flannery), p. 102.

40   'Pe-mall' or 'bamal' means earth or clay: Troy, in *Macquarie Aboriginal Words*, p. 68; Smith, *Bennelong*, p. 84.

41   Collins, vol. I, pp. 117–19; Phillip, *Voyage*, 13 December 1790.

42   Tench (ed. Flannery), pp. 164–9; Collins, vol. I, p. 118; Reece, R.H.W., *Aborigines and Colonists: Aborigines and colonial society in New South Wales in the 1830s and 1840s*, SUP, 1974, p. 8.

43   Hunter, February 1791; Collins, vol. I, p. 461.

44   Collins, vol. I, pp. 121–2.

45   Tench (ed. Flannery), pp. 184, 264.

46   *Ibid.*, p. 118; Macarthur, letter quoted in Crowley, *A Documentary History*, vol. 1, p. 40.

47   Collins, vol. I, pp. 485, 488–9, vol. II, p. 9.

48   Arago, Jacques, *Souvenirs d'un aveugle: Voyage autour du monde*, Paris, 1839, tome 4, pp. 51, 87, 93.

49   Collins, vol. I, pp. 466, 463–4, 485–6.

50   *Ibid.*, vol. II, p. 25.

51   Collins, vol. II, pp. 90, 25, vol. I, 498–9; Tench (ed. Flannery), pp. 264–5; Stanner [1963], 'The history of indifference thus begins', in Stanner, *White Man*, p. 189.

52   Collins, vol. I, pp. 466–86.

53   *Ibid.*, vol. I, pp. 499–504; Smith, *Bennelong*, pp. 123–6.

54   King to Banks (25 October 1791), Letter Books 1788–96, 1797–1806, and papers, Mss. A1687, C187, ML; Tench (ed. Flannery), p. 271.

55   Hunter, July 1789, pp. 150, 153. 'Yam' was a generic name used by Hunter and others for all tubers, but the walnut-sized tubers seen by Hunter were daisy 'yams' (*Microseris lanceolata*, previously *scapigera*), a staple food in Southeast Australia: Gott, B., '*Microseris scapigera*: A study of a staple food of Victorian Aborigines', *AAS*, 1983, 2: 2–18. Only one true yam (*Dioscorea transversa*) occurred in the Sydney region and this has small, carrot-shaped tubers and grows on vines in woodland: Attenbrow, *Sydney's Aboriginal Past*, pp. 41, 76–8, plate 4. The fern root chewed by Sydney Aborigines was native bracken, bungwall (*Blechnum indicum*) or gristle fern (*Blechnum cartilagineum*).

56   Collins, vol. I, pp. 348–9; Connor, *The Australian Frontier Wars*, pp. 35–82.

57   Atkins, R. (May 1795), quoted in Connor, *The Australian Frontier Wars*, pp. 36, 134 note 4.

58   Kohen, J., *The Darug and their Neighbours*, Blacktown and District Hist. Soc., Sydney, 1993; Kohen, J., 'The Dharug of the western

Cumberland Plain: Ethnography and demography', in B. Meehan and R. Jones (eds), *Archaeology with Ethnography: An Australian perspective*, ANU, 1988, pp. 238–50; Turbet, P., *The Aborigines of the Sydney District Before 1788*, Kangaroo Press, Sydney, 2001, p. 4.

59 Willmot, E., *Pemulwuy: Rainbow Warrior*, Weldon, Sydney, 1987; Collins, vol. II, p. 96; King to Lord Hobart (30 October 1802), in *HRNSW*, vol. 4, p. 867.

60 Willey, K., *When the Sky Fell Down*, Collins, Sydney, 1979, p. 167.

61 King to Lord Hobart, (20 December 1804), *HRA*, series I, vol. V, pp. 166–7.

62 King, proclamation of June 1802, in *HRA*, series I, vol. III, pp. 592–3.

63 Atkins, Judge Advocate, to Governor King (8 July 1805), in *HRA*, series I, vol. IV, p. 653.

64 Flannery, T. (ed.), *Terra Australis: Matthew Flinders' great adventures in the circumnavigation of Australia*, Text, Melbourne, 2000, pp. xxi–iii, 189–92. The Aboriginal rescue of lost crew was at Keppel Bay, Queensland, and the fatality was on Woodah Island, Northern Territory.

65 Flannery, *Terra Australis*, pp. 152–5.

66 *Sydney Gazette*, 17 April 1819.

67 *Sydney Gazette*, 7 July 1829; Clendinnen, *Dancing with Strangers*, pp. 273–9.

68 Macquarie in *HRA*, series I, vol. VIII, pp. 368–9, 338.

69 *Sydney Gazette*, 4 May 1816.

70 Leigh, S., appendix 2, The Reverend Samuel Leigh's account of the Aborigines of New South Wales, written about October, 1821, in N. Gunson (ed.), *Australian Reminiscences of Papers of L.E. Threkeld, Missionary to the Aborigines, 1824–1859*, vol. 2, pp. 333–7, Australian Aboriginal Studies, no. 40, Ethnohistory Series 2, AIAS, Canberra.

71 Field, B., *Geographical Memoirs on New South Wales*, London, 1825, p. 224.

Box—Boomerangs (p. 54)

a *Sydney Gazette*, 23 December 1804.

b Jones, P., *Boomerang: Behind an Australian icon*, Wakefield Press, Kent Town, SA, 1996; Musgrove, P., 'Why a boomerang returns', *New Scientist*, 1974, 61: 186–9; Musgrove, P., 'Prehistoric aeronautics', *Hemisphere*, 1975, 19(9): 10–14; Drake, F., 'What goes around comes around', *Sunday Telegraph*, 29 August 2004.

CHAPTER 3—CONFRONTATION

1 Re. French explorers see C. Dyer, *The French Explorers and the Aboriginal Australians 1772–1839*, UQP, 2005, pp. 1–2 (my spelling of French names follows Dyer); Lovejoy, A.O., and Boas, G., *Primitivism and Related Ideas in Antiquity*, John Hopkins Press, Baltimore, 1955, p. 240.

2 Ryan, L. [1981], *The Aboriginal Tasmanians*, UQP, 1996, p. 49; Smith, B., *European Vision and the South Pacific 1768–1850*, OUP, 1960, p. 25.

3 Plomley, N.J.B., *Friendly Mission: The Tasmanian journals and papers of George Augustus Robinson 1829–1834*, Tasmanian Historical Research Association, Hobart, 1966, pp. 38–9.

4 Smith, *European Vision*, p. 87.

5 Re. Aboriginal speculations on ships see Clarke, P., *Where the Ancestors Walked: Australia as an Aboriginal landscape*, A&U, 2003, p. 191.

6 Bonwick, J., *The Last of the Tasmanians*, London, 1870, pp. 18–19; Clark, J. [1983], *The Aboriginal People of Tasmania*, Tasmanian Museum, Hobart, 1986, pp. 47–65; Plomley, B., and Piard-Bernier, J., *The General: The visits of the expedition led by Bruny d'Entrecasteaux to Tasmanian waters in 1792 and 1793*, Queen Victoria Museum, Launceston, 1993, pp. 283–4.

7 Plomley, N.J.B., *The Baudin Expedition and the Tasmanian Aborigines*, Blubber Head Press, Hobart, 1983, plate 4 (Petit plate 20.021.4); re. pustules see Plomley, *Friendly Mission*, p. 533; re. hunchback see Samwell on Cook's 1777 expedition, quoted by Plomley, *Baudin Expedition*, pp. 199–200.

8 Labillardière, vol. I, pp. 308–9, 303, 127.

9 Plomley, *Friendly Mission*, pp. 581–2.

10 James Backhouse in N.J.B. Plomley, *Weep in Silence*, Blubber Head Press, Hobart, 1987, p. 225; Labillardière, vol. I, pp. 308–9, 303, 127; Cook, J. [1768–1779] (ed. J.C. Beaglehole), *The Journals of Captain James Cook on His Voyages of Discovery*, Hakluyt Society, Cambridge, 1955–67, vol. 3, pp. 54–6; Péron in Plomley, *Baudin Expedition*, pp. 57–60.

11 Re. heights, figures come from measurements made on the Dufresne, d'Entrecasteaux and Baudin expeditions and at Wybalenna c. 1836, see Plomley, *Baudin Expedition*, p. 165 (Plomley's imperial figures are correct but his metric equivalents were wrong and have been corrected here); Re. hair, see Dyer, *French Explorers*, pp. 37–8.

12 Pardoe, C., 'Isolation and evolution in Tasmania', *Current Anthropology*, 1991, 31: 1–21, and personal communication, 2004; Pardoe, C., 'Population genetics and population size in prehistoric Tasmania', *AA*, 1986, 22: 1–6; Presser, J.C. *et al.*, 'Tasmanian Aborigines and DNA', *Papers & Proc. Roy. Soc. Tas*, 2002, 136: 35–8.

13 Flood, J. [1983], *Archaeology of the Dreamtime*, A&R, 2001, pp. 118–38, 195–211; re. artefacts see R. Jones, 'The Tasmanian paradox', in R.V.S. Wright (ed.), *Stone Tools as Cultural Markers*, AIAS, 1977, pp. 189–204.

14 Plomley, *Baudin Expedition*, pp. 184–94; Flood, *Archaeology*, pp. 196–211, 205, 118–120; re. nomadism, bag-making and grass ropes see J. Backhouse in Plomley, *Weep in Silence*, pp. 223, 244, 263–4; Jones, R., 'Man as an element of a

continental fauna: The case of the sundering of the Bassian bridge', in J. Allen, J. Golson and R. Jones (eds), *Sunda and Sahul: Prehistoric studies in Southeast Asia, Melanesia and Australia*, Academic Press, London, 1977, pp. 317–86, esp. p. 325.

15 Vanderwal, R.L., and Horton, D.R., 'Coastal southwest Tasmania', *Terra Australis*, ANU, 1984, 9; Bowdler, S., 'Hunter Hill, Hunter Island', *Terra Australis*, ANU 1984, 8; Jones, 'Man as an element', in Allen, Golson and Jones, pp. 326–7, 331; Plomley, *Friendly Mission*, pp. 183 (re. swimming to Doughboys and Trefoil), 379, 554.

16 Robinson's invaluable field journals were discovered in Britain in the 1950s, edited by Brian Plomley and analysed by Rhys Jones; Plomley, *Friendly Mission*; Jones, R., 'The demography of hunters and farmers in Tasmania', in D. J. Mulvaney and J. Golson (eds), *Aboriginal Man and Environment in Australia*, ANU Press, 1971, pp. 271–87; Jones, R., 'Tasmanian tribes', in N.B. Tindale, *Aboriginal Tribes of Australia*, UCP, 1974, pp. 319–54.

17 Jones, 'The demography of hunters', in Mulvaney and Golson, *Aboriginal Man*, pp. 280–1; Lourandos, H., 'Aboriginal spatial organisation and population: Southwestern Victoria reconsidered', *APAO*, 1978, 12: 202–25, esp. p. 220; for revised figures see Critchett, J., *A Distant Field of Murder: Western District frontiers 1834–1848*, MUP, 1990, pp. 68–85, esp. pp. 74–5.

18 Plomley, *Friendly Mission*, pp. 970–5, 1971 supplement to *Friendly Mission*, map 4 and pp. 21–2; Jones, 'Tasmanian tribes', in Tindale, pp. 323–30, map on p. 327; Jones, 'The demography of hunters', in Mulvaney and Golson, *Aboriginal Man*, pp. 280–5.

19 Duclesmeur quoted in Dyer, *French Explorers*, p. 2; Windschuttle, K., *The Fabrication of Aboriginal History: Volume One, Van Diemen's Land 1803–1847*, Macleay Press, Sydney, 2002, pp. 364–72, quote is on p. 371.

20 Jones, R., 'Hunting forbears', in M. Roe (ed.), *The Flow of Culture: Tasmanian studies*, AAH, 1987, pp. 14–49, esp. pp. 28–9.

21 Bonwick, *The Last of the Tasmanians*, p. 85.

22 Plomley, *Friendly Mission*, pp. 113, 225, 526; Robinson to Colonial Secretary (6 August 1831), Colonial Secretary's Office 1/318.

23 Physical anthropologist Colin Pardoe has argued for a much higher population because of the lack of physical differences between Tasmanians and mainlanders, but this cannot be quantified and has not been substantiated: Pardoe, C., 'Isolation and evolution in Tasmania', *Current Anthropology*, 1991, 31: 1–21.

24 Plomley, *Friendly Mission*, pp. 57, 742.

25 Dyer, *French Explorers*, p. 154; Plomley, *Friendly Mission*, p. 280.

26 Plomley, *Friendly Mission*, p. 187.

27 *Ibid.*, p. 529.

28 *Ibid.*, p. 83.

29 *Ibid.*, pp. 560, 888.

30 Flood, J., *Rock Art of the Dreamtime*, A&R, 1997, pp. 223–39; re. circles see Plomley, *Friendly Mission*, p. 581–2 note 69; re. west coast engravings see *ibid.*, p. 915, note 49; re. post-contact art see S. Brown, 'Art and Tasmanian prehistory: Evidence for changing cultural traditions in a changing environment', in P. Bahn and A. Rosenfeld (eds), *Rock Art and Prehistory*, Oxbow Monograph 10, Oxbow Books, Oxford, 1991, pp. 96–119.

31 Plomley, *Friendly Mission*, pp. 373–7.

32 Plomley, *Friendly Mission*, p. 373; Maddock, K. 'Myths of the acquisition of fire in northern and eastern Australia', in R.M. Berndt (ed.), *Australian Aboriginal Anthropology*, UWA Press, 1970, p. 177.

33 Flood, J. [1990], *The Riches of Ancient Australia*, UQP, 1999, pp. 331–4, 358.

34 Labillardière quoted in Plomley, *The General*, p. 293; re. violin *ibid.*, p. 281; David, B., *Landscapes, Rock-Art and the Dreaming: An archaeology of preunderstanding*, Leicester University Press, London, 2003, pp. 13–110.

35 Anderson, W. in Cook, *Journals*, vol. III, pp. 54–6.

36 McGregor, R., *Imagined Destinies: Aboriginal Australians and doomed race theory, 1880–1939*, MUP, 1997.

37 Chappell's most recent estimate of when Tasmania was isolated from the mainland is 14 000 years: Lambeck, K., and Chappell, J., 'Sea level change through the last glacial cycle', *Science*, 2001, 292: 679–86.

38 Tip-damage on bone points is 'consistent with damaged spears being repaired at these sites and with tips being returned to them inside game carcasses': Webb, C., and Allen, J., 'A functional analysis of Pleistocene bone tools from two sites in southwest Tasmania', *AO*, 1990, 25: 75–8.

39 Flood, *Archaeology*, pp. 205–8, 133; Jones, 'The Tasmanian paradox', in Wright, *Stone Tools*, p. 194.

40 Colley, S., and Jones, R., 'New fish bone data from Rocky Cape, northwest Tasmania', *AO*, 1987, 22(2): 67–71.

41 Allen, H., 'Left out in the cold: Why the Tasmanians stopped eating fish', *Artefact*, 1979, 4: 1–10; Horton, D., *The Pure State of Nature: Sacred cows, destructive myths and the environment*, A&U, 2000, pp. 39–52; Lourandos, H., *Continent of Hunter-Gatherers: New perspectives in Australian prehistory*, CUP, 1997, pp. 274–7.

42 Jones, R., 'Why did the Tasmanians stop eating fish?' in R. Gould (ed.) *Explorations in ethnoarchaeology*, University of New Mexico Press, Santa Fe, 1978, pp. 11–47 (p. 41 re. Arnhem Land); re. using fish as threat see Plomley, *Friendly Mission*, p. 653.

43 <www.fishingcairns.com.au>; Colley and Jones,

'New fish bone data'. To avoid being poisoned, stick to safe fish such as mullet, whiting, bream and flathead, never eat or handle red bass, chinaman-fish, paddle-tail or Moray eels and do not eat any fish if your hands sting or feel numb after cleaning it!

44 Ferguson, W.C., 'Mokaré's domain', in D.J. Mulvaney and J.P. White (eds), *Australians: A historical library, Australians to 1788*, Fairfax, Syme & Weldon, Sydney, 1987, pp. 120–45, esp. p. 124; Anderson, D.M., 'Red tides', *Sci. Am.*, 1994, 271(2): 52–9.

45 Isaacs, J. (ed.), *Australian Dreaming: 40 000 years of Aboriginal history*, Lansdowne Press, Sydney, 1980; Dixon, R.M.W., *The Dyirbal Language of North Queensland*, CUP, 1972; Flood, *Riches*, p. 128. The volcanic lakes are Lakes Eacham, Barrine and Euramoo.

46 Flinders, M., *A Voyage to Terra Australis . . .* (21 March 1802), 1814, p. 169.

47 Jones, 'The Tasmanian paradox', in Wright, *Stone Tools*, pp. 202–3; re. climate see Lourandos, *Continent of Hunter-Gatherers*, pp. 265–81.

48 Jones, R., 'Tasmanian Aborigines and dogs', *Mankind*, 1970, 7(4): 256–71.

49 Backhouse, J., *A Narrative of a Visit to the Australian Colonies*, Hamilton Adams, London, 1843, p. 58.

50 Plomley, *Friendly Mission*, pp. 264, 487, 647–52.

51 *Hobart Town Courier*, 14 January 1832, p. 2.

52 Plomley, *Baudin Expedition*, p. 127.

53 Plomley, *Friendly Mission*, pp. 296–7.

54 *Ibid.*, p. 82.

55 Bowden, K.M., *Captain James Kelly of Hobart Town*, MUP, 1964, pp. 35–44.

56 Plomley, *Weep in Silence*, pp. 13, 22.

57 Plomley, *Friendly Mission*, p. 357; Bartolomé de Las Casas [1542] (ed. A. Pagden), *A Short Account of the Destruction of the Indies*, Penguin, London, 1992 (this book became well known in Britain after 1583, when it was translated into English). My discussion of atrocities in Tasmania is based on Windschuttle's re-examination of Robinson and other sources: Windschuttle, *Fabrication*, pp. 29–60, 379–86.

58 Details in Windschuttle, *Fabrication*, pp. 32–40.

59 Plomley, *Friendly Mission*, pp. 457–60 note 166; minutes of evidence taken before the Committee for the Affairs of Aborigines, *British Parliamentary Papers, Colonies, Australia*, 1830, vol. 4; Jones, R., and Haydon, T., *The Last Tasmanian*, film produced and directed by Tom Haydon, Artis Film Productions, Sydney, 1978.

60 Péron, F. [1802], *Voyage de découvertes aux Terres Australes*, ch. 12, quoted in translation in Plomley, *Baudin Expedition*, pp. 32, 37; Plomley, *Friendly Mission*, pp. 187, 529, 560, 888, 966; Jeffreys, C., *Van Diemen's Land: Geographical and descriptive delineation of the island of Van Diemen's Land*, London, 1820, pp. 118–19.

61 Plomley, *Friendly Mission*, pp. 652–3.

62 Ryan, *Aboriginal Tasmanians*, p. 71. Cape Barren Island was returned to Aborigines in 2005.

63 Ryan, *Aboriginal Tasmanians*, pp. 175–6; Baudin, N. [1802], *The Journal of Post Captain Nicholas Baudin* (trans. C. Cornell), Libraries Board of SA, Adelaide, 1974, p. 345; Calder, J.E., *Some Account of the Wars, Extirpation, Habits, etc. of the Native Tribes of Tasmania*, Hobart, 1875.

64 West, J. [1852] (ed. A.G.L. Shaw), *The History of Tasmania*, A&R, 1971, p. 262, quoted in Ryan, *Aboriginal Tasmanians*, p. 75.

65 Minutes of evidence taken before the Committee for the Affairs of Aborigines, *British Parliamentary Papers, Colonies, Australia*, 1830, vol. 4, pp. 53, 209, 223, 225; Windschuttle, *Fabrication*, pp. 16–28; Tardif, P., 'Risdon Cove', in R. Manne (ed.), *Whitewash: On Keith Windschuttle's Fabrication of Aboriginal History*, Schwartz, Melbourne, 2003, pp. 218–24.

66 Ryan, *Aboriginal Tasmanians*, p. 75; Reynolds, H., *Fate of a Free People: A radical re-examination of the Tasmanian Wars*, Penguin, Melbourne, 1995, pp. 76–7; 'Copies of all correspondence . . . on the subject of the military operations . . . against the Aboriginal inhabitants of Van Diemen's Land', *Military Operations, Parliamentary Papers, Great Britain*, 1831, vol. 19, no. 259, pp. 47–55; Walker, J.B., *Early Tasmania*, Government Printer, Hobart, 1902, pp. 48–52; Crowther, W.E.L., 'The passing of the Aboriginal race', *Medical Journal of Australia*, 1934, vol. 1: 147–60; Bonwick, *The Last of the Tasmanians*, pp. 32–6.

67 McGowan, A., *Archaeological Investigations at Risdon Cove Historic Site 1978–1980*, NPWS, Hobart, 1985, pp. 35, 69; Contos, N., *Pinjarra Massacre Site Research and Development Project*, Murray Districts Aboriginal Association, Pinjarra, WA, 1998.

68 Elder, B., *Blood on the Wattle: Massacres and maltreatment of Aboriginal Australians since 1788*, New Holland, Sydney, 1988, pp. 31–3.

69 Tardif in Manne, *Whitewash*, p. 222.

70 Reynolds, *Fate of a Free People*, pp. 45, 47; Plomley, *Friendly Mission*, pp. 81, 508, 510, 891; Windschuttle, *Fabrication*, p. 78.

71 Hiatt, B., 'The food quest and the economy of the Tasmanian Aborigines', *Oceania*, 1968–9, 38: 99–133 and 190–219.

72 Twenty-six Aboriginal children were baptised (i.e. their existence in settlers' homes was registered) between 1809 and 1819: *HRA*, series I, vol. III, p. 510; Windschuttle, *Fabrication*, p. 56.

73 Ryan, *Aboriginal Tasmanians*, pp. 78–9; Windschuttle, *Fabrication*, p. 56.

74 Calder, J.E. (ed.), *The Circumnavigation of Van Diemen's Land in 1815 by James Kelly and in 1824 by James Hobbs*, Hobart, 1984, pp. 21–34.

75 Only 3.1 per cent of the land had been formally

granted; the rest was occupied by leaseholders holding tickets of occupation or by ex-convicts and others illegally: Ryan, *Aboriginal Tasmanians*, pp. 79, 87–8, 90; Boyce, J., 'Fantasy Island', in Manne, *Whitewash*, pp. 17–80.

76 Plomley, N.J.B. (ed.), *Jorgen Jorgenson and the Aborigines of Van Diemen's Land*, Blubber Head Press, Hobart, 1991, p. 63.

77 The quote is from the *Colonial Times*, 3 September 1830.

78 Windschuttle, *Fabrication*, p. 129; William Darling (commandant of Aboriginal exiles in Bass Strait 1832–34) to Governor Arthur (4 May 1832), ML, ms A2188; Reynolds, *Fate of a Free People*, p. 32.

79 Broome, R., 'The struggle for Australia: Aboriginal-European warfare, 1770–1930', in M. McKernan and M. Browne (eds), *Australia: Two centuries of warfare*, Canberra, 1988, pp. 97–9; Connor, J., *The Australian Frontier Wars 1788–1838*, UNSW Press, 2002, pp. 18–19.

80 Robinson Report (30 April 1838), Robinson Papers, ML, ms A7044.

81 Bonwick, *The Last of the Tasmanians*, p. 219; Plomley, *Friendly Mission*, pp. 186, 837; Reynolds, *Fate of a Free People*, p. 49; Clark, *Aboriginal People*, p. 46; Ryan, *Aboriginal Tasmanians*, pp. 150–1.

82 Arthur to Murray (12 September 1829), *HRA*, series I, vol. XIV, p. 446, quoted in Reynolds, *Fate of a Free People*, p. 66; Plomley, *Friendly Mission*, p. 552.

83 Calder, *Some Account*, p. 7; Jorgenson to Burnett (24 February 1830) Colonial Secretary's Office 1/320, p. 375, quoted in Reynolds, *Fate of a Free People*, pp. 36–7.

84 Plomley, *Friendly Mission*, pp. 175–6, 181, 182–3, 231–2, quote is on p. 183; For detailed re-examination of the Cape Grim massacre see Windschuttle, *Fabrication*, pp. 249–69 and Ian McFarlane, 'Cape Grim', in Manne, *Whitewash*, 2003, pp. 277–98, esp. p. 289.

85 McFarlane, in Manne, *Whitewash*; Plomley, *Friendly Mission*, pp. 577–8, 700 note 159, 927, 936 notes 2 and 4, 937 notes 5 and 7.

86 Arthur to Goderich (10 January 1828), quoted in C. Turnbull, *Black War: The extermination of the Tasmanian Aborigines*, Melbourne, 1948, p. 83.

87 *Military Operations* (1831), p. 4; Ryan, *Aboriginal Tasmanians*, pp. 92–4.

88 Anstey to Burnett (4 December 1827), Colonial Secretary's Office I/320, quoted in Reynolds, *Fate of a Free People*, p. 123.

89 *Military Operations* (1831), pp. 4–7, 24–5 quoted in Reynolds, *Fate of a Free People*, pp. 105–7.

90 *Military Operations* (1831), p. 11, quoted in Reynolds, *Fate of a Free People*, p. 108; the definition of martial law is from the *Macquarie Dictionary*.

91 Executive Council (27 August 1830), p. 570, quoted in Reynolds, *Fate of a Free People*, p. 117.

92 Plomley, *Friendly Mission*, p. 277.

93 Reynolds, *Fate of a Free People*, p. 77.

94 Ryan, *Aboriginal Tasmanians*, p. 174.

95 Willis, H.A., 'A tally of those killed during the fighting between Aborigines and Settlers in Van Diemen's Land 1803–34', 2002, <http://www.historians.org.au/forumsupport/Tally-VDL.PDF>; Reynolds, *Fate of a Free People*, pp. 81–2; Windschuttle, *Fabrication*, pp. 361–4, 86–7.

96 Plomley, *Friendly Mission*, p. 52, re. motto p. 816 note 147; Robinson Papers, vol. 40, ML, mss. A7061, A7042, quoted in Reynolds, *Fate of a Free People*, pp. 132–3.

97 Calder, in Reynolds, *Fate of a Free People*, p. 142.

98 Curr to Lee-Archer (27 July 1841), Governor's Office 1/45, quoted in Reynolds, *Fate of a Free People*, p. 44, and see Ryan, *Aboriginal Tasmanians*, pp. 197–9.

99 Plomley, *Weep in Silence*, pp. 938–42, 946–47; Rowley, C.D., *The Destruction of Aboriginal Society*, Penguin, Melbourne, 1970, p. 52.

100 Ryan, *Aboriginal Tasmanians*, pp. 182–203; Reynolds, *Fate of a Free People*, pp. 159–89; Board of Inquiry (March 1839), report, Colonial Secretary's Office 5/180/4240.

101 Hughes, R., *The Fatal Shore: A history of the transportation of convicts to Australia, 1787–1868*, Harvill Press, London, 1986, pp. 83, 423; Ryan, *Aboriginal Tasmanians*, p. 185; Plomley, *Weep in Silence*, pp. 224, 262, 281.

102 Ryan, *Aboriginal Tasmanians*, p. 191; Reynolds, *Fate of a Free People*, pp. 165–6.

103 *Ibid.*, pp. 169–74.

104 Ryan, *Aboriginal Tasmanians*, pp. 79, 124; Reynolds, *Fate of a Free People*, p. 142.

105 Ryan, *Aboriginal Tasmanians*, pp. 175–6; Plomley, *Baudin Expedition*, pp. 201, 204 (the French word translated as 'yaws' is *pian*, meaning Mediterranean yaws or *framboesia*); Plomley, *Weep in Silence*, pp. 943, 945; Webb, S., *Palaeopathology of Aboriginal Australians: Health and disease across a hunter-gatherer continent*, CUP, 1995, pp. 138, 143–4; Meyer, C. et al., 'Syphilis 2001—A palaeopathological reappraisal', *Homo*, 2002, 53(1): 39–58.

106 Plomley, *Friendly Mission*, pp. 132, 77: 'Loath-some disorder' was the euphemism used by Robinson and his contemporaries for venereal disease but in the Bruny Island Mission journal his clerk, Sterling, called it venereal disease.

107 Plomley, *Weep in Silence*, pp. 937–47; Ryan, *Aboriginal Tasmanians*, p. 193; Journal of George Robinson, jr., Robinson Papers (28 March 1839), vol. 50, ML A7071. Robinson left Tasmania in 1839 to become Protector of Aborigines in New South Wales, based in Melbourne.

108 Plomley, *Friendly Mission*, pp. 534, 556–7.

109 Arthur to Spring-Rice (27 January 1835), Select Committee on Native People, *British Parliamentary Papers*, vol. 7, no. 425, p. 126, quoted in Reynolds, *Fate of a Free People*, p. 122.

110 *Military Operations* (1831), pp. 82, 84, 79.

111 Flannery, T., *The Explorers*, Text, Melbourne, 1998, pp. 163–170.

112 The treaty is displayed in NMA, Canberra. The treaty text is in G. Dawson [1881], *Australian Aborigines*, George Robertson, Melbourne (facsimile by ASP), 1981, pp. 111–12; Barwick, D., 'Mapping the past: An atlas of Victorian clans 1835–1904, *AH*, 1984, 8: 100–31, quote is on p. 107; Reynolds, H. [1987], *Law of the Land*, Penguin, London, 1992, pp. 125–8.

113 Morgan, J. [1852], *The Life and Adventures of William Buckley*, ANU Press, 1980, pp. 33, 119–20; Flannery, T. (ed.), *The Life and Adventures of William Buckley*, Text, Melbourne, 2002; Plomley, *Weep in Silence*, pp. 408, 410.

Box—Fire-making (p. 61)

a   Gott, B., 'Fire-making in Tasmania: Absence of evidence is not evidence of absence', *Current Anthropology*, 2002, 43(4): 650–6; Plomley, N.J.B., *The Baudin Expedition and the Tasmanian Aborigines*, Blubber Head Press, Hobart, 1983, pp. 188, 201–2; Volger, G., 'Making fire by percussion in Tasmania', *Oceania*, 1973, 44: 58–63; Plomley, *The General*, pp. 270–3; Labillardière, J.J.H. de (ed. J. Stockdale), *An Account of a Voyage in Search of La Perouse*, Debrett, London, 1800, vol. I, p. 177; Furneaux quoted in G.W. Anderson, *A New, Authentic and Complete Collection . . . of Captain Cook's First, Second, Third and Last Voyages*, London, 1784, p. 131; Cox, J., in G. Mortimer, *Observations and Remarks Made During a Voyage to . . . Maria's Island . . .*, London, 1791, p. 17; William Bligh in R.W. Giblin, *The Early History of Tasmania: The Geographical Era 1642–1804*, London, 1928, p. 93.

b   Plomley, *Friendly Mission*, p. 113.

c   *Ibid.*, pp. 837, 567, 399; Bonwick, J., *Daily Life and Origin of the Tasmanians*, Sampson, Low, Son & Marston, London, 1870, p. 205.

d   Banks, vol. II, pp. 123–37.

e   Mountford, C.P., and Berndt, R.M., 'Making fire by percussion in Australia', *Oceania*, 1941, XI(4): 342–4; Calley, M., 'Fire-making by percussion on the east coast of Australia', *Mankind*, 1957, 5(4): 168–71; Volger, 'Making fire', p. 61.

Box—Grave-robbing (p. 91)

a   Ryan, *Aboriginal Tasmanians*, pp. 214–17, 220; Petrow, S., 'The last man: The mutilation of William Lanney in 1869 and its aftermath', *AH*, 1997, 21: 90–112.

CHAPTER 4—DEPOPULATION

1   Worgan, G.B. [1788], *Journal of a First Fleet Surgeon*, Library of Australian History, Sydney, 1978, p. 10.

2   Blaxland, G., *A Journal of a Tour of Discovery across the Blue Mountains in New South Wales*, London, 1823; Richards, J.S. (ed.), *Blaxland-Lawson-Wentworth*, Blubber Head Press, Hobart, 1979, quoted in T. Flannery (ed.), *The Explorers*, Text, Melbourne, 1998, pp. 111–15; Perry, T.M., *Australia's First Frontier*, Melbourne, 1963; Stockton, E., *Blue Mountains Dreaming: The Aboriginal heritage*, Three Sisters Publications, Winmalee, 1993, pp. 118–19.

3   Macquarie, L., *Journal*, quoted in B. Elder [1988], *Blood on the Wattle: Massacres and maltreatment of Aboriginal Australians since 1788*, New Holland, Sydney, 1998, pp. 51–2; Read, P., *A Hundred Years War*, ANU Press, 1994, pp. 2–3; Tindale, N.B., *Aboriginal Tribes of Australia*, UCP, 1974, p. 201; Pearson, M., 'Bathurst Plains and beyond: European colonisation and Aboriginal resistance', *AH*, 1984, 8: 63–79.

4   Robinson, G.A., to La Trobe (30 December 1843), 'Aborigines (Australian Colonies), Return to an Address', *British Parliamentary Papers*, 1844, vol. 34, p. 282.

5   McMillan, A. [1898], in T.F. Bride (ed.), *Letters from Victorian Pioneers*, Heinemann, Melbourne, 1969, p. 204.

6   Elder, *Blood on the Wattle*, pp. 49–63; Clayton, I., and Barlow, A., *Wiradjuri of the Rivers and Plains*, Heinemann, Melbourne, 1997, pp. 51–62; Read, *A Hundred Years War*, pp. 5–11.

7   Grassby, A., and Hill, M., *Six Australian Battlefields*, A&R, 1988, pp. 134–68; Elder, *Blood on the Wattle*, p. 59; *Sydney Gazette*, 29 July, 12 August 1824.

8   Governor's Proclamation (14 August 1824), *HRA*, series I, vol. XI, p. 410; Coe, M., *Windradyne: A Wiradjuri koorie*, Blackbooks, Sydney, 1986, p. 53.

9   Connor, J., *The Australian Frontier Wars 1788–1838*, UNSW Press, 2002, pp. 53–62; letter Brisbane to Bathurst (31 December 1824), *HRA*, series I, vol. XI, p. 431.

10 Connor, *The Australian Frontier Wars*, pp. 59–61; *Sydney Gazette*, 16 September, 14 October, 25 November, 30 December 1824; *Australian*, 30 December 1824; letter Brisbane to Bathurst (31 December 1824); Governor's Proclamation (11 December 1824), *HRA*, series I, vol. XI, p. 431–2.

11 *Sydney Gazette*, 30 September 1824; Coe, *Windradyne*, pp. 56–7.

12 By 1981, historian Michael Pearson had completed his PhD on European colonisation and Aboriginal resistance in the Bathurst region, and found no evidence of these three alleged massacres: Pearson, M., 'Seen through different eyes: Changing land-use and settlement patterns in the upper Macquarie River', PhD thesis, ANU, 1981; Pearson, M., 'Bathurst Plains and beyond: European colonisation and Aboriginal resistance', *AH*, 1984, 8: 75; Windschuttle, K., 'The

myths of frontier massacres in Australian history, Parts I–III', *Quadrant*, 2000, 44(10–12): 8–21, 17–24, 6–20.

13 Re. Threlkeld's alleged massacre, see N. Gunson (ed.), *Australian Reminiscences and Papers of L.E. Threlkeld, Missionary to the Aborigines, 1824–1859*, AIAS, 1974, 1, p. 49.

14 Suttor, W.H., *Australian Stories Retold*, Glyndwr Whalan, Bathurst, 1887.

15 Gresser's local history, *The Aborigines of the Bathurst District*, was serialised in the *Bathurst Times* in 1962. Under the headline 'Massacre' Gresser wrote, 'An old resident . . . told me years ago that "hundreds of blacks" had been rounded up and shot at Bells Falls . . . Probably, if not undoubtedly, some were shot there, but in the course of time the number would become greatly exaggerated.' This vague tradition did not feature in any of William Suttor Senior's stories as he guided G.C. Mundy, who published stories about the Sofala area in 1853, i.e. this 'local tradition' was unknown to the leading local family. Gresser's annotated copy of his manuscript reveals he later decided all Aborigines escaped the soldiers in 1824. This retraction was omitted in the 1971 book, *Windradyne of the Wiradjuri: Martial law at Bathurst in 1824* published by Wentworth Books, Sydney, under the names of T. Salisbury and P. J. Gresser, although Gresser had died in 1969. All subsequent versions of the Bells Falls massacre are based on Gresser's 1962 story, e.g. Mary Coe, *Windradyne*. See D.A. Roberts, 'Bells Falls massacre and Bathurst's history of violence: Local tradition and Australian historiography', *Australian Historical Studies*, 1995, pp. 615–33; Roberts, D.A., 'The Bells Falls massacre and oral tradition', in B. Attwood and S.G. Foster (eds.), *Frontier Conflict: The Australian experience*, NMA, 2003, pp. 150–7.

16 Windschuttle, K., 'How not to run a museum', *Quadrant*, 2001, 45(379): 11–9; Davison, G., 'Conflict in the museum', in *Frontier Conflict*, 2003, pp. 201–14.

17 Read, *A Hundred Years War*, p. 11; Grassby and Hill, *Six Australian Battlefields*, p. 167.

18 *Ibid.*, p. 146.

19 Wills Cooke, T.S., *The Currency Lad: A biography of Horatio Spencer Howe Wills 1811–1861*, T.S. Wills Cooke, Melbourne, 1997, pp. 42–54; Wilson, G., *Murray of Yarralumla*, OUP, 1968; Durack, M., *Kings in Grass Castles*, Constable, London, 1959; Durack, M., *Sons in the Saddle*, Constable, London, 1983, pp. 50, 84, 137, 192–3; Gunn, Mrs Aeneas, *We of the Never-Never*, Hutchinson, London, 1907.

20 Governor King to Earl Camden (30 April 1805) in *HRA*, series I, vol. V, pp. 306–7.

21 Pike, D.H., 'The Diary of James Coutts Crawford: Extracts on Aborigines and Adelaide

1839 and 1841', *South Australiana*, 1965, 4(1): 4.

22 Broome, R., 'Aboriginal victims and voyagers: Confronting frontier myths', *JAS*, 1994, 42: 70–7; Any incident involving a convict had to be reported, for instance.

23 Broome, R., *Aboriginal Victorians: A history since 1800*, A&U, 2005, pp. xxiv, 80–1; Broome, R., 'The statistics of frontier conflict', in *Frontier Conflict*, pp. 88–98, esp. pp. 90–7; Clark, I., *Scars in the Landscape: A register of massacre sites in Western Victoria 1803–1859*, ASP, 1995.

24 Meyrick, H.H., Letters, H15789–15816, La Trobe Collection, State Library of Victoria, Melbourne, 1846; Pepper, P., and De Arauago, T., *The Kurnai of Gippsland*, Hyland House, Melbourne, 1985, pp. 58–9; Morgan, P., 'Gippsland settlers and the Kurnai dead', *Quadrant*, 2004, 410: 26–8.

25 Curr, E.M. [1883] (ed. H. Foster), *Recollections of Squatting in Victoria*, Robertson, Melbourne, 1965, p. 106 (son of the E. Curr mentioned in ch. 4); Bride, *Letters*, pp. 132, 187.

26 Flood, J., *The Moth Hunters: Aboriginal prehistory of the Australian Alps*, AIAS, Canberra, 1980.

27 Reynolds, H. [1981], *The Other Side of the Frontier*, Penguin, Melbourne, 1995, pp. 121–5.

28 Green, N., *Broken Spears: Aborigines and Europeans in the southwest of Australia*, Focus Education, Perth, 1984, Appendix 1.

29 Lang, G.S., *The Aborigines of Australia*, Melbourne, pp. 41–2.

30 Blainey, G., 'Drawing up the balance sheet of our history', *Quadrant*, 1993, 37(7–8): 11, 15.

31 Knightley, P., *Australia: Biography of a Nation*, Jonathan Cape, London, 2000.

32 Roberts, A.J., *Frontier Justice: A history of the Gulf country to 1900*, UQP, 2005, pp. 235, 65–7, 230–44.

33 Green, N., 'Windschuttle's debut', in R. Manne (ed.), *Whitewash: On Keith Windschuttle's Fabrication of Aboriginal History*, Schwartz, Melbourne, 2003, pp. 187–98; Connor, *The Australian Frontier Wars*, pp. 76–83.

34 *HRA*, series I, vol. XX, p. 440; Milliss, R., *Waterloo Creek: The Australia Day Massacre of 1838, George Gipps and the British conquest of New South Wales*, McPhee Gribble, Ringwood, 1992; Ryan, L., 'Waterloo Creek, northern New South Wales, 1838', in *Frontier Conflict*, pp. 33–43; Elder, *Blood on the Wattle*, pp. 74–82; Windschuttle, K., 'The myths of frontier massacres in Australian history, Part I', *Quadrant*, 2000, 44(10): 8–21; Connor, *The Australian Frontier Wars*, pp. 102–22.

35 Elder, *Blood on the Wattle*, pp. 83–94; Milliss, *Waterloo Creek*, p. 66.

36 Reid, G., *A Nest of Hornets*, OUP, 1982; Elder, *Blood on the Wattle*, pp. 135–48; Wood, J.D. (10 April 1862), remarks on the Aborigines, letter to Queensland Colonial Secretary, 1118 of 1862, Qld State Archives, quoted in Reynolds, *The Other Side of the Frontier*, pp. 81–2.

37 Elder, *Blood on the Wattle*, pp. 149–58; Mulvaney,

D.J., *Encounters in Place: Outsiders and Aboriginal Australians 1606–1985*, UQP, 1989, pp. 95–104; Wills Cooke, *The Currency Lad*.

38   Green, N., *The Forrest River Massacres*, Fremantle Arts Press, Fremantle, 1995, but see R. Moran, *Massacre Myth: An investigation into allegations concerning the mass murder of Aborigines at Forrest River, 1926*, Access Press, Bassendean, WA, 1999, pp. 17–8, 18–20, 23; re. Royal Commission see *SMH*, 9 December 1926, 16, 19, 23, 24 and 26 March 1927.

39   Moran, *Massacre Myth*, pp. 186–202; Elder, *Blood on the Wattle*, pp. 168–76; Rowley, C.D., *The Destruction of Aboriginal Society*, Penguin, Melbourne, 1970, pp. 200–2; Reynolds, H., *This Whispering in Our Hearts*, A&U, 1998, pp. 191–200; Knightley, *Australia: Biography of a Nation*; Shaw, B., *My Country of the Pelican Dreaming*, AIAS, 1981.

40   Moran, R., *Sex, Maiming and Murder: Seven case studies into the reliability of Reverend E.R.B. Gribble, Superintendent, Forrest River Mission 1913–1928, as a witness to the truth*, Access Press, Bassendean, WA, 2002, p. xiii.

41   Moran, *Massacre Myth*, pp. 45–7, 192, 201.

42   All Aboriginal stories about the massacre conflict with proven facts, e.g. Frank Chulung claimed his father found a 'massacre site', but Gribble's search party recorded in the Mission journal, 'no traces of natives having been shot': Moran, *Massacre Myth*, pp. 227–8, 232–8.

43   Moran, *Massacre Myth*, pp. 121–4, 200, re. firewood pp. 108–12, 190; Moran, *Sex, Maiming and Murder*, pp. 111–31.

44   Green, N., 'The evidence for the Forrest River Massacres', *Quadrant*, 2003, 398: 39–43, but see R. Moran, 'Grasping at the straws of "evidence"', *Quadrant*, 2003, 401: 20–4. Web sites are full of massacre stories, but when compared with written records, most are found to be untrue or implausible. For example, in 2001 the Governor-General attended a remembering ceremony for Mistake Creek massacre victims in the Kimberley. No whites were involved in the massacre, which was an entirely Aboriginal affair. In 1915, two Aborigines (Joe Wynn and Nipper Carogbiddy) stole rifles from their white boss, Mick Rhatigan. They then found and shot another Aboriginal man, Hopples (who had stolen Wynn's wife) and seven other Aborigines, including two children. The three women in the group were forced to collect fuel to burn the corpses before being killed. Others survived but Wynn was shot trying to escape and Carogbiddy surrendered. Eyewitnesses all testified that Mick Rhatigan was not involved. Carogbiddy was charged but he could not be prosecuted as the witnesses escaped from Wyndham jail. The event was well-documented in a contemporary 84-page official report, and writer Ion Idriess, in his book *Tracks of Destiny*, published in the 1960s, gave a factually correct account based on statements taken in 1915.

Another supposed massacre by poisoning at Bedford Downs station was portrayed in a play *Fire, Fire Burning Bright*, but there is no evidence or even hearsay that it took place: Clement, C., 'Mistake Creek', in Manne, *Whitewash*, pp. 199–214; Moran, R., 'Was there a massacre at Bedford Downs?' *Quadrant*, 2002, 391: 48–51.

45   Cribbin, J., *The Killing Times: The Coniston Massacre*, Fontana, Sydney (and film of the same name), 1984, pp. 42, 91, 163–4.

46   Moran, R., 'Paradigm of the postmodern museum', *Quadrant*, 2002, XLVI(383): 43–9; Moran, R., 'Millennia-old oral culture puts down written roots', *West Australian*, 2 April 1994.

47   Attwood, quoted by A. Stevenson, 'Trio's role a turn-up for history books', *SMH*, 17 December 2001.

48   Rose, D.B., 'Oral histories and knowledge', in Attwood and Foster, *Frontier Conflict*, pp. 120–31.

49   Reynolds, H., *Aborigines and Settlers: The Australian experience*, Cassell Australia, Melbourne, 1972, ch. 5; Broome, *Aboriginal Victorians*, pp. 91–2.

50   Kimber, R., 'The end of the bad old days: European settlement in central Australia 1871–1894', State Library of NT, *Occasional Papers*, vol. 25, 1991, p. 16; Kimber, R., 'Smallpox in Central Australia: Evidence for epidemics and postulations about the impact', *AA*, 1988, 27: 6; Reynolds, H., *An Indelible Stain? The question of genocide in Australia's history*, Viking, Melbourne, 2001, p. 134.

51   Broome, R. [1982], *Aboriginal Australians: Black responses to white dominance*, A&U, 2001, p. 64; Broome, *Aboriginal Victorians*, pp. 86–7.

52   Flannery, T. (ed.), *The Life and Adventures of William Buckley*, Text, Melbourne, 2002, pp. xi, xii, 189–200. Some historians blame Aboriginal violence on the disruption of traditional society caused by the 1789 smallpox epidemic. Pockmarked survivors were seen at Port Phillip Bay in 1803 but the Wathaurong were not affected. Buckley had suffered smallpox himself in England but commented that in Australia, 'I never observed any European contagious disease prevalent, in the least degree . . . There was at one time, however, I now recollect, a complaint which spread through the country, occasioning the loss of many lives, attacking generally the healthiest and strongest . . . It was a dreadful swelling of the feet, so that they were unable to move about, being also afflicted with ulcers of a very painful kind': Morgan, J. [1852], *The Life and Adventures of William Buckley*, ANU Press, 1980, pp. 94–5. This sounds like hearsay about the aftermath of smallpox among distant groups and it seems clear that none of Buckley's own group had been afflicted.

53 Morgan, *Buckley*, pp. 49–51, 68–9, 74, 75, 76, 81.

54 *Ibid.*, pp. 81–3; re. betrothal pp. 72–3.

55 Warner, W.L. [1937], *A Black Civilization: A social study of an Australian tribe*, Harper and Row, London, 1958, pp. 155, 148, 159, 163; Blainey, G., *Triumph of the Nomads*, Macmillan, Sydney, 1975, pp. 108–11.

56 Berndt, R.M., and C.H. [1964], *The World of the First Australians*, ASP, 1988, pp. 153–4; Howitt, A.W. [1904], *The Native Tribes of South-East Australia*, Macmillan, London, 1996, and ASP, pp. 748–50.

57 Cowlishaw, G., 'Infanticide in Aboriginal Australia', *Oceania*, 1978, XLVIII(4): 262–83, esp. 264–7.

58 Re infanticide, see Collins, vol. I, p. 504.

59 Blainey, *Triumph of the Nomads*, pp. 95–100; Hilliard, W.M., *The People in Between: The Pitjantjatjara People of Ernabella*, Hodder & Stoughton, London, 1968, p. 237; Curr, *Recollections*, p. 116.

60 Bates, D., *The Passing of the Aborigines*, Murray, London, 1937, pp. 192–3 (this book is reasonably reliable on infanticide, but *not* on cannibalism); Hall, R., 'Fantasies in the desert: The unhappy life of Daisy Bates', in Hall, R., *Black Armband Days*, Random House, Sydney, 1998, pp. 147–70.

61 Rose, F.G.G., *Traditional Mode of Production of the Australian Aborigines*, A&R, 1987, pp. 38, 194–5, 217. Malnutrition adversely affects women's fertility, as shown by studies in Bangladesh and of *!Kung* women in Africa. Well-nourished women have shorter birth-spacing and suffer fewer miscarriages and stillbirths than poorly nourished ones. Among the malnourished, menarche (onset of menstruation) is later and amenorrhea (cessation of menstrual cycle) more frequent. Amenorrhea through starvation is well-documented. It also often occurs when women are very active, for example, ballet dancers, runners and Himalayan mountaineers. Among hunter-gatherers, women's collecting was inevitably strenuous and amenorrhea common, leading to greater spacing between births. Frequent and prolonged suckling of a child prevented ovulation for a long period among *!Kung* and nomadic Australian Aboriginal women: Scott, E.C., and Johnston, F.E., 'Science, nutrition, fat, and policy: Tests of the critical-fat hypothesis', *Current Anthropology*, 1985, 26(4): 463–73.

62 Abbie, A.A., *The Original Australians*, Reed, Sydney, 1969, p. 95.

63 Marks of childhood suffering from famine or disease are visible on X-rays of leg-bones as 'Harris lines', dense lines of bone laid down when growth temporarily ceases. Since the bones continue to grow from each end, these 'growth arrest' lines are left behind and last well into adulthood. The most logical reason for formation of multiple Harris lines, according to Webb, lies in annual 'nutritional deprivation, or a regime of feast and famine'. The other main indicators, anaemia and dental enamel hypoplasia, suggest a longer episode of stress: Webb, S., *Palaeopathology of Aboriginal Australians: Health and disease across a hunter-gatherer continent*, CUP, 1995, pp. 279–80.

64 Webb, *Palaeopathology*, pp. 278–81; Williams, E., *Complex Hunter-Gatherers: A late Holocene example from temperate Australia*, S423, British Archaeological Reports, Oxford, 1988.

65 Webb, *Palaeopathology*, pp. 188–216.

66 *Ibid.*, pp. 161–87.

67 Tench (ed. Flannery), pp. 103–4.

68 Fenner, *Smallpox*, pp. 117–18; Campbell, J., *Invisible Invaders: Smallpox and other diseases in Aboriginal Australia 1780–1880*, MUP, 2002.

69 Fowell in Butler, *The Myth of Terra Nullius*, p. 113; King, in Hunter, p. 270; Hunter, p. 272; Collins, vol. I, p. 53.

70 Marriott, E.W., *The Memoirs of Obed West: A portrait of early Sydney*, Barcom Press, Bowral, 1988. The 'large overhanging rock' forming a cave 'about 200 yards back from the beach' is at Long Bay.

71 Bradley, *A Voyage*, p. 118. Lapérouse stopped in Canton from 1 January 1787 to 5 February 1787 and took on Chinese sailors there, but smallpox could not have survived on board for 12 months before reaching Australia.

72 Butlin, N.G., *Our Original Aggression: Aboriginal populations of southeastern Australia 1788–1850*, A&U, 1983, pp. 21, 22, 175, 65–700; Butlin, N., 'Macassans and Aboriginal smallpox: the "1789" and "1829" epidemics', *Historical Studies*, 1985, 21(84): 315–35; Stearn and Stearn, *The Effect of Smallpox*, pp. 44–5 et passim.

73 Frost, A., *Botany Bay Mirages: Illusions of Australia's convict beginnings*, MUP, 1995, pp. 190–210; Wilson, C., 'History, hypothesis and fiction', *Quadrant*, 1985, 29(3): 26–32; Wilson, C., *Australia: The creation of a nation*, Weidenfeld & Nicolson, London, 1987, pp. 75–84; Day, D. [1996], *Claiming a Continent: A new history of Australia*, HarperCollins, Sydney, 2001, p. 43; Reynolds, H., *An Indelible Stain? The question of genocide in Australia's history*, Viking, Melbourne, 2001, p. 36.

74 Smallpox was not finally eradicated until 1977. Experiments in Bangladesh showed smallpox scabs were adversely affected by high temperatures and humidity, and even at only 26°C and 10 per cent relative humidity, the virus was inactivated after 12 weeks. Similarly, in Afghanistan where variolation was still practised in the 1970s, even when smallpox virus was kept in jars in cool caves, 'most variolators stated that it was necessary to obtain new material each year'. Both temperatures and humidity are high in summer in Sydney. Hunter and Dawes kept

records for 1788: maximum temperatures in the open air were 34°C in October, 39°C in November and 44°C in December. Surgeon Arthur Bowes said that on 20 February 1788 'in the hospital tent the temperature was up to 105 degrees [F]' (40°C). This is 15°C hotter than maximum outside temperature recorded for that month. On the voyage out, cabin temperatures were sometimes high enough to melt pitch sealing the timbers; Fenner, F., personal communication, 2001.

75 Fenner, *Smallpox*, pp. 192, 115–16, 480, 682–3.

76 Stirling, E.C., 'Preliminary report on the discovery of native remains with an enquiry into a pandemic among Australian Aboriginals', *Trans. Roy. Soc. SA*, 1911, 35: 4–46; Cleland, J.B. [1911], 'Some diseases peculiar to, or of interest in, Australia', in J.H.L. Cumpston, *The History of Smallpox in Australia, 1788–1900*, C. of A, Melbourne, 1914, pp. 163–70; re. Dr Mair, pp. 150–4; re. Clark, pp. 151–2; Cleland, J.B., 'Ecology, environment and diseases', in B.C. Cotton (ed.), *Aboriginal Man in South and Central Australia*, Govt. Printer, Adelaide, 1966, pp. 111–58, esp. pp. 155–6.

77 Butlin, N.H., *Our Original Aggression: Aboriginal populations of southeastern Australia 1788–1850*, A&U, 1983, pp. 34–5; Fenner, F. *et al., Smallpox and its Eradication*, WHO, Geneva, 1988, pp. 194, 480; Campbell, J., 'Smallpox in Aboriginal Australia, 1829–31', *Historical Studies*, 1983, 20(81): 536–56; Sturt, C. [1833] (ed. L. Hiddins), *Two Expeditions into the Interior of South Australia*, Corkwood Press, Adelaide, 1999, pp. 58, 65.

78 Campbell, J. and Frost, A., 'Aboriginal smallpox: the 1789 and 1829 epidemics', *Historical Studies*, 1985, 21(84); Campbell, *Invisible Invaders*, *passim*; Macknight, C.C., personal communication, 2005.

79 Flinders, *A Voyage to Terra Australis*, pp. 228–33; Brown, R. [1803], *Journal*, quoted in C.C. Macknight, 'Macassans and Aborigines', *Oceania*, 1972, 42: 292.

80 Foelsche, P., 'Notes on the Aborigines of North Australia', *Trans. & Proc. Roy. Soc. SA*, 1881–82, 5: 8.

81 Flood, *Moth Hunters*; Mackaness, G. (ed.), *George Augustus Robinson's Journey into South-Eastern Australia, 1844*, Australian Historical Monographs, XIX, Review Publications, Dubbo, 1978.

82 Teichelmann, C.G., and Schurmann, C.W. [1840], *Outlines of a Grammar, Vocabulary and Phraseology of the Aboriginal Language of South Australia . . .* (facsimile edn), Tjintu Books, Largs Bay, 1982.

83 Rose, D.B., *Hidden Histories: Black stories from Victoria River Downs, Humbert River and Wave Hill Stations*, ASP, 1991, pp. 5, 75–8, 113–18.

84 *Ibid.*, p. 75.

85 Diamond, J., *Guns, Germs, and Steel: A short history*

86 Campbell, *Invisible Invaders*, *passim*.

87 Diamond, *Guns, Germs and Steel*, pp. 210, 357.

88 *Ibid.*, p. 210; Fyans, in Bride, *Letters*, p. 181.

89 Flood, *Moth Hunters*, pp. 32, 37, 42, 43.

90 Davidson, A., *Geographical Pathology*, Pentland, Edinburgh, 1892; Mulvaney, *Encounters in Place*, pp. 183–94; Reynolds, *The Other Side of the Frontier*, p. 57; Sturt, *Two Expeditions*, pp. 192, 209, 57–8, 65; Butlin, *Our Original Aggression*, pp. 38–9; Eyre, E.J., *Journal of an Expedition of Discovery into Central Australia*, Boone, London, 1845, vol. II, pp. 379–80; Westgarth, W., *Australia Felix*, London, 1848, pp. 81–2; Webb, *Palaeopathology*, pp. 154–5.

91 Basedow, H., *The Australian Aboriginal*, Preece, Adelaide, 1925, p. 194.

92 The scientific name for yaws is *Treponema pallidum pertenue*, and treponarid is *Treponema pallidum endemicum*. Symptoms are ulcers and large crusty sores on hands, feet, the face, anus and groin: Hackett, C., 'The human treponematoses', in *Diseases in Antiquity* (eds D. Brothwell and A.T. Sandison), Thomas, Springfield, IL, 1967; Moodie, P. M., *Aboriginal Health: Aborigines in Australian Society*, ANU Press, 1973, pp. 163–8; Webb, *Palaeopathology*, pp. 135–60. Webb found lesions from endemic treponemal infection on prehistoric skeletons, especially in arid and tropical regions. Frequencies in relatively crowded settlements on the central Murray River reached 16 per cent. He concluded yaws or treponarid 'had a much wider distribution than we have previously thought'. It affected people in northern Western Australia, Northern Territory, South Australia, western Queensland and western New South Wales and 'possibly further east': Webb, *Palaeopathology*, p. 155.

93 According to Fenner, 'measles caused the deaths of about 25 per cent of Fijians when introduced by Indian immigrant workers brought to the island by the British, then settled back to a lower fatality rate'. The pattern in Australia was probably similar.

94 Briscoe, G., 'Queensland Aborigines and the Spanish influenza pandemic of 1918–1919', *AIATSIS*, 1996, Occasional paper 3.

95 Thomson, N., 'A review of Aboriginal health status', in J. Reid, and P. Trompf (eds), *The Health of Aboriginal Australia*, Harcourt-Brace-Jovanovich, Sydney, 1991, pp. 37–79.

96 Black, R.H., *Malaria in Australia*, AGPS, 1972; Spencer, M., *Malaria: The Australian Experience 1843–1991*, Australasian College of Tropical

of everybody for the last 13 000 years, Chatto & Windus, London, 1997, pp. 21, 197–205; Moorehead, A., *The Fatal Impact: An account of the invasion of the South Pacific, 1767–1840*, Hamish Hamilton, London, 1966; Goldsmid, J., *The Deadly Legacy*, UNSW Press, 1988; Stearn and Stearn, *The Effect of Smallpox*, pp. 44–5 et passim.

Medicine, JCU, 1994, pp. 10–14, 80–1; Groube, L., 'Contradictions and malaria in Melanesian and Australian prehistory', in M. Spriggs *et al.* (eds), *A Community of Culture . . .*, ANU, 1993, pp. 164–86.

97 Hargrave, J., 'Leprosy in the Northern Territory', in Reid and Trompf, *Health*, 1991, pp. 62–3, 61.

Box—Native police (p. 107)

a   Fels, M., *Good Men and True: The Aboriginal Police of the Port Phillip District 1837–1853*, MUP, 1988.

b   Quoted in Elder, *Blood on the Wattle*, p. 135.

Box—Cannibalism (p. 118)

a   Flannery, *Life and Adventures of William Buckley*, p. 197; Morgan, *Buckley*, p. 81; Hollingham, R., 'Natural born cannibals', *New Scientist*, 2004, 183(2455): 30–3; White, T.D., 'Once were cannibals', *Scientific American*, 2003, 13(2): 86–93.

b   Pickering, M.P., 'Cannibalism amongst Aborigines? A critical review of the literary evidence', BLitt thesis, ANU, 1985; Lumholtz, C. [1889], *Among Cannibals . . .*, ANU Press, Canberra, 1980, pp. 271–4; Morgan, *Buckley*, pp. 50, 76, 97, 108; Elkin, A. P. [1938], *The Australian Aborigines: How to understand them*, A&R, 1954, pp. 171, 313, 317; Howitt, *Native Tribes*, pp. 247, 443, 448–50, 457–8, 470, 749–56.

c   Berndt and Berndt, *The World*, pp. 467–70; Spencer, W.B., and Gillen, E.J., *The Northern Tribes of Central Australia*, MacMillan, London, 1904, pp. 608–9; Cowlishaw, 'Infanticide', pp. 264–5.

d   Durack, *Kings in Grass Castles*, p. 228.

e   Flannery, *Life and Adventures of William Buckley*, p. 197, in notes by Rev. George Langhorne.

f   Berndt and Berndt, *The World*, p. 470.

g   Pickering, *Cannibalism*, pp. 115–17.

CHAPTER 5—TRADITION

1   Collins, D. [1798] (ed. B.H. Fletcher), *An Account of the English Colony in New South Wales*, Reed, Sydney, 1975, vol. I, p. 497.

2   Stanner, W.E.H., *After the Dreaming*, Boyer Lecture, ABC, Sydney, 1968, p. 44, reprinted in W.E.H. Stanner, *White Man Got No Dreaming: Essays 1938–1973*, ANU Press, 1979, p. 230.

3   Rose, D.B., *Nourishing Terrains: Australian Aboriginal views of landscape and wilderness*, AHC, 1996; Neidjie, B., *Story about Feeling*, Magabala Books, Broome, 1989; Neidjie, B., Davis, S., and Fox, A., *Kakadu Man: Bill Neidjie*, Mybrood, NSW, 1985.

4   Stanner [1958], 'Continuity and change among the Aborigines', in *White Man*, pp. 41–66, quotes on pp. 48–9.

5   Stanner [1962], 'Religion, totemism and symbolism', in *White Man*, pp. 109–14; Guenther, M., 'From totemism to shamanism: Hunter-gatherer contributions to world mythology and spirituality', in R.B. Lee and R. Daly (eds), *Cambridge Encyclopedia of Hunters and Gatherers*, CUP, 1999, pp. 426–33.

6   Edwards, W.H., *An Introduction to Aboriginal Societies*, Social Science Press, Wentworth Falls, 1988, p. 66.

7   Stanner, W.E.H. [1976], 'Some aspects of Aboriginal religion', in M. Charlesworth (ed.), *Religious Business: Essays on Australian Aboriginal spirituality*, CUP, 1998, pp. 1–24, esp. p. 14.

8   Reed, A.W. [1969], *An Illustrated Encyclopedia of Aboriginal Life*, Reed, Sydney, 1974, p. 16; Howitt, A.W. [1904], *The Native Tribes of South-East Australia*, ASP, 1996, pp. 426–34.

9   Elkin, A.P. [1938], *The Australian Aborigines: How to understand them*, A&R, 1954, pp. 287–8; Berndt, R.M., and C.H., *The World of the First Australians . . .*, ASP, 1988; Eliade, M., *Australian Religions*, Cornell University Press, Ithaca, 1973; Freud, S. [1913], *Totem and Taboo* (trans. J. Strachey), Routledge & Kegan Paul, London, 1960.

10 Peterson, N., 'Introduction to Australia', in R.B. Lee and R. Daly (eds), *Cambridge Encyclopedia*, 1999, pp. 317–23.

11 Guenther, 'From totemism', p. 426.

12 Stanner [1953], 'The Dreaming', in *White Man*, pp. 23–40; also in W.H. Edwards (ed.) [1987], *Traditional Aboriginal Society*, Macmillan, Melbourne, 1998, pp. 227–38.

13 Walker and Penrith interviews recorded under the Oral History Program for the Australian Museum, Sydney, exhibition, *Indigenous Australians: Australia's First Peoples*, 1997; Roberts, quoted in Edwards, *An Introduction*, p. 21.

14 Isaacs, J., *Australian Dreaming*, Lansdowne Press, Sydney, 1980.

15 Chatwin, B., *Songlines*, Jonathan Cape, London, 1987; Berndt and Berndt, *The World*, pp. 368–81.

16 Berndt and Berndt, *The World*, p. 392.

17 *Ibid.*; Isaacs, J. (ed.), *Australian Aboriginal Music*, Aboriginal Artists Agency, Sydney, 1979, pp. 8–9, 15–18, 237.

18 Stanner, W.E.H. [1961], *On Aboriginal Religion*, Oceania Monographs 36, UOS, 1989, pp. 81–4; Berndt, R.M., and C.H., *The Speaking Land: Myth and story in Aboriginal Australia*, Penguin, Melbourne, 1988, pp. 73–125; re. whirlwind see Harney, W.E., *Life among the Aborigines*, Robert Hale, London, 1957, p. 36.

19 Dixon, R.M.W., *The Languages of Australia*, CUP, 1980.

20 Blake, B.J. [1981], *Australian Aboriginal Languages: A general introduction*, UQP, 1991.

21 Elkin, A.P., *Aboriginal Men of High Degree: Initiation and sorcery in the world's oldest tradition*, UQP, 1977.

22 Edwards, *An Introduction*, p. 75; Reed, *An Illustrated Encyclopedia*, pp. 56, 123–5.

23 Guenther, 'From totemism', p. 429.

24 Isaacs, J., *Aboriginal Bush Food and Herbal Medicine*, Weldon, Sydney, 1987.

25 Berndt and Berndt, *The World*, pp. 150–66.

26 Quoted in Flood, *Rock Art*, p. 164; Basedow, H. 'Aboriginal rock carvings of great antiquity in South Australia', *Journal of the Royal Anthropological Institute*, 1914, vol. 44, pp. 95–211, esp. p. 201.

27 Reed, *An Illustrated Encyclopedia*, pp. 19–20, 72–3, 81, 142, 151.

28 Dunlop, I., *Desert People*, Film Australia, Sydney, 1967. For anthropology, see I. Keen, *Aboriginal Economy and Society: Australia at the threshold of colonisation*, OUP, Melbourne, 2004.

29 Berndt, R.M., and C.H. [1952], *The First Australians*, Ure Smith, Sydney, 1974, p. 52; Berndt and Berndt, *The World*, pp. 180–9.

30 Berndt and Berndt, *The World*, p. 182; Howitt, A.W. [1904], *The Native Tribes of South-East Australia*, ASP, 1996, pp. 746–7; re. Western Desert, Sutton, P., personal communication, 2005.

31 Berndt and Berndt, *The World*, pp. 166–180.

32 Rose, F.G.G., *The Traditional Mode of Production of the Australian Aborigines*, A&R, 1987, p. 29; Maddock, K. [1972], *The Australian Aborigines: A portrait of their society*, Penguin, Melbourne, 1982, pp. 67–75.

33 Introcision by male relatives was widespread using a stone knife or cylindro-conical stone: Berndt and Berndt, *The World*, pp. 181–2, 185. Re. Central Australia: Spencer, B., and Gillen, F. [1899], *The Native Tribes of Central Australia*, Macmillan, London, 1938, pp. 92–4, 269, 458–65.

34 Berndt and Berndt, *The World*, pp. 191–2.

35 *Ibid.*, p. 193.

36 Berndt and Berndt, *First Australians*, pp. 106–7; Stanner [1959], 'Durmugam: A Nangiomeri', in *White Man*, pp. 91–2.

37 Mountford, C.P., *Nomads of the Australian Desert*, Rigby, Adelaide, 1976, p. 213 and plate 206.

38 Arndt, W., 'The interpretation of the Delamere lightning paintings and rock engravings', *Oceania*, 1962, vol. 32, pp. 163–77; Flood, J. and David, B., 'Traditional systems of encoding meaning in Wardaman rock art, Northern Territory, Australia', *The Artefact*, 1994, vol. 17, pp. 6–22.

39 Berndt and Berndt, *First Australians*, pp. 115–18; Reed, *An Illustrated Encyclopedia*, pp. 30–2.

40 Berndt and Berndt, *The World*, pp. 347–50; re. northern hierarchy, Sutton, P., personal communication, 2003.

41 Squires, N., 'Aborigines seek return of tribal justice', *Daily Telegraph*, 6 June 2005.

42 Harney, *Life among the Aborigines*, p. 19.

43 Sutton, P., personal communication, 2005.

44 Flood, J., *The Moth Hunters: Aboriginal prehistory of the Australian Alps*, AIAS, Canberra, 1980. The moth hunters were the subject of my doctorate and my first archaeological book. The research involved experimental archaeology, including eating moths! The recipe is—cook them on a pre-heated granite slab for a minute on each side, pick them out of the fire with a pointed stick and winnow away the ashes. The abdomens are only peanut-sized but full of oily protein and taste like roast chestnuts.

45 Mulvaney, D.J., 'The chain of connection: The material evidence', in N. Peterson (ed.), *Tribes and Boundaries in Australia*, AIAS, 1976, pp. 72–94; McCarthy, F.D., 'Trade in Aboriginal Australia', *Oceania*, 1939, 9: 405–38, 10: 80–104, 171–95; Watson, P., *This Precious Foliage*, Oceania Monograph, UOS, 1983.

Box—Fishing methods (p. 160)

a Reed, *An Illustrated Encyclopedia*, pp. 11, 24, 83–6, 125, 160, 66–7.

b Hunter, p. 44.

c Collins, vol. I, p. 499.

Box—Torres Strait Islanders (p. 164)

a Australian Bureau of Statistics 2002, *Population Distribution Aboriginal and Torres Strait Islander Australians 2001*, ABS.4705.0, CofA.

b Beckett, J.R., *Torres Strait Islanders: Custom and colonialism*, CUP, 1987; Sharp, N., *Stars of Tagai: The Torres Strait Islanders*, ASP, 1993.

CHAPTER 6—ORIGINS

1 Isaacs, J. (ed.), *Australian Dreaming*, Lansdowne Press, Sydney, 1980, p. 5.

2 Interglacial periods happen about every 100 000 years, when variations in the Earth's orbit and tilt of its polar axis cause polar ice to melt. The last interglacial was about 125 to 110 kya (thousand years ago).

3 Oppenheimer, S., *Out of Eden: The peopling of the world*, Constable, London, 2003, pp. 51–3; re. 'hominin', previously we used the word 'hominid' to describe humans and their ancestors, but recently a better understanding of the evolutionary relationship between humans and the other great apes has led to re-classification. 'Now, the African apes, including humans, are separated from orang-utans and lumped together in the sub-family Homininae. This group is further divided into Hominini (humans plus their ancestors and extinct "cousins"), making "hominin" the new word for "hominid"': *New Scientist*, 18 June 2005, p. 41.

4 Gabunia, L. *et al.*, 'Earliest Pleistocene hominid cranial remains from Dmanisi, Republic of Georgia: Taxonomy, geological setting and age', *Science*, 2000, 288: 1019–25; Gore, R., 'New Find', *National Geographic*, 2002, 202(2): i–x; Swisher, C.C., Curtis, G.H., and Lewin, R., *Java*

Man: How two geologists' dramatic discoveries changed our understanding of the evolutionary path to modern humans, Scribner, New York, 2000; Huffman, O.F., 'Geologic context and age of the Perning/Mojokerto *Homo erectus*, East Java', *JHE*, 2001, 40: 353–62; Simanjuntak, T., Prasetyo, B., and Handini, R. (eds), *Sangiran: Man, culture and environment in Pleistocene times*, National Research Centre of Archaeology, Jakarta, 2001, pp. 160–7; Morwood, M.J. *et al.*, 'Revised age for Mojokerto 1, an early *Homo erectus* cranium from East Java, Indonesia', *AA, 2003*, 57: 1–4. For genetic evidence, see Templeton, A.R., 'Out of Africa again and again', *Nature*, 2002, 416: 45–51; for archaeological evidence see Burenhult, G. (ed.), *The First Humans: Human origins and history to 10 000 BC*, UQP, 1993.

5   Morwood, M.J. *et al.*, 'Fission-track ages of stone tools and fossils on the east Indonesian island of Flores', *Nature*, 1998, 392: 173–6; Bednarik, R.G., 'Seafaring in the Pleistocene', *CAJ*, 2003, 13(1): 41–66; elephants are superb long-distance swimmers—one African herd swam 48 km (30 miles) at sea, averaging 2.7 km per hour; Johnson, D.L., 'Problems in the land vertebrate zoogeography of certain islands and the swimming powers of elephants', *Journal of Biogeography*, 1980, 7: 383–98.

6   For tools see Burenhult, *The First Humans*, pp. 64–5; Simanjuntak, *Sangiran*, pp. 143–70, 375–99.

7   Brown, P., Sutikna, T., Morwood, M.J., Soejono, R.P. *et al.*, 'A new small-bodied hominin from the Late Pleistocene of Flores, Indonesia', *Nature*, 2004, 431: 1055–61; Morwood, M.J., Soejon, R.P., Roberts, R.G., Sutikna, T., Turney, C.S.M. *et al.*, 'Archaeology and age of a new hominin from Flores in eastern Indonesia', *Nature*, 2004, 431: 1087–91; *New Scientist*, 30 October 2004, pp. 5, 8–10; Morwood, M., Sutikna, T., and Roberts, R., 'The people time forgot', *National Geographic*, 2005, 207(4): 2–15; Wong, K., 'The littlest human', *Scientific American*, 2005, 292(2): 40–49; Kohn, M., 'The little troublemaker', *New Scientist*, 18 June 2005, pp. 41–5.

8   Lahr, M.M., and Foley, R., 'Human evolution writ small', *Nature*, 2004, 431: 1043–4. Adult status was diagnosed from tooth eruption and wear.

9   *Weekly Telegraph*, 9 November 2004, no. 693, pp. 9, 23; *SMH*, 28 October 2004, pp. 1, 4; Wong, 'The littlest human', pp. 42, 49; Forth, G., in *Anthropology Today*, 2005, 21(1): 22.

10   Thorne, A.G., and Wolpoff, M.H., 'The multiregional evolution of humans', *Sci. Am.*, 1992, 266(4): 28–33 and update in *Sci. Am.*, 2003, 13(2): 46–53; Thorne, A.G., and Raymond, R., *Man on the Rim: The peopling of the Pacific*, A&R, 1989; Templeton, A.R., 'Out of Africa again and again', *Nature*, 2002, 416: 45–51; Tattersall, I.,

'Out of Africa again . . . and again?' *Sci. Am.*, 2003, 13(2): 38–45.

11   Stringer, C., and McKie, R., *African Exodus: The origins of modern humans*, Jonathan Cape, London, 1996. For 'Eve' and 'Adam' see Oppenheimer, *Out of Eden*, pp. xx, 37–43, 46, 84, 141–2, 171.

12   There are two types of DNA, nuclear and mitochondrial. Nuclear DNA is in the nucleus inside each cell and is passed to us from both parents. Other DNA is in bean-shaped, energy-producing parts outside the nucleus called mitochondria. Mitochondrial DNA clones itself rather than recombining and is passed to the next generation only by the mother. There are many more mitochondria in the body than cell nuclei, so they are easier to find and mitochondrial DNA mutates twenty times faster than nuclear DNA. The mtDNA mutation rate is about one mutation per 20 000 years along a single lineage, but timings on the molecular clock are very much approximations: Sykes, B., *The Seven Daughters of Eve*, Corgi Books, Transworld, 2001, p. 197.

13   Two species descended from a common ancestor start out with identical DNA, but gradually changes accumulate. The more different the DNA, the longer since the two populations split. DNA analysis has answered the question Thor Heyerdahl sailed a raft across the Pacific to try to solve—Polynesians came from Southeast Asia, not South America as he suggested: Hagelberg, E. *et al.*, 'DNA from ancient Easter Islanders', *Nature*, 1994, 369: 25; Cann, R.L., Stoneking, M., and Wilson, A.C., 'Mitochondria, DNA and human evolution', *Nature*, 1987, 325: 31–6; Wilson, A.C., and Cann, R.L., 'The recent African genesis of human genes', *Sci. Am.*, 1992, 266: 68–73 and update in *Sci. Am.*, 2003, 13(2): 54–61; Relethford, J.H., *Genetics and the Search for Modern Human Origins*, Wiley, New York, 2001; Ke, Y. *et al.*, 'African origin of modern humans in East Asia: A tale of 12 000 Y chromosomes', *Science*, 2001, 292: 1151–3. For the Y chromosome, one single mutation (M168) on the African tree defines all non-African lineages: see P.A. Underhill *et al.*, 'Y-chromosome sequence variation and the history of human populations', *Nature Genetics*, 2000, 26: 358–61; Wells, S., *The Journey of Man: A genetic odyssey*, Penguin, London, 2002; Wells quoted by Callaghan, G., 'State of Origin', *Weekend Australian Magazine*, 30 July 2005, pp. 24–30.

14   Foley, R., and Lahr, M., quoted in S. Woodward, 'Out of Africa', *Cambridge Alumni Magazine*, 2003, 38: 14–6; Schultz, H. *et al.*, 'Correlation between Arabian Sea and Greenland climate oscillations of the past 110 000 years', *Nature*, 1998, 393: 54–7.

15   Oppenheimer, *Out of Eden*, pp. 80–2, 355; Wells, *The Journey of Man*, p. 30.

The Original Australians

16 Kirk, R.L., *Aboriginal Man Adapting*, OUP, 1981, pp. 112–13, 118.

17 van Holst Pellekaan, S. *et al.*, 'Mitochondrial control-region sequence variation in Aboriginal Australians', *Am. J. Human Genetics*, 1998, 62: 435–49.

18 *Ibid.*, p. 446.

19 Lambeck, K., and Nakada, M., 'Late Pleistocene and Holocene sea-level change along the Australian coast', *Palaeogeography, Palaeoclimatology, Palaeoecology*, 1990, 89: 143–76; Ingman and Gyllensten, 'Mitochondrial genome variation'; Wells, *Journey of Man*, pp. 73–6, 104; Wells, quoted by Callaghan, *Weekend Australian Magazine*, pp. 29–30.

20 Howells, W.W., *Skull Shapes and the Map: Craniometric analyses in the dispersion of the modern Homo*, HUP, 1989, pp. 37–79; Pietrusewsky, M., 'Pacific-Asian relationships: A physical anthropological perspective', *Oceanic Linguistics*, 1994, 33: 407–29.

21 Oppenheimer, *Out of Eden*, pp. 67–76, 78–82; Taylor, B.W., personal communication, 2003; Bellwood, *Prehistory*, pp. 88, 100. At low sea-level the strait of Bab-al-Mandab is reduced to a narrow channel only a few kilometres wide, broken up by islets and reefs.

22 From 80–60 kya was the second coldest period of the last 100 000 years and sea-level fluctuated from –50 to 85 metres (–160 to 260 ft). At 62 kya sea-level was minus 85 m $\pm$ 5 m: Lambeck, K. and Chappell, J., 'Sea-level change through the last glacial cycle', *Science*, 2001, 292: 679–86; Oppenheimer, *Out of Eden*, pp. 79, 156; Wells, *Journey of Man*, p. 59.

23 Foley, R., and Lahr, M.M., 'Technologies and the evolution of modern humans', *CAJ*, 1997, 7(1): 3–36; Stringer, C., 'Coasting out of Africa', *Nature*, 2000, 405: 24–6; Rowley-Conwy, P. in Burenhult, *The First Humans*, p. 62.

24 *SMH*, 14/15 May 2005; Macaulay, V. *et al.*, 'Single rapid coastal settlement of Asia revealed by analysis of complete mitochondrial genomes', *Science*, 2005, 308: 1034–6; <http://arts.anu.edu.au/bullda/S_Asia_Austral_homepage.html>.

25 Neves, W.A., Powell, J.F. and Ozolins, E.G., 'Modern human origins as seen from the peripheries', *JHE*, 1999, 37: 129–33; Dillehay, T.D., *The Settlement of the Americas: A new prehistory*, Basic Books, New York, 2000; Dillehay, T.D., 'Tracking the first Americans', *Nature*, 2003, 425: 23–4; Gamble, C., *Timewalkers: The Prehistory of Global Colonisation*, Penguin, London, 1993, pp. 203–14; Oppenheimer, *Out of Eden*, pp. 27–342, but see Wells, *Journey of Man*, pp. 134–45.

26 McBrearty, S., and Brooks, A.S., 'The revolution that wasn't: A new interpretation of the origin of modern human behaviour', *JHE*, 2000, 39: 453–63.

27 Flood, J. [1983], *Archaeology of the Dreamtime*,

A&R, 2001; in Australia, pierced shell beads have been found in four WA sites (Mandu Mandu, Riwi, Carpenter's Gap rock-shelters and Devil's Lair Cave) dated to c. 40 kya: Jane Balme, UWA, personal communication, 2004; Henshilwood, C., d'Errico, H., *et al.*, 'Middle Stone Age shell beads from South Africa', *Science*, 2004, 304: 404, 369; Wong, K., 'The morning of the modern mind', *Scientific American*, 2005, 292(6): 64–73. Blades are twice as long as wide, microliths are less than 3 centimetres long.

28 Eurasia includes the Middle East, Europe, North Africa and Central and South Asia.

29 Flood, J., *Rock Art of the Dreamtime*, A&R, 1997; Bednarik, R., 'The origins of navigation and language', *The Artefact*, 1997, 20: 16–56; Tacon, P.S., Aung, D.Y.Y., and Thorne, A., 'Myanmar prehistory: Rare rock-markings revealed', *AO*, 2004, 39: 138–9.

30 Bahn, P.G., and Vertut, J., *Images of the Ice-age*, Windward, London, 1988; Clottes, J., and Courtin, J., *La Grotte Cosquer*, Editions du Seuil, Paris, 1994.

31 For latest sea-level estimates, see Lambeck, K., and Chappell, J., 'Sea-level change through the Last Glacial Cycle', *Science*, 2001, 292: 679–86; Chappell, J., 'Pleistocene seedbeds of western Pacific maritime cultures and the importance of chronology', in S. O'Connor and P. Veth (eds), *East of Wallace's Line: Studies of past and present maritime cultures of the Indo-Pacific region*, Modern Quaternary Research in Southeast Asia, 16, Balkema, Rotterdam & Brookfield, USA, 2000, pp. 77–98; see also Oppenheimer, *Out of Eden*; Cavalli-Sforza, L.L., *Genes, Peoples and Languages*, Penguin, London, 2000, p. 94.

32 Flood, *Archaeology*, pp. 31–2; re. antiquity of monsoon, see Chappell, 'Pleistocene seedbeds', pp. 88–9, and Magee, J.W. *et al.*, 'Stratigraphy, sedimentology, chronology and palaeohydrology of Quaternary lacustrine deposits at Madigan Gulf, Lake Eyre, South Australia', *Palaeogeography, Palaeoclimatology, Palaeoecology*, 1995, 113: 3–42.

33 Ingman, M., and Gyllensten, U., 'Mitochondrial genome variation and evolutionary history of Australian and New Guinean Aborigines, *Genome Research*, 2003, 13: 1600–6 (and references therein).

34 Bednarik, R.G., 'The origins of navigation and language', *Artefact*, 1997, 20: 16–56; Bednarik, R.G., *et al.*, 'Nale Tasih 2: Journey of a Middle Palaeolithic raft', *International Journal of Nautical Archaeology*, 1999, 28: 25–33; at 3–4 kya, Polynesian colonists headed out into the vast Southern Ocean, their sophisticated outrigger sailing canoes laden with food plants and animals to sustain them on the distant islands they hoped to discover. Navigating by stars, currents and birds, these Argonauts of the Pacific crossed

incredible expanses of ocean to reach Hawaii, Tahiti and even remotest Easter Island: see Bellwood, P. [1978], *The Polynesians: Prehistory of an island people*, Thames & Hudson, London, 1987; Irwin, G., *The Prehistoric Exploration and Colonisation of the Pacific*, CUP, 1992.

35 Roberts, R.G., Jones, R., and Smith, M.A., 'Thermoluminescence dating of a 50 000-year-old human occupation site in northern Australia', *Nature*, 1990, 345: 153–6; Roberts, R.G., Jones, R., and Smith, M.A., 'Optical dating at Deaf Adder Gorge, Northern Territory, including human occupation between 53 000 and 60 000 years', *AA*, 1993, 37: 58–9; Roberts, R.G. *et al.*, 'The human colonisation of Australia: Optical dates of 53 000 and 60 000 years bracket human arrival at Deaf Adder Gorge, Northern Territory', *Quaternary Science Review*, 1994, 13: 575–83; Roberts, R.G. *et al.*, 'Single-aliquot and single grain optical dating confirm thermoluminescence age estimates at Malakunanja II rock shelter in northern Australia', *Ancient Thermoluminescence*, 1998, 16: 19–24. Beyond 10 kya, age determinations are accurate only within a few thousand years. The main methods used in Australia are radiocarbon dating, which measures the decay of minute traces of naturally radioactive carbon atoms within the organic remains, and luminescence dating of naturally deposited sands to date the time since artefact-bearing quartz sand was last exposed to sunlight. Optically stimulated luminescence (OSL) dating of single grains of quartz sand is the most accurate of the luminescence methods. The lowest artefacts at Nauwalabila I have OSL dates between 53.4±5.4 and 60.3±6.7 kya; at Malakunanja II the OSL dates are 45±7 and 61±10 kya. Leading sceptics are Jim Allen and James O'Connell, see 'The long and the short of it: Archaeological approaches to determining when humans first colonised Australia and New Guinea', *AA*, 2003, 57: 5–20.

36 Turney, C.S.M., *et al.*, 'Early human occupation at Devil's Lair, southwestern Australia 50 000 years ago', *Quaternary Research*, 2001, 55: 3–13.

37 O'Connor, S. and Veth, P., 'The world's first mariners: Savannah dwellers in an island continent', in *East of Wallace's Line*, pp. 99–137.

38 Flood, *Archaeology*, pp. 95–7.

39 Bowler, J.M., Jones, R., Kirk, R.C. and Thorne, A.G., 'Pleistocene human remains from Australia: A living site and human cremation from Lake Mungo, western New South Wales', *World Archaeology*, 1970, 2: 39–60; Bowler, J.M. and Thorne, A.G., 'Human remains from Lake Mungo: Discovery and excavation of Lake Mungo III', in R.C. Kirk and A. Thorne (eds), *The origin of the Australians*, AIAS, 1976, pp. 127–38; Bowler, J.M., 'Willandra Lakes revisited: Environmental framework for human occupation', *AO*, 1998, 33: 120–55.

40 Closest approximation is 60 000±6000 years: Thorne, A.G., Grun, R., Mortimer, G., Taylor, N., and Curnoe, D., 'Australia's oldest human remains: Age of the Lake Mungo 3 skeleton', *JHE*, 1999, 36: 591–612.

41 Bowler, J. M., Johnston, H., Olley, J.M. *et al.*, 'New ages for human occupation and climatic change at Mungo, Australia', *Nature*, 2003, 421: 837–40. According to Bowler, Mungo Man was buried 40±2 kya, i.e. between 42 000 and 38 000 years ago. The grave, which was 80–100 centimetres deep, was dug into sands OSL-dated to 42±3 kya and the overlying unit sealing the grave to 38±2 kya. The editors of *Nature* and its American equivalent *Science* will not publish new discoveries unless different laboratories have replicated the results, and Bowler's results are now well accepted.

42 Barrows, T.T., *et al.*, 'Late Pleistocene glaciation of the Kosciuszko Massif, Snowy Mountains, Australia', *Quaternary Research*, 2001, 55: 179–89.

43 Flood, *Archaeology*, ch. 3.

44 *The Australian*, 9 January 2001; Adcock, G.J. *et al.*, 'Mitochondrial DNA sequences in ancient Australians: Implications for modern human origins', *Proc. National Academy of Science USA*, 2001, 98(2): 537–42.

45 Thorne, A.G. and Macumber, P.G., 'Discoveries of Late Pleistocene man at Kow Swamp, Australia', *Nature*, 1972, 238: 316–9; Thorne, A.G., 'Mungo and Kow Swamp: Morphological variation in Pleistocene Australians', *Mankind*, 1971, 8: 85–9; Stone, T., and Cupper, M.L., 'Last glacial maximum ages for robust humans at Kow Swamp, southern Australia', *JHE*, 2003, 45: 99–111; Thorne in *The Age*, 8 January 2004; Stone, T., 'Robust and gracile', *Australasian Science*, 2004 (March), 18–20.

46 Birdsell, 'Preliminary data'; Birdsell, *Microevolutionary Patterns*, pp. 22–3; Photographs of Barrineans are reproduced in K. Windschuttle and D. Gillin, 'The extinction of the Australian Pygmies', *Quadrant*, 2002 (June), pp. 7–18; Groves, C., letter, in *Quadrant*, 2002 (September), p. 5; Gillin, T., reply, in *Quadrant*, 2002 (October), pp. 5–7; re. links with India see van Holst Pellekaan, 'Mitochondrial control'.

47 Jablonski, N.G. and Chaplin, G., 'Skin deep', *Sci. Am.*, 2002, 287(4): 50–7; Jablonski, N.G., and Chaplin, G., 'The evolution of human skin coloration', *JHE*, 2000, 39(1): 57–106; Oppenheimer, *Out of Eden*, pp. 198–200.

48 Birdsell, 'Preliminary data', pp. 120–1.

49 Redd, A.J., and Stoneking, M., 'Peopling of Sahul: mtDNA variation in Aboriginal Australian and Papua New Guinean populations', *Am. J. Human Genetics*, 1999, 65: 808–28.

50 van Holst Pellekaan *et al.*, 1998; Kayser, M. *et al.*, 'Independent histories of human Y chromosomes from Melanesia and Australia', *Am. J.*

Human Genetics, 2001, 68: 173–90; Underhill, P.A. et al., 'The phylogeography of Y chromosome binary haplotypes and the origins of modern human populations', *Annals of Human Genetics*, 2001, 65: 43–62.

51 White, N., 'Genes, languages and landscapes in Australia', in P. McConvell and N. Evans (eds), *Archaeology and Linguistics: Australia in Global Perspective*, MUP, 1997, pp. 45–81.

52 Flood, *Archaeology*, ch. 12; Webb, R.E., 'Megamarsupial extinction: The carrying capacity argument', *Antiquity*, 1998, 72: 46–55; Flannery, T., *The Future Eaters*, Reed, Melbourne, 1994.

53 Barrows, T.T. et al., 2002, 'The timing of the last glacial maximum in Australia', *Quaternary Science Reviews*, 21: 159–73; Barrows, T.T. et al., 'The timing of late Pleistocene periglacial activity in Australia', *Quaternary Science Reviews*, 2004, 23: 697–708.

54 Miller, G.H., Magee, J.W. et al., 'Pleistocene extinction of *Genyornis newtoni*: Human impact on Australian megafauna', *Science*, 1999, 283: 205–8; Magee, J., Miller, G., and Johnson, B., 'Why did Australia's megafauna become extinct?' *Australasian Science*, 1999 (August), pp. 27–32.

55 Miller, G.H. et al., 'Ecosystem collapse in Pleistocene Australia and a human role in megafaunal extinction', *Science*, 2005, 309: 287–90, quote is on p. 287; Johnson, C.N., 'The remaking of Australia's ecology', *Science*, 2005, 309: 255–6.

56 Smith, M., personal communication, 2003.

57 Pate, D.F. et al., 'Last recorded evidence for megafauna at Wet Cave, Naracoorte, South Australia 45 000 years ago', *AA*, 2002, 54: 53–5.

58 Field, J., and Dodson, J., 'Late Pleistocene megafauna and archaeology from Cuddie Springs, southeastern Australia', *Proc. Prehist. Soc.*, 1999, 65: 275–301; Wroe, S., and Field, J., 'Mystery of megafaunal extinctions remains', *Australasian Science*, 2001 (September), pp. 21–5; papers by Judith Field, Jim Allen and Joe Dortch at AAA conference, December 2003.

59 Roberts, R.G. et al., 'New ages for the last Australian megafauna: Continent-wide extinction about 46 000 years ago', *Science*, 2001, 292: 1888–92; Flannery, T., *Country*, Text, Melbourne, 2004, pp. 167–80; Flood, *Archaeology*, pp. 15–26; re. articulation see Diamond, J.M., 'Australia's last giants', *Nature*, 2001, 411: 755–7.

60 Martin, P.S., and Steadman, D.W., in R.D.E. MacPhee (ed.), *Extinctions in Near Time: Causes, contexts and consequences*, Kluwer Academic/Plenum, New York, 1999, pp. 17–55.

61 Taylor, B.W., personal communication, 2003; Flannery, *Future Eaters*, pp. 180–6, 199–207; Flannery, T., 'Debating extinction', *Science*, 1999, 283: 182–3; Nolch, G., 'Where is the smoking gun?' *Australasian Science*, 2001 (September),

pp. 19–20; Murray, P., 'Pleistocene megafauna', in P. Vickers-Rich et al. (eds), *Vertebrate Palaeontology of Australasia*, Monash University, Melbourne, 1991, pp. 1072–164.

62 Flannery, T., *Beautiful Lies: Population and environment in Australia*, Quarterly Essay, Black Inc., Schwartz, Melbourne, 2003, pp. 40–1.

63 Murray, 'Pleistocene megafauna', p. 1142.

64 Jones, R., 'Fire-stick farming', *Australian Natural History*, 1969, 16: 224–78; Hallam, S., *Fire and Hearth: A study of Aboriginal usage and European usurpation in south-western Australia*, AIAS, 1975; Jones, R., 'The neolithic, palaeolithic and the hunting gardeners: Man and land in the Antipodes', in R.P. Suggate and M.M. Cresswell (eds), *Quaternary Studies*, 1975, Roy. Soc. NZ, Wellington, pp. 21–34.

65 Jones, 'The neolithic', p. 25.

66 Taylor, B.W., personal communication, 2003. At a 1964 UNESCO conference, ecologists reached consensus that tropical savannahs resulted from man's use of fire.

67 Kershaw, A.P., 'Climatic change and Aboriginal burning in northeast Australia during the last two glacial/interglacial cycles', *Nature*, 1986, 322: 47–9; Flood, *Archaeology*, chs 7 and 8.

68 Roberts, D.A, and Parker, A., *Ancient Ochres: The Aboriginal rock paintings of Mount Borradaile*, J.B. Books, Adelaide, 2003.

69 Flannery, *Future Eaters*, pp. 217–36; Flannery, *Beautiful Lies*, pp. 20–1, 38–42.

70 Flood, *Rock Art*, pp. 178–222.

71 Flood, J., *The Moth Hunters: Aboriginal prehistory of the Australian Alps*, AIAS, Canberra, 1980, pp. 254–75.

72 Lambeck and Chappell, 'Sea-level change'.

73 Flood, *Rock Art*, pp. 278–85; Layton, R., *Australian Rock Art: A new synthesis*, CUP, 1992, p. 245; Tacon, P.S.C., and Chippindale, C., 'Australia's ancient warriors: Changing depictions of fighting in the rock-art of Arnhem Land, N.T.', *CAJ*, 1994, 4: 211–48; Tacon, P.S.C., 'Regionalisation in the recent rock-art of western Arnhem Land, Northern Territory', *AO*, 1993, 28: 112–20.

74 Tacon, P.S.C., Wilson, M., and Chippindale, C., 'Birth of the Rainbow Serpent in Arnhem Land rock-art and oral history', *AO*, 1996, 31: 103–24.

75 Flood, *Archaeology*, ch. 15; Mulvaney, D.J., and Kamminga J., *Prehistory of Australia*, A&U, 1999, pp. 223–56.

76 Kennedy, K.A.R., *God-Apes and Fossil Men: Paleoanthropology in South Asia*, University of Michigan Press, Ann Arbor, 2000; Bulbeck, D. et al., 'The contribution of South Asia to the Peopling of Australasia . . .', *Bulletin Soc. Suisse d'Anthrop.*, 2003, 9(2): 49–70, esp. pp. 59–60.

77 Slack, M.J., Fullagar, R.L.K., Field, J.H., and Border, A., 'New Pleistocene ages for backed artefact technology in Australia', *AO*, 2004, 39: 131–7.

78 Hiscock, P., 'Pattern and context in the Holocene proliferation of backed artefacts in Australia', *Archaeological Papers of American Anthropological Association*, 2002, 12: 163–77; Hiscock, P., and Attenbrow, V., 'Early Holocene backed artefacts from Australia', *AO*, 1998, 33: 49–62.

79 O'Connor, S., *30 000 Years of Aboriginal Occupation: Kimberley, North West Australia*, ANH, 1999, pp. 74–5, 137; Walsh, G.L. and Morwood, M.J., 'Spear and spearthrower evolution in the Kimberley region, N.W. Australia: Evidence from rock-art', *AO*, 1999, 34: 45–58.

80 Flood, *Archaeology*, pp. 146–7.

81 Tacon, P.S.C., and Pardoe, C., 'Dogs make us human', *Nature Australia*, 2002 (Autumn), 53–61.

82 The earliest reliable radiocarbon date for dingo bones is 3450 ± 95 years BP (the present being 1950). This date calibrates to c. 4000 calendar years.

83 Gollan, K., 'The Australian dingo: In the shadow of man', in M. Archer and G. Clayton (eds), *Vertebrate Zoogeography and Evolution in Australasia*, Hesperian Press, Perth, 1984, pp. 921–7; Gollan, K., 'Prehistoric dogs in Australia: An Indian origin?' in V.N. Misra and P. Bellwood (eds), *Recent Advances in Indo-Pacific Prehistory*, Oxford and IBH, New Delhi, 1985, pp. 439–43. Research on dingo DNA was by Dr Alan Wilton of Biotechnology Department, UNSW, reported at 'Modern Human Origins: Australian Perspectives', conference, UNSW, September 2003 and *SMH*, 30 September 2003.

84 Walsh and Morwood, 'Spear and spearthrower'; Walsh, G.L., *Bradshaw Art of the Kimberley*, Takarakka Nowan Kas Publications, Toowong Qld 4066, 2000, pp. 420–4; re. Arnhem Land see G. Chaloupka, *Journey in Time*, Reed, Sydney, 1993.

85 Roberts, R., Walsh, G. *et al.*, 'Luminescence dating of rock art and past environments using mud-wasp nests in northern Australia', *Nature*, 1997, 387: 696–9; Watchman, A., 'Perspectives and potentials for absolute dating of prehistoric rock paintings', *Antiquity*, 1993, 67: 58–65.

86 Gum Tree Valley excavated by Michel Lorblanchet; date on trumpet shell 18 500 BP, see Flood, *Rock Art*, p. 323; Tacon, P.S.C. and Brockwell, S., 'Arnhem Land prehistory', in J. Allen and J.F.O'Connell (eds), 'Transitions: Pleistocene to Holocene in Australia and Papua New Guinea', *Antiquity*, 1995, pp. 676–95, 69(265); Morwood, M.J. and Hobbs, D.R., 'Themes in tropical Australia', *ibid.*, pp. 747–68.

87 Dixon, R.M.W., *The Languages of Australia*, CUP, 1980; McConvell, P., 'Backtracking to Babel: The chronology of Pama-Nyungan expansion in Australia', *AO*, 1996, 31: 125–44; McConvell, P., 'Language shift and language spread among hunter-gatherers', in C. Panter-Brick, R. Layton and P. Rowley-Conwy (eds), *Hunter-Gatherers: An Interdisciplinary Perspective*, CUP, 2001, pp. 143–69, esp. pp. 158–60.

88 Blake, B.J. [1981], *Australian Aboriginal Languages: A general introduction*, UQP, 1991, pp. 61–2.

89 *Ibid.*

90 Flood, *Archaeology*, pp. 212–20; Flood, *Moth Hunters*.

91 Lourandos, H., *Continent of Hunter-Gatherers: New perspectives in Australian prehistory*, CUP, 1997, pp. 218–22; Lourandos, H., 'Swamp managers of southwestern Victoria', in D.J. Mulvaney and J.P. White (eds), *Australians: A historical library, Australians to 1788*, Fairfax, Syme & Weldon, Sydney, 1987, pp. 292–307.

92 Williams, E., 'Estimation of prehistoric populations of archaeological sites in southwestern Victoria: Some problems', *AO*, 1985, 20(3): 73–80.

93 Flood, *Archaeology*, ch. 16; Williams, E., *Complex Hunter-Gatherers: A late Holocene example from temperate Australia*, S423, British Archaeological Reports, Oxford, 1988; re. Buckley, see Morgan, J. [1852], *The Life and Adventures of William Buckley*, ANU Press, 1980, pp. 33, 119–20; Flannery, T. (ed.), *The Life and Adventures of William Buckley*, Text, Melbourne, 2002; Hallam, *Fire and Hearth*, pp. 29–30.

94 Ferguson, W.C., 'Mokaré's domain', in Mulvaney and White, *Australians*, pp. 121–45, esp. pp. 128–9, 134.

95 Pulleine, R.W., Presidential address at anthropological congress in Tasmania in 1928.

96 Ross, A., 'Archaeological evidence for population change in the middle to late Holocene in southeastern Australia', *AO*, 1985, 20(3): 81–9; Rowland, M.J., 'Holocene environmental variability: Have its impacts been underestimated in Australian prehistory?' *The Artefact*, 1999, 22: 11–48; David, B., *Landscapes, Rock Art and the Dreaming*, Leicester University Press, London, 2002, pp. 154–213.

Box—Watercraft (p. 180)

a Edwards, R., *Aboriginal Bark Canoes of the Murray Valley*, Rigby, Adelaide, 1972; Davidson, D.S., 'The chronology of Australian watercraft', *Polynesian Society Journal*, 1935, 44: 1–16, 69–84, 137–52, 193–207.

b Hunter, p. 63.

c Bradley quoted in Flannery, *Birth of Sydney*, pp. 54–5.

Box—Physical characteristics (p. 186)

a Abbie, A.A., *The Original Australians*, Muller, London, 1969; Elkin, A.P. [1938], *The Australian Aborigines: How to understand them*, A&R, 1954; Birdsell, J.B., *Microevolutionary Patterns in Aboriginal Australia: A gradient analysis of clines*, OUP, 1993.

b   Groves C., personal communication, 2004.

c   Bellwood, P., *Prehistory of the Indo-Malaysian Archipelago*, Academic Press, Sydney, 1985, pp. 69–101, 132–3; Venkateswar, S., 'The Andaman Islanders', *Sci. Am.*, 1999, 280(5): 72–8.

d   Tindale, N.B., and Lindsay, H.A., *Aboriginal Australians*, Jacaranda Press, Brisbane, 1963, p. 34; Birdsell, *Microevolutionary Patterns*, pp. 207–46; Birdsell, J.B., 'Preliminary data on the trihybrid origin of the Australian Aborigines', *APAO*, 1967, 2(2): 100–55, esp. plates 1–6, pp. 123–4.

CHAPTER 7—ASSIMILATION

1   Clark, M. [1963], *A Short History of Australia*, Penguin, Melbourne, 1995, p. 75; Harris, J., *One Blood: 200 years of Aboriginal encounter with Christianity, a story of hope*, Albatross, Sutherland, NSW, 1990.

2   Rowley, C.D., *The Destruction of Aboriginal Society*, Penguin, Melbourne, 1970, p. 100.

3   *Select Committee on Aborigines. British settlements. Report*, British Parliamentary Papers, 1837, vol. 7, no. 425, pp. 10–11, 83, quoted in F. Crowley, *A Documentary History of Australia: Volume 1, Colonial Australia 1788–1840*, Thomas Nelson, Melbourne, 1980, pp. 112, 526.

4   Mulvaney, D.J., *Encounters in Place: Outsiders and Aboriginal Australians 1606–1985*, UQP, 1989, pp. 88–94, 41–5.

5   Broome, R. [1982], *Aboriginal Australians: Black responses to white dominance*, A&U, 1994, pp. 30–5, 71–96, 101–19, 105.

6   Gsell, F.X., *'The Bishop with 150 Wives': Fifty Years as a Missionary*, A&R, 1956, pp. 22, 24, 34, 152.

7   Roughsey, D., *Moon and Rainbow: The autobiography of an Aboriginal*, Reed, Sydney, 1971; Roughsey, E., *An Aboriginal Mother Tells of the Old and the New*, McPhee Gribble, Melbourne, 1984.

8   Durack, M., *The Rock and the Sand*, Constable, London, 1969, p. 52.

9   Lang, J.D., *An Historical and Statistical Account of New South Wales*, Sampson Low, London, 1875, vol. 1, p. 28.

10 Darwin, C. [1839], *Journal of Researches . . .*, published in C.W. Eliot (ed.), *Charles Darwin: The Voyage of the Beagle*, P.F. Collier & Son, Harvard Classics, 1909–14, vol. 29, ch. XIX, entries for 16 January 1836, 6 March 1836.

11 Reece, R.H.W., *Aborigines and Colonists: Aborigines and colonial society in New South Wales in the 1830s and 1840s*, SUP, 1974, p. 21.

12 *NSW Legislative Assembly, Votes and Proceedings*, 1843, p. 542.

13 Durack, M., *Kings in Grass Castles*, Constable, London, 1959; Durack, M., *The Rock and the Sand*, Constable, London, 1969; Holthouse, H. [1973], *S'pose I Die: The Evelyn Maunsell Story*, A&R, 1994.

14 Broome, *Aboriginal Australians*, p. 122–3.

15 McGrath, A., *'Born in the Cattle': Aborigines in Cattle Country*, A&U, 1987, pp. 141, 100–1, 122–3, 150–1.

16 Stevens, F., *Aborigines in the Northern Territory Cattle Industry*, ANU Press, 1974, p. 164.

17 McGrath, A. (ed.), *Contested Ground: Australian Aborigines under the British Crown*, A&U, 1995, pp. 24–5; Reynolds, H., and May, D., 'Queensland', in McGrath, *Contested Ground*, pp. 168–207, esp. pp. 198–9; McGrath, *'Born in the Cattle'*, pp. 138–9; re. stolen wages see Kidd, R., *In the Land of the 'Fair Go': Black lives, government lies*, UNSW Press, 2000.

18 Horton, D. (ed.), *Encyclopaedia of Aboriginal Australia*, AIATSIS, 1994, pp. 672–3.

19 Rowley, C.D., *Outcasts in White Australia*, Penguin, 1972, pp. 401, 403–5, 414.

20 Wilson, J., 'The Pilbara Aboriginal social movement', in R.M. and C.H. Berndt (eds), *Aborigines of the West: Their past and present*, UWA Press, 1980, pp. 151–68, esp. p. 166.

21 Broome, *Aboriginal Australians*, pp. 138–44; Rowley, C.D., *The Remote Aborigines*, ANU Press, 1970, pp. 167–70, 251–62.

22 Rowley, *The Remote Aborigines*, pp. 337–43.

23 Tatz, C., quoted in P. Howson, 'Land rights—The next battleground', *Quadrant*, 2005, vol. 417: 24–33.

24 Quoted by Toussaint, S., 'Western Australia', in McGrath, *Contested Ground*, pp. 240–68, esp. 259–60; Broome, *Aboriginal Australians*, p. 141.

25 Broome, *Aboriginal Australians*, pp. 56–8.

26 Bryson, B., *Down Under*, Doubleday, London, 2000, p. 283.

27 Kimber, R., personal communication, 1999.

28 Broome, *Aboriginal Australians*, pp. 174–5.

29 Saggers, S., and Gray, D., *Dealing with Alcohol: Indigenous usage in Australia, New Zealand and Canada*, CUP, 1998; Merlan, F., *Caging the Rainbow*, University of Hawaii Press, Honolulu, 1998, p. 41; Duguid, *Doctor*, pp. 202, 203.

30 Reynolds, H. [1987], *The Law of the Land*, Penguin, Melbourne, 1992, pp. 133–42; Reserves were in Cape York Peninsula, Central Australia, Arnhem Land, Daly River and the Kimberley; Rowley, *Destruction*, pp. 60–3, 247–54.

31 Singh, S. et al. (eds), *Aboriginal Australia and the Torres Strait Islands*, Lonely Planet Publications, Melbourne, 2001, pp. 212–24.

32 Maconochie, A., 'Observations on the treatment of the Aborigines, New South Wales', in *Extracts from the Papers and Proceedings of the Aborigines Protection Society*, London, 1839, vol. 1, pp. 109–15.

33 Reynolds, *The Law of the Land*, pp. 146–53.

34 By the late 1850s, there were six Australian colonies. Detached from New South Wales were Victoria (1851) and Queensland (1859). The others were South Australia (founded 1836), Tasmania (founded 1855, previously Van Diemen's Land), and Western Australia (founded

1829). Each colony had its own representative government and parliament. The governor of New South Wales became Governor-General, but the colonies did not federate until 1901. South Australia had administrative authority for the Northern Territory from 1863 until 1911, when the Federal Government assumed responsibility, although the Territory now has its own parliament.

35 Broome, *Aboriginal Australians*, pp. 75–87; Barwick, D., 'And the lubras are ladies now', in F. Gale (ed.), *Woman's Role in Aboriginal Society*, AIAS, 1974, pp. 51–63.

36 Barwick, D., 'Changes in the Aboriginal population of Victoria, 1863–1966', in D.J. Mulvaney and J. Golson (eds), *Aboriginal Man and Environment in Australia*, ANU Press, 1971, pp. 288–315, esp. p. 313; Moodie, P.M., *Aboriginal Health*, ANU Press, 1973, p. 38.

37 Broome, *Aboriginal Australians*, pp. 86, 101–4. Legislation governing reserves was enacted in Queensland in 1897 (*Queensland Aborigines Protection and Restriction of the Sale of Opium Act*), Western Australia in 1905, South Australia and Northern Territory in 1911.

38 Abbie, A.A., *The Original Australians*, Frederick Muller, London, 1969, p. 13.

39 Jupp, J. (ed.) [1988], *The Australian People: An encyclopedia of the nation, its people and their origins*, CUP, 2001, pp. 51, 610–14.

40 Quoted by Neill, R., *Whiteout: How politics is killing black Australia*, A&U, 2002, p. 126.

41 Conference Report (1937), quoted in H. Reynolds, *An Indelible Stain? The question of genocide in Australia's history*, Penguin, Melbourne, 2001, pp. 153–4; Anon., *Aboriginal Welfare: Initial Conference of Commonwealth and States Aboriginal Authorities, 1937*. Commonwealth Government Printer, Canberra, 1937, p. 5.

42 Haebich, A., *Broken Circles: Fragmenting indigenous families, 1800–2000*, Fremantle Arts Centre Press, Perth, 2000.

43 Stone, S. (ed.), *Aborigines in White Australia: A documentary history of the attitudes affecting official policy and the Australian Aborigine 1697–1973*, Heinemann, Melbourne, 1974, p. 196; Hasluck, P., *Native Welfare in Australia*, Patterson Brokenshaw, Perth, 1953, p. 16.

44 Lippmann, M., *Generations of Resistance: Aborigines demand justice*, Longman, Cheshire, 1991, p. 29.

45 McConnochie, K., Hollinsworth, D., and Pettman, J., *Race and Racism in Australia*, Social Science Press, Wentworth Falls, 1988, pp. 30, 27, 182.

46 McCorquodale, J., *Aborigines and the Law: A Digest*, ASP, 1987.

47 Wilson, R. and Dodson, M., *Bringing Them Home: National inquiry into the separation of Aboriginal and Torres Strait Islander children from*

their families, Human Rights and Equal Opportunity Commission, Commonwealth of Australia, 1997, p. 6.

48 Australian Museum, 'Indigenous Australians', Oral histories exhibition, Sydney, 1999.

49 Rintoul, S., 'Going home', *The Australian Magazine*, 21 April 2001, pp. 12–17.

50 O'Donoghue, L., 'A journey of healing or a road to nowhere?' in M. Grattan (ed.), *Reconciliation*, Black Inc., Bookman Press, Melbourne, 2000, pp. 288–96, esp. pp. 289–91.

51 *Bringing Them Home*, p. 17.

52 O'Donoghue, *ibid.*, p. 290; Andrew Bolt, *Herald Sun*, 23 February 2001; O'Donoghue, press release, 1 March 2001.

53 Keefe, K., *Paddy's Road: Life stories of Patrick Dodson*, ASP, 2003.

54 Roberts, A., *Sister Eileen—A life with the lid off*, Access Press, Bassendean, 2002, pp. 30–5, 37–9, 161, 192–3, 282–3.

55 *Ibid.*, pp. 176–7.

56 Harney, B. (Yidumduma) and Wositsky, J., *Born Under the Paperbark Tree: A man's life*, ABC Books, Sydney, 1996, pp. 73–7.

57 Randall, B., *Songman: The story of an Aboriginal elder of Uluru*, ABC Books, Sydney, 2003.

58 *Bringing Them Home*, p. 13.

59 *Ibid.*, pp. 21, 285.

60 *Ibid.*, pp. 275, 280–3.

61 Jopson, D., 'G-word a "distraction" from stolen generation', *SMH*, 7 June 2001, p. 13.

62 Reynolds, *An Indelible Stain*, pp. 21–3; Lemkin, R., *Axis Rule in Occupied Europe*, Carnegie Endowment for International Peace, Washington, 1944, pp. 79, 147.

63 *Bringing Them Home*, pp. 4, 29.

64 *Bringing Them Home*, pp. 35–7; Manne, R. 'In Denial: The Stolen Generations and the Right', *Australian Quarterly Essay*, Schwartz, Melbourne, 2001, pp. 24–7.

65 Manne, 'In Denial', pp. 77–85; Neill, *Whiteout*, A&U, 2002, pp. 116–20, 140–1.

66 Neill, *Whiteout*, p. 75; *Bringing Them Home*, p. 37; *Australian*, 16 May 2001, p. 11; *SMH*, 26 May 2000, p. 21.

Box—Ernabella/Pukatja (p. 206)

a Duguid, C., *Doctor and the Aborigines*, Rigby, Adelaide, 1972, pp. 115–16.

b *Ibid.*, p. 167; Hilliard, W.M., *The People in Between: The Pitjantjatjara People of Ernabella*, Hodder & Stoughton, London, 1968, p. 141.

c *Weekend Australian Magazine*, 24 November 2001, pp. 24–8.

CHAPTER 8—RESILIENCE

1 ATSIC definition of self-determination, quoted in R. Neill, *Whiteout: How politics is killing black Australia*, A&U, 2002, pp. 47, 23.

2   Perkins, C., 'Political objectives', in J. Jupp (ed.), *The Australian People*, A&R, 1988, pp. 233–9.

3   Principal political parties in Australia are Labor on the left and the Liberal Party on the right usually in coalition with the National Party (previously Country Party). The federal government ministry is known by the name of the Prime Minister, e.g. the Whitlam government.

4   Whitlam, G., 6 April 1973 speech in House of Representatives, quoted in G.F. Gale and A. Brookman (eds), *Race Relations in Australia: The Aborigines*, McGraw-Hill, Sydney, 1975, pp. 100–2.

5   McLaughlin, H., 'Are we headed in the right direction?' in G. Johns (ed.), *Waking Up to Dreamtime*, Media Masters, Singapore, 2001, pp. 125–51.

6   *Weekend Australian*, 17 May 2004, p. 16, 6 November 2004; *Australian*, 8 November, 9 November 2004; *SMH*, 12 November, 15 November 2004.

7   Flood, J., 'Tread softly, for you tread on my bones: The development of cultural resource management in Australia', pp. 79–101 in H.F. Cleare (ed.), *Archaeological Heritage Management in the Modern World*, Unwin Hyman, London, 1989; Flood, J., 'Cultural resource management in Australia: The last three decades', in M. Spriggs *et al.* (eds), *Community of Culture . . .* , ANU, 1993, pp. 259–65; Sullivan, S. (ed.), *Cultural Conservation: Towards a national approach*, AHC, AGPS, 1995.

8   Press, A. *et al.* (eds), *Kakadu: Natural and cultural heritage and management*, ANCA, NARU ANU, 1995; Bell, D., *Ngarrindjeri Wurruwarrin: A world that is, was and will be*, Spinifex Press, Melbourne, 1998, pp. 1–39; Simons, M., *The Meeting of the Waters: The Hindmarsh Island affair*, Hodder Headline, Sydney, 2003.

9   Butt, P. and Eagleson, R., *Mabo, Wik and Native Title*, Federation Press, Sydney, 1998; Attwood, B. (ed.), *In the Age of Mabo: History, Aborigines and Australia*, A&U, 1996.

10 Brennan, F., *The Wik Debate: Its Impact on Aborigines, pastoralists and miners*, UNSW Press, 1998.

11 Johns, G., 'The poverty of Aboriginal self-determination', in G. Johns (ed.), *Waking Up to Dreamtime*, pp. 20–45; Howson, P., 'Land rights: The next battleground', *Quadrant*, 2005, 417: 24–9; McDonnell, J., 'Land rights and Aboriginal development', *Quadrant*, 2005, 417: 30–3; Hughes, H. and Warin, J., *A New Deal for Aborigines and Torres Strait Islanders in Remote Communities*, Centre for Independent Studies, Sydney, 2005.

12 Johnston, E., *National Report, Royal Commission into Aboriginal Deaths in Custody*, 5 vols, AGPS, Canberra, 1991; Cuneen, C., *The Royal Commission into Aboriginal deaths in custody: An overview of its establishment, findings and outcomes*, ATSIC, Canberra, 1997; Statistics from ATSIC <www.atsic.gov.au>, Australian Institute of Criminology <www.aic.gov.au> and Australian Bureau of Statistics <www.abs.gov.au>; *SMH*, 21 February 2004; re. car crashes, data are from Western Australia in 1999: *The West Australian*, 19 March 1999.

13 Council for Aboriginal Reconciliation, *Reconciliation: Australia's Challenge*, Commonwealth of Australia, Ausinfo, GPO Box 1920, Canberra ACT 2601, 2000, pp. 109–14.

14 Maddock, K., 'Sceptical thoughts on customary law', in Johns (ed.), *Waking Up to Dreamtime*, pp. 152–71.

15 *Weekend Australian*, 9 December 2000, p. 4.

16 Newspoll, Saulwick and Muller, 2000; Mackay, H., 'Public opinion on Reconciliation', in Grattan (ed.), *Reconciliation*, pp. 33–52, esp. pp. 39–40.

17 Scott, E., 'A personal reconciliation journey', in Grattan (ed.), *Reconciliation*, pp. 18–24; *SMH*, 22 May 2000, p. 2.

18 Dodson, M., *First annual report of Australian Aboriginal and Torres Strait Islander Social Justice Commissioner*, HREOC, AGPS, Canberra, 1993; Ridgeway, A., 'An impasse or a relationship in the making?' in Grattan (ed.), *Reconciliation*, pp. 12–17, esp. p. 14.

19 Dodson, *First annual report*, p. 19.

20 Clark, G., reported in *SMH*, 29 May 2000, p. 17.

21 Mansell, M., quoted in 'Trouble among the tribes', *SMH*, 8 June 2000.

22 *SMH*, 30 May 2000, 6 June 2000.

23 *Weekend Australian*, 9 December 2000, p. 4; Brennan, S., Behrendt, L., Strelein, L. and Williams, G., *Treaty*, Federation Press, Sydney, 2005.

24 Jull, P., 'Embracing new voices: Reconciliation in Canada', in Grattan (ed.), *Reconciliation*, pp. 220–7; *SMH*, 22 May 2000, p. 19; re. Mohawks, *SMH*, 12 May 2001, p. 22; Flanagan, T., 'Aboriginal orthodoxy in Canada', in Johns (ed.), *Waking Up to Dreamtime*, pp. 1–19, esp. pp. 6–7, 16–17.

25 *Australian*, 19 February 2001; re. marrying out, Peterson, N. and Taylor, J., 'Aboriginal intermarriage and economic status in Western New South Wales', *People and Places*, 2002, 10(4): 11–16.

26 *Aboriginal and Torres Strait Islander Commission Act 1989*.

27 Australian Bureau of Statistics, *Population Distribution, Indigenous Australians*, 4705.0 & 2015.0, ABS, 2002.

28 Dutter, B., 'Battle of "last Tasmanians"', *Daily Telegraph*, 25 July 2002; Squires, N., 'Tasmania embroiled in dispute over white tribe of Aborigines', *Daily Telegraph*, 14 July 2005.

29 Editorial, *Australian*, 22 March 2001.

30 Editorial, *Australian*, 11 November 2004.

31 Statistics from ABS, *The Health and Welfare of Australia's Aboriginal and Torres Strait Islander*

Peoples, Report 4704.0, Australian Institute of Health & Welfare, GPO Box 570, Canberra ACT 2601, <http://www.aihw.gov.au>, 2003, pp. 120–1, 86–90.

32 Statistics from <http://www.hollows.org>.

33 Thomson, N., 'A review of Aboriginal health status', in J. Reid and P. Trompf (eds), *The Health of Aboriginal Australia*, Harcourt-Brace-Jovanovich, Sydney, 1991, pp. 37–79; ABS, *The Health and Welfare . . .*, pp. 92–4.

34 Neill, *Whiteout*, pp. 157–8.

35 Rosser, B., *Return to Palm Island*, ASP, 2004, p. 147.

36 ABS, *The Health and Welfare . . .*, pp. 93–4; National Centre in HIV Epidemiology and Clinical Research, *HIV/AIDS, Hepatitis C and Sexually Transmitted Infections in Australia . . . 2000*, NCHECR, UNSW, 2000.

37 *SMH*, 15 August, 21 August 2000; *Weekend Australian*, 5 August 2000; *Australian*, 6 January, 21 February 2001; Squires, N., 'Shameful secret in the shadow of Uluru', *Daily Telegraph*, 13 August 2005.

38 Trudgen, R.I., *Why Warriors Lie Down and Die*, Aboriginal Resource and Development Services, Darwin, 2000, pp. 239–44.

39 Information from <http://www.bp.com.au/news_information/press_releases/opal.pdf>.

40 Pearson, N., quoted in B. Robertson, *Aboriginal & Torres Strait Islander Women's Task Force on Violence Report*, Gumurri Centre, Griffith University, Brisbane, 1999, p. 71.

41 *Ibid.*, pp. xxviii, 5, 65, 147; re. heroin, *SMH*, 17 May 2004.

42 Robertson, ATSI *Women's Task Force on Violence Report*, pp. 30–1.

43 *SMH*, 17 February, 17 May 2004.

44 Mow, K., *Tjunparni: Family violence in Indigenous Australia*, ATSIC, 1992, p. 10.

45 ABS, <http://www.abs.gov.au/census>; Edwards, R.W. and Madden, R., *The Health and Welfare of Australia's Aboriginal and Torres Strait Islander Peoples*, ABS, 2001; *SMH*, 27 May 2000; Neill, *Whiteout*, pp. 76–88, 62; Toohey, P., 'Sticks and stones', *Weekend Australian*, 14 April 2001, pp. 21, 24.

46 Robertson, ATSI *Women's Task Force on Violence Report*, p. 91.

47 Neill, *Whiteout*, pp. 76–88.

48 *Ibid.*, p. 215.

49 Robertson, ATSI *Women's Task Force on Violence Report*, p. 101.

50 Memmott, P., Stacy, R., Chambers, C. and Keys, C., *Violence in Indigenous Communities*, Attorney General's Dept, Canberra, 2001, pp. 6, 18.

51 Trudgen, *Why Warriors*, p. 174; re. Christianity see Peterson, N. *et al.*, 'Social and cultural life', in W. Arthur and F. Morphy (eds), *Macquarie Atlas of Indigenous Australia*, Macquarie Press, Sydney, 2005, pp. 88–107, esp. pp. 101–7.

52 Robertson, ATSI *Women's Task Force on Violence Report*, p. x.

53 Pearson, N., *Our Right to Take Responsibility*, Discussion Paper, Noel Pearson and associates, Trinity Beach, Qld, 1999; Pearson, N., 'Light on the Hill', Ben Chifley Lecture, Bathurst, NSW, 2000; *SMH*, 16 August, 19 August, 25 August, 24 October 2000, 6 July 2002; *Australian*, 7 August 2002.

54 *SMH*, 19 August 2000; Pearson, N., 'Australia needs you', *Weekend Australian*, 10 April 2004, p. 20.

55 Pearson, *Our Right*, p. 1.

56 *Ibid.*, p. 20.

57 Pearson, quoted in *Weekend Australian*, 30 October 2004.

58 *SMH*, 16 August 2000.

59 Chaney, F., quoted in 'Lessons from Redfern can be put to use', *SMH*, 23 February 2004; *Australian*, 20 April 2004.

60 *SMH*, 18 August 2000.

61 Robertson, ATSI *Women's Task Force on Violence Report*, p. viii.

62 *Weekend Australian*, 4 December 2004; re. mutual obligation see McDonnell, J., 'Land rights and Aboriginal development', *Quadrant*, 2005, 417: 30–3.

63 Gordon, S. quoted in *SMH*, 12 November 2004.

64 Cane, S., *Pila Nguru: The Spinifex people*, Fremantle Arts Centre Press, Fremantle, 2002, pp. 158, 203, 215–21, 217.

Box—The development of Aboriginal art (p. 235)

a Caruana, W. [1987], *Aboriginal Art*, Thames & Hudson, London, 2003; Morphy, H., *Ancestral Connections: Art and an Aboriginal system of knowledge*, Chicago University Press, 1991; Morphy, H., *Aboriginal Art*, Phaidon, London, 1998; Sutton, P. (ed.), *Dreamings: The art of Aboriginal Australia*, Viking, Penguin, Ringwood, 1988; Kleinert, S. and Neale, M. (eds), *The Oxford Companion to Aboriginal Art and Culture*, OUP, Melbourne, 2000.

b Batty, J.D., *Namatjira: Wanderer between two worlds*, Hodder & Stoughton, Melbourne, 1963, pp. 19–32.

c French, A., *Seeing the Centre: The art of Albert Namatjira, 1902–1959*, NGA, 2002, pp. 2–12, 18–21.

d Edwards, R. and Guerin, B., *Aboriginal Bark Paintings*, Rigby, Adelaide, 1969.

e Quoted from Yunupingu, G., 'The black/white conflict', in W. Caruana (ed.), *Windows on the Dreaming*, NGA, Ellsyd Press, Sydney, 1989, p. 14.

f Bardon, G., *Papunya Tula: Art of the Western Desert*, McPhee Gribble, Penguin, Ringwood, Vic, 1991; Stokes, D., *Desert Dreamings*, Heinemann Library, Reed, Melbourne, 1997.

Box—Schooling (p. 261)

a   Harris, S., *Two-way Aboriginal Schooling: Education and cultural survival*, ASP, 1990, pp. 55–8, 1, 15.

b   Trudgen, *Why Warriors*, pp. 44–5, 178.

c   *Ibid.*, p. 122; NT Department of Education, *Learning Lessons: An independent review of Indigenous education in the Northern Territory*, Darwin, 1999, p. 2.

d   *SMH*, 27 May 2000, pp. 10–11; Beresford, Q., and Partington, G., *Reform and Resistance in Aboriginal Education: The Australian experience*, UWA Press, 2004.

e   *SMH*, 5 April 2004, p. 4.

f   Grattan (ed.), *Reconciliation*, pp. 165–75, esp. pp. 167–8. Pidgin is a mixed contact language which is not a first language; if it becomes the first language of children it is then a creole.

g   <http://www.smartstate.qld.gov.au/resources/publications/catalyst/2004/issue_11/seven.shtm> the State of Queensland, Dept. of the Premier and Cabinet, 2005.

h   Cherbourg State School <http://www.cherbourss.qld.edu.au>.

FURTHER READING

Arthur, W. and Morphy, F. (eds), *Macquarie Atlas of Indigenous Australia*, Macquarie Library, Sydney, 2005.

Beckett, J.R., *Torres Strait Islanders: Custom and colonialism*, CUP, 1987.

Berndt, R.M. and C.H., *The Speaking Land: Myth and story in Aboriginal Australia*, Penguin, Melbourne, 1989.

Berndt, R.M. and C.H., *The World of the First Australians: Aboriginal Traditional Life— Past and Present*, ASP, 1988.

Blainey, G., *Triumph of the Nomads*, Macmillan, Sydney, [1975] 1988.

Broome, R., *Aboriginal Australians: Black responses to white dominance*, A&U, [1982] 1994.

Burenhult, G. (ed.), *The First Humans: Human origins and history to 10 000 BC*, UQP, 1993.

Cane, S., *Pila Nguru: The Spinifex people*, Fremantle Arts Centre Press, Fremantle, 2002.

Caruana, W., *Aboriginal Art*, Thames & Hudson, London, 1993.

Chaloupka, G., *Journey in Time*, Reed, Sydney, 1993.

Charlesworth, M., Dussart, F. and Morphy, H. (eds), *Aboriginal Religions in Australia: An anthology of recent writings*, Ashgate, Aldershot, Hants, England, 2005.

Chatwin, B., *Songlines*, Jonathan Cape, London, 1987.

Clarke, P., *Where the Ancestors Walked: Australia as an Aboriginal landscape*, A&U, 2003.

Clendinnen, I., *Dancing with Strangers*, Text, Melbourne, 2003.

Diamond, J., *Guns, Germs and Steel: A short history of everybody for the last 13 000 years*, Chatto & Windus, London, 1997.

Edwards, W.H., *An Introduction to Aboriginal Societies*, Social Science Press, Wentworth Falls, NSW, [1988] 2004.

Edwards, W.H. (ed.), *Traditional Aboriginal Society*, Macmillan, Melbourne, [1987] 1998.

Elkin, A.P., *The Australian Aborigines: How to understand them*, A&R, [1938] 1954.

Flood, J., *Archaeology of the Dreamtime*, J.B. Books, Adelaide, [1983] 2004.

Flood, J., *The Riches of Ancient Australia*, UQP, [1990] 1999.

Flood, J., *Rock-art of the Dreamtime*, J.B. Books, Adelaide, 1997.

Grattan, M. (ed.), *Reconciliation*, Black Inc., Bookman Press, Melbourne, 2000.

Hallam, S., *Fire and Hearth: A study of Aboriginal usage and European usurpation in south-western Australia*, AIAS, 1975.

Harney, B. (Yidumduma) and Wositsky, J., *Born Under the Paperbark Tree: A man's life*, ABC Books, Sydney, 1996.

Harris, J., *One Blood: 200 years of Aboriginal encounter with Christianity—A story of hope*, Albatross, Sutherland, NSW, 1990.

Harris, S., *Two-way Aboriginal schooling: Education and cultural survival*, ASP, 1990.

Hilliard, W., *The People In Between: The Pitjantjatjara People of Ernabella*, Hodder & Stoughton, London, 1968.

Horton, D. (ed.), *Encyclopaedia of Aboriginal Australia*, AIATSIS, 1994.

Isaacs, J., *Aboriginal Bush Food and Herbal Medicine*, Weldon, Sydney, 1987.

Isaacs, J. (ed.), *Australian Aboriginal Music*, Aboriginal Artists Agency, Sydney, 1979.

Isaacs, J. (ed.), *Australian Dreaming: 40 000 years of Aboriginal history*, Lansdowne Press, Sydney, 1980.

Jupp, J. (ed.), *The Australian People: An encyclopedia of the nation, its people and their origins*, CUP, [1988] 2001.

Kauffman, P., *Travelling Aboriginal Australia: Discovery and reconciliation*, Hyland House, Melbourne, 2000.

Keefe, K., *Paddy's Road: Life stories of Patrick Dodson*, ASP, 2003.

Keen, I., *Aboriginal Economy and Society: Australia at the threshold of colonisation*, OUP, 2004.

Latz, P., *Bushfires and Bushtucker: Aboriginal plant use in Central Australia*, IAD Press, Alice Springs, 1995.

Layton, R., *Australian Rock-art: A new synthesis*, CUP, 1992.

Maddock, K., *The Australian Aborigines: A portrait of their society*, Penguin, Melbourne, [1972] 1982.

McGrath, A., *'Born in the Cattle': Aborigines in cattle country*, A&U, 1987.

Morgan, S., *My Place*, Fremantle Arts Centre Press, Fremantle, 1987.

Morphy, H., *Aboriginal Art*, Phaidon Press, London, 1998.

Muecke, S. and Shoemaker, A., *Aboriginal Australians: First Nations of an ancient continent*, Thames & Hudson, London, 2004.

Mulvaney, D.J., *Encounters in Space: Outsiders and Aboriginal Australians 1606–1985*, UQP, 1989.

Mulvaney, D.J. and Kamminga, J., *Prehistory of Australia*, A&U, 1999.

Neidjie, B., *Story about Feeling*, Magabala Books, Broome, 1989.

Neidjie, B., Davis, S. and Fox, A., *Kakadu Man: Bill Neidjie*, Mybrood, NSW, 1985.

Neill, R., *Whiteout: How politics is killing black Australia*, A&U, 2002.

Pilkington, D. (Nugi Garimara), *Follow the Rabbit-Proof Fence*, UQP, 1996.

Randall, B., *Songman: The story of an Aboriginal Elder of Uluru*, ABC Books, Sydney, 2003.

Reed, A.W., *An Illustrated Encyclopedia of Aboriginal Life*, Reed, Sydney, [1969] 1974.

Reynolds, H., *The Other Side of the Frontier*, Penguin, Melbourne, [1981] 1995.

Rose, D.B., *Nourishing Terrains: Australian Aboriginal views of landscape and wilderness*, AHC, 1996.

Stanner, W.E.H., *White Man Got No Dreaming: Essays 1938–1973*, ANU Press, 1979.

Taylor, R., *Unearthed: The Aboriginal Tasmanians of Kangaroo Island*, Wakefield Press, Kent Town, SA, 2002.

Trudgen, R.I., *Why Warriors Lie Down and Die*, Aboriginal Resource and Development Services, Darwin, 2000.

PHOTO ACKNOWLEDGEMENTS

Inside cover: Photo by R. Edwards.
p. vii: Photo by G. Walsh.

CHAPTER 1—EXPLORATION

p. 2: Data from C.C. Macknight, 1994; courtesy of Professor Susan Bambrick, *Cambridge Encyclopedia of Australia*, Cambridge, 1994, and Cambridge University Press.
p. 4: Photo by Dr Herbert Basedow, National Museum of Australia, Canberra.
p. 13: Courtesy of DAA, AIATSIS.
p. 14: Photo by Thomas Dick, courtesy of the Australian Museum, Sydney.
p. 22: Photo by J. Flood.

CHAPTER 2—COLONISATION

p. 31: Based on I. Clendinnen (2003).
p. 39: Courtesy of Rex Nan Kivell collection, National Library of Australia, Canberra.
p. 43: Courtesy of Rex Nan Kivell collection, National Library of Australia, Canberra.
p. 48: Courtesy of the National Parks and Wildlife Service, New South Wales.
p. 51: From Terra Cognita (1859) by William Blandowski, Mitchell Library, State Library of New South Wales.
p. 55: Photo by Dr Herbert Basedow. Used with the permission of the Central Land Council in Alice Springs. Courtesy of the National Museum of Australia, Canberra <www.nma.gov.au>.

CHAPTER 3—CONFRONTATION

p. 62: Courtesy of DAA.
p. 64: C.A. Lesueur, *Voyage de découvertes aux Terres Australia . . .*, 1807/1811, Le Havre Museum, Paris.
p. 65: Photo by Dr Herbert Basedow. Used with the permission of the Central Land Council in Alice Springs. Courtesy of the National Museum of Australia, Canberra <www.nma.gov.au>.
p. 68: Painting by B. Duterrau. Courtesy of Tasmanian Museum and Art Gallery, Hobart.
p. 70: Photo by R. Edwards.
p. 73: Photo by J. Flood.
p. 80: Photo by R. Maynard, AIATSIS.
p. 85: Courtesy of National Library of Australia, Canberra.
p. 92: Painting by Thomas Bock 1832–33, courtesy of Tasmanian Museum and Art Gallery, Hobart.

CHAPTER 4—DEPOPULATION

p. 97: Photo from Taplin collection, #AA319, South Australian Museum, Adelaide. Courtesy of Ngarrindjeri Heritage Committee.
p. 98: Courtesy of R. Broome. Map conceived by Richard Broome, originally published in *Aboriginal Australians*, Allen & Unwin, Sydney, 2001.
p. 99: Courtesy of Rex Nan Kivell collection, National Library of Australia, Canberra.
p. 101: Courtesy of National Library of Australia, Canberra.
p. 106: Mitchell Library, State Library of New South Wales, Sydney.
p. 108: Photo by Australians News and Information Bureau, Australia House, London.
p. 112: First reproduced in E.B. Kennedy, *The Black Police of Queensland*, London 1902, courtesy of National Library of Australia, Canberra.
p. 131: Courtesy of The Battye Library 7816B, State Library of Western Australia, Perth; collection of Susan Stretch.

CHAPTER 5—TRADITION

p. 134: Photo by J. Flood.
p. 137: Photo by G. Walsh.
p. 141: Photo by D. Baglin, AIATSIS.
p. 147: Photo by C. Duguid, courtesy of National Library of Australia, Canberra.
p. 150: Frobenius Institute, Frankfurt.
p. 151: Photo by R. Edwards.
p. 156: Photo by J. Flood.
p. 161: Courtesy of the Australian Museum, Canberra.
p. 165: Photo by AIATSIS.
p. 166: Photo by AIATSIS.
p. 168: Information courtesy of D.J. Mulvaney.
p. 169: Photo by J. Flood.

CHAPTER 6—ORIGINS

p. 174: Data courtesy of Spencer Wells, *The Journey of Man: A genetic odyssey*, Penguin 2002 and *Weekend Australian Magazine*, 30 July 2005.
p. 177: Photo by R. Edwards.
p. 180: Photo by Dr Herbert Basedow, 1916, National Museum of Australia, Canberra.
p. 181: Photo by R. Edwards.
p. 183: Photo by C. Groves.
p. 186: Photo by J. Flood at Papunya, Northern Territory, 1980.

The Original Australians

p. 187: Photo by Kerry and King, courtesy of Tyrrell's Bookshop, Sydney.

CHAPTER 7—ASSIMILATION

p. 205: Photographer unknown; courtesy of Mitchell Library, State Library of New South Wales, Sydney.
p. 210: National Library of Australia, Canberra.
p. 226: Still from *Rabbit-Proof Fence*; courtesy of Jabal Films Pty Ltd.

CHAPTER 8—RESILIENCE

p. 235: Reproduced by permission of Legend Press, Sydney.
p. 239: Photo by DAA, AIATSIS #N452813a.
p. 243: Photo by DAA, AIATSIS.
p. 248: Photo by Lee Chittick, National Library of Australia, Canberra.
p. 263: Photo by Madonna Cullinan; courtesy of Cyberstyle.

COLOUR PHOTOS

1. Photo by H. McNickle.
2. Photo by A. Massola, AIATSIS.
3. Photo by J. Flood, courtesy of SA Museum, Adelaide, #A66823.
4. Photo by J. Flood.
5. Photo courtesy of DAA.
6. Courtesy of Museum d'Histoire Naturelle, Le Havre, France.
7. Courtesy of Tasmanian Museum and Art Gallery, Hobart.
8. Mitchell Library.
9. Photo by G. Chaloupka.
10. Photo by J. Flood.
11. Photo by J. Flood.
12. Photo by J. Flood.
13. Photo by J. Flood.
14. Photo by J. Flood.
15. Photo courtesy of G. Pretty and the South Australian Museum.
16. Photo by P. Clark.
17. Photo by E. Harvey, 1955, AIATSIS.
18. Photo by J. Flood.
19. Photo by G. Walsh.
20. Photo by H. McNickle.
21. Photo by D. Baglin, AIATSIS.
22. Photo by J. Flood.
23. Photo by J. Flood.
24. Photo by R. Jones.
25. Photo by G. Chaloupka.
26. Photo by P. Cooke, AIATSIS.
27. Photo from V. Megaw collection, AIATSIS.
28. Photo by J. Flood.
29. Photo by J. Flood.
30. Photographed by J. Flood with the painter's permission on completion of the canvas at Papunya in 1980.
31. Photo by J. Flood.
32. Photo by S. Cane, AIATSIS.
33. Photo by P. Tweedie, AIATSIS.
34. Photo by Leon Mead. Photo courtesy of Mamabulanjin Aboriginal Corporation.
35. Photo by R. Baker, AIATSIS.
36. Photo by J. Flood.
37. Photo by M. Bowers, Fairfax Photo Library.
38. Photo by R. Stevens, Fairfax Photo Library.
39. Photo from Meehan Jones collection, AIATSIS.
40. Photo by J. Klatchko, AIATSIS.
41. Photo by J. Flood.

INDEX

Numbers in *italic* refer to illustrations